X/1999

VOL. 13
LAMENT
Shōjo Edition

STORY & ART BY CLAMP

ENGLISH ADAPTATION BY FRED BURKE

Translation/Lillian Olsen
Touch-Up Art & Lettering/Stephen Dutro
Cover and Interior Design/Yuki Ameda
Supervising Editor/Julie Davis
Editor/P. Duffield

Managing Editor/Annette Roman
Editorial Director/Alvin Lu
Director of Production/Nobi Watanabe
Sr. Director of Licensing & Acquisitions/Rika Inouye
VP of Sales & Marketing/Liza Coppola
Executive Vice President/Hyoe Narita
Publisher/Seiji Horibuchi

© 1999 CLAMP
Originally published in 1999 by KADOKAWA SHOTEN PUBLISHING CO., LTD., Tokyo. English translation rights arranged with KADOKAWA SHOTEN PUBLISHING CO., LTD., Tokyo.

Printed in Canada

Published by VIZ, LLC
P.O. Box 77010 • San Francisco, CA 94107

Shōjo Edition
10 9 8 7 6 5 4 3 2
First printing, December 2003
Second printing, October 2004

X/1999 ™

Vol. 13
LAMENT
Shōjo Edition

Story and Art by
CLAMP

X/1999
THE STORY THUS FAR

The End of the World has been prophesied …and time is running out. Kamui Shiro is a young man who was born with a special power—the power to decide the fate of the Earth itself.

Kamui had grown up in Tokyo, but had fled with his mother after the suspicious death of a family friend. Six years later, his mother too, dies under suspicious circumstances, engulfed in flames. Her last words to him are that he should return to Tokyo…that his destiny awaits.

Kamui obeys his mother's words, but almost immediately upon his arrival, he's challenged to a psychic duel—a first warning that others know of his power, and of his return.

Kamui is also reunited with his childhood friends, Fuma and Kotori Monou. Although Kamui attempts to push his friends away, hoping to protect them, they too are soon drawn into the web of destiny that surrounds him.

Meanwhile, the two sides to the great conflict to come are being drawn. On one side is the dreamseer Hinoto, a blind princess who lives beneath Japan's seat of government, the Diet Building. On the other side is Kanoe, Hinoto's dark sister with similar powers, but a different vision of Earth's ultimate future. Around these two women gather the Dragons of Heaven and the Dragons of Earth, the forces that will fight to decide the fate of the planet. The only variable in the equation is Kamui, whose fate it will be to choose which side he will join.

And Kamui finally does make a choice. He chooses to defend the Earth as it stands now. But by making this choice, he pays a terrible price. For fate has chosen his oldest friend to be his "twin star"—the other "Kamui" who will fight against him. And in this first battle, the gentle Kotori is the first casualty.

Now Kamui must face the consequences of his decision…and try to come to terms with not only his ultimate fate, but that of the Earth….

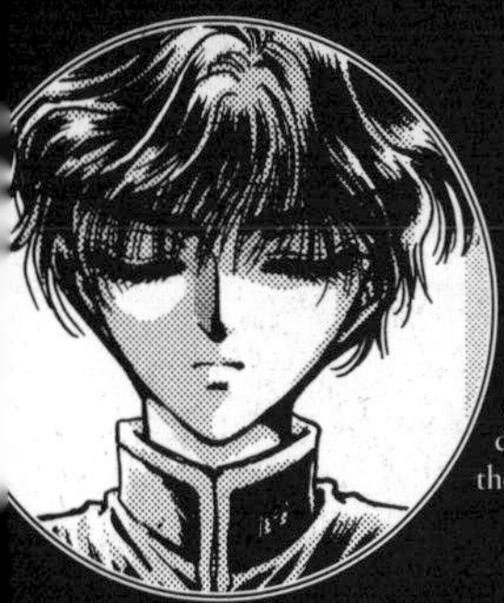

Kamui Shiro
A young man with psychic powers whose choice of destiny will decide the fate of the world.

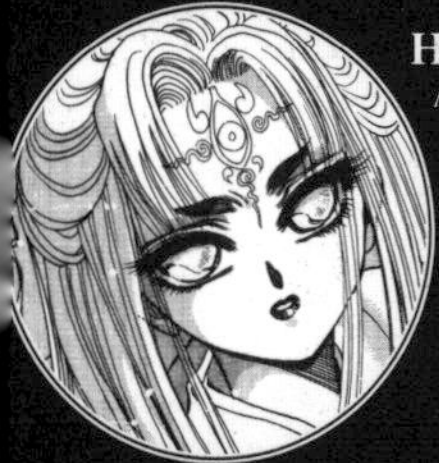

Hinoto
A powerful prophetess who communicates with the power of her mind alone. She lives in a secret shrine located beneath Tokyo's Diet Building.

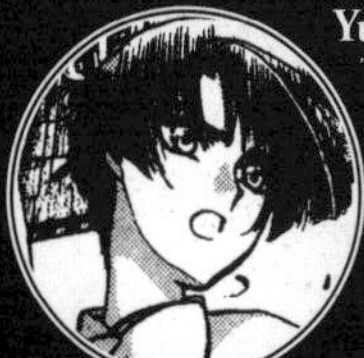

Yuzuriha Nekoi
The youngest of the Dragons, she is always accompanied by a spirit dog named Inuki.

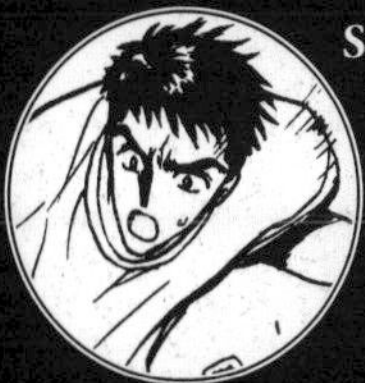

Sorata Arisugawa
A brash, but good-natured priest of the Mt. Koya shrine.

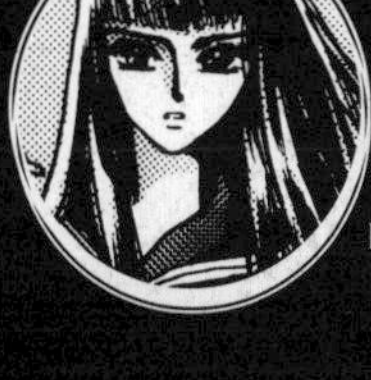

Arashi Kishu
Priestess of the Ise Shrine, Arashi can materialize a sword from the palm of her hand.

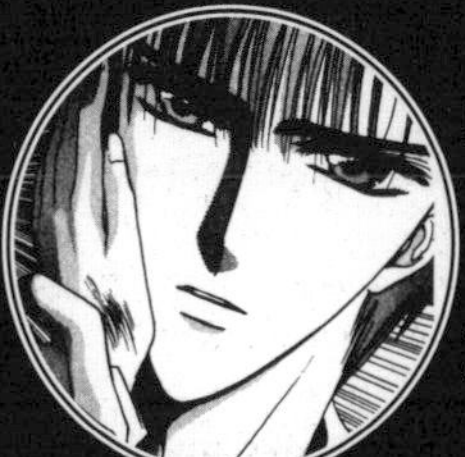

Fuma Monou
Kamui's childhood friend. When Kamui made his choice, Fuma was chosen by fate to become his "Twin Star"—the other "Kamui."

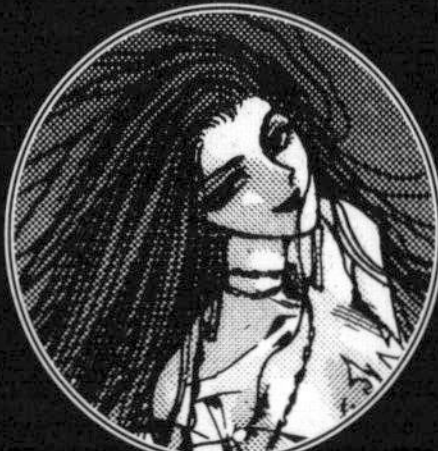

Kanoe
Hinoto's sister shares her ability to see the future… but Kanoe has predicted a different final result.

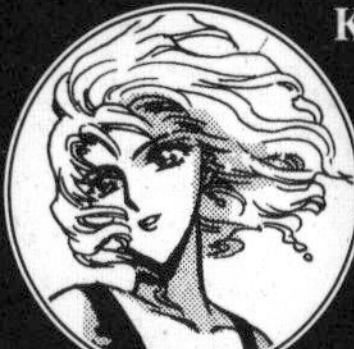

Karen Kasumi
A young woman who works in a Japanese bathhouse (massage parlor). She can control fire.

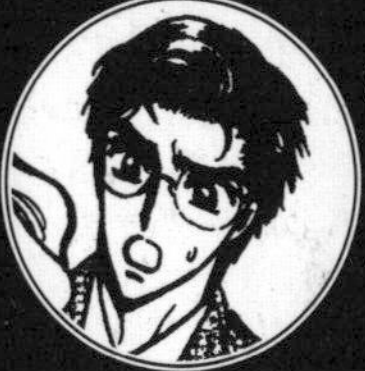

Seiichiro Aoki
A magazine editor, Seiichiro is a devoted family man. He can control the wind.

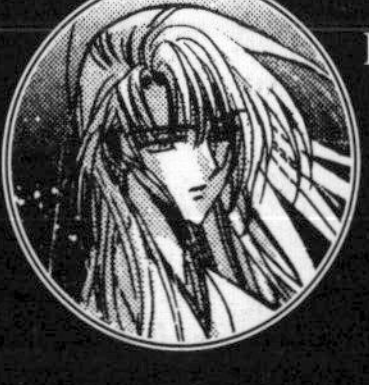

Kakyo Kuzuki
A dreamseer like Hinoto, Kakyo is a hospital-bound invalid kept alive by machines.

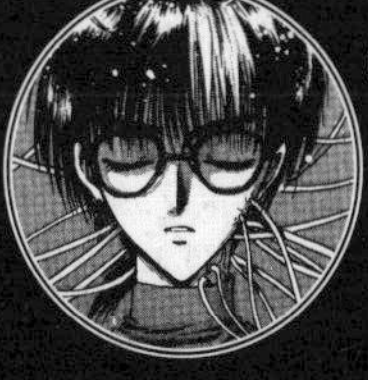

Satsuki Yatoji
A computer expert, Satsuki can interface directly with her personal machine, "The Beast."

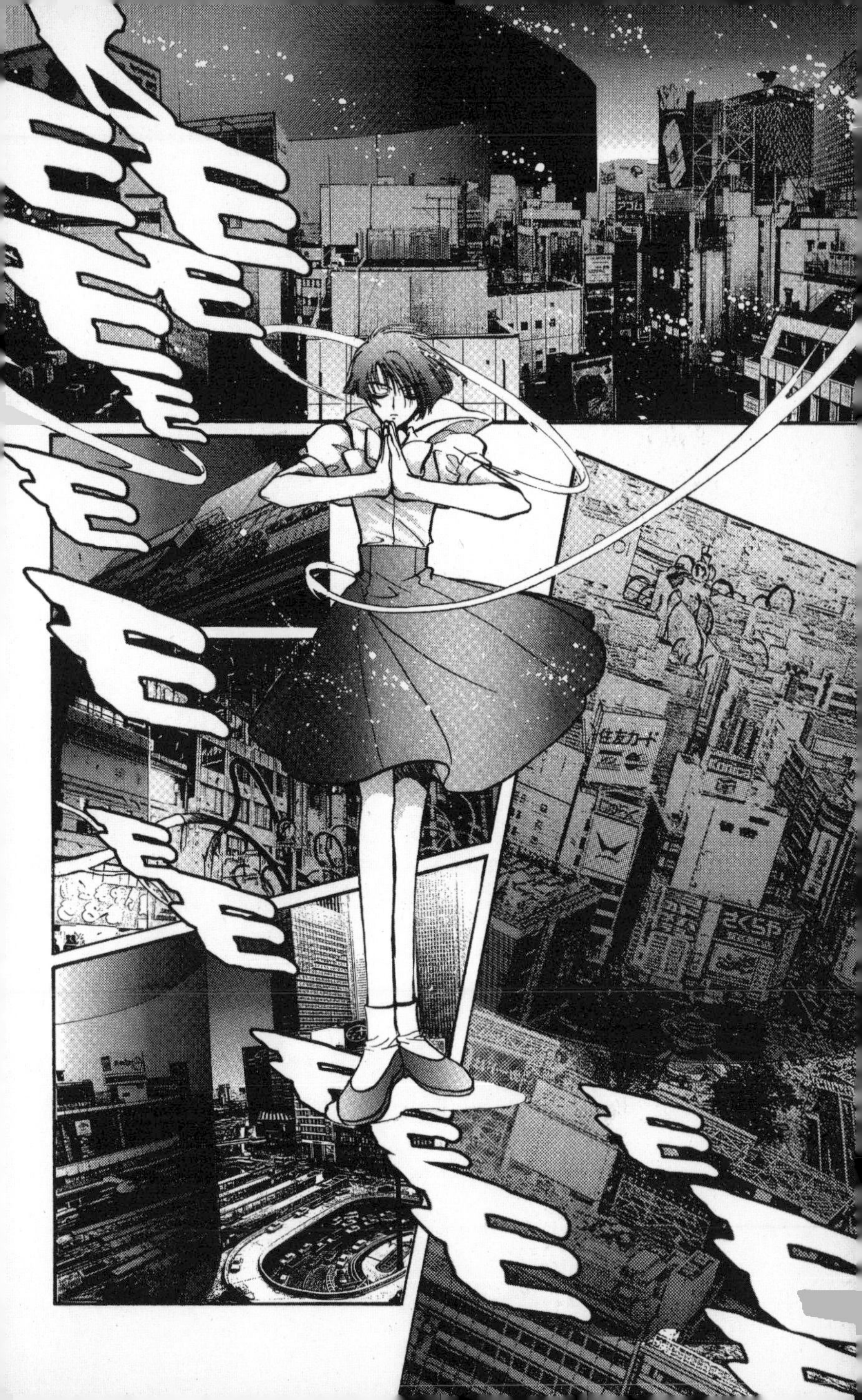
住友カード

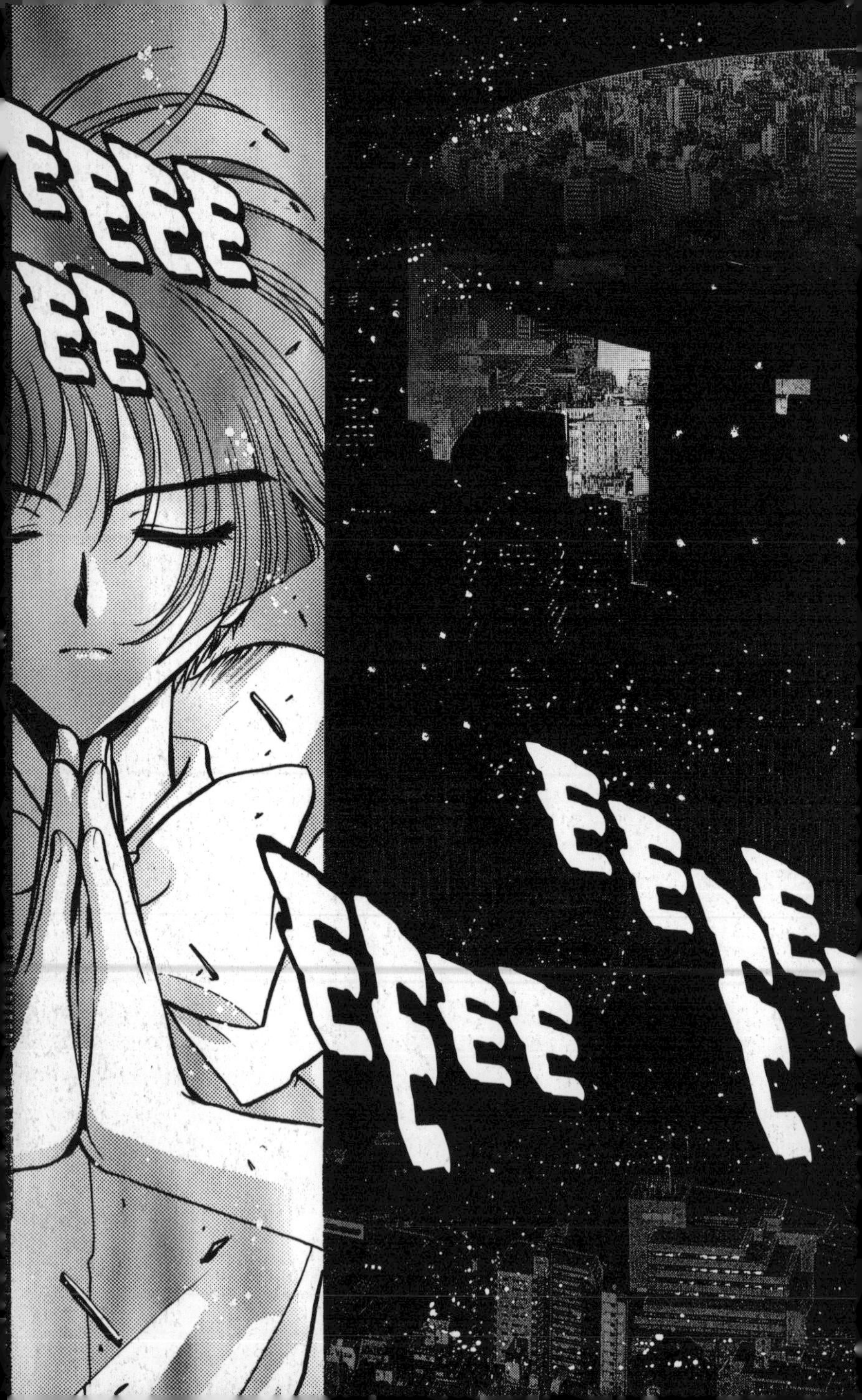
EEEEEE
EEEEE
EEEEEE

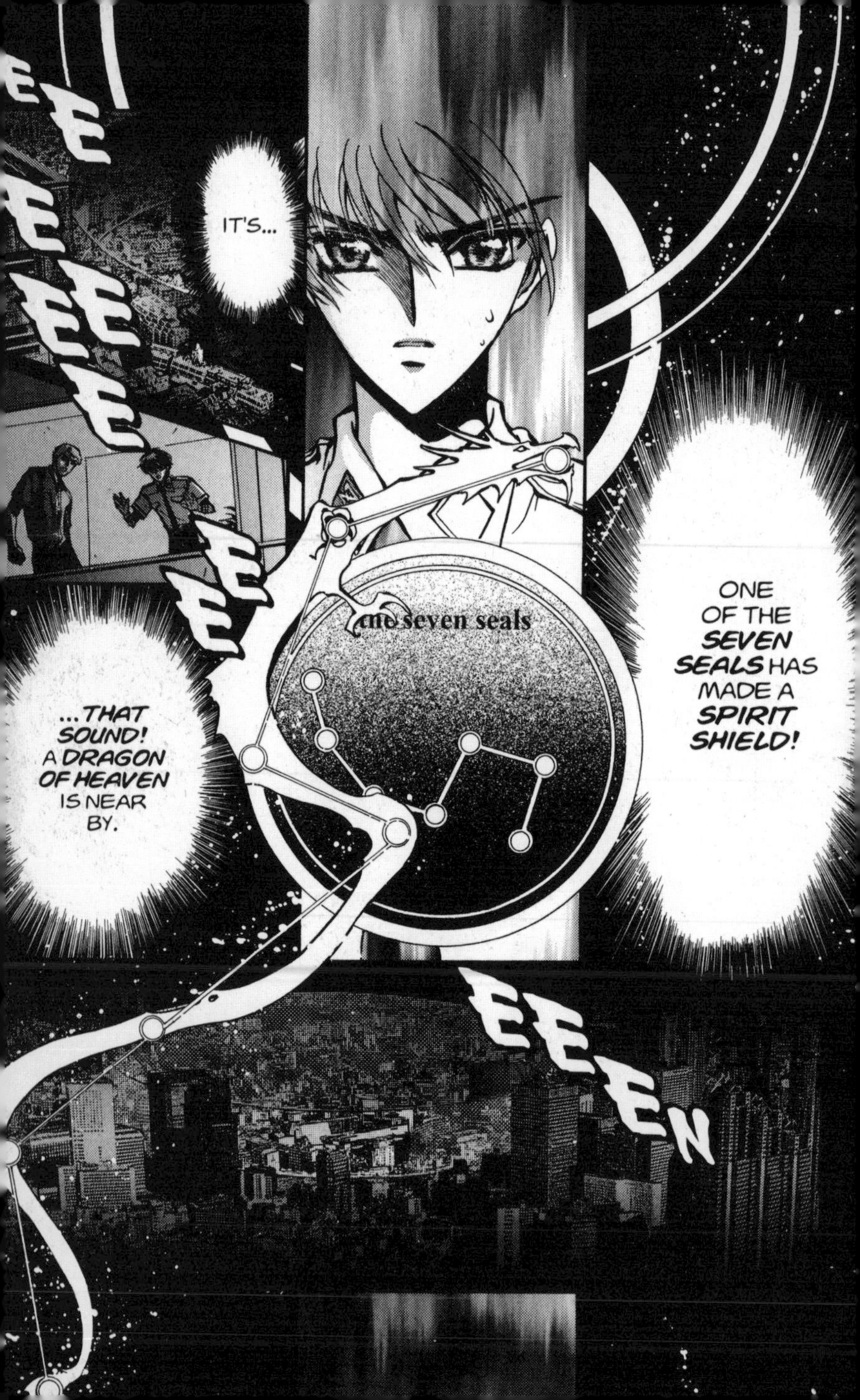
IT'S...
EEEEEEEEEE
...THAT SOUND! A DRAGON OF HEAVEN IS NEAR BY.
seven seals
ONE OF THE SEVEN SEALS HAS MADE A SPIRIT SHIELD!
EEEEN

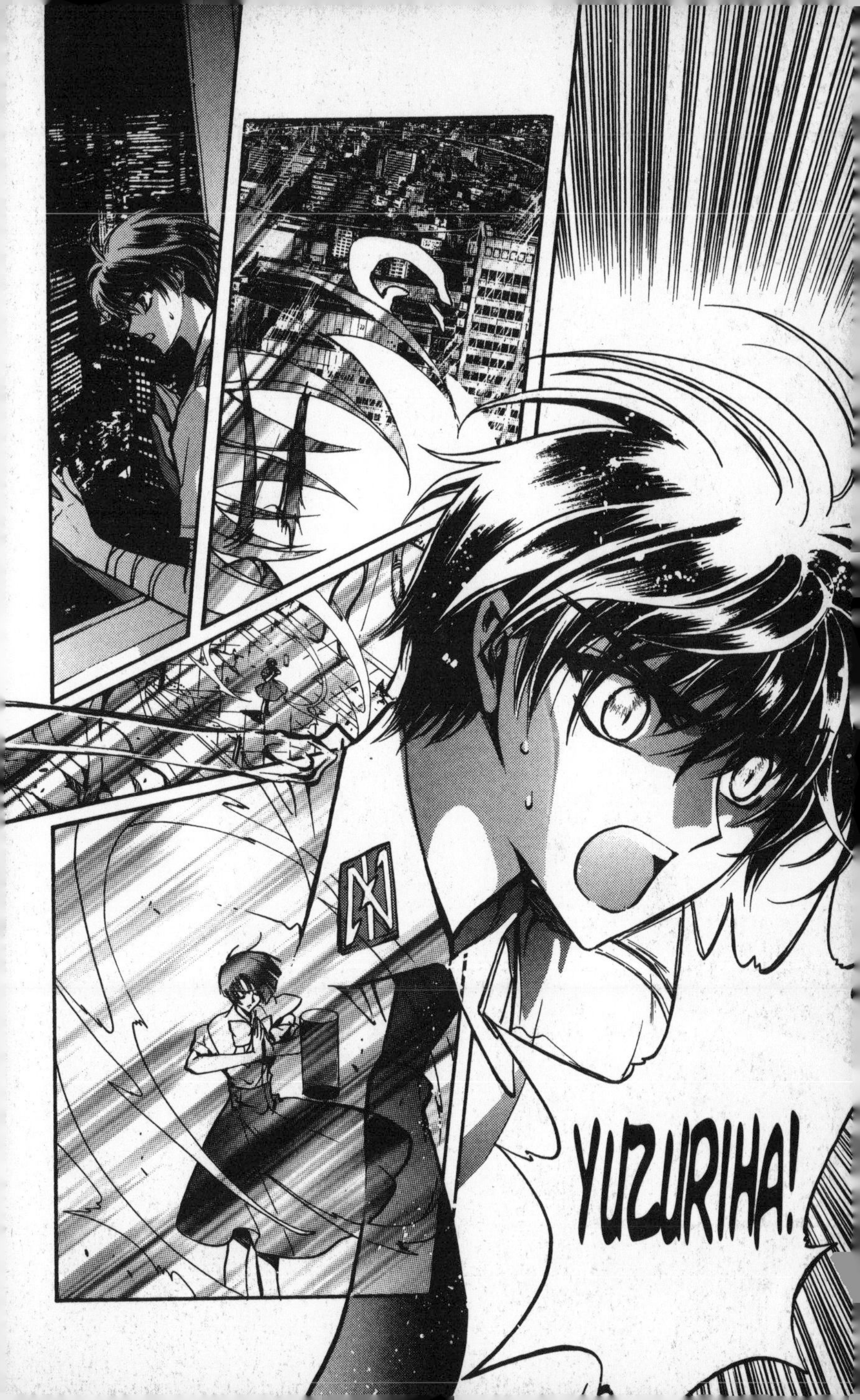
YUZURIHA!

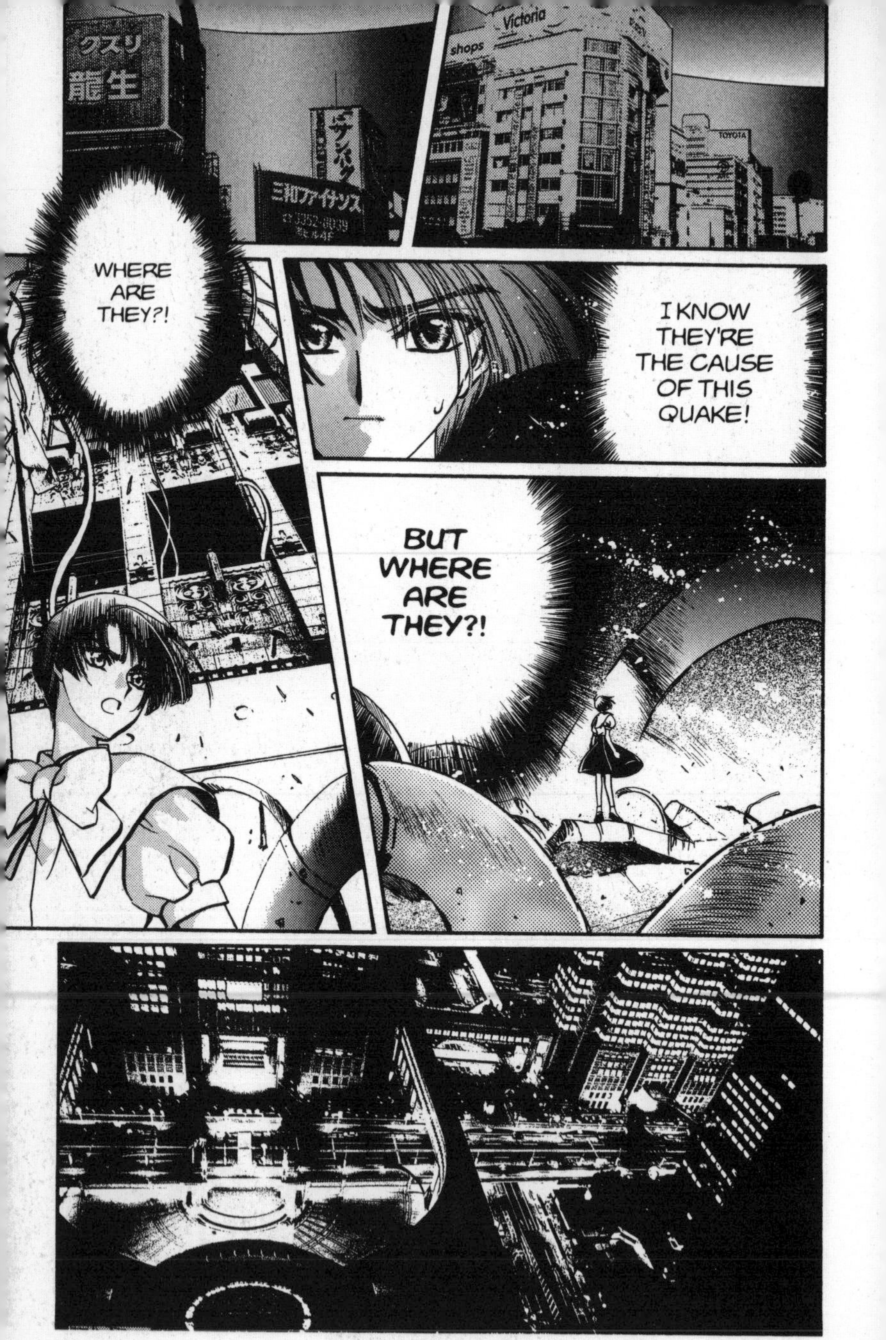
Victoria
shops
WHERE ARE THEY?!
I KNOW THEY'RE THE CAUSE OF THIS QUAKE!
BUT WHERE ARE THEY?!

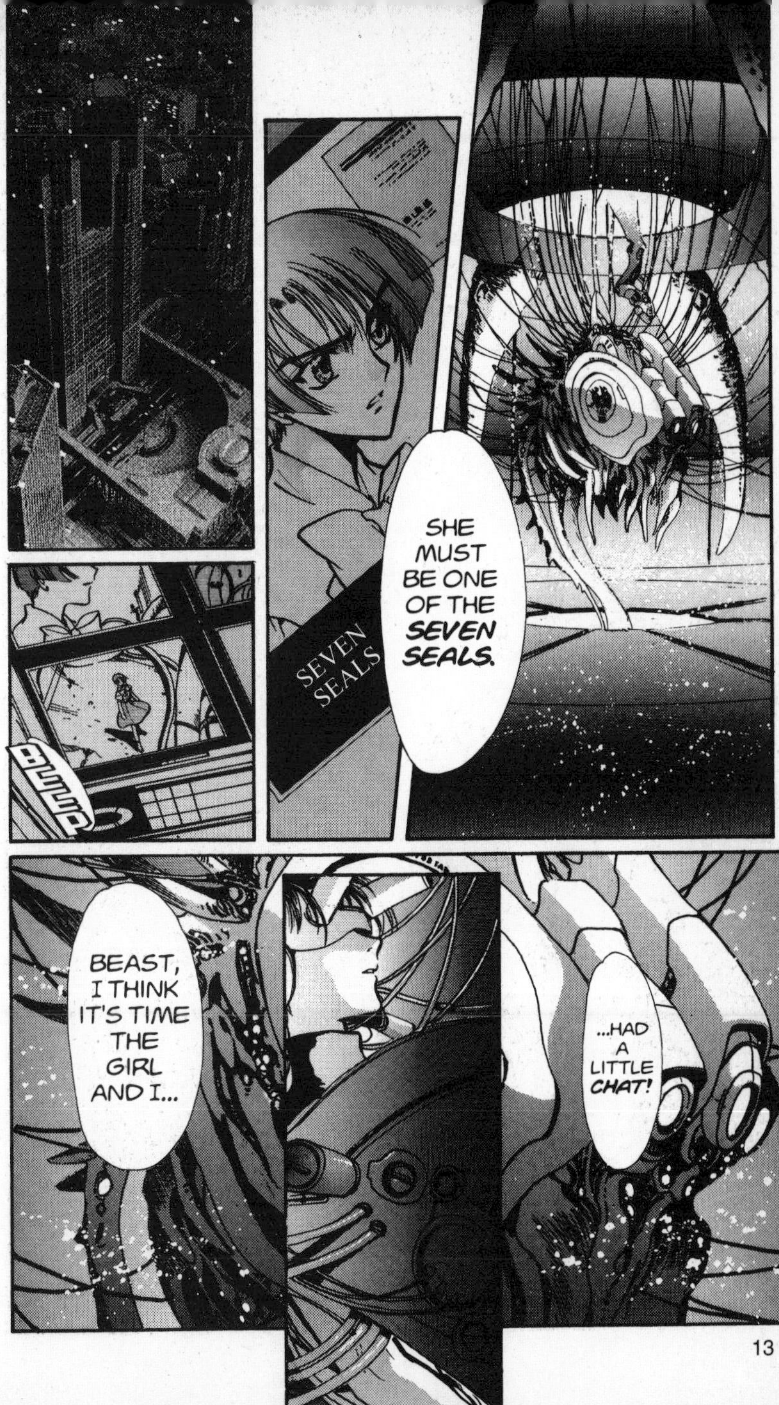
BEEP
SEVEN SEALS
SHE MUST BE ONE OF THE SEVEN SEALS.
BEAST, I THINK IT'S TIME THE GIRL AND I...
...HAD A LITTLE CHAT!

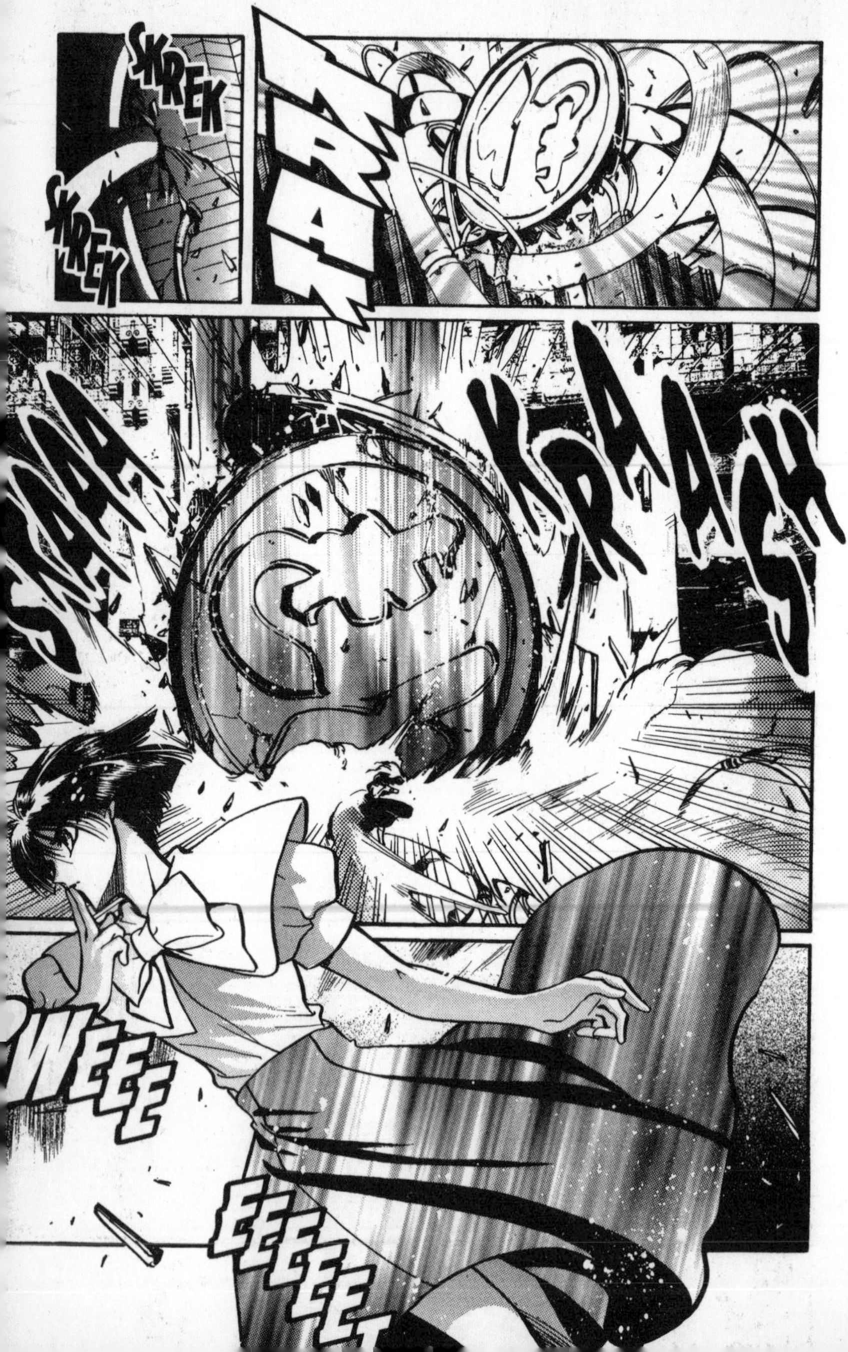
SKREK
SKREK
KRAASH
WEEE
EEEEE

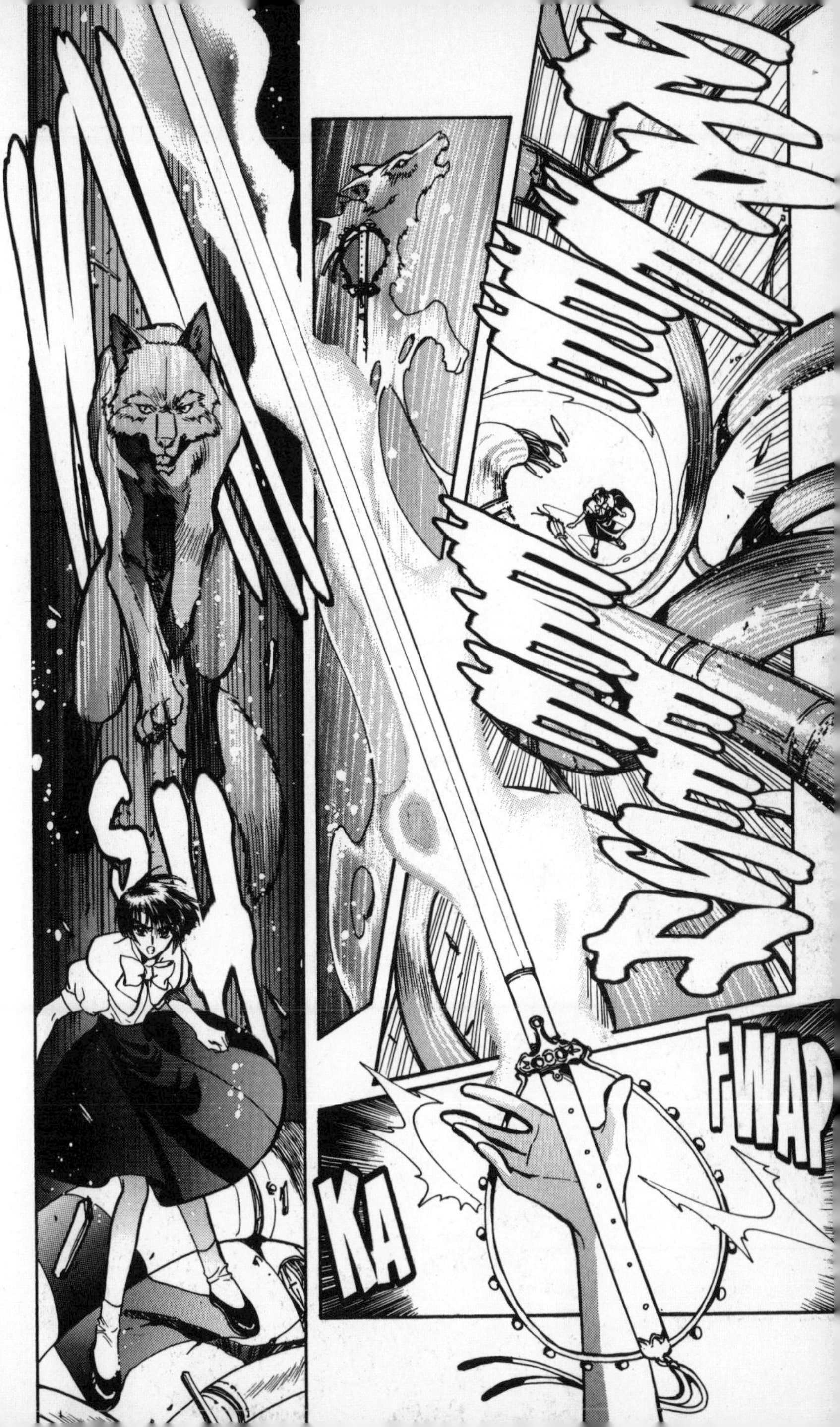
KA
FWAP

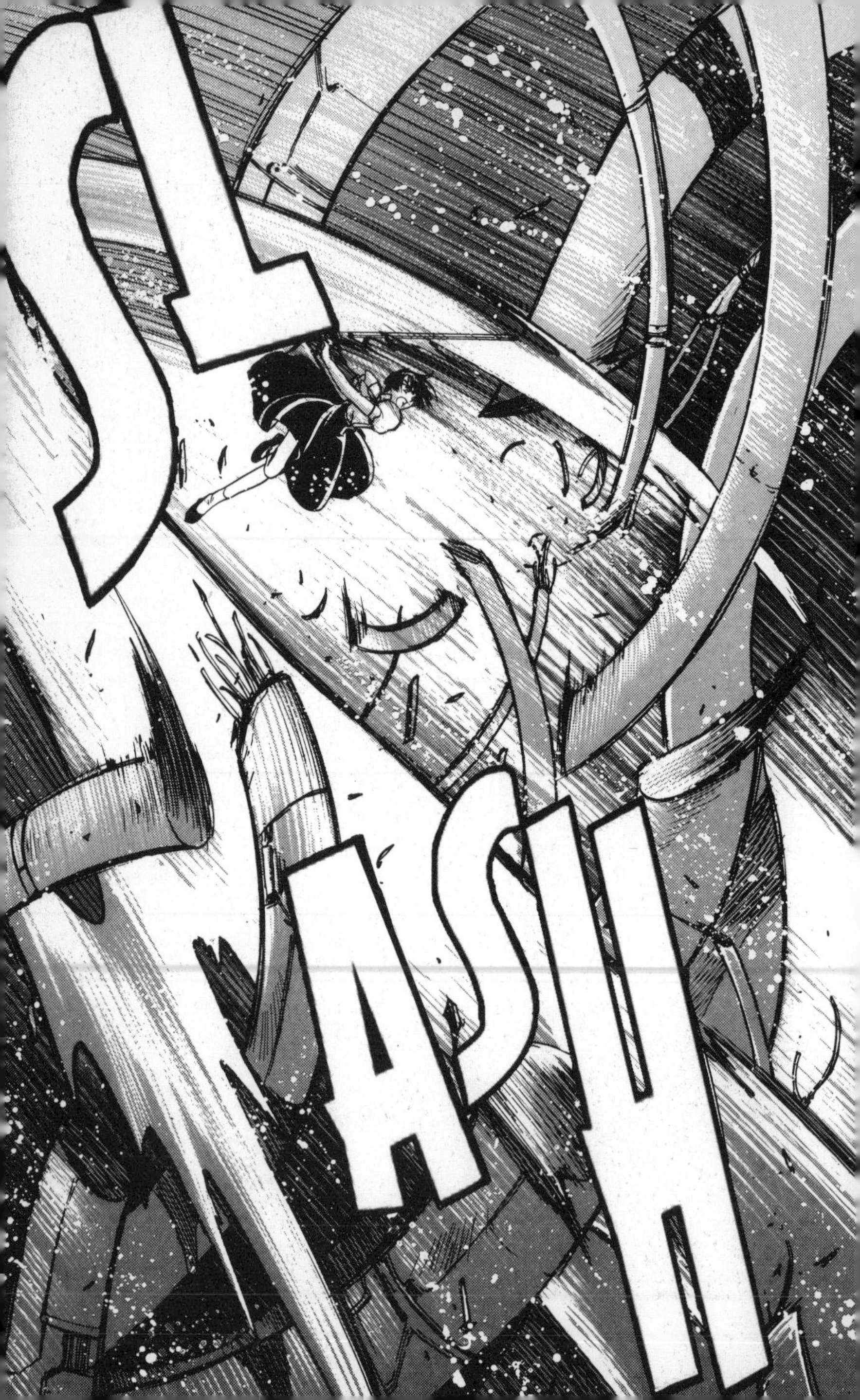
SLASH

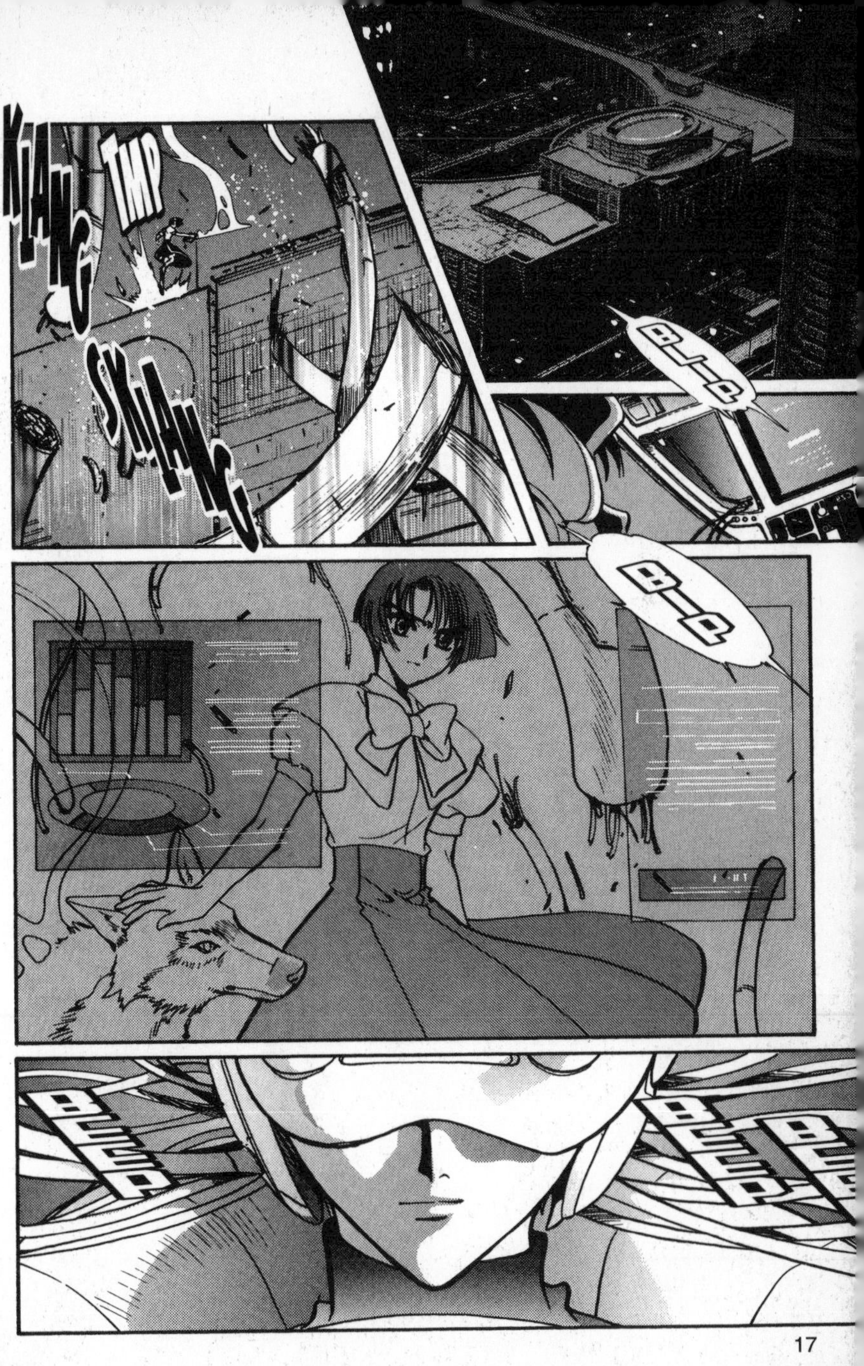
KLANG
TMP
SKLANG
BIP
BIP
BEEP
BEEP
BEEP

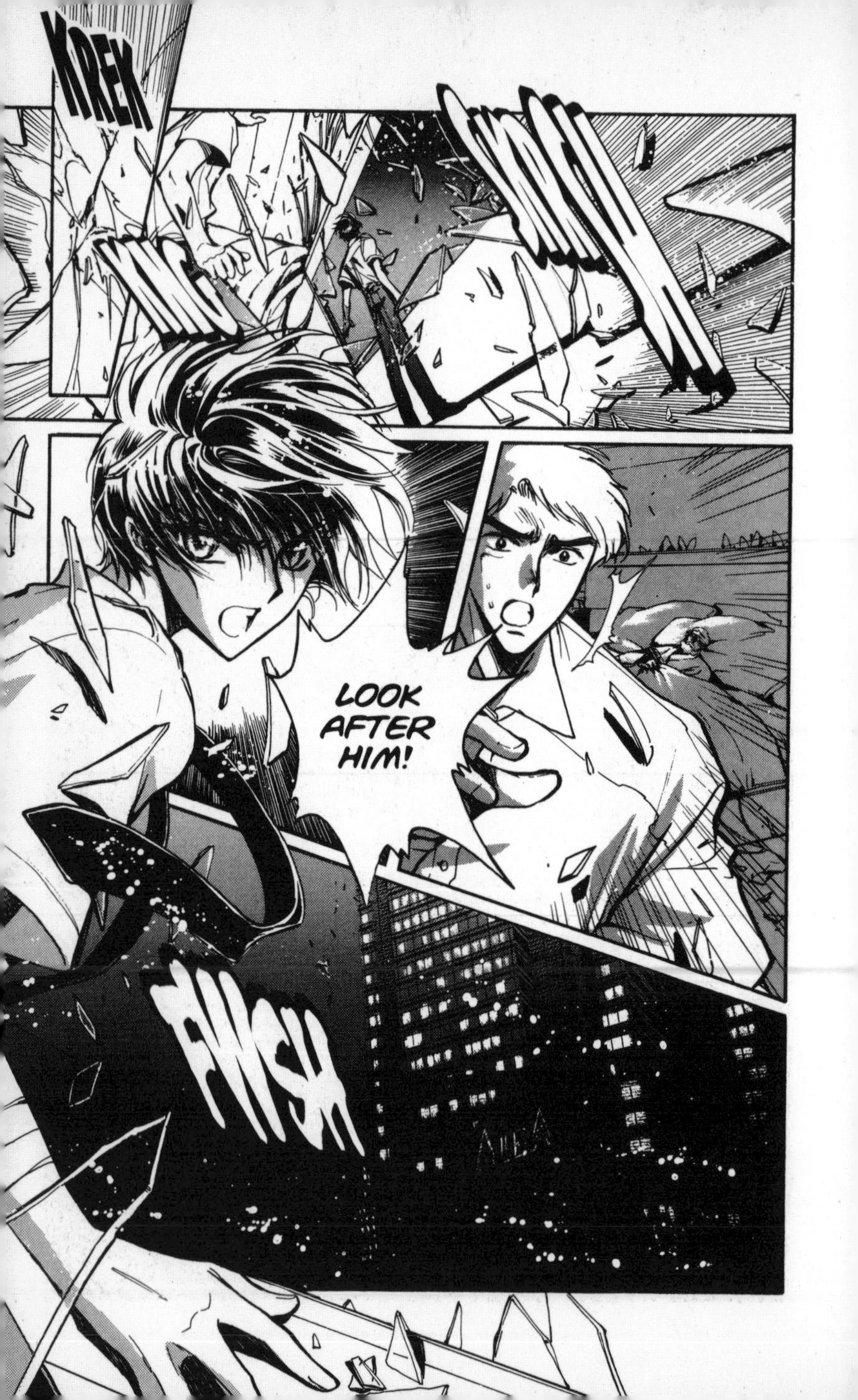
KREK
KLANG
CRASH
LOOK AFTER HIM!
FWSH

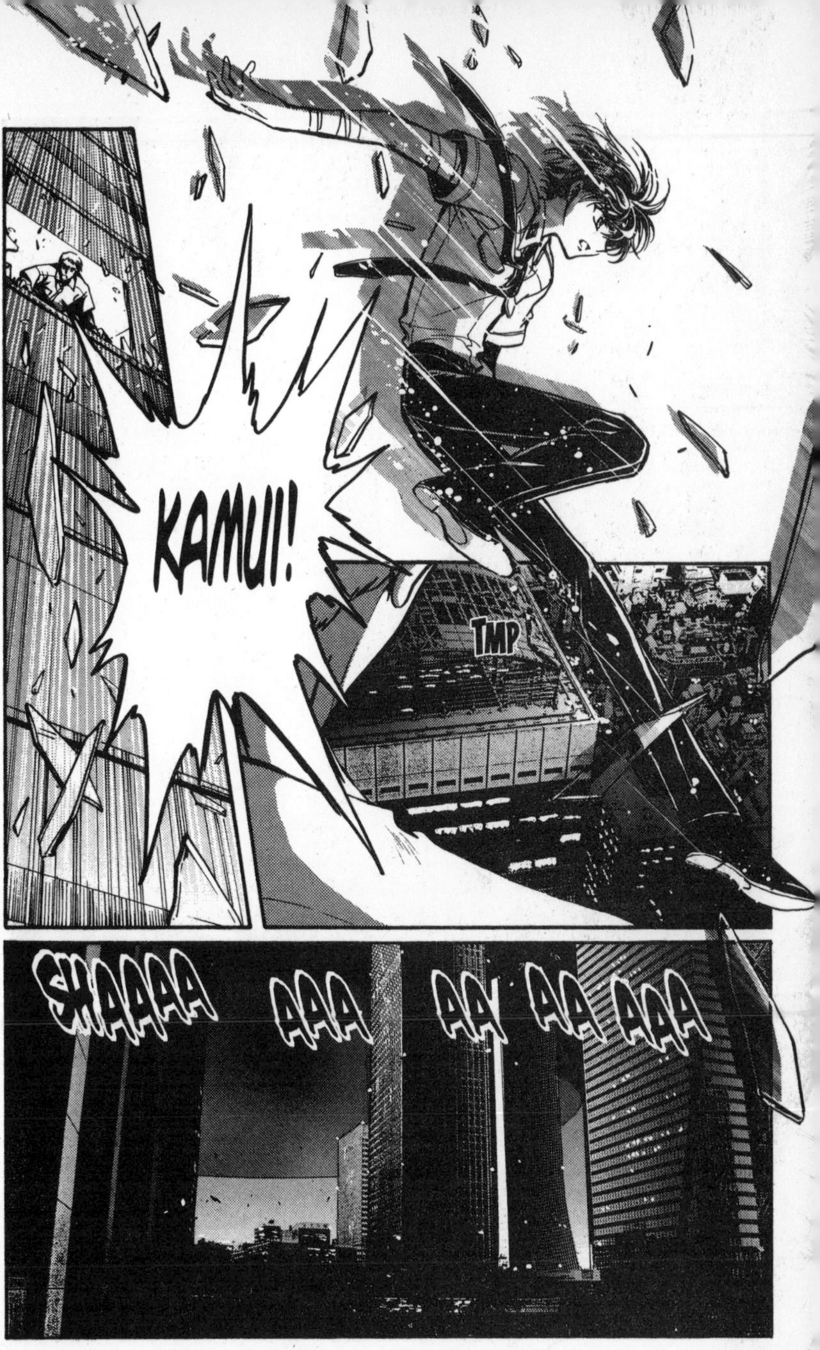
KAMUI!
TMP
SHAAAA AAA AA AA AAA

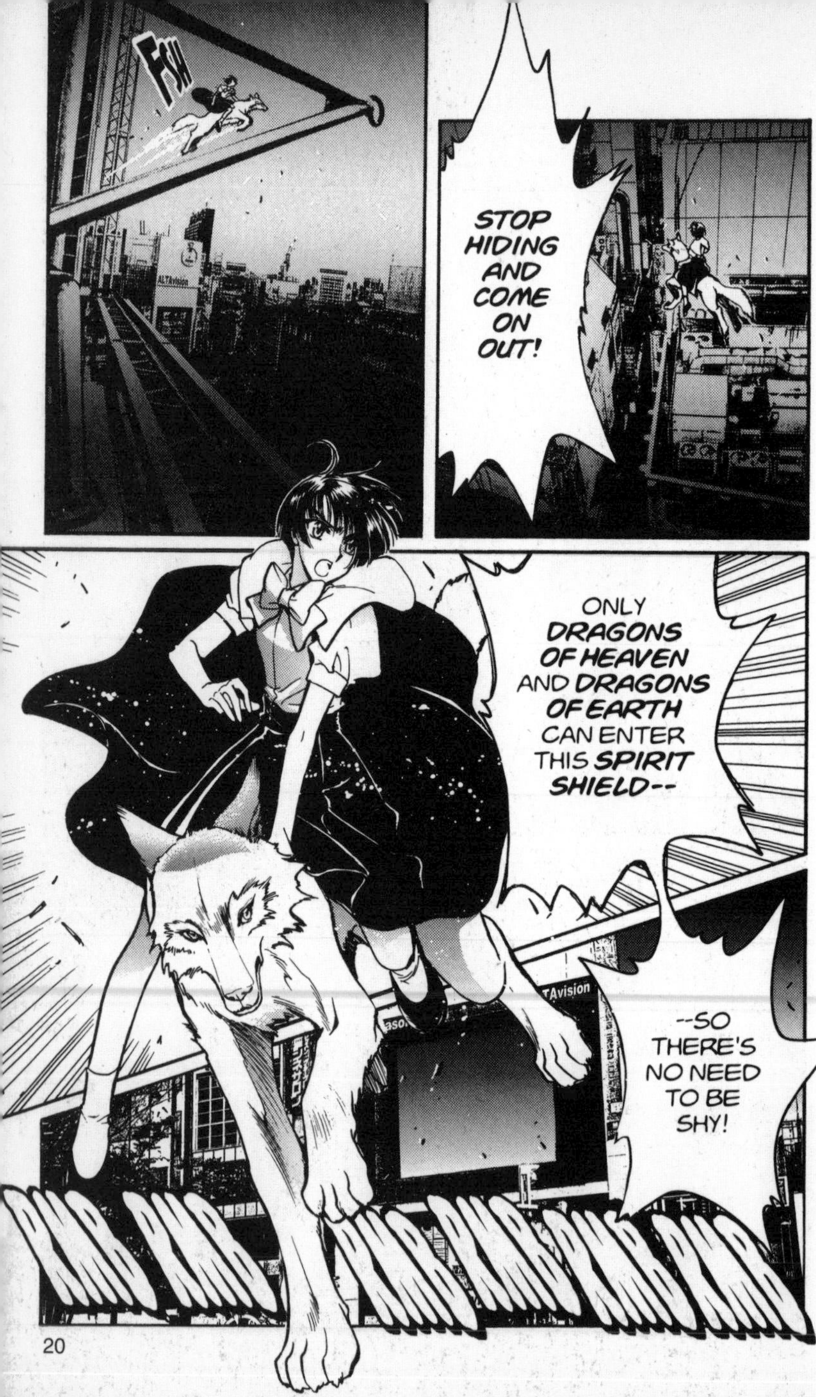
FSH
ALTAvision
STOP HIDING AND COME ON OUT!
ONLY DRAGONS OF HEAVEN AND DRAGONS OF EARTH CAN ENTER THIS SPIRIT SHIELD--
TAvision
--SO THERE'S NO NEED TO BE SHY!

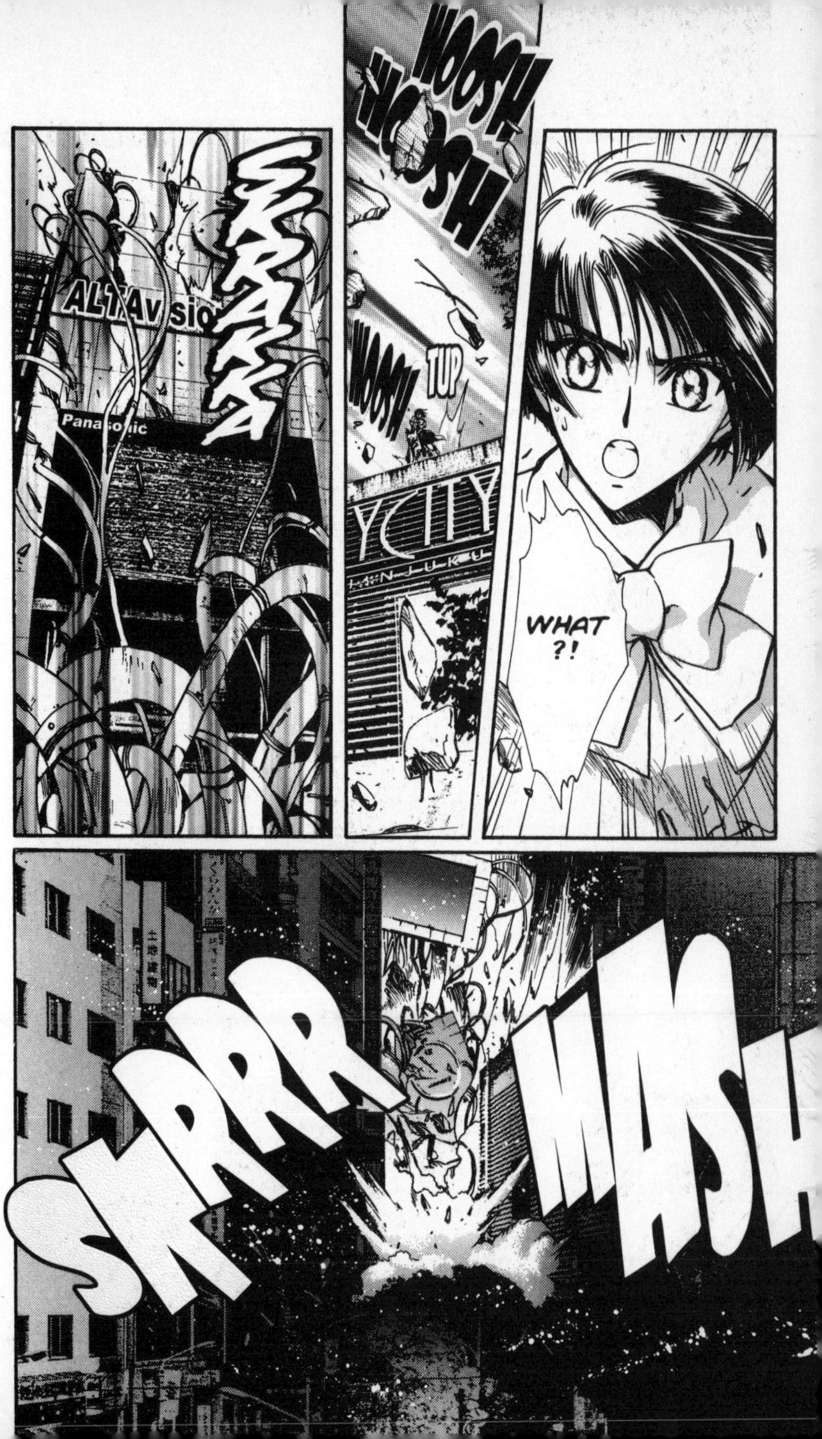
ALTAvsio
Panasonic
WOOSH, WOOSH
WOOSH
TUP
Y CITY
WHAT ?!
SMRRR-MASH

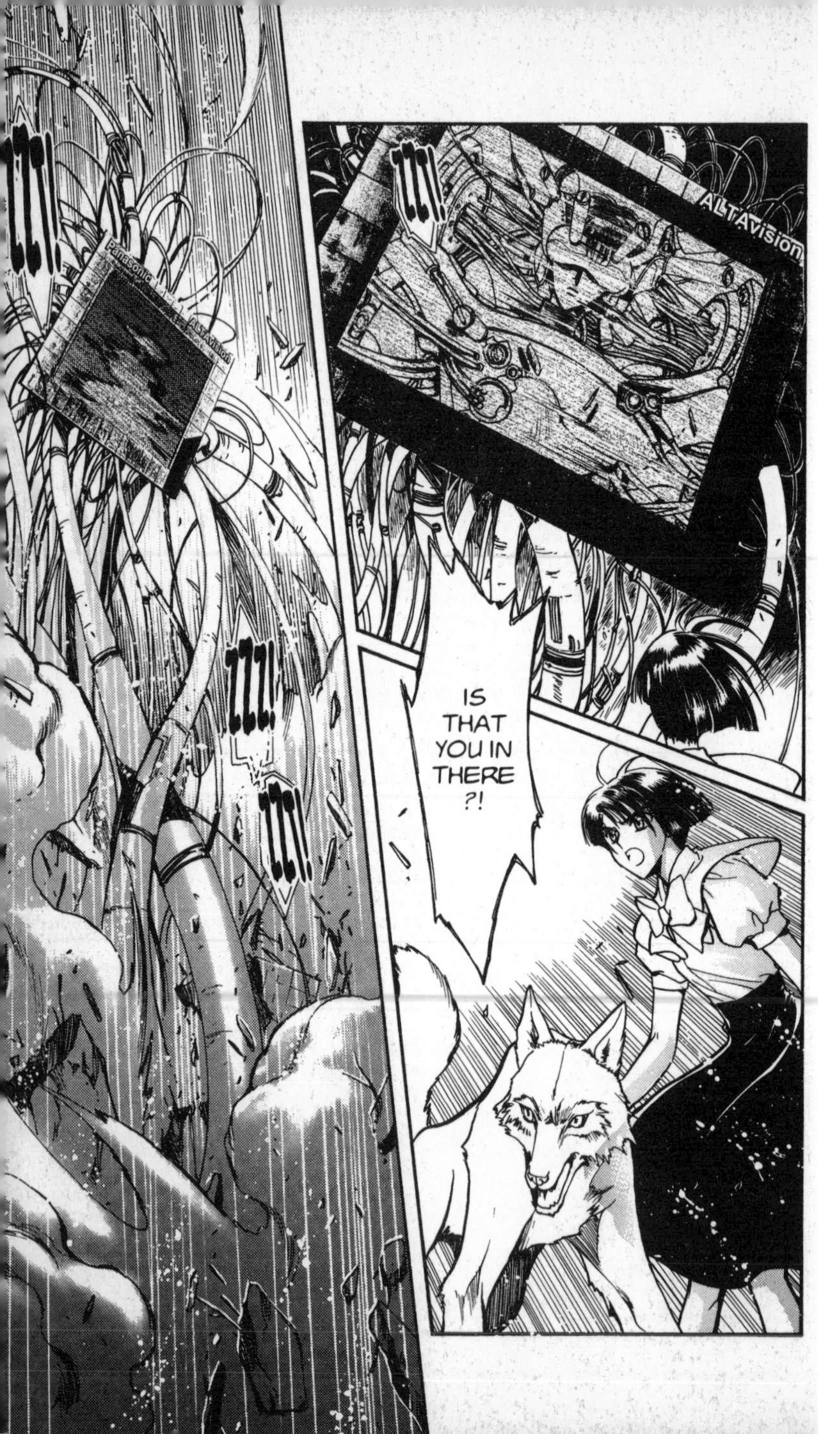
ZZZ!
Panasonic
ALTAvision
ZZZ!
ZZZ!
ZZZ!
ALTAvision
IS THAT YOU IN THERE ?!

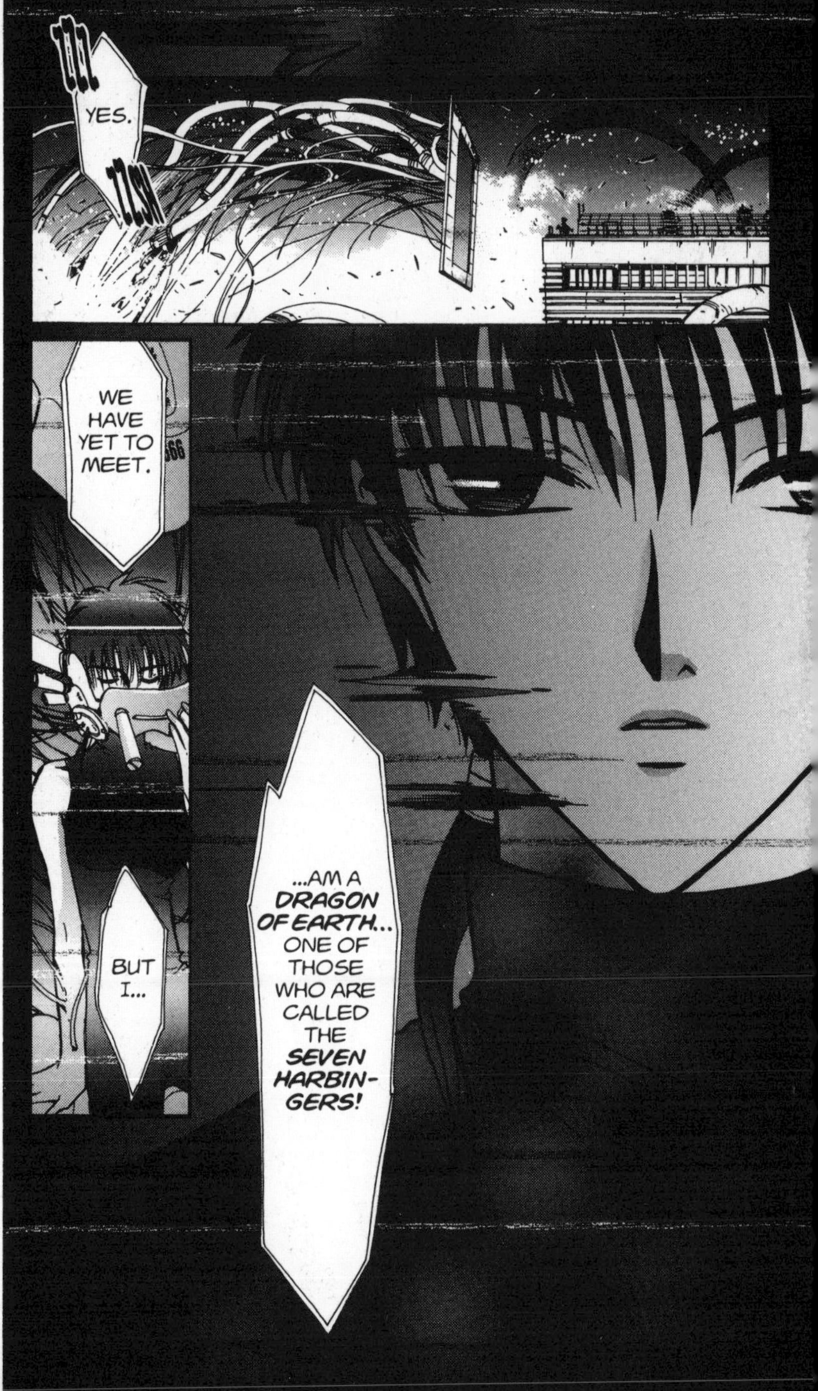
YES.
WE HAVE YET TO MEET.
BUT I...
...AM A DRAGON OF EARTH... ONE OF THOSE WHO ARE CALLED THE SEVEN HARBINGERS!

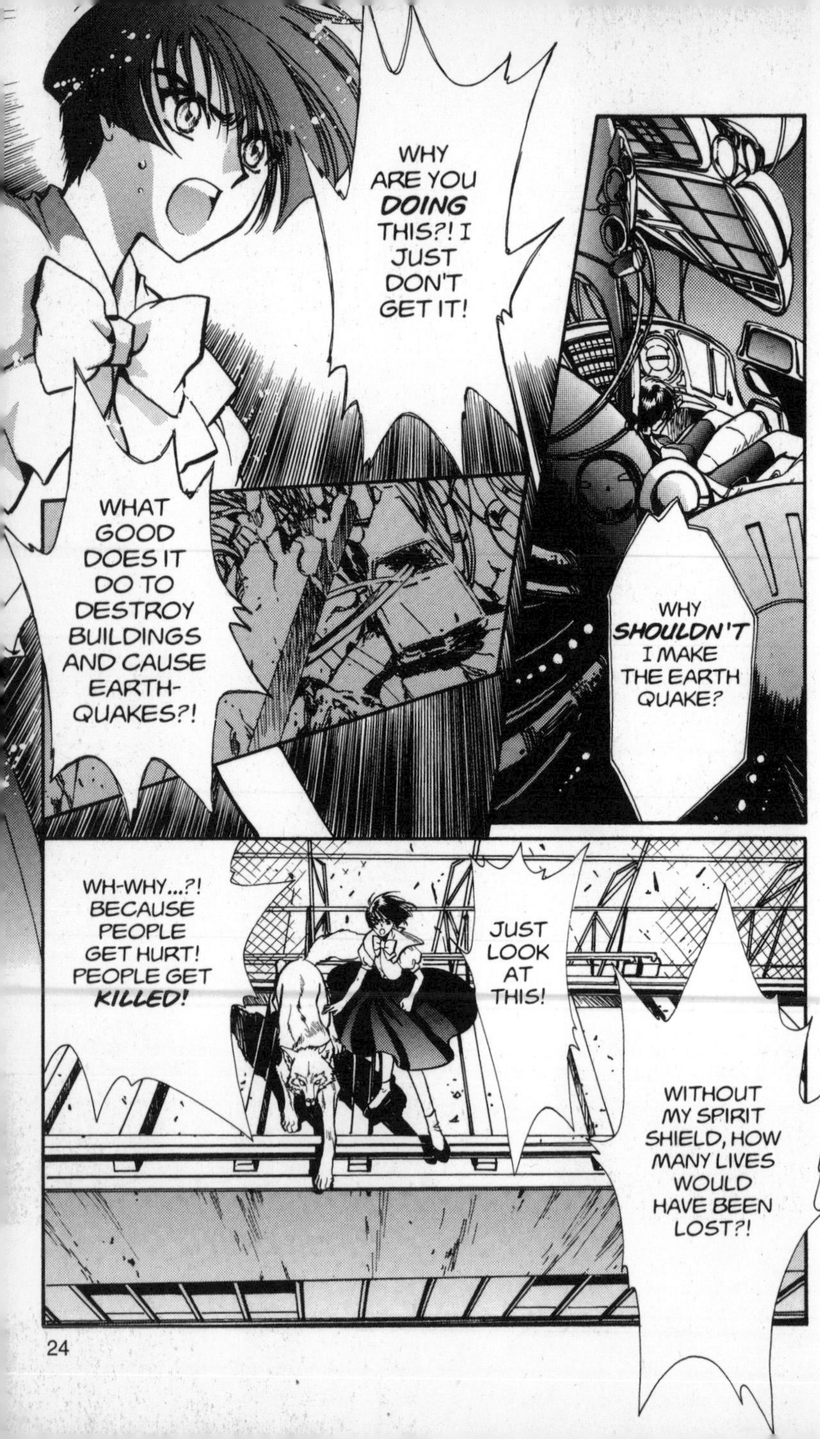
WHY ARE YOU DOING THIS?! I JUST DON'T GET IT!
WHAT GOOD DOES IT DO TO DESTROY BUILDINGS AND CAUSE EARTH-QUAKES?!
WHY SHOULDN'T I MAKE THE EARTH QUAKE?
WH-WHY...?! BECAUSE PEOPLE GET HURT! PEOPLE GET KILLED!
JUST LOOK AT THIS!
WITHOUT MY SPIRIT SHIELD, HOW MANY LIVES WOULD HAVE BEEN LOST?!

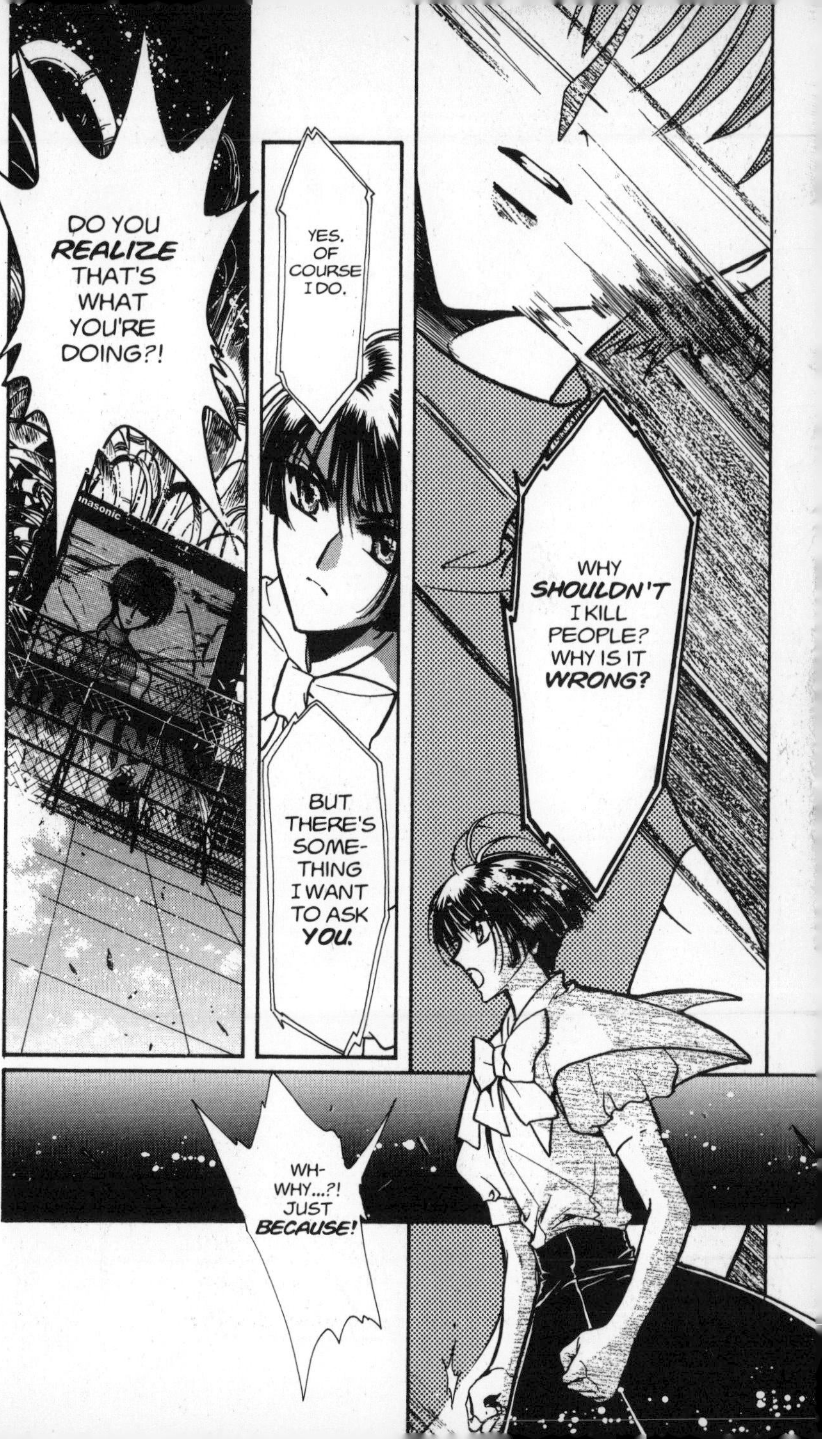
DO YOU **REALIZE** THAT'S WHAT YOU'RE DOING?!
YES. OF COURSE I DO.
BUT THERE'S SOME-THING I WANT TO ASK **YOU.**
WHY **SHOULDN'T** I KILL PEOPLE? WHY IS IT **WRONG?**
WH-WHY...?! JUST **BECAUSE!**

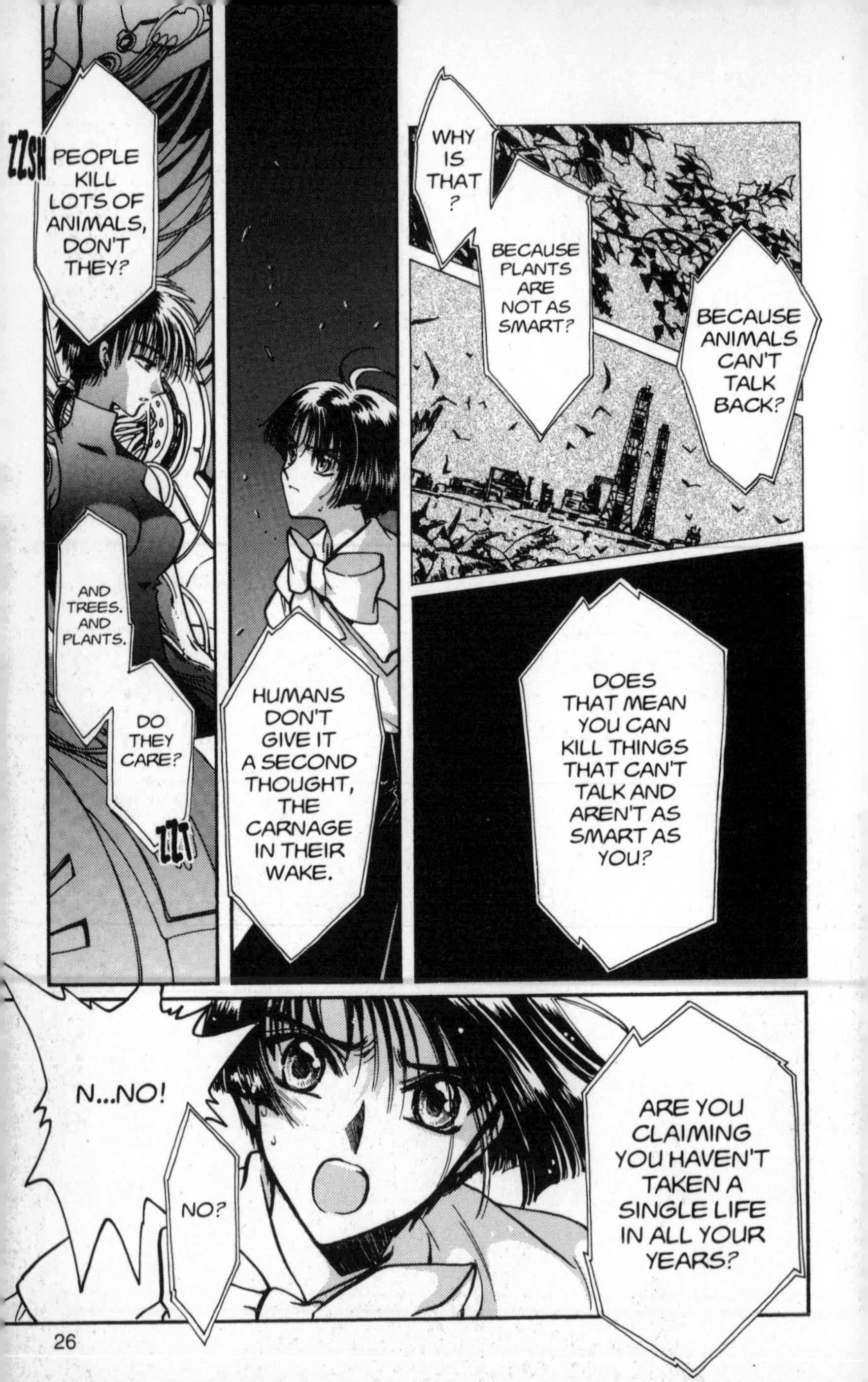
ZZSH
PEOPLE KILL LOTS OF ANIMALS, DON'T THEY?
AND TREES. AND PLANTS.
DO THEY CARE?
ZZT
HUMANS DON'T GIVE IT A SECOND THOUGHT, THE CARNAGE IN THEIR WAKE.
WHY IS THAT?
BECAUSE PLANTS ARE NOT AS SMART?
BECAUSE ANIMALS CAN'T TALK BACK?
DOES THAT MEAN YOU CAN KILL THINGS THAT CAN'T TALK AND AREN'T AS SMART AS YOU?
N...NO!
NO?
ARE YOU CLAIMING YOU HAVEN'T TAKEN A SINGLE LIFE IN ALL YOUR YEARS?

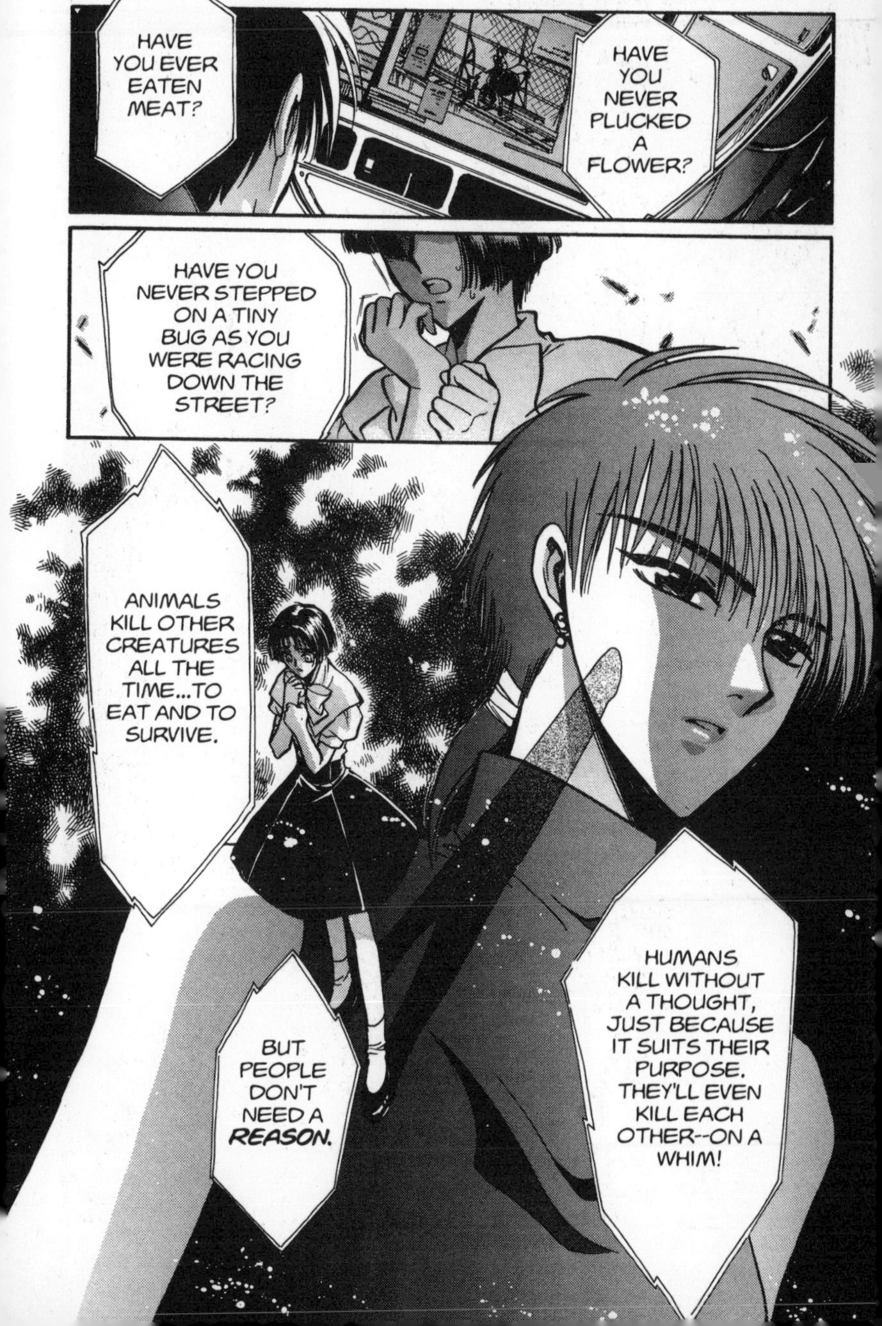
HAVE YOU EVER EATEN MEAT?
HAVE YOU NEVER PLUCKED A FLOWER?
HAVE YOU NEVER STEPPED ON A TINY BUG AS YOU WERE RACING DOWN THE STREET?
ANIMALS KILL OTHER CREATURES ALL THE TIME...TO EAT AND TO SURVIVE.
BUT PEOPLE DON'T NEED A REASON.
HUMANS KILL WITHOUT A THOUGHT, JUST BECAUSE IT SUITS THEIR PURPOSE. THEY'LL EVEN KILL EACH OTHER--ON A WHIM!

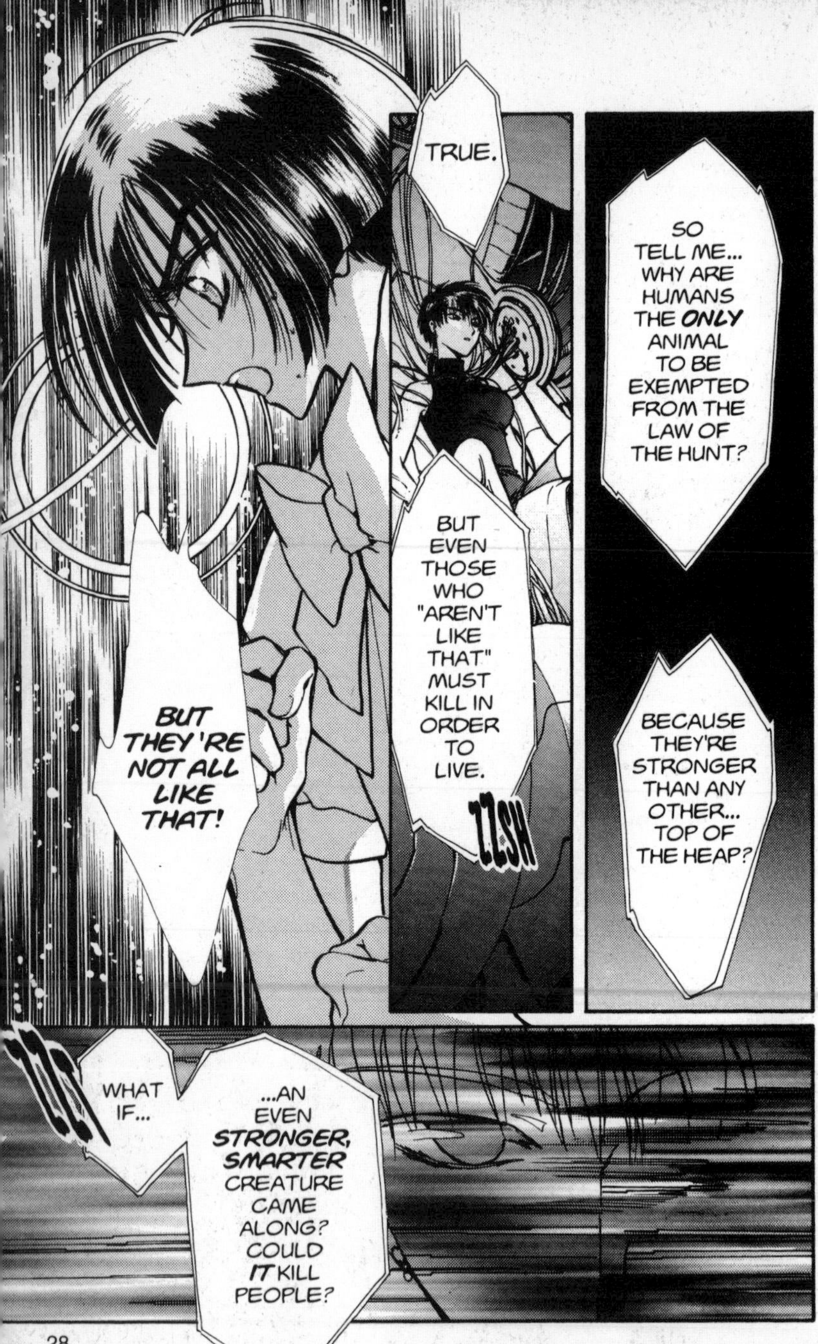
BUT THEY'RE NOT ALL LIKE THAT!
TRUE.
BUT EVEN THOSE WHO "AREN'T LIKE THAT" MUST KILL IN ORDER TO LIVE.
ZZSH
SO TELL ME... WHY ARE HUMANS THE ONLY ANIMAL TO BE EXEMPTED FROM THE LAW OF THE HUNT?
BECAUSE THEY'RE STRONGER THAN ANY OTHER... TOP OF THE HEAP?
WHAT IF...
...AN EVEN STRONGER, SMARTER CREATURE CAME ALONG? COULD IT KILL PEOPLE?

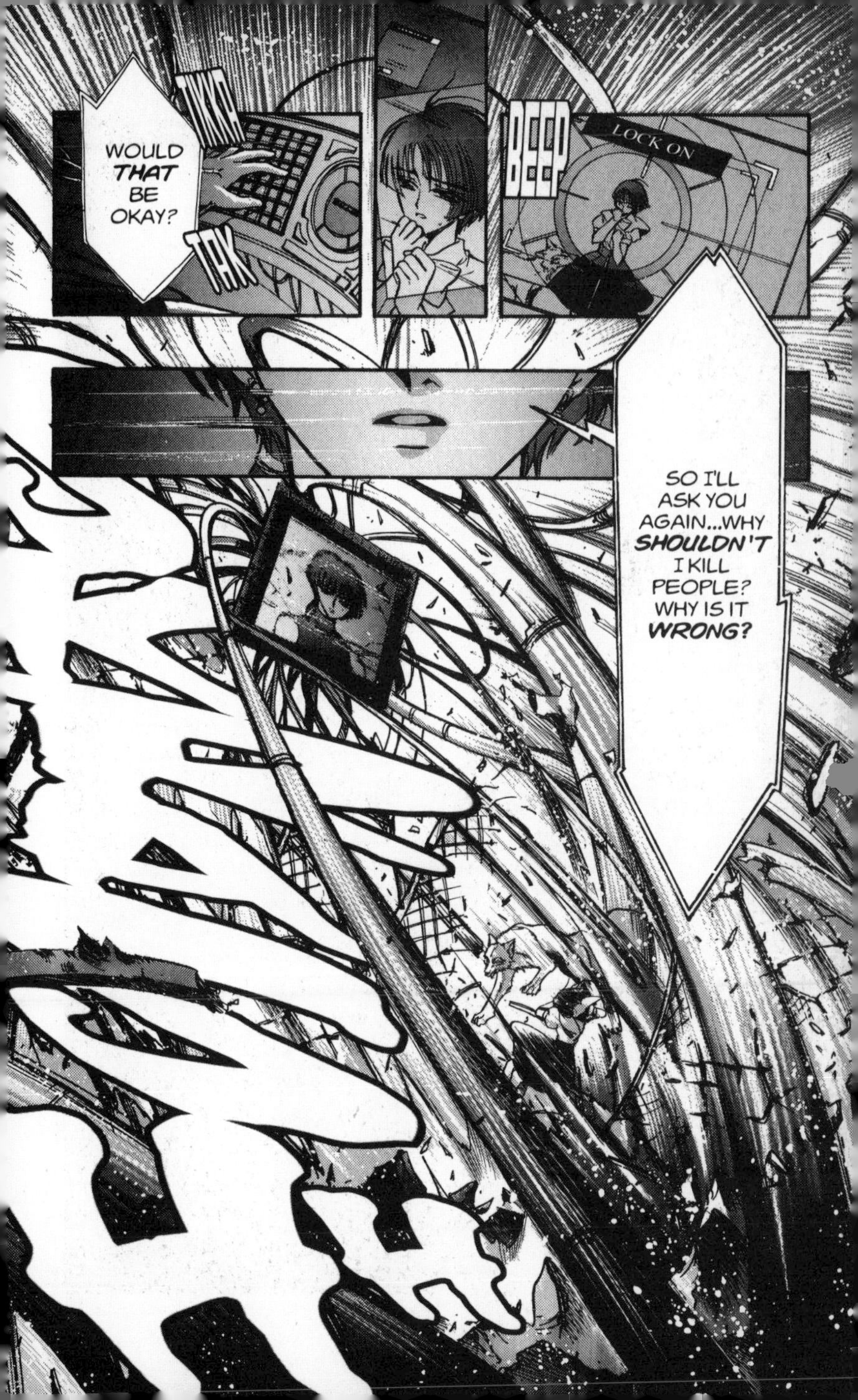
WOULD THAT BE OKAY?
TIKKA
TAK
BEEP
LOCK ON
SO I'LL ASK YOU AGAIN...WHY SHOULDN'T I KILL PEOPLE? WHY IS IT WRONG?

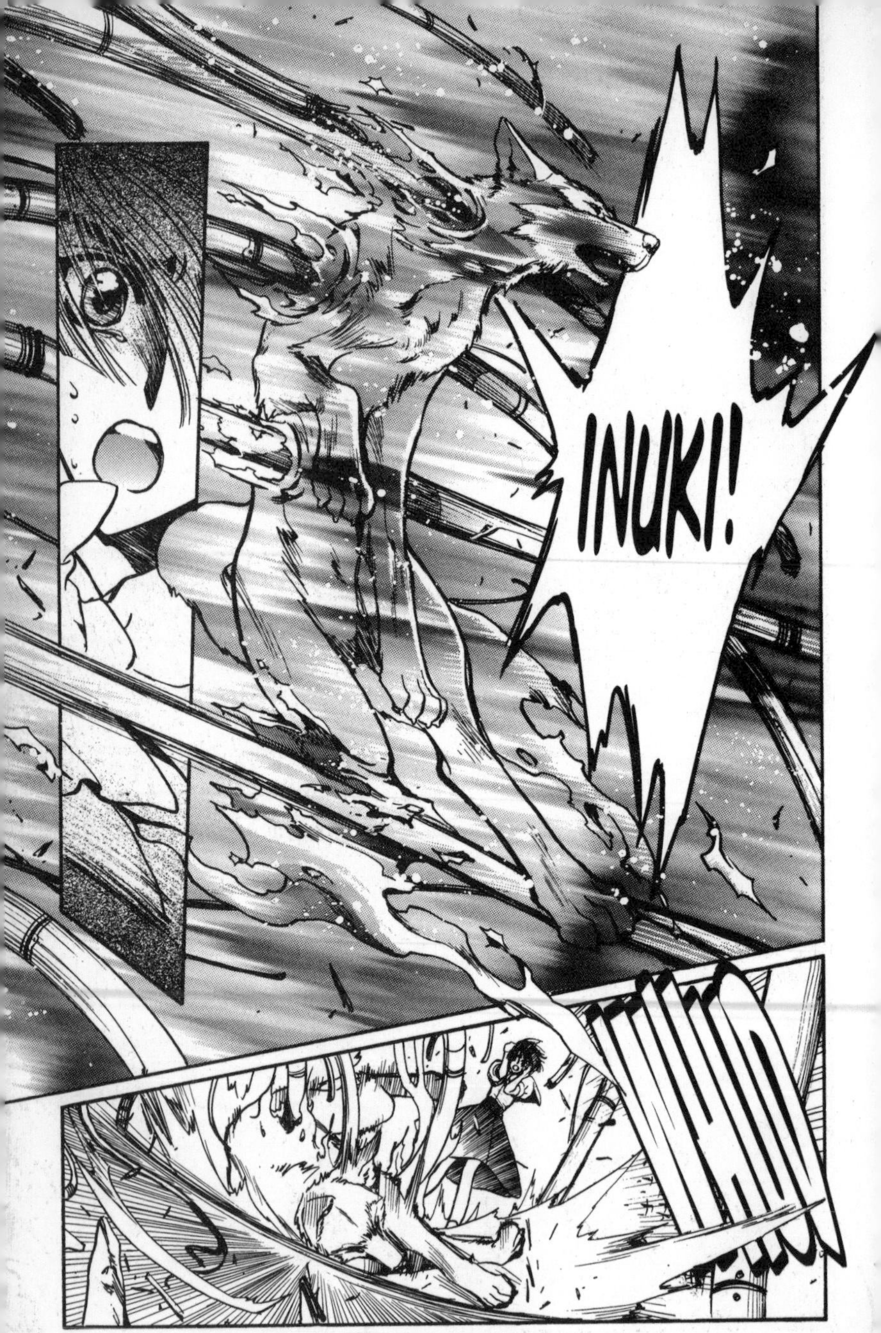
INUKI!

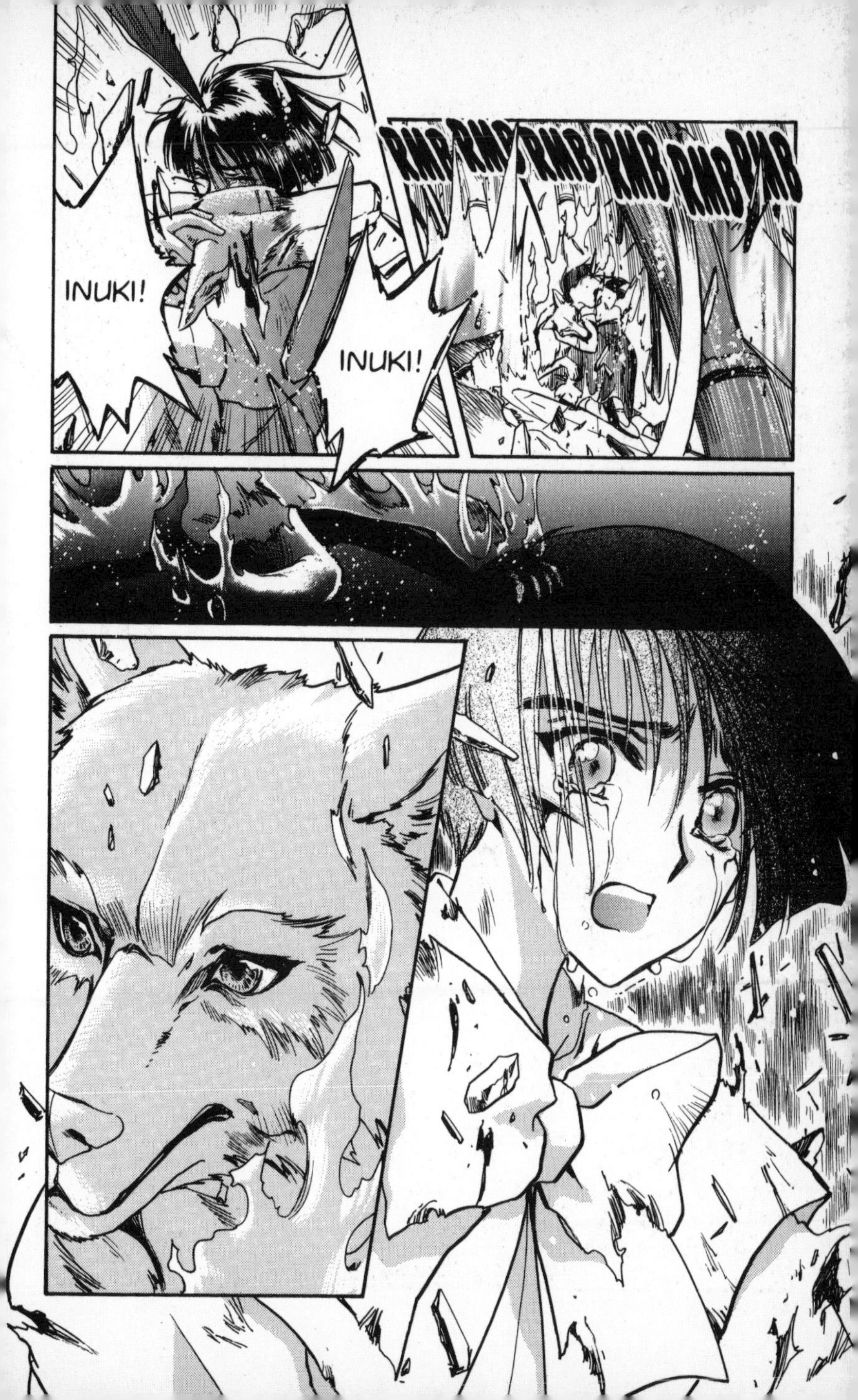

INUKI!
RMB RMB RMB RMB RMB RMB
INUKI!

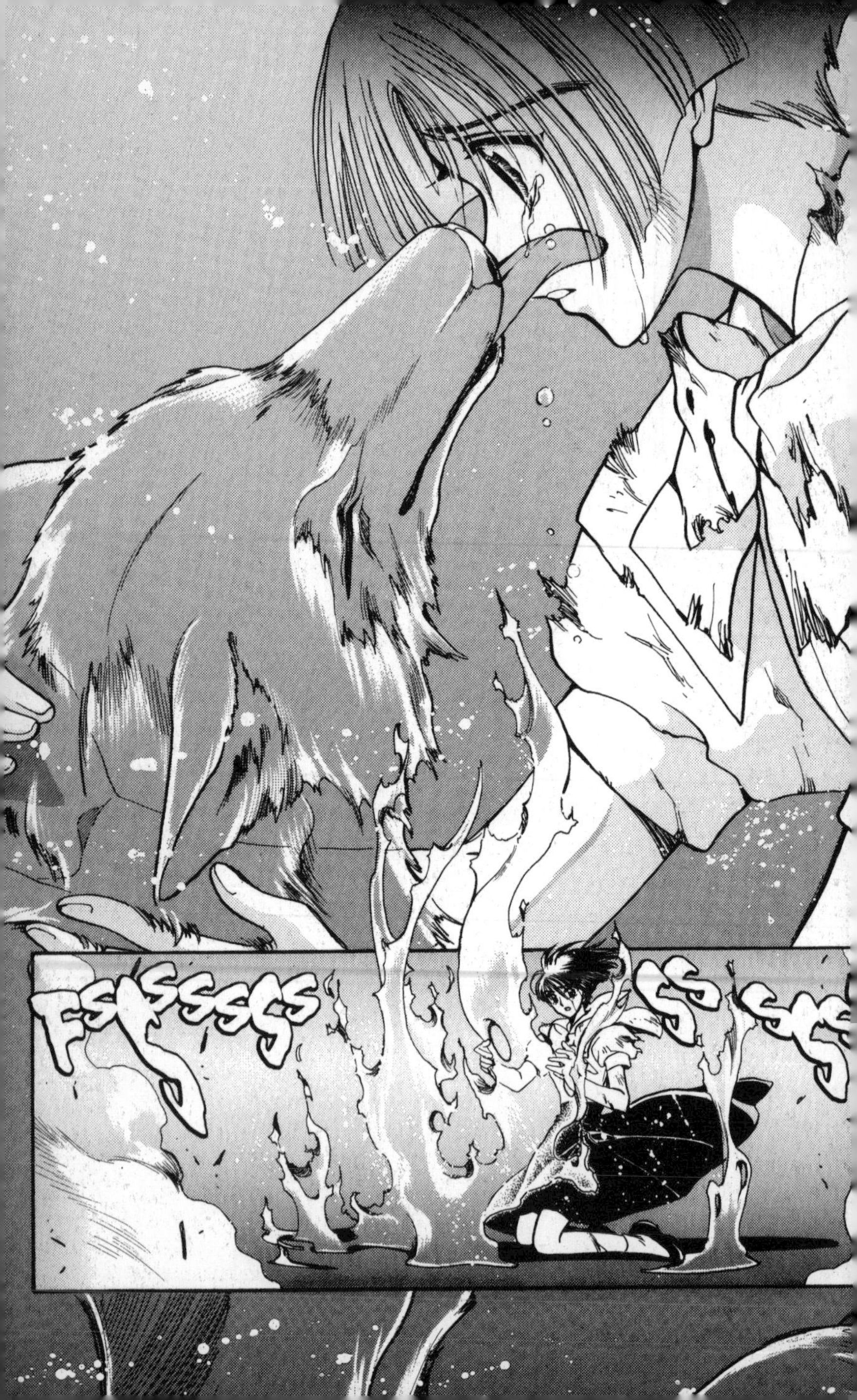
FSSSSSS
SSSS

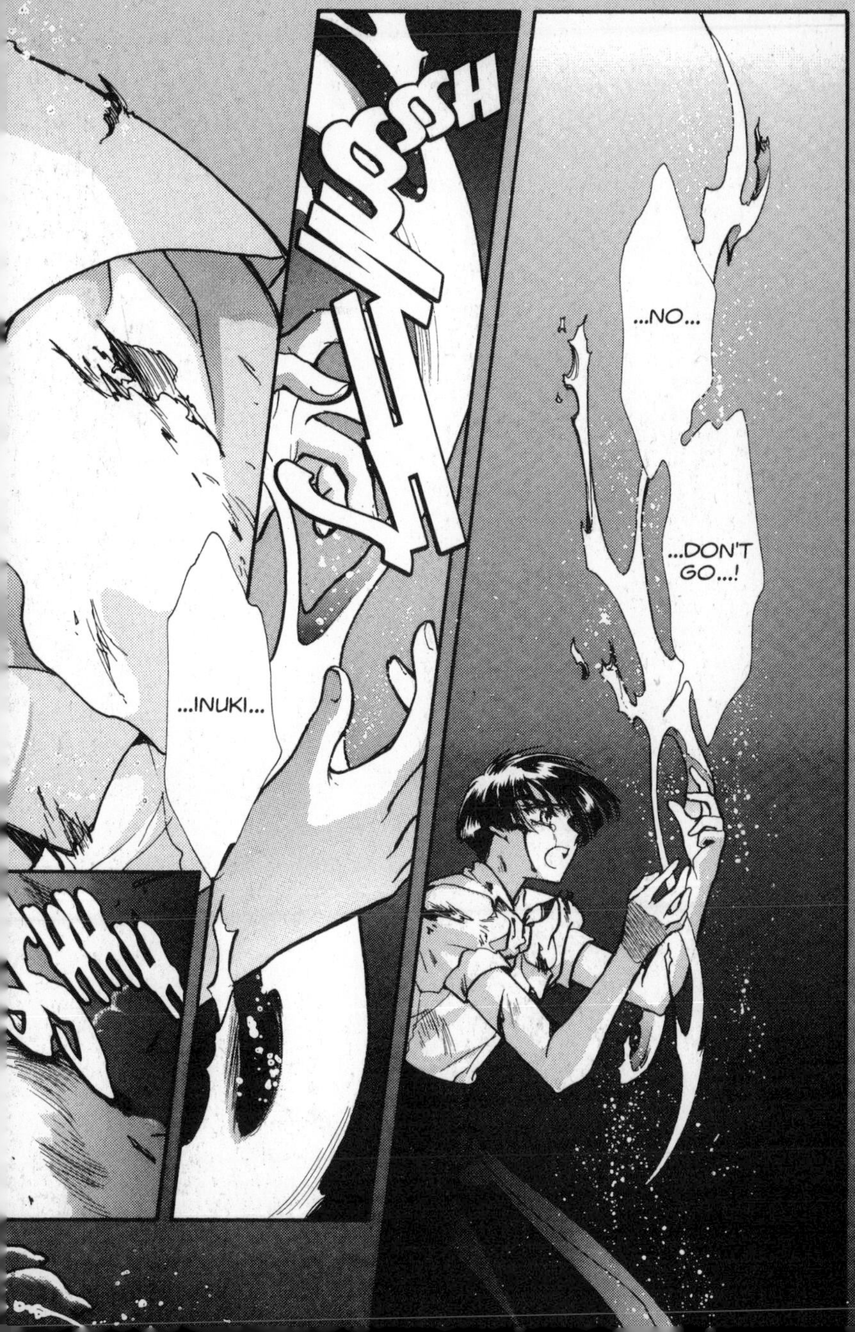
...INUKI...
...NO...
...DON'T GO...!

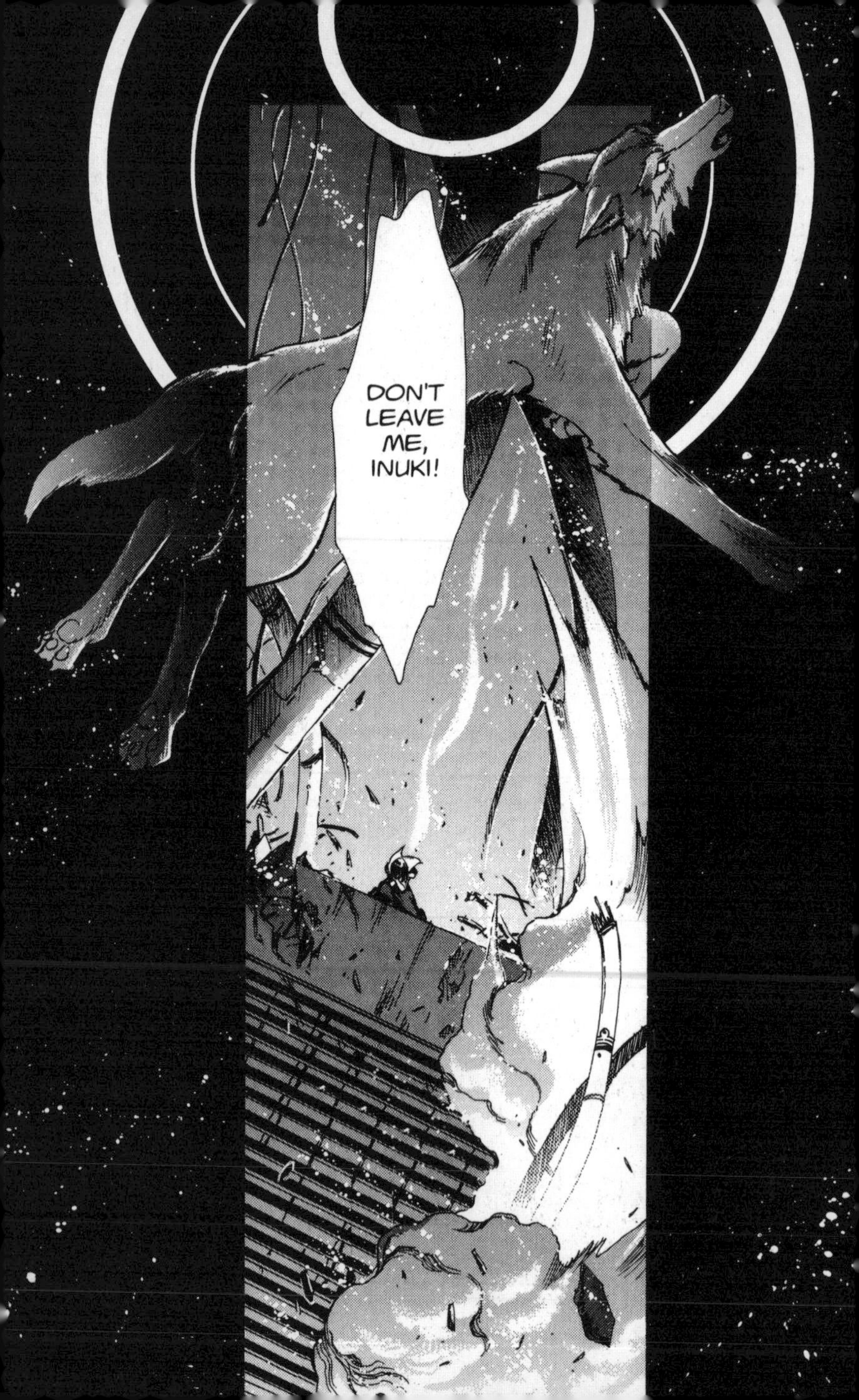
DON'T LEAVE ME, INUKI!

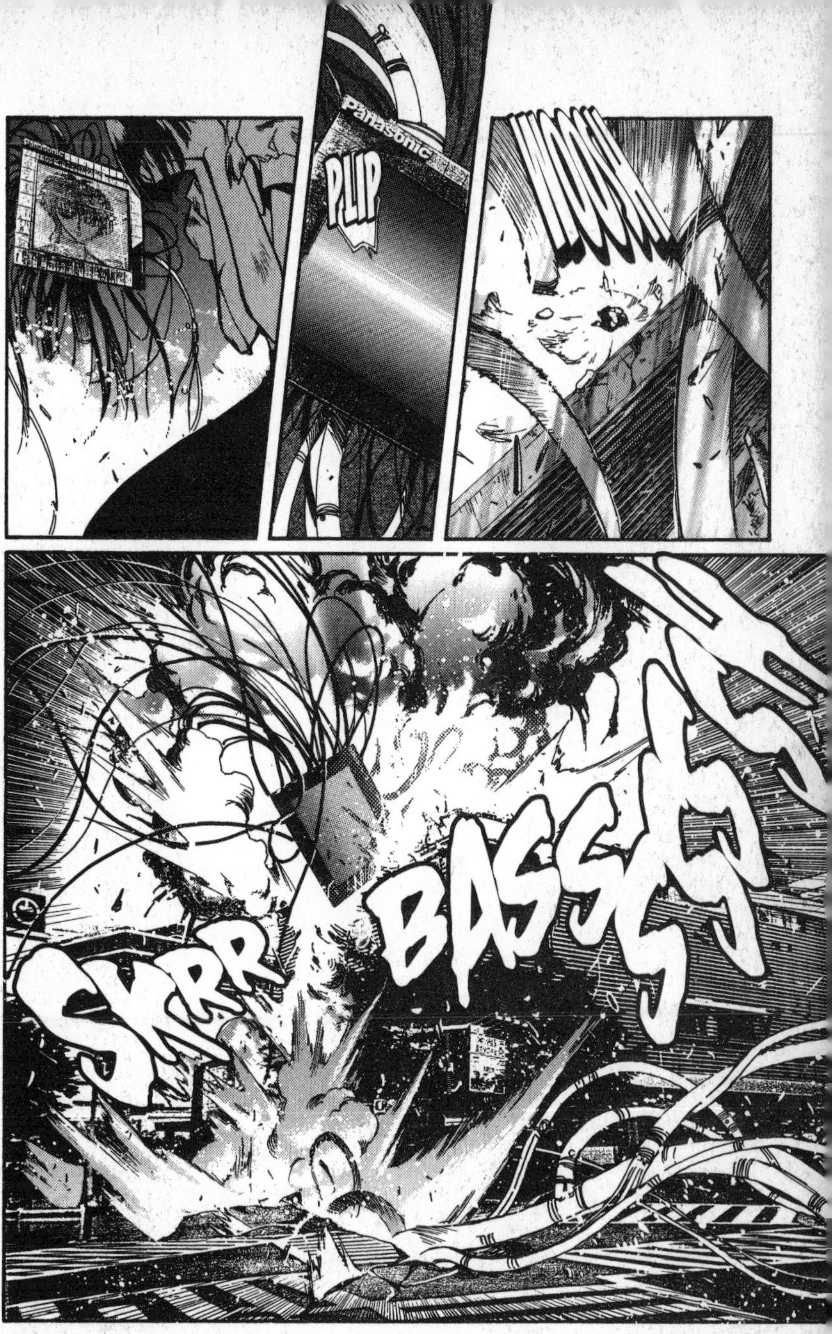
Panasonic
PLIP
WOOSH
SKRR
BASSSS

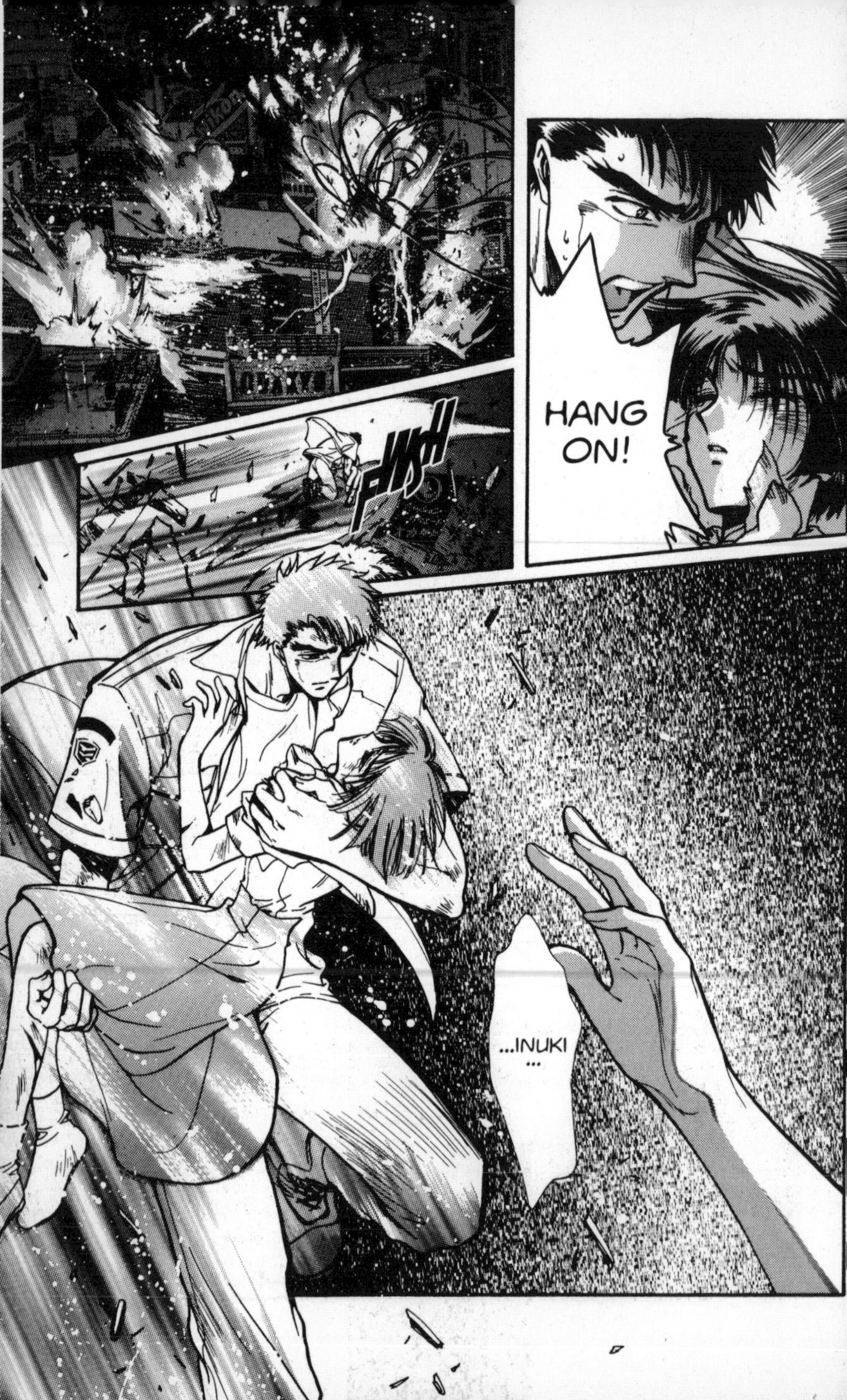
FWISH
HANG ON!
...INUKI ...

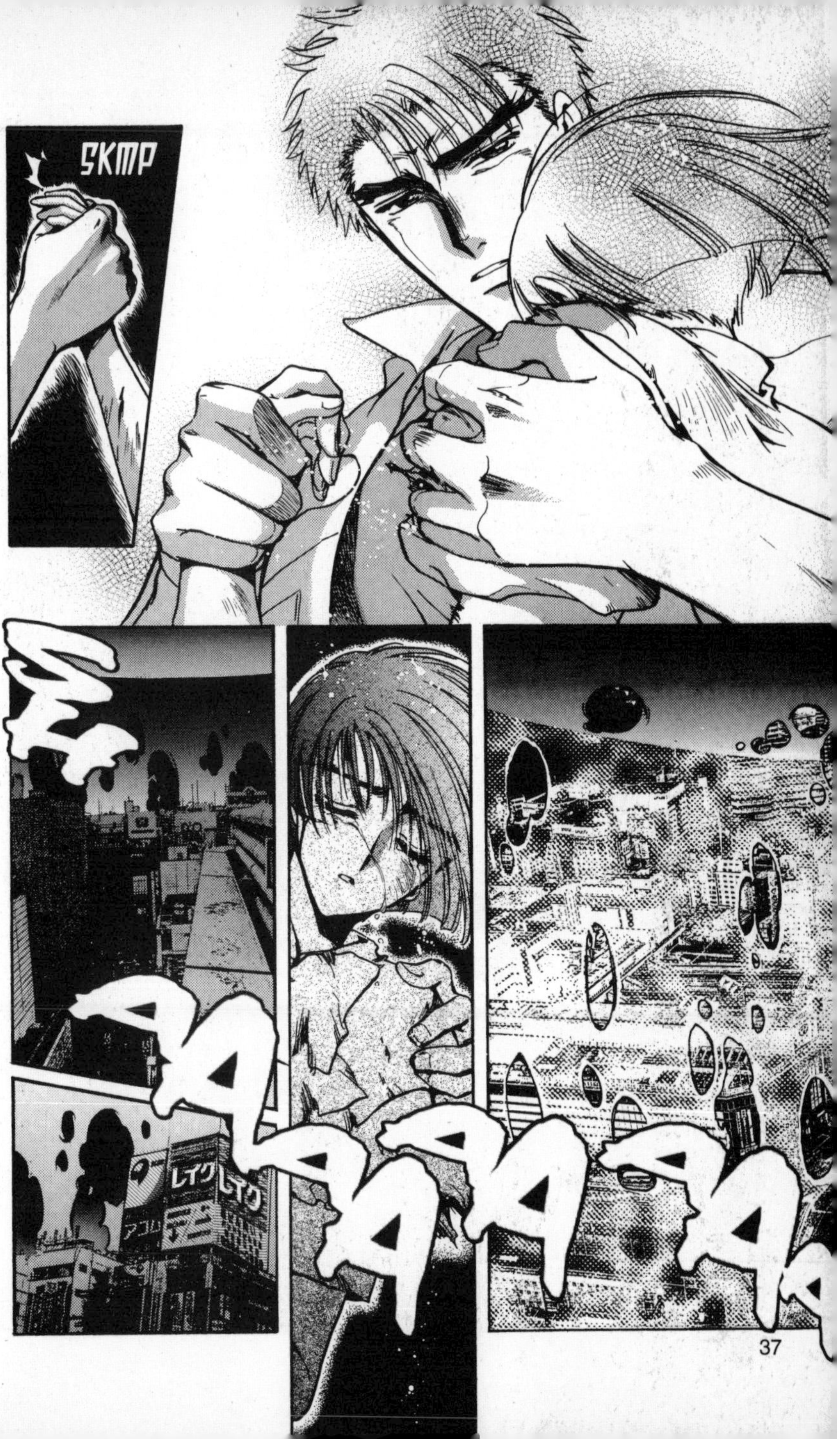
SKMP
ZAAAAAAAA
レイク
レイク
アコム

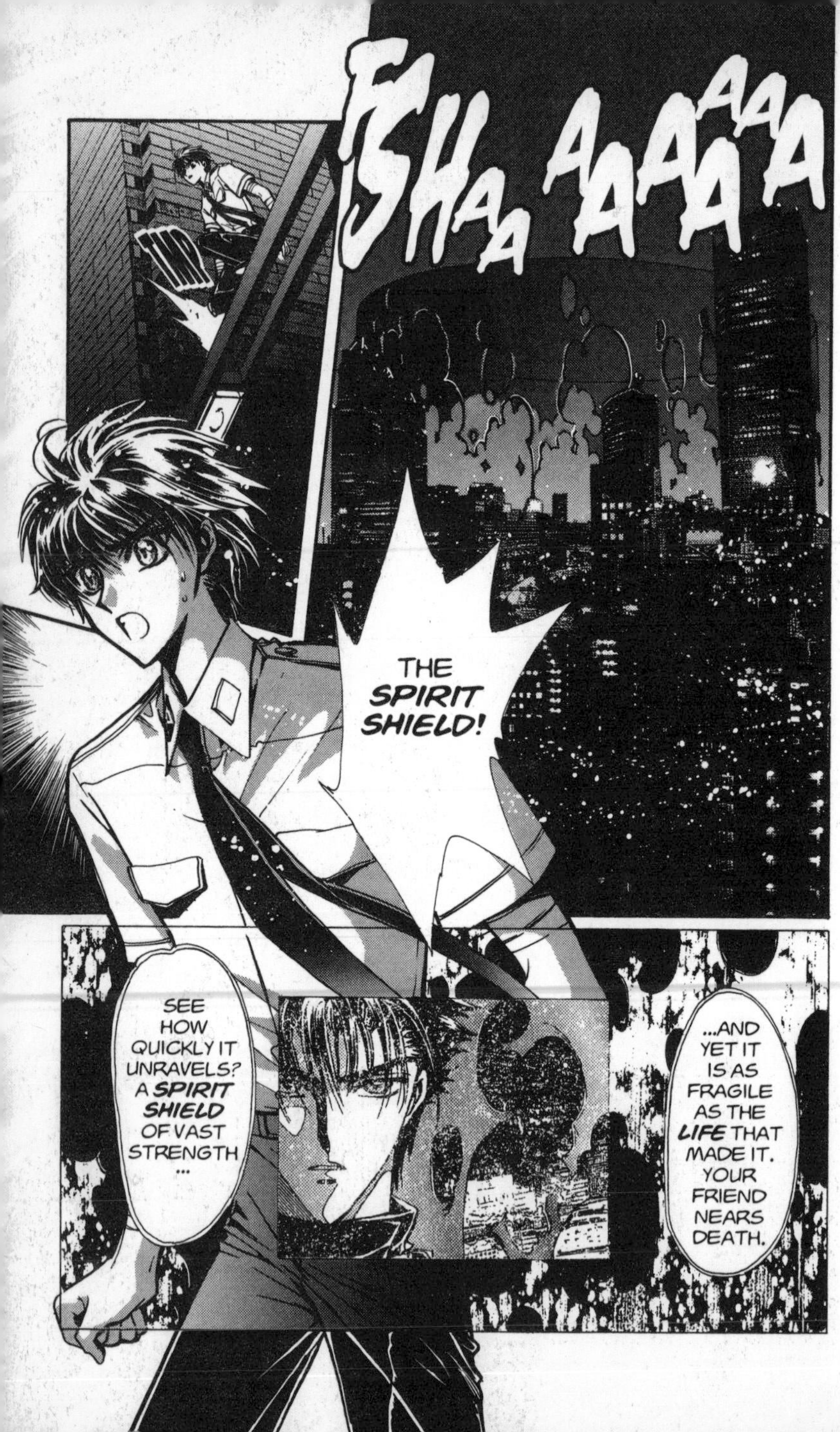
FSHAAAAAAAAAAA
THE SPIRIT SHIELD!
SEE HOW QUICKLY IT UNRAVELS? A SPIRIT SHIELD OF VAST STRENGTH...
...AND YET IT IS AS FRAGILE AS THE LIFE THAT MADE IT. YOUR FRIEND NEARS DEATH.

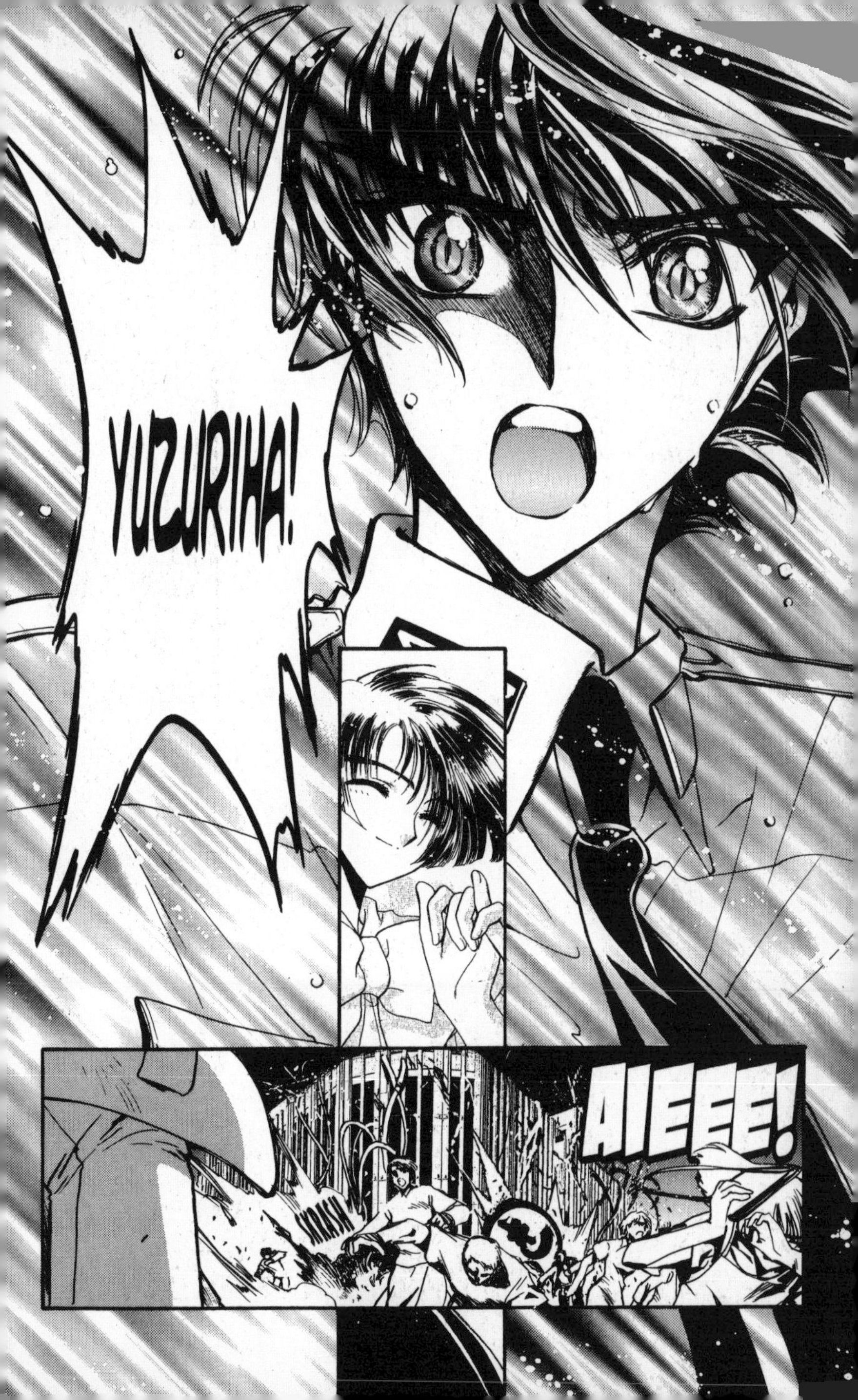
YUZURIHA!
SKRASH
AIEEE!

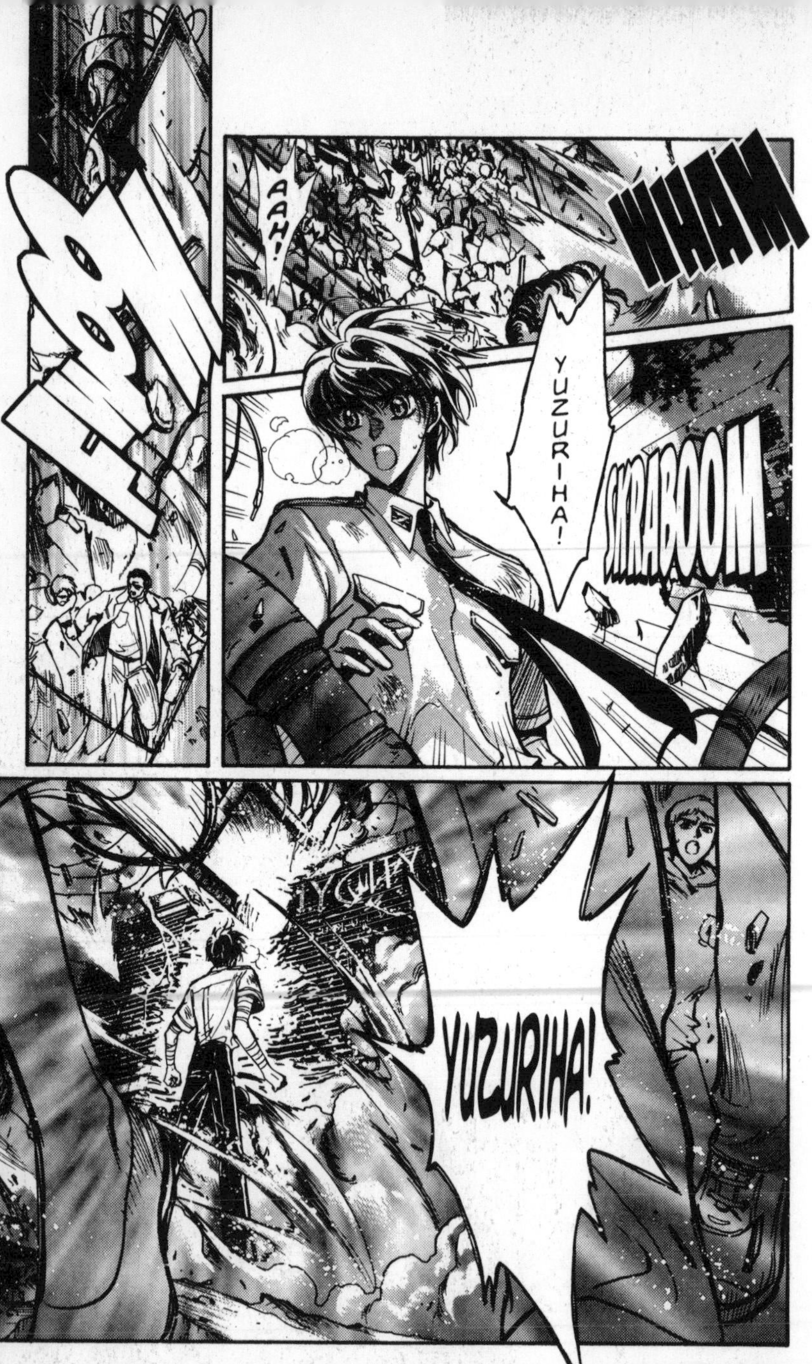
AAH!
WHAM
YUZURIHA!
SKRABOOM
YUZURIHA!

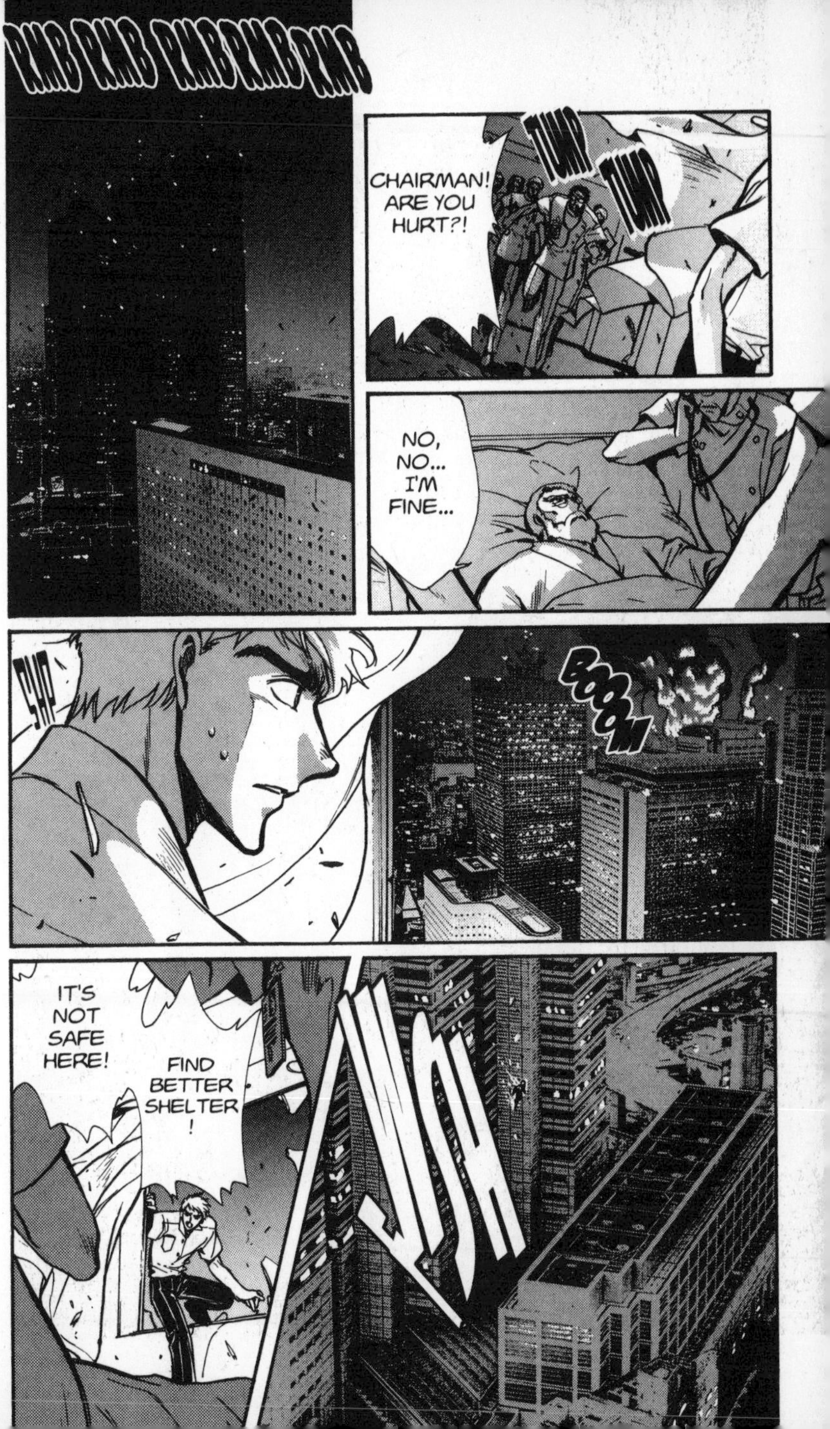
RMB RMB RMBRMBRMB
CHAIRMAN! ARE YOU HURT?!
TUMP TUMP
NO, NO... I'M FINE...
SHP
BOOOM
IT'S NOT SAFE HERE!
FIND BETTER SHELTER!

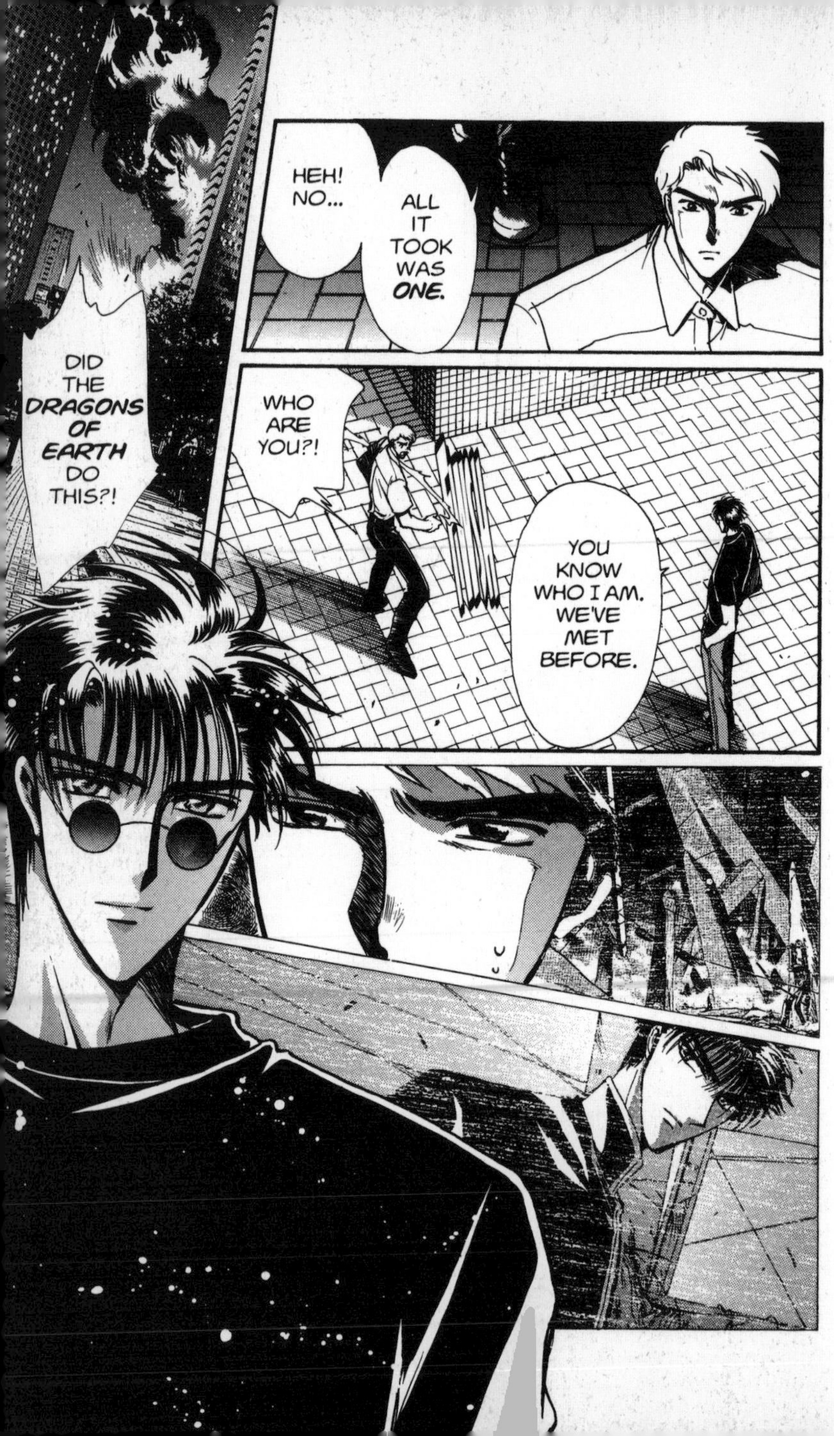
DID THE DRAGONS OF EARTH DO THIS?!
HEH! NO...
ALL IT TOOK WAS ONE.
WHO ARE YOU?!
YOU KNOW WHO I AM. WE'VE MET BEFORE.

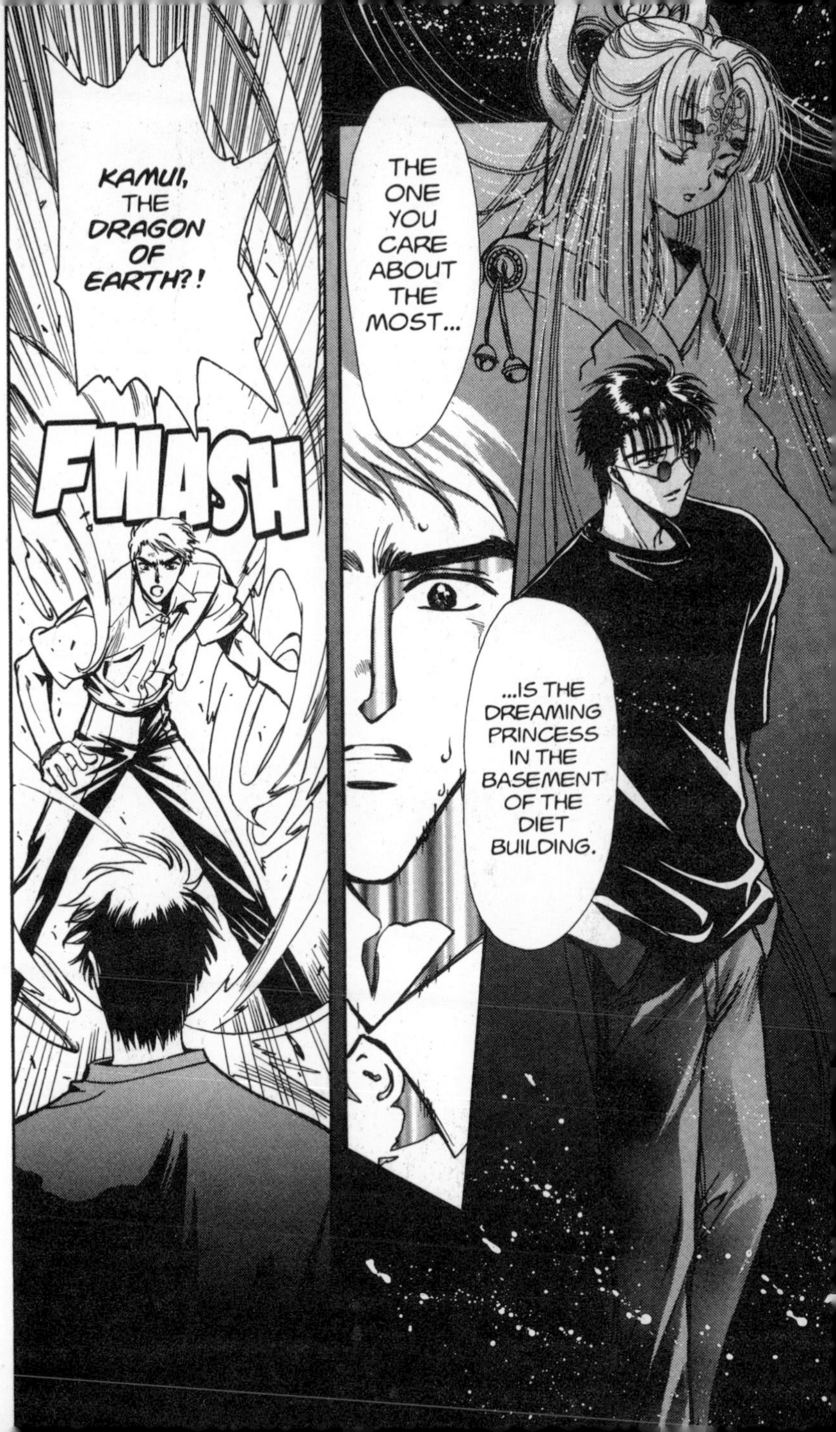
KAMUI, THE DRAGON OF EARTH?!
FWASH
THE ONE YOU CARE ABOUT THE MOST...
...IS THE DREAMING PRINCESS IN THE BASEMENT OF THE DIET BUILDING.

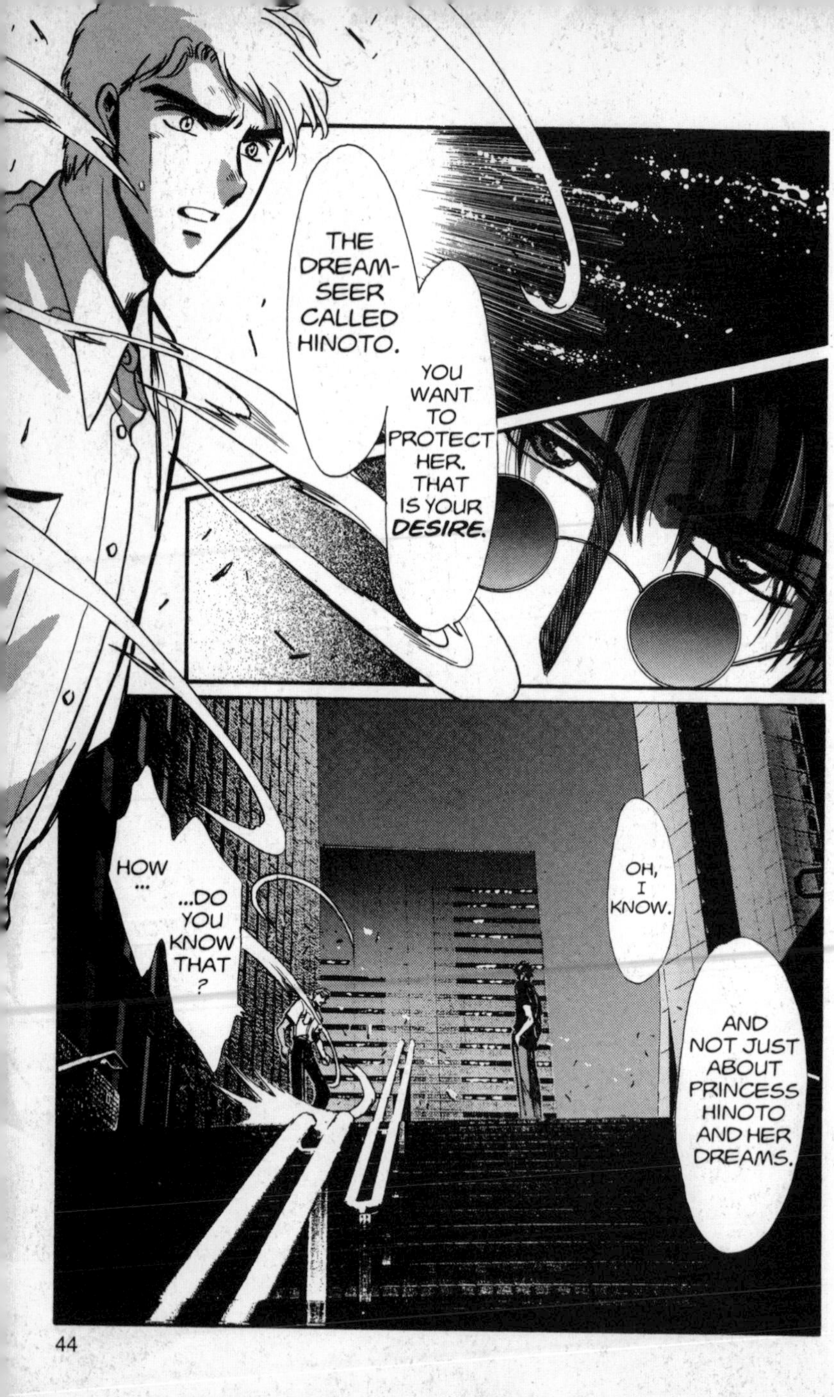
THE DREAM-SEER CALLED HINOTO.
YOU WANT TO PROTECT HER. THAT IS YOUR DESIRE.
HOW ...
...DO YOU KNOW THAT?
OH, I KNOW.
AND NOT JUST ABOUT PRINCESS HINOTO AND HER DREAMS.

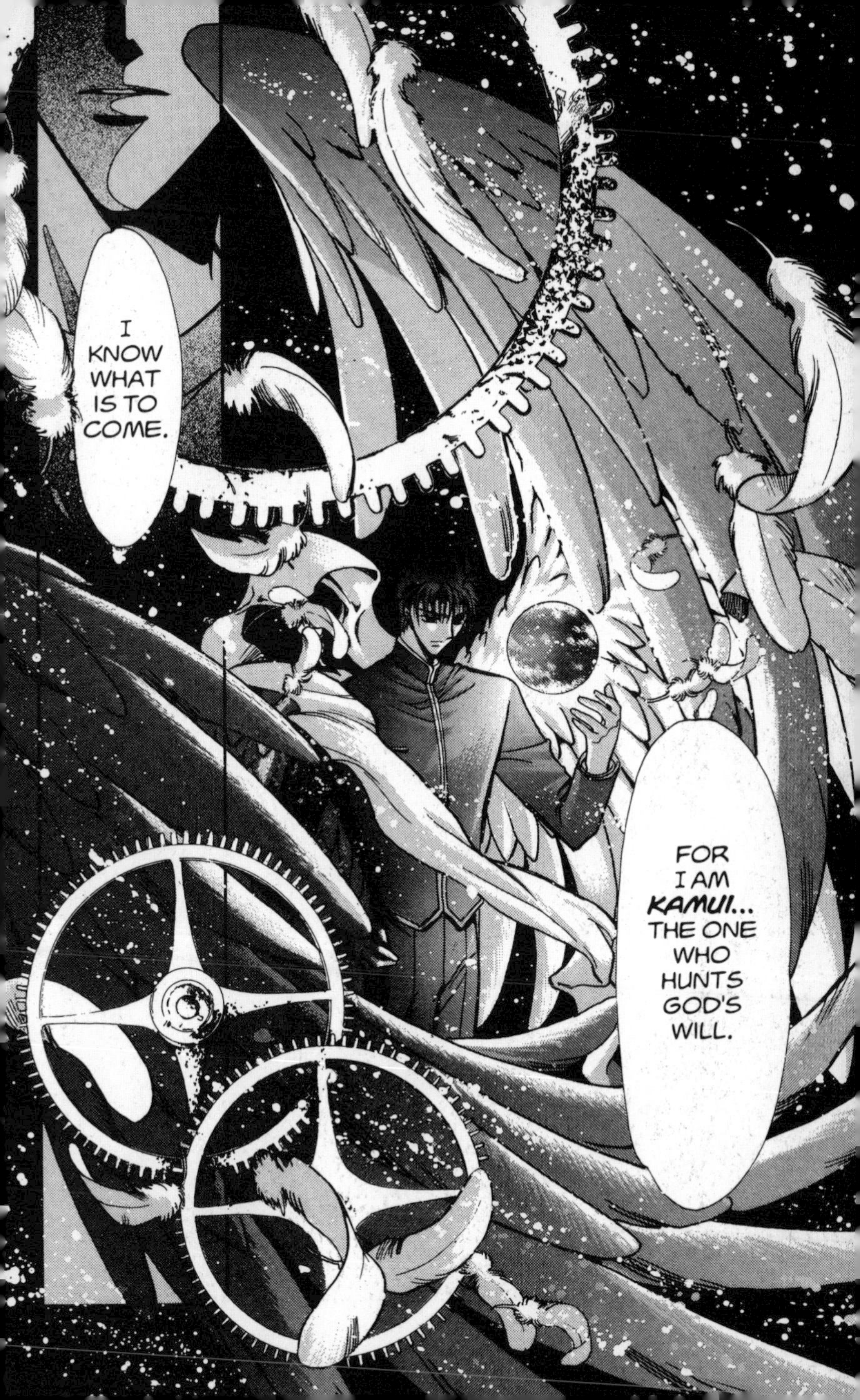
I KNOW WHAT IS TO COME.
FOR I AM ***KAMUI...*** THE ONE WHO HUNTS GOD'S WILL.

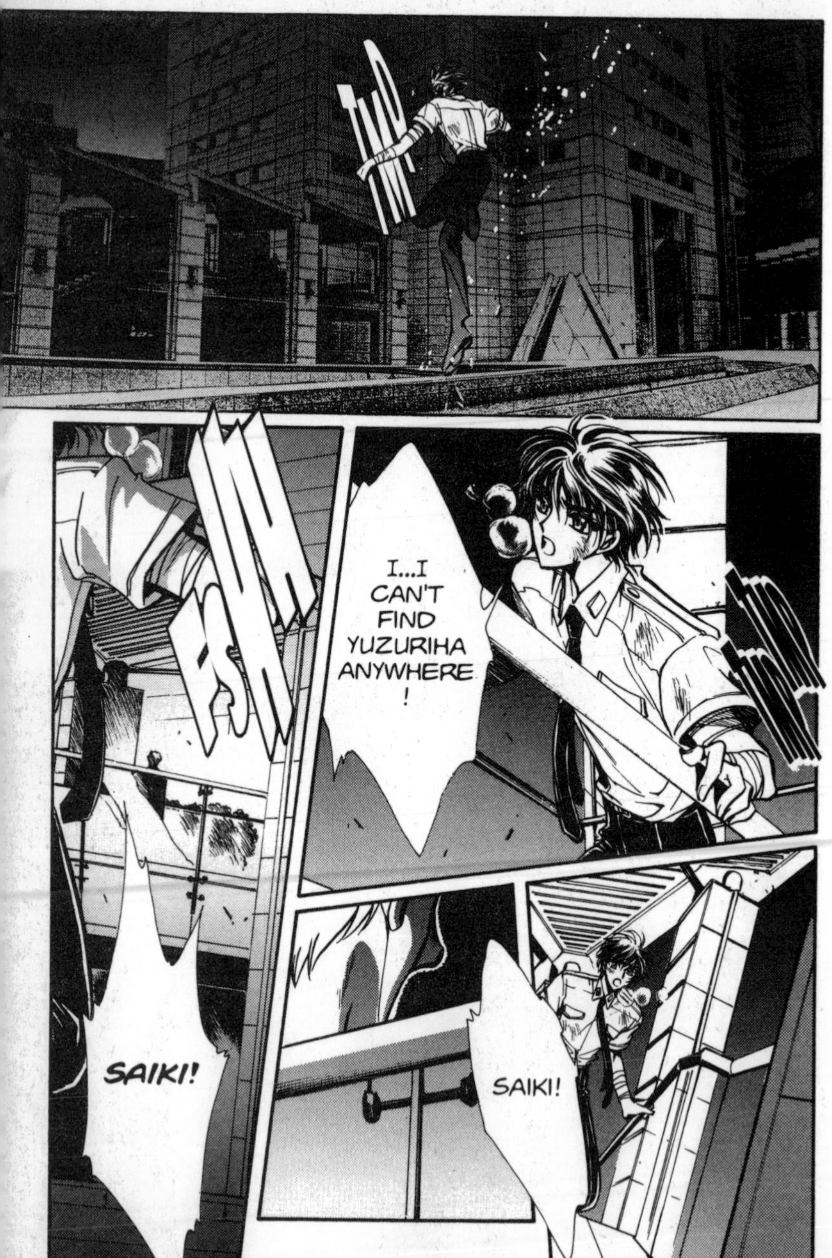
I...I CAN'T FIND YUZURIHA ANYWHERE!
SAIKI!
SAIKI!

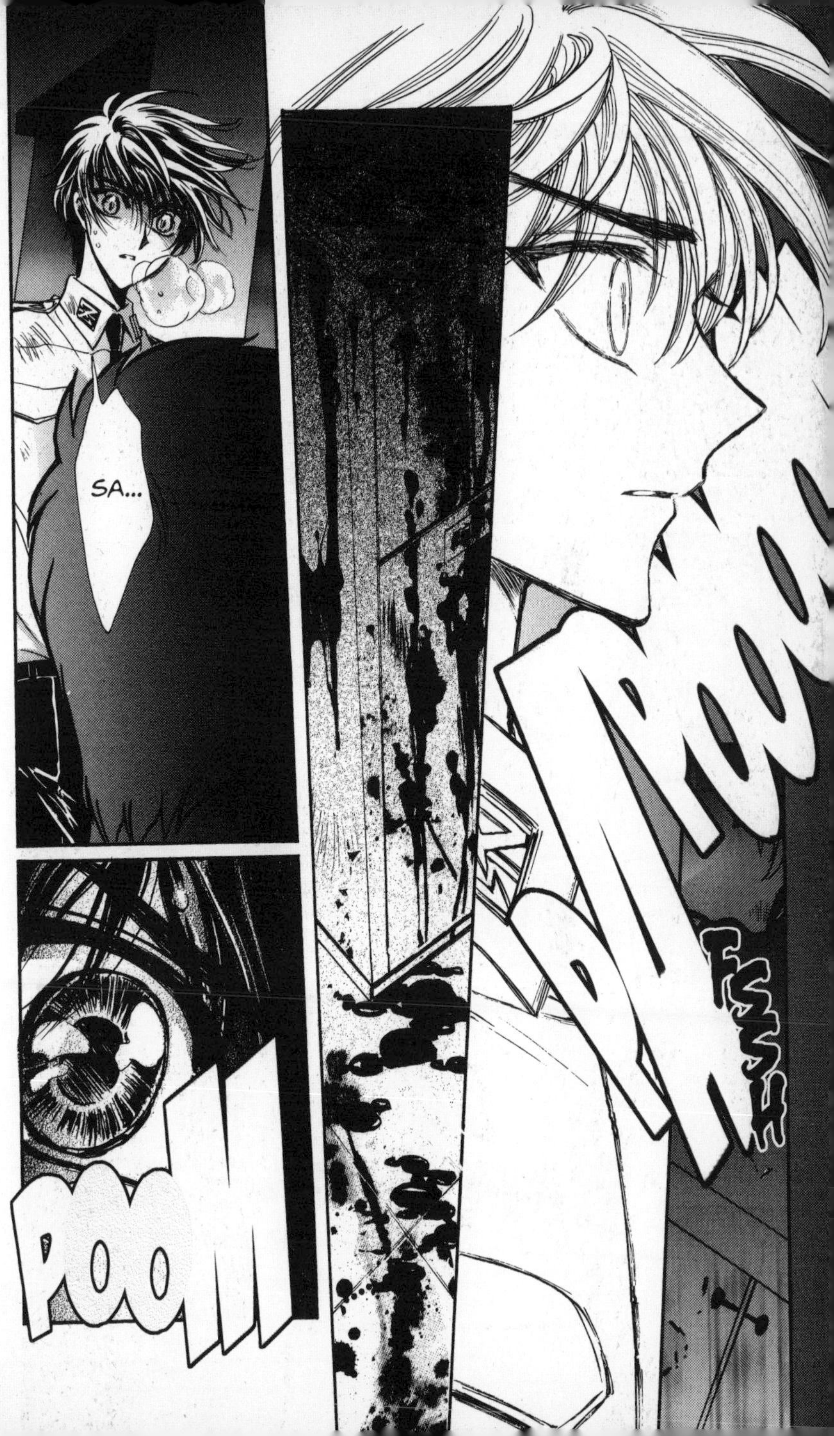
SA...
POOM

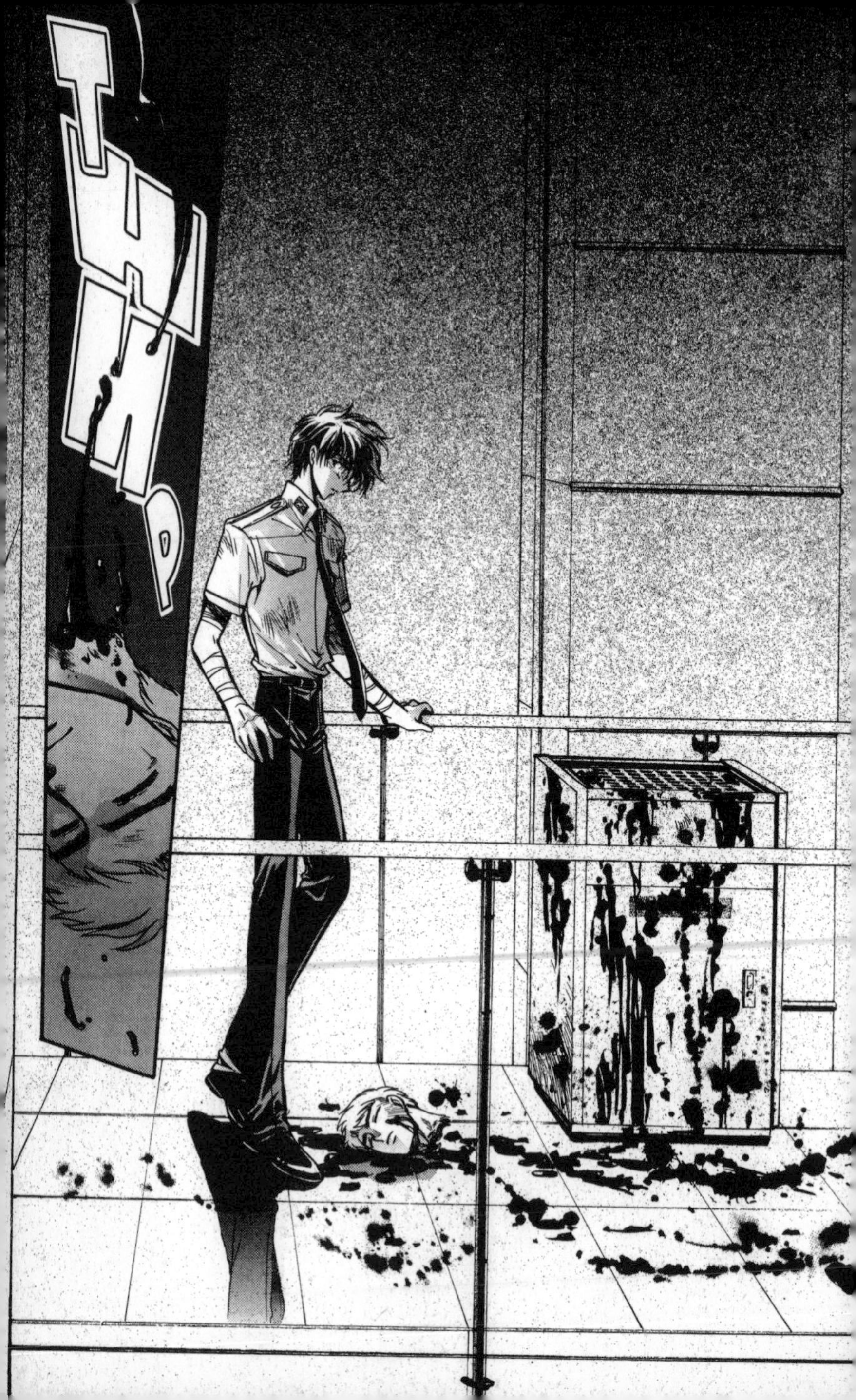
THUMP

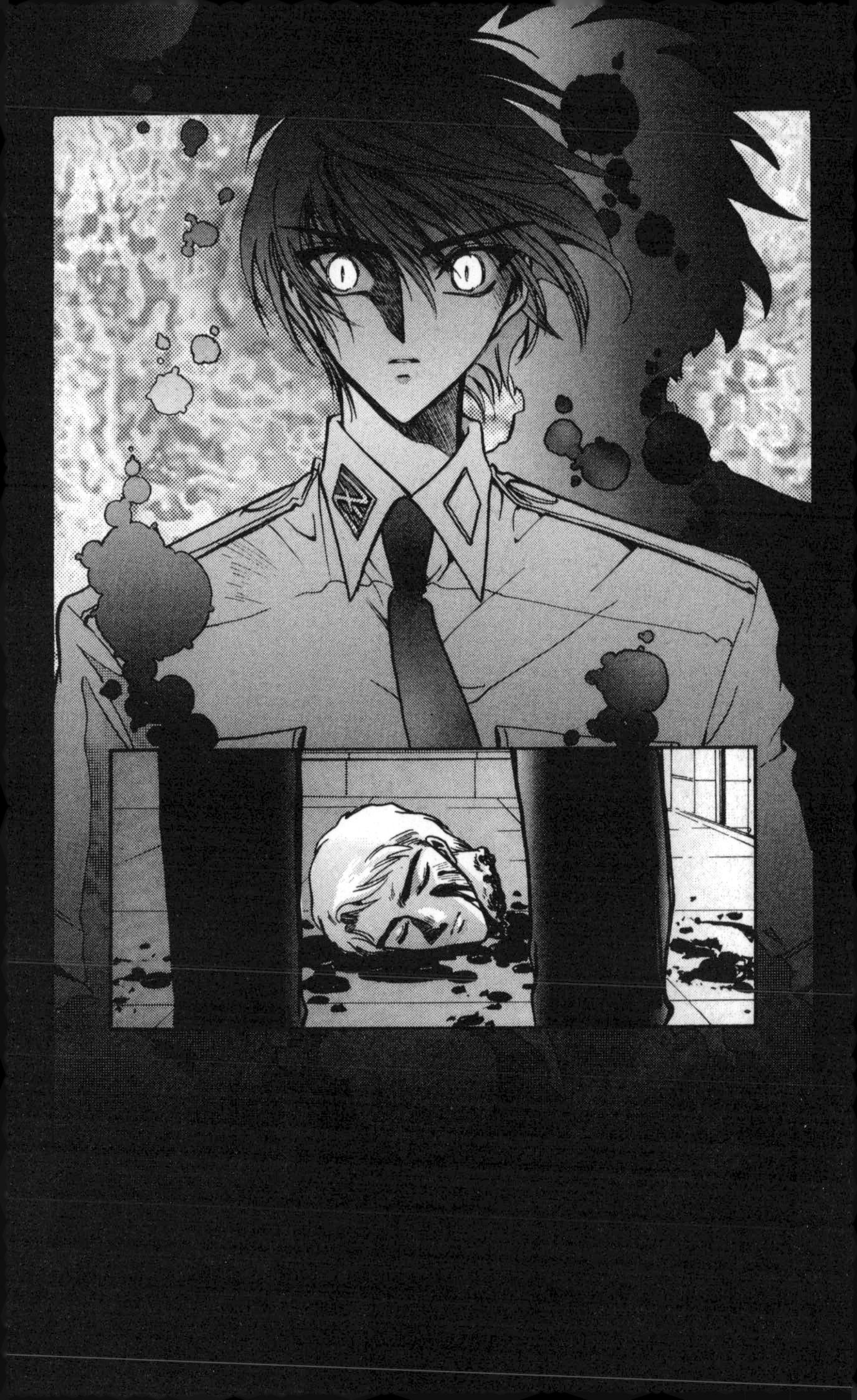

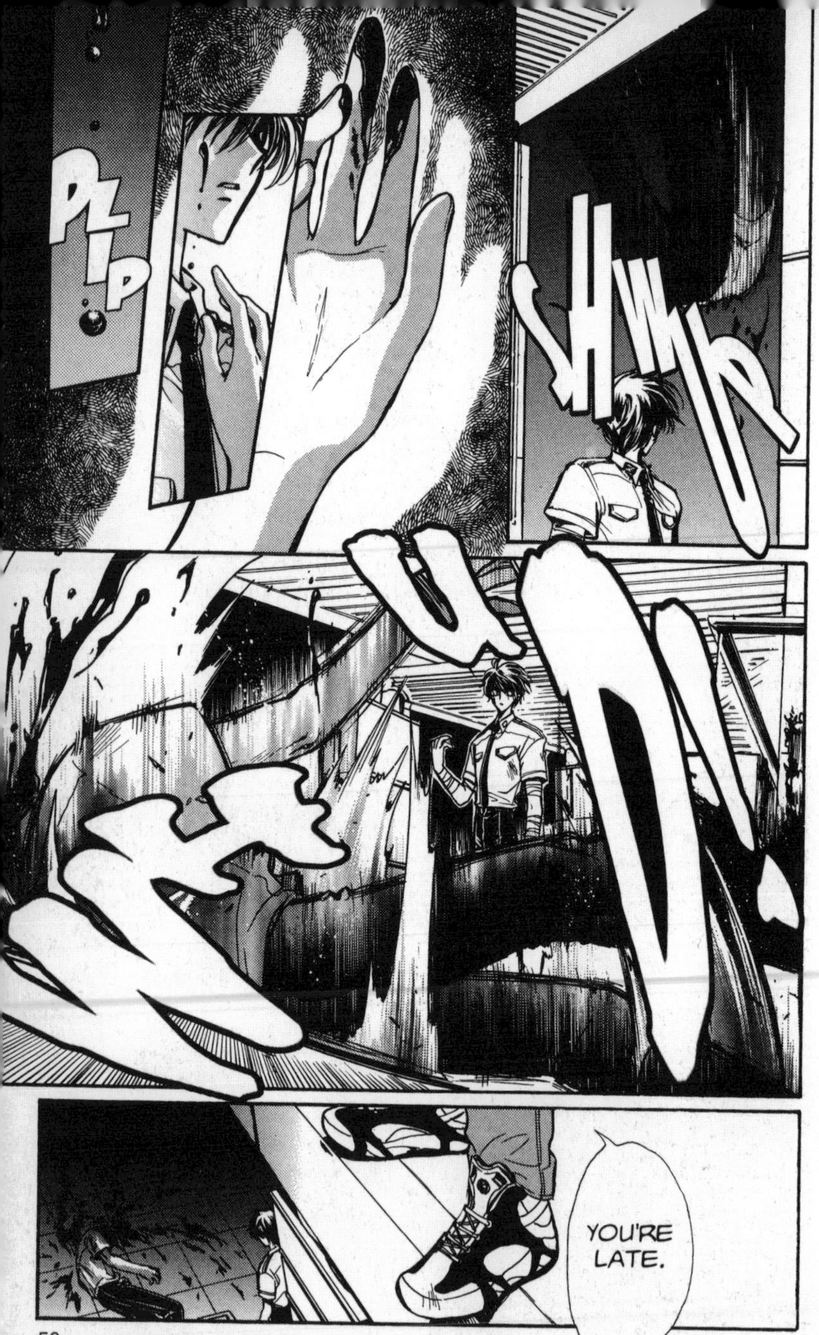
PLIP
SHWMP
YOU'RE LATE.

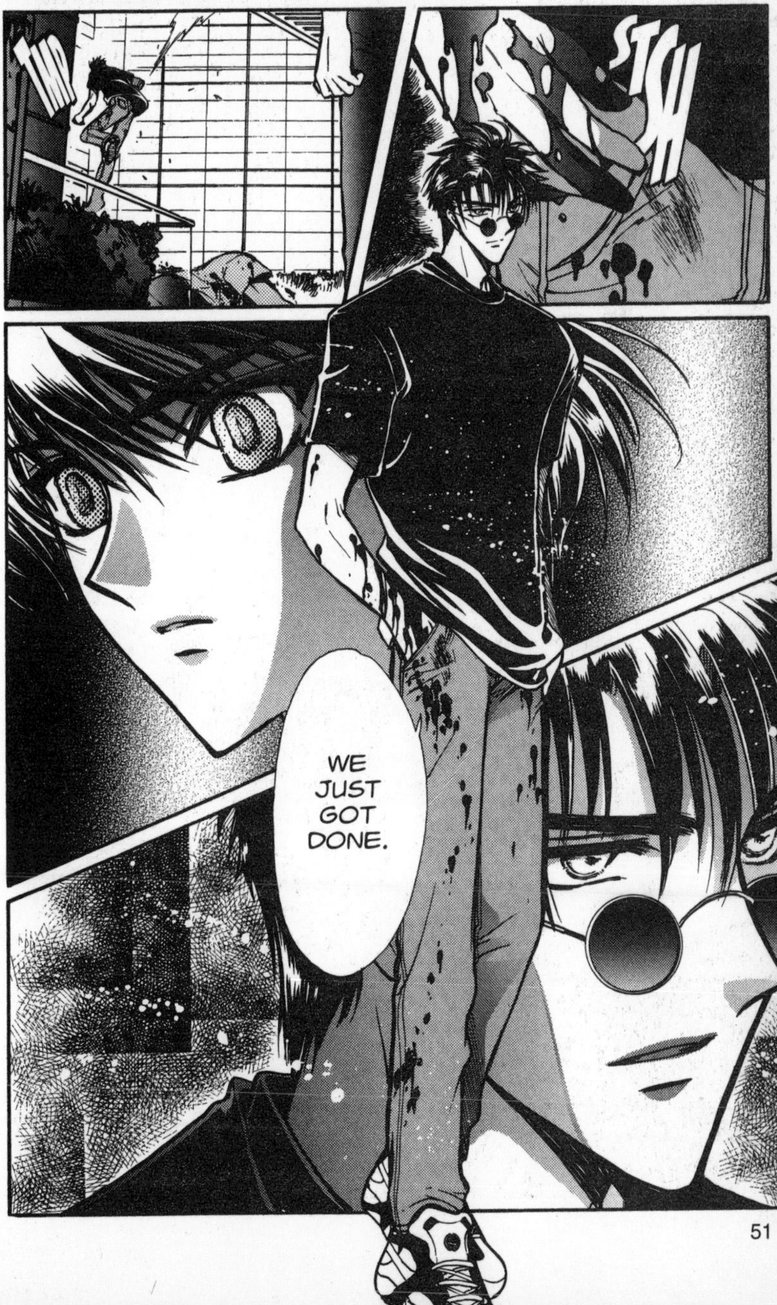
THP
STCH
WE JUST GOT DONE.

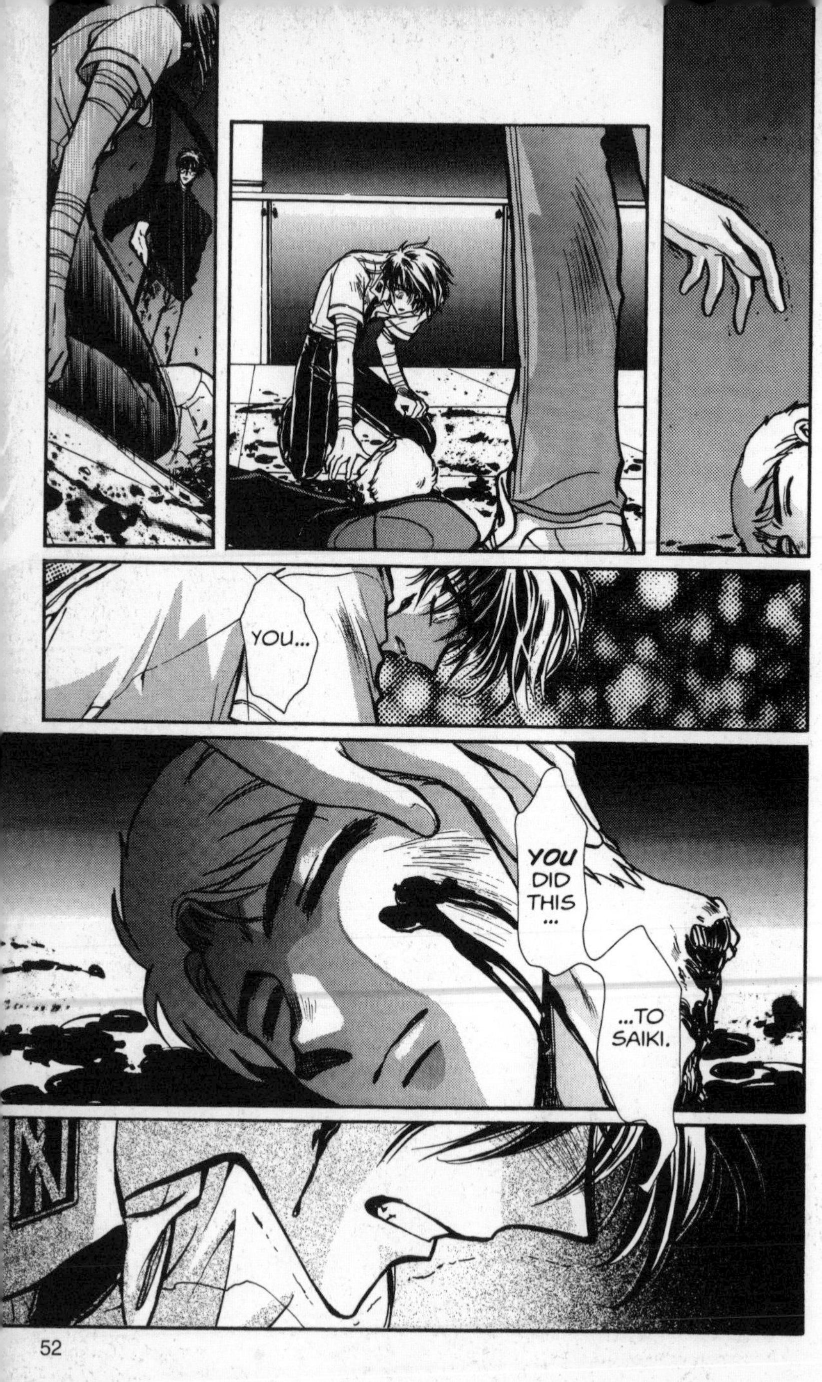
YOU...
YOU DID THIS ...
...TO SAIKI.

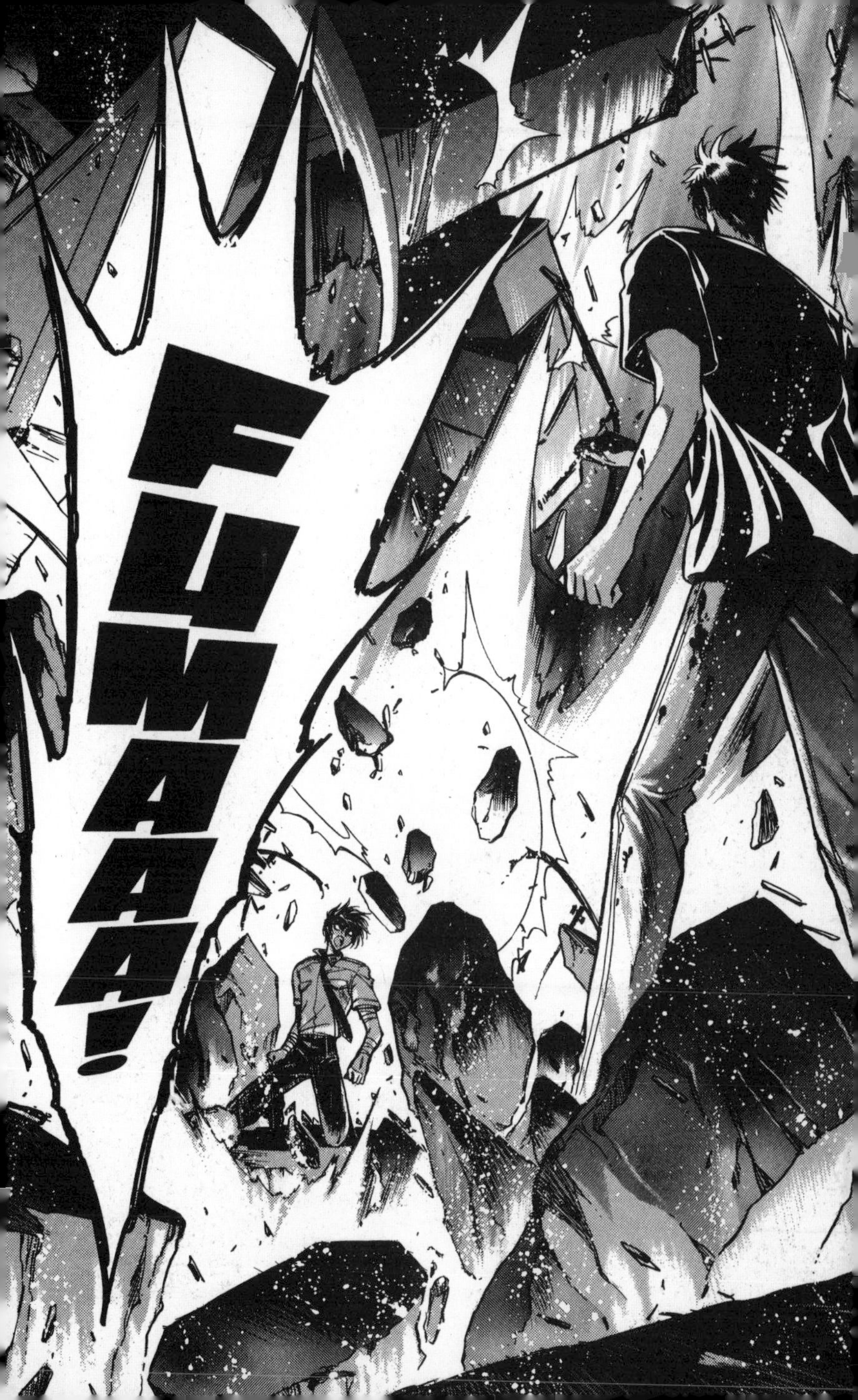
FUMAAA!

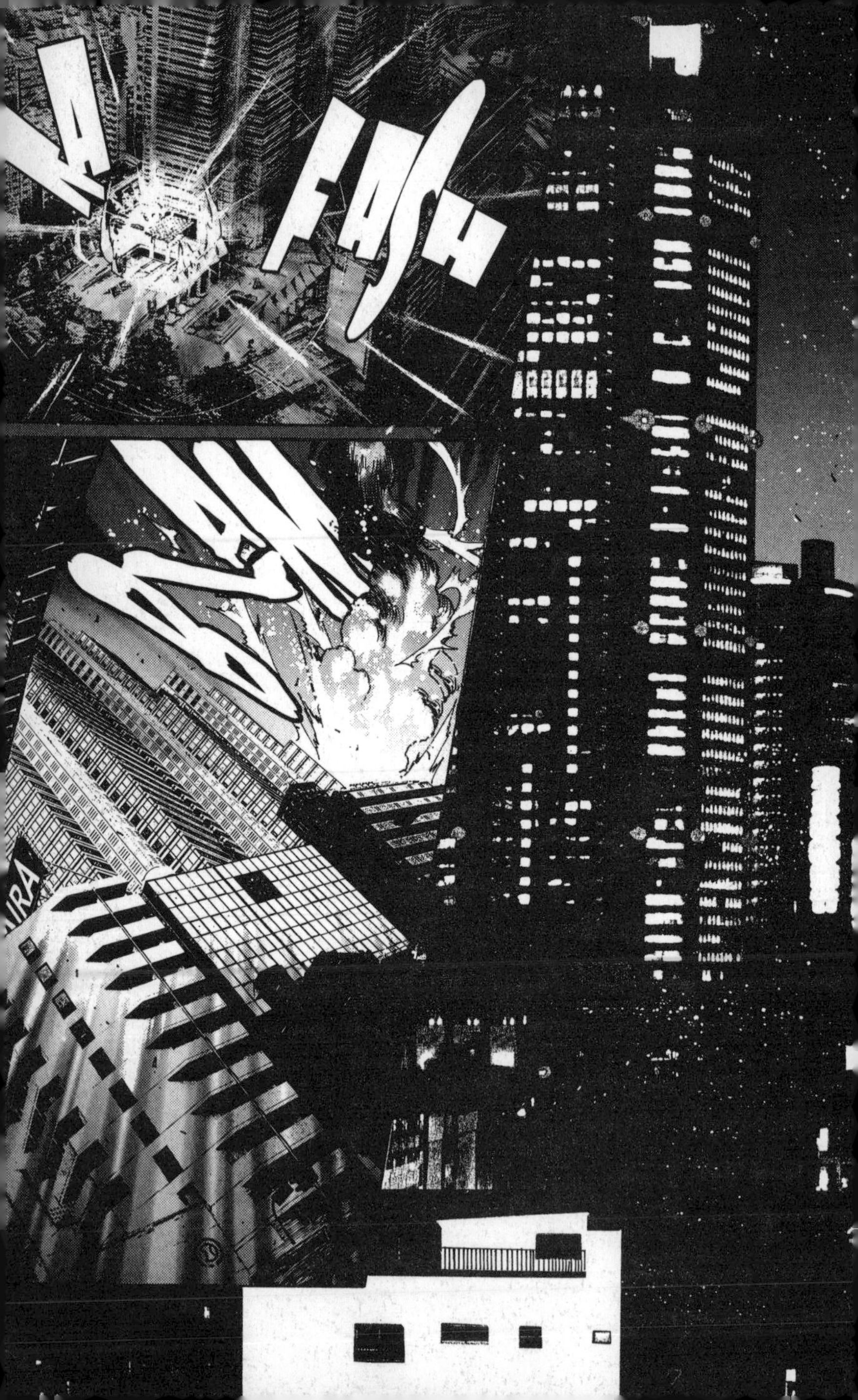
FASH

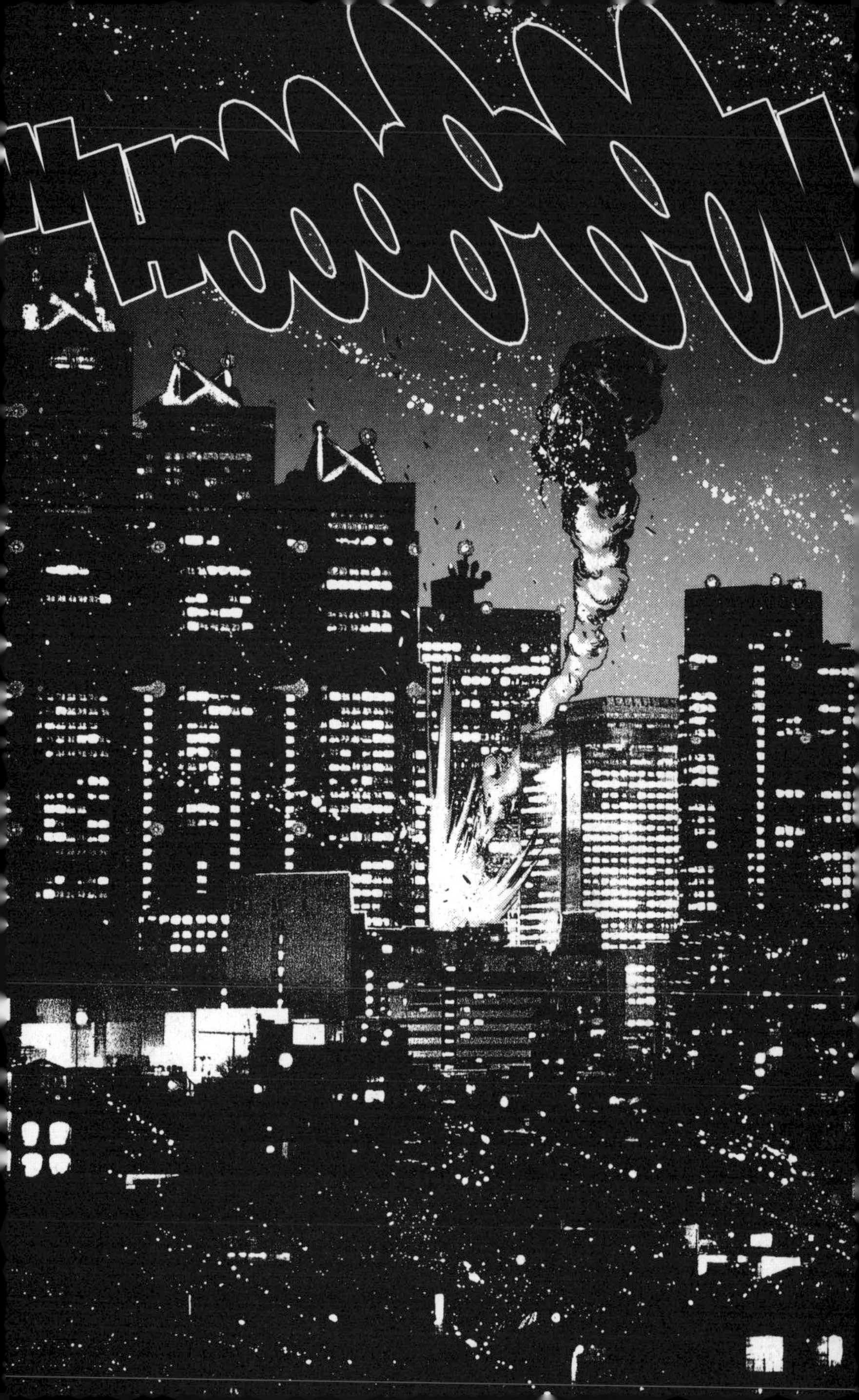

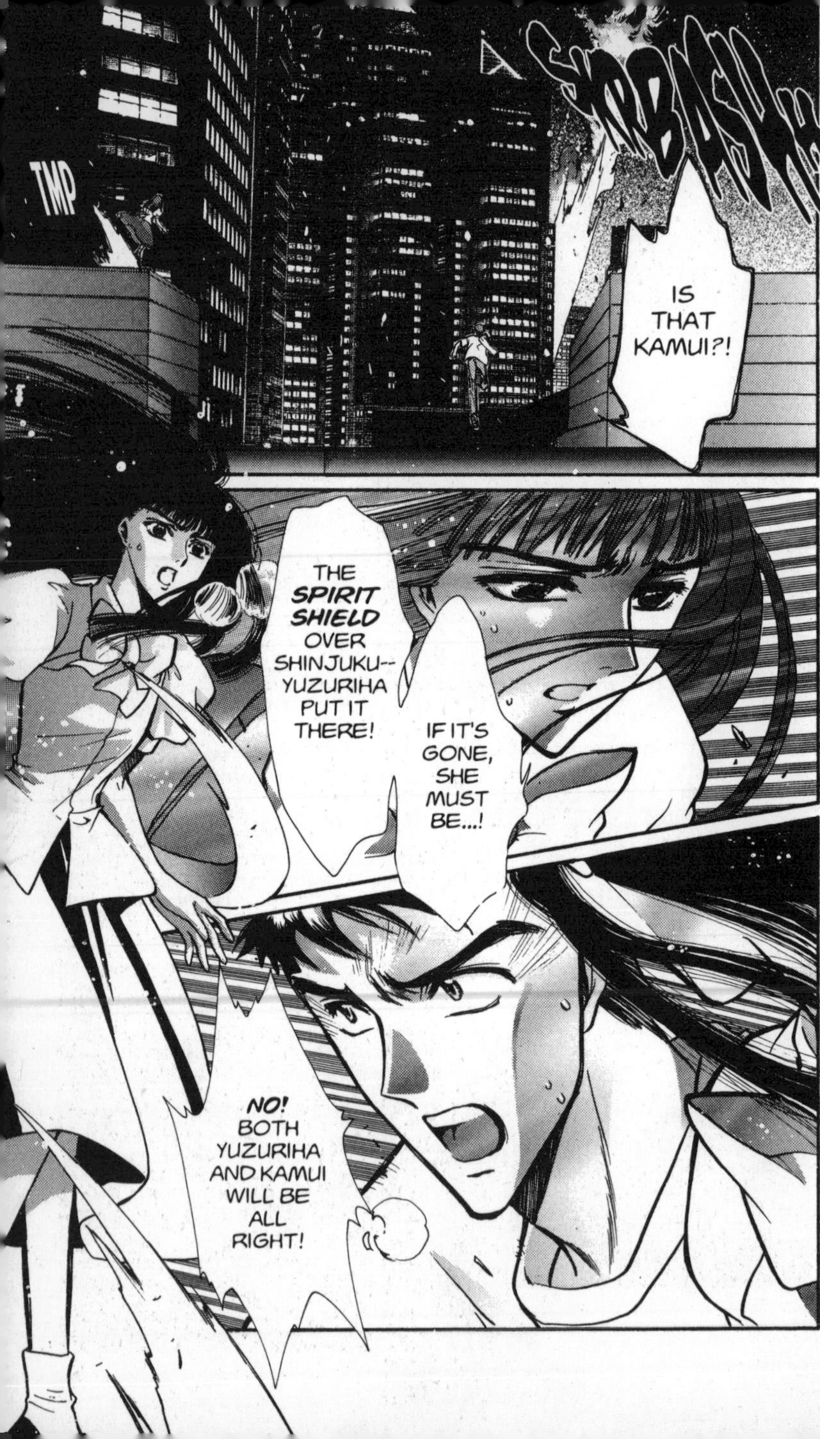

TMP
IS THAT KAMUI?!
THE SPIRIT SHIELD OVER SHINJUKU-- YUZURIHA PUT IT THERE!
IF IT'S GONE, SHE MUST BE...!
NO! BOTH YUZURIHA AND KAMUI WILL BE ALL RIGHT!

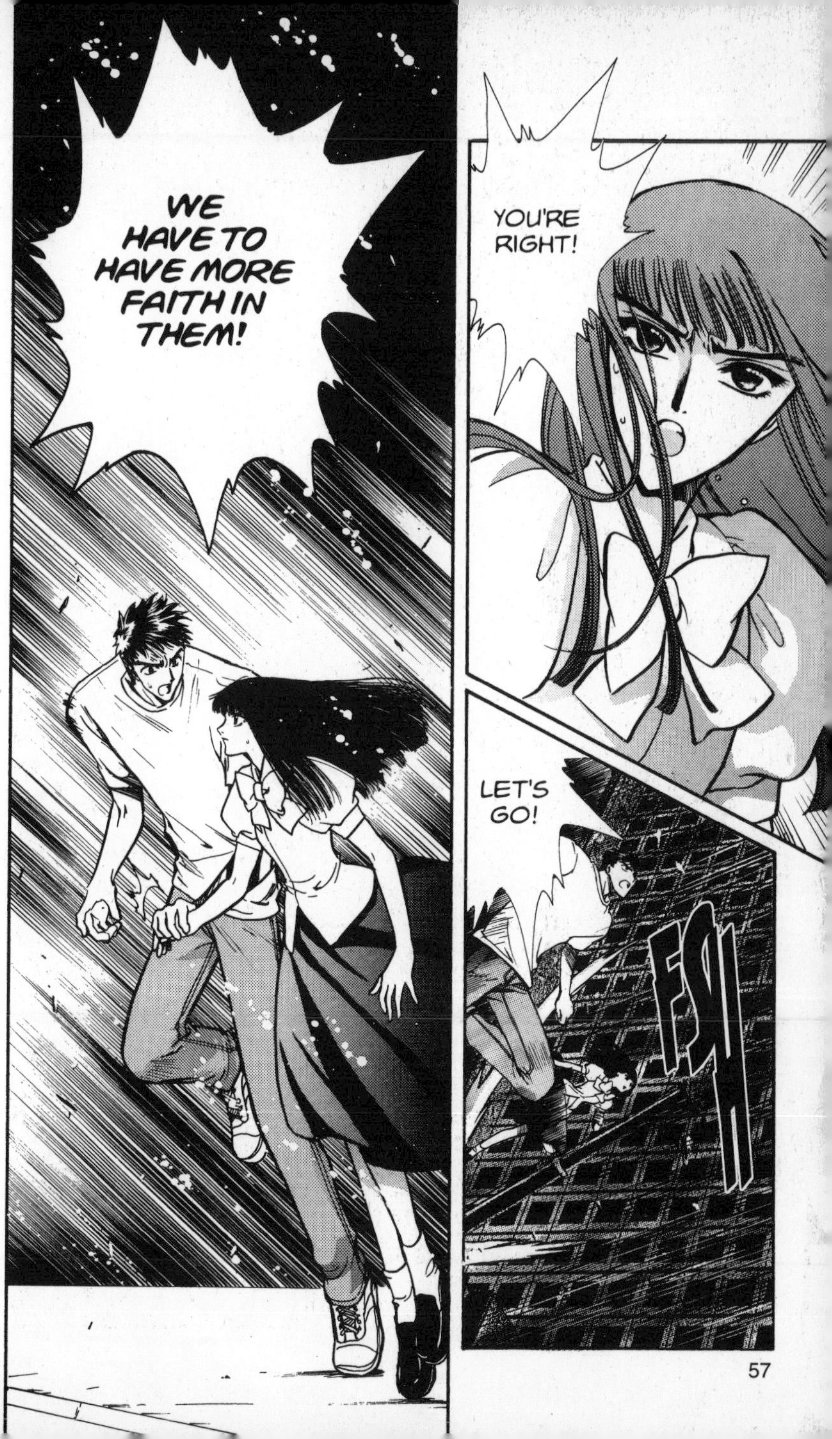
WE HAVE TO HAVE MORE FAITH IN THEM!
YOU'RE RIGHT!
LET'S GO!
FSH

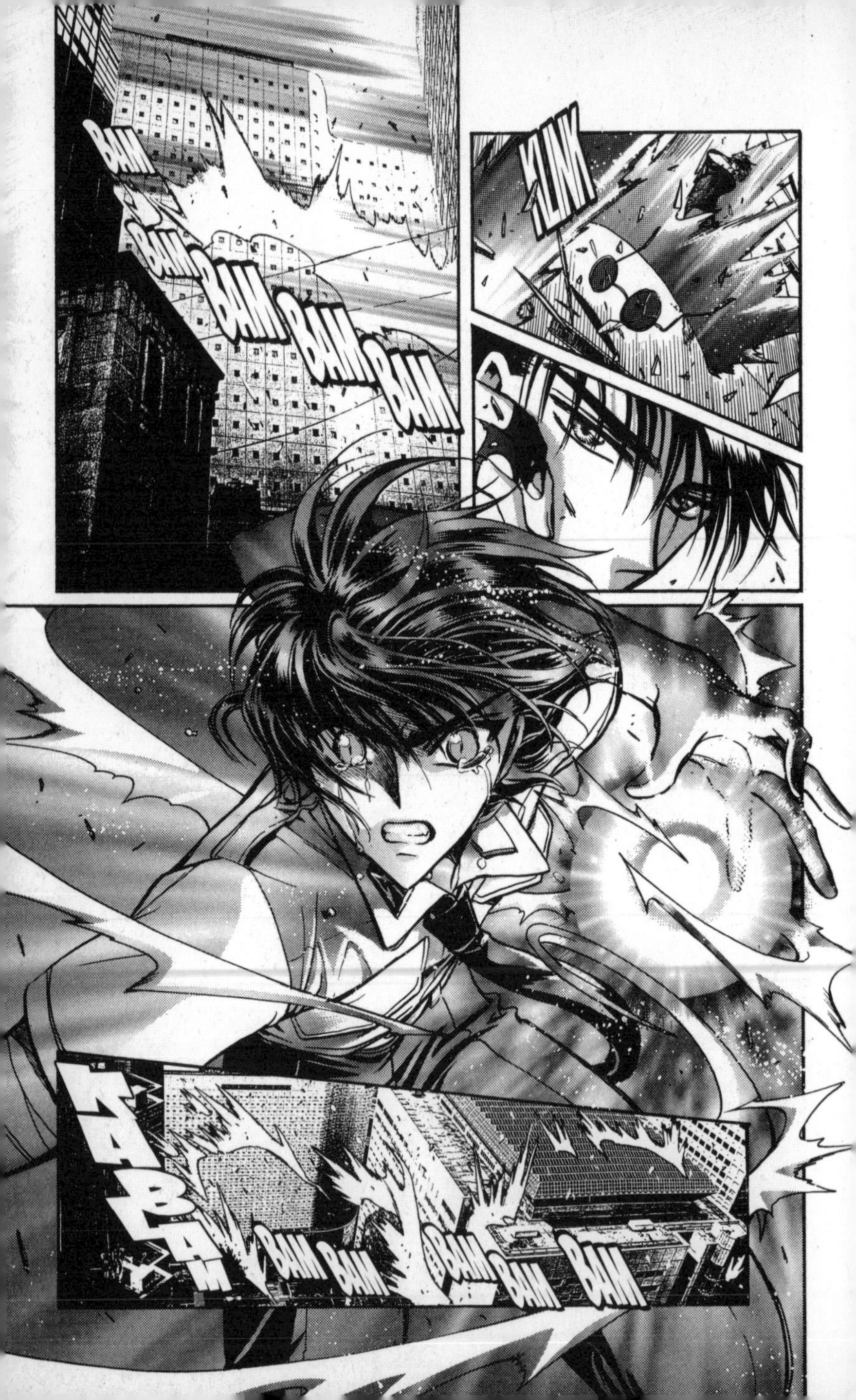
BAM
BAM BAM BAM BAM BAM
KLINK
BLAM
BAM BAM
BAM BAM BAM

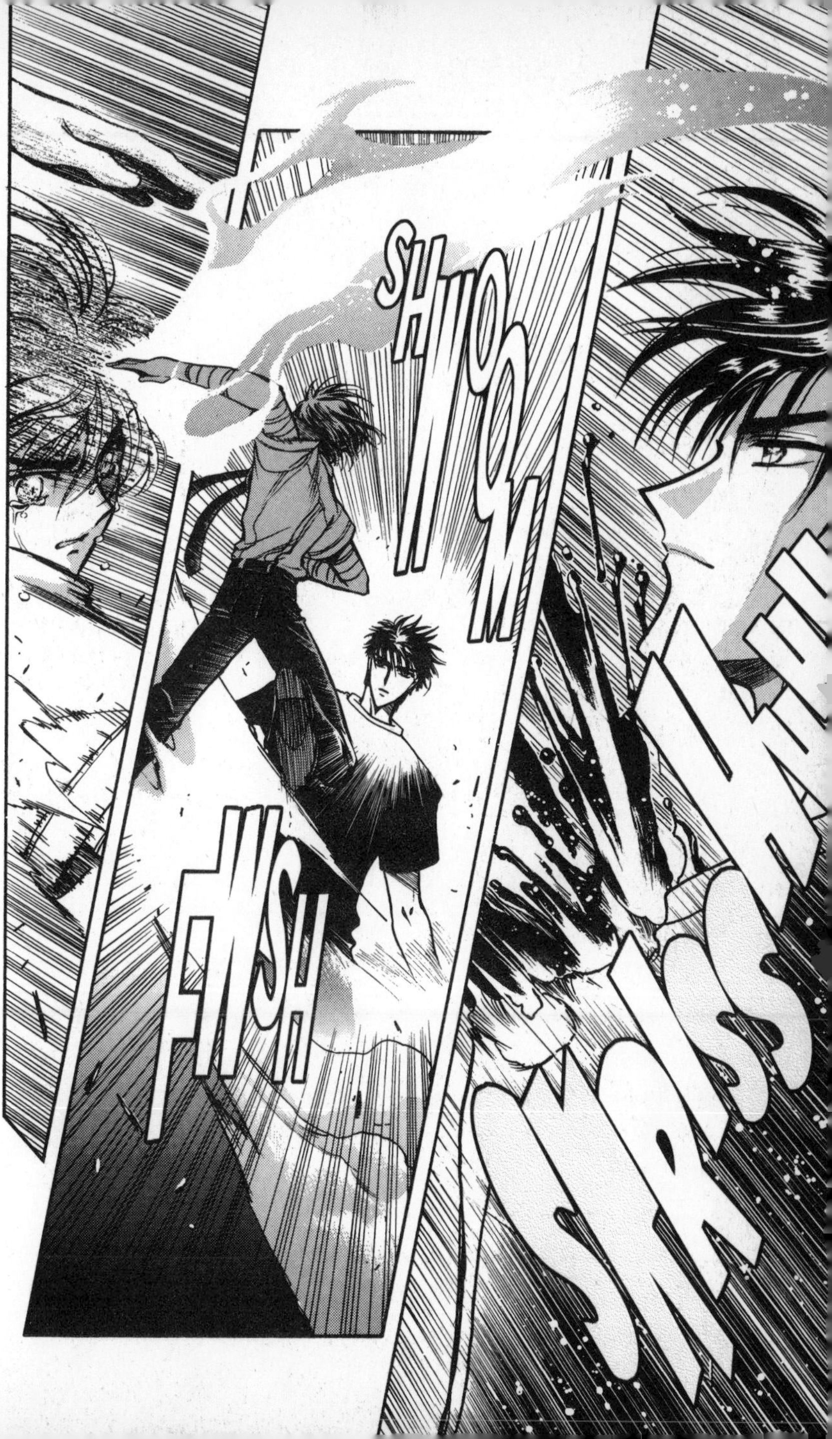
SHWOOM
FWISH
SPRSSH

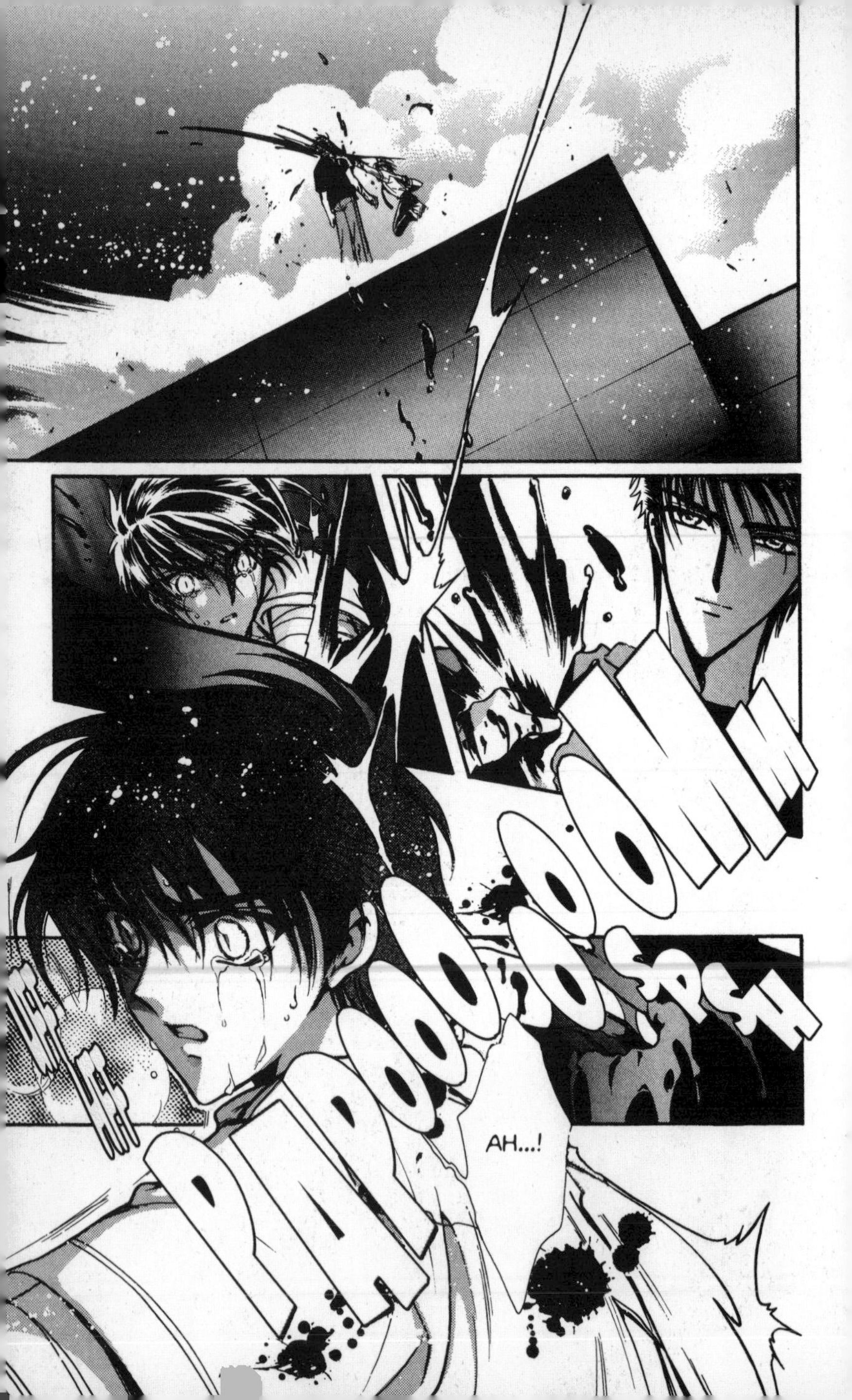
SPSH
AH...!

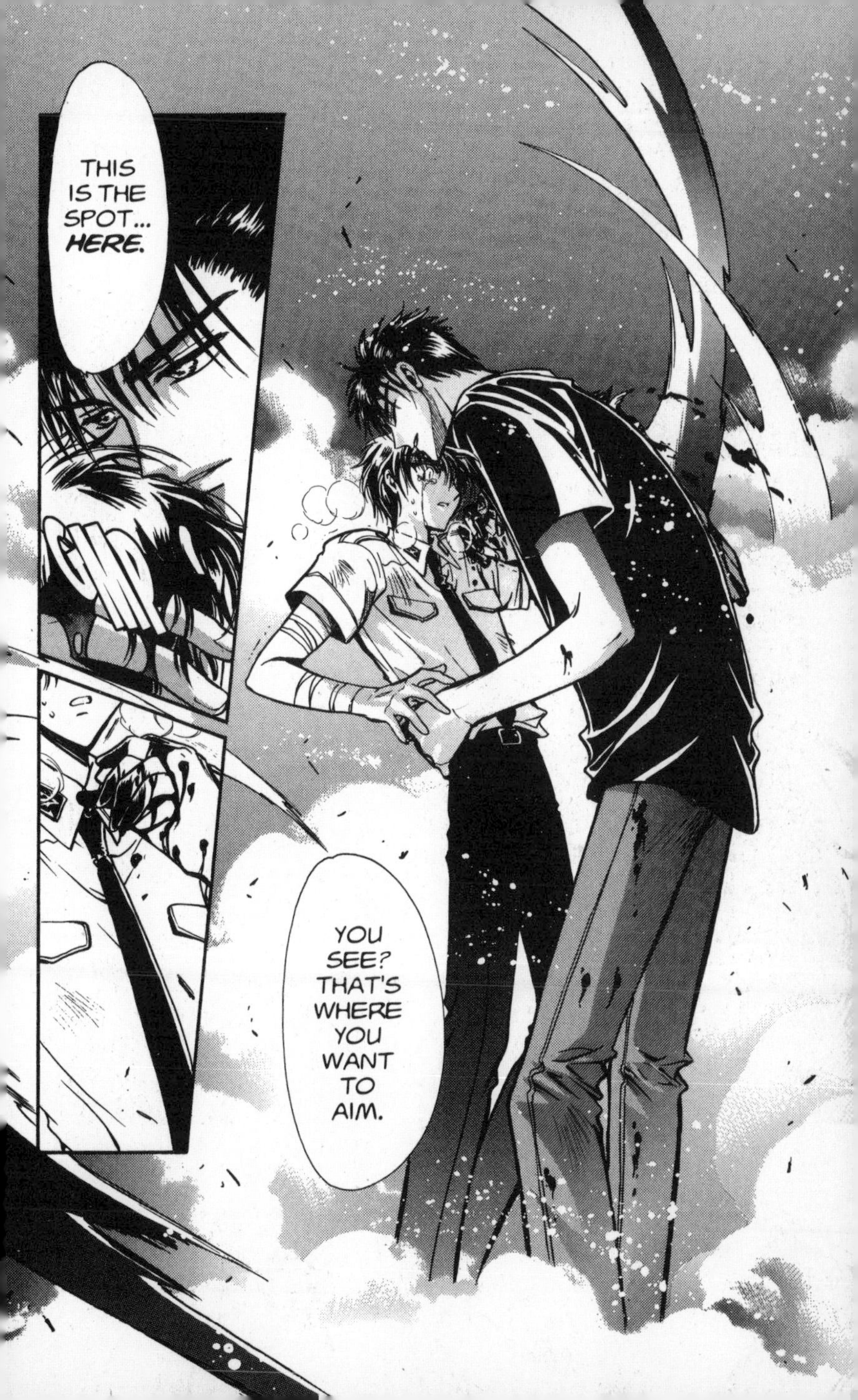
THIS IS THE SPOT... ***HERE.***
YOU SEE? THAT'S WHERE YOU WANT TO AIM.

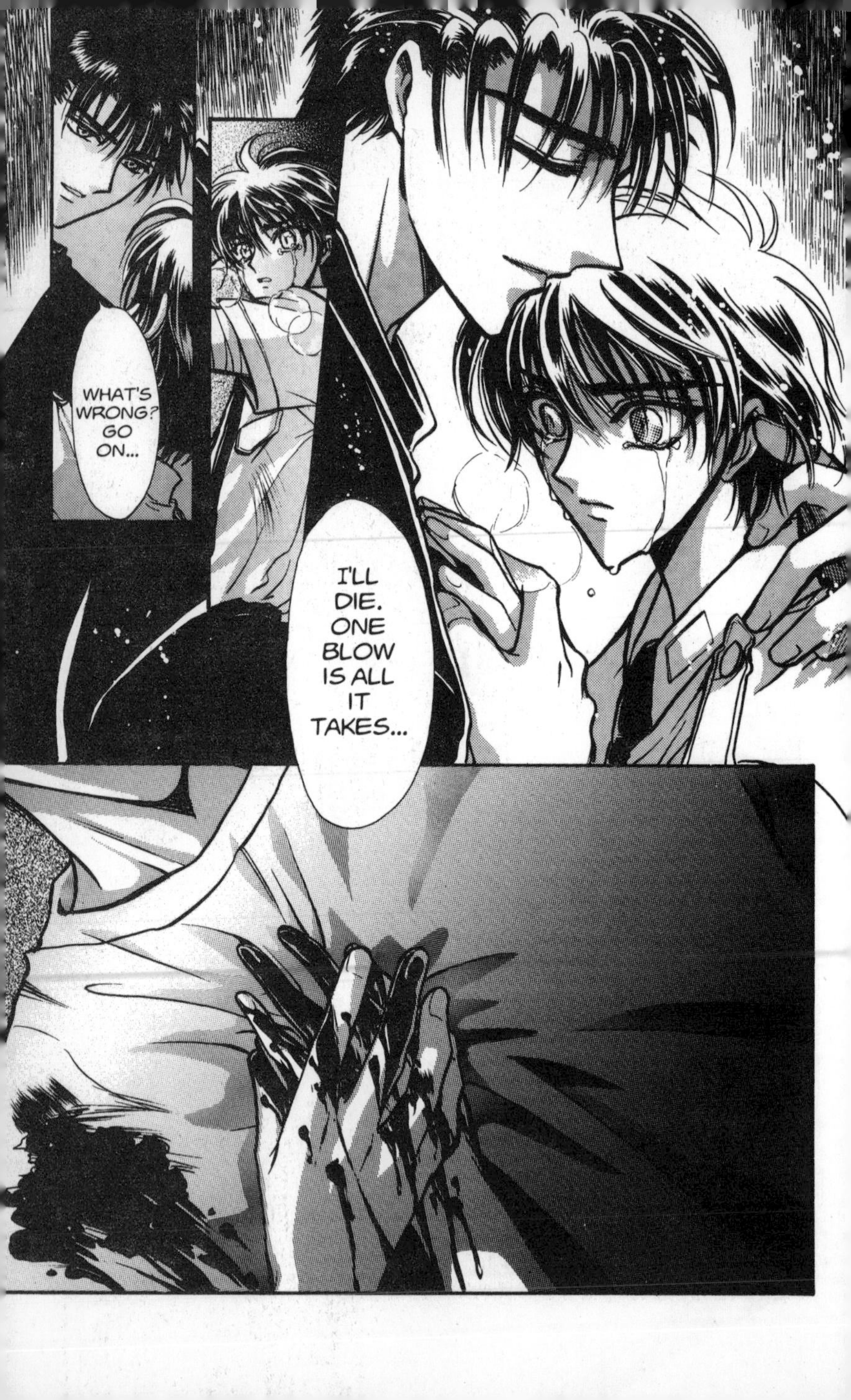
WHAT'S WRONG? GO ON...
I'LL DIE. ONE BLOW IS ALL IT TAKES...

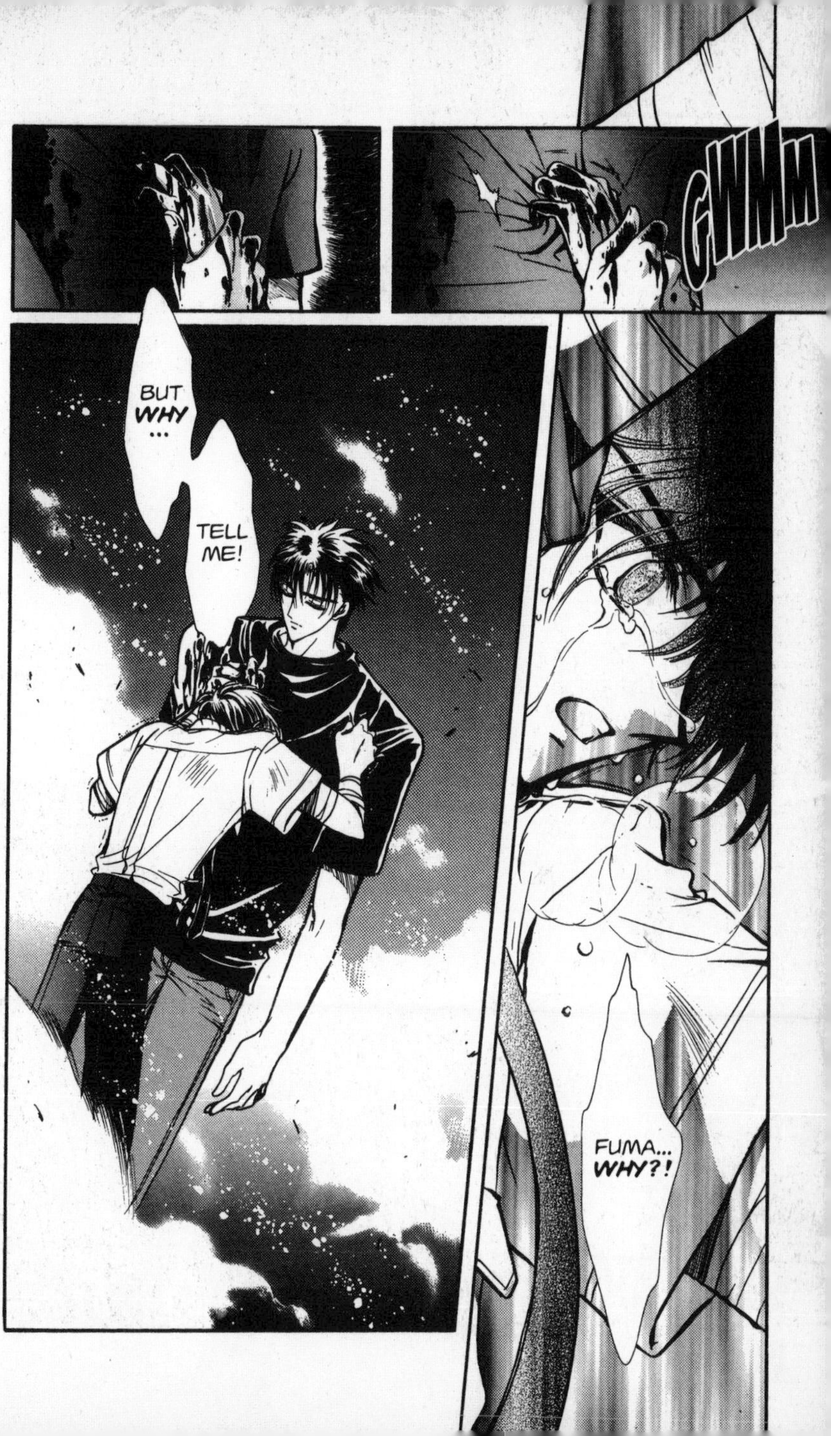
GWMm
BUT WHY ...
TELL ME!
FUMA... WHY?!

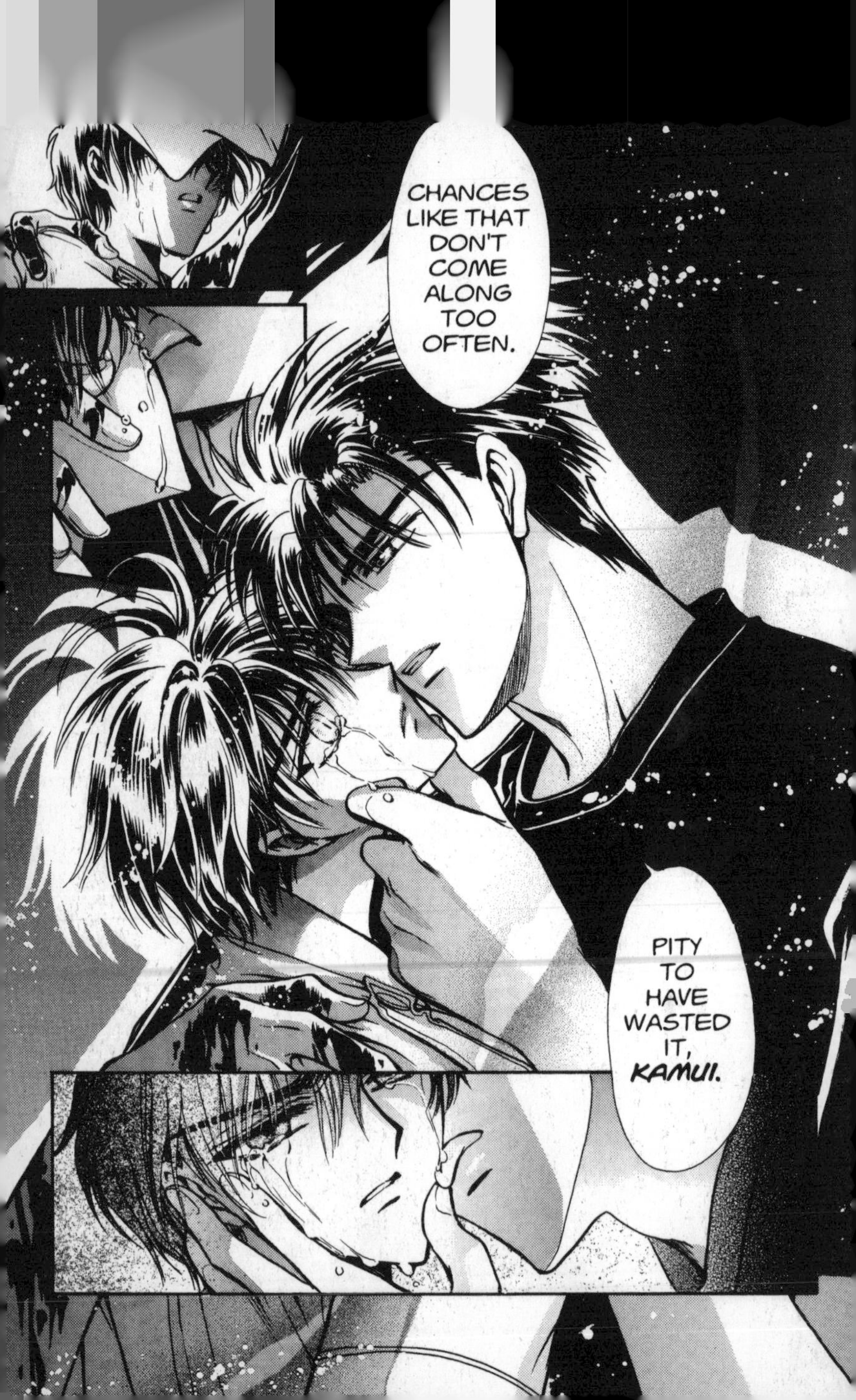
CHANCES LIKE THAT DON'T COME ALONG TOO OFTEN.
PITY TO HAVE WASTED IT, *KAMUI.*

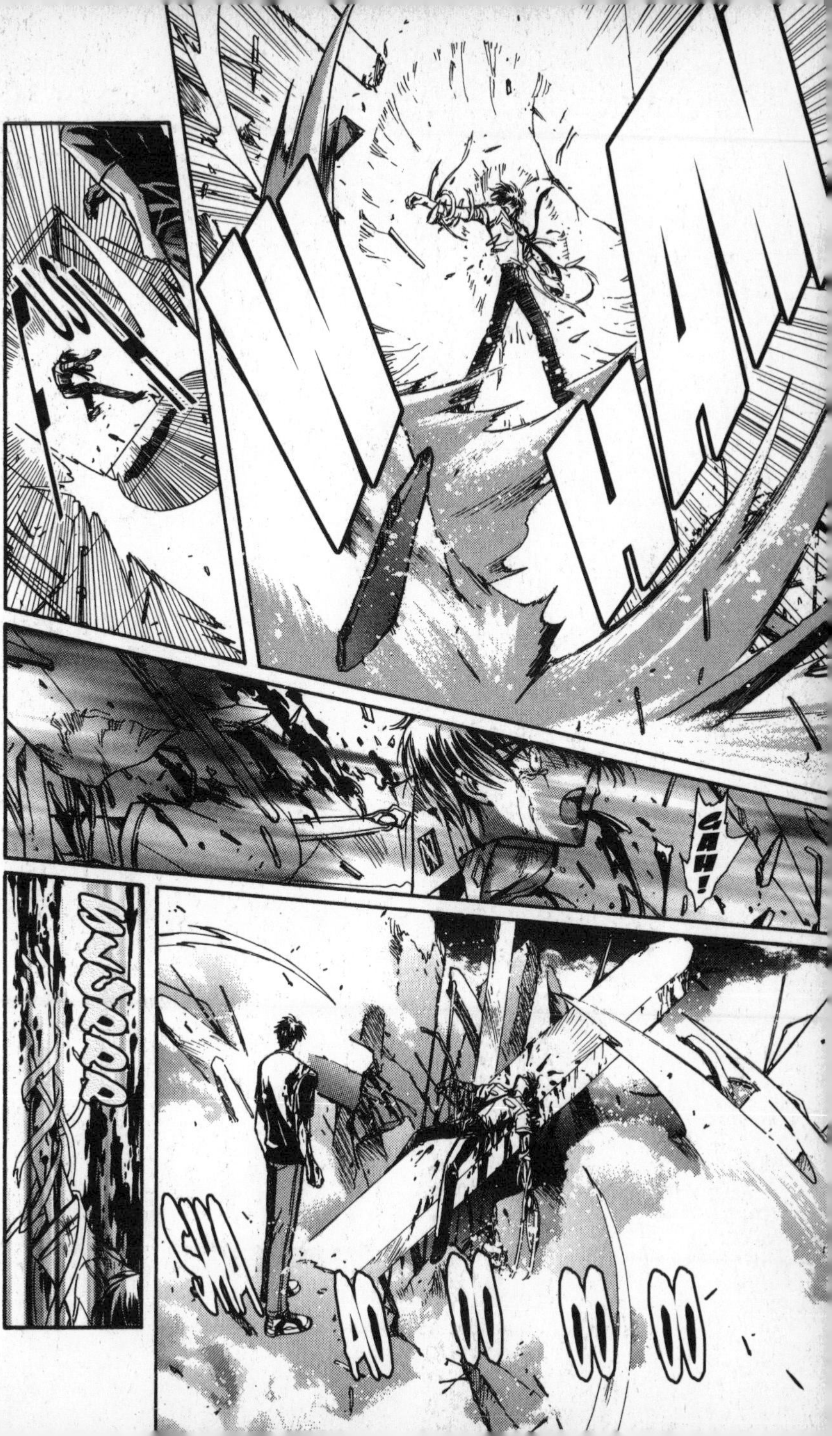
GAH!

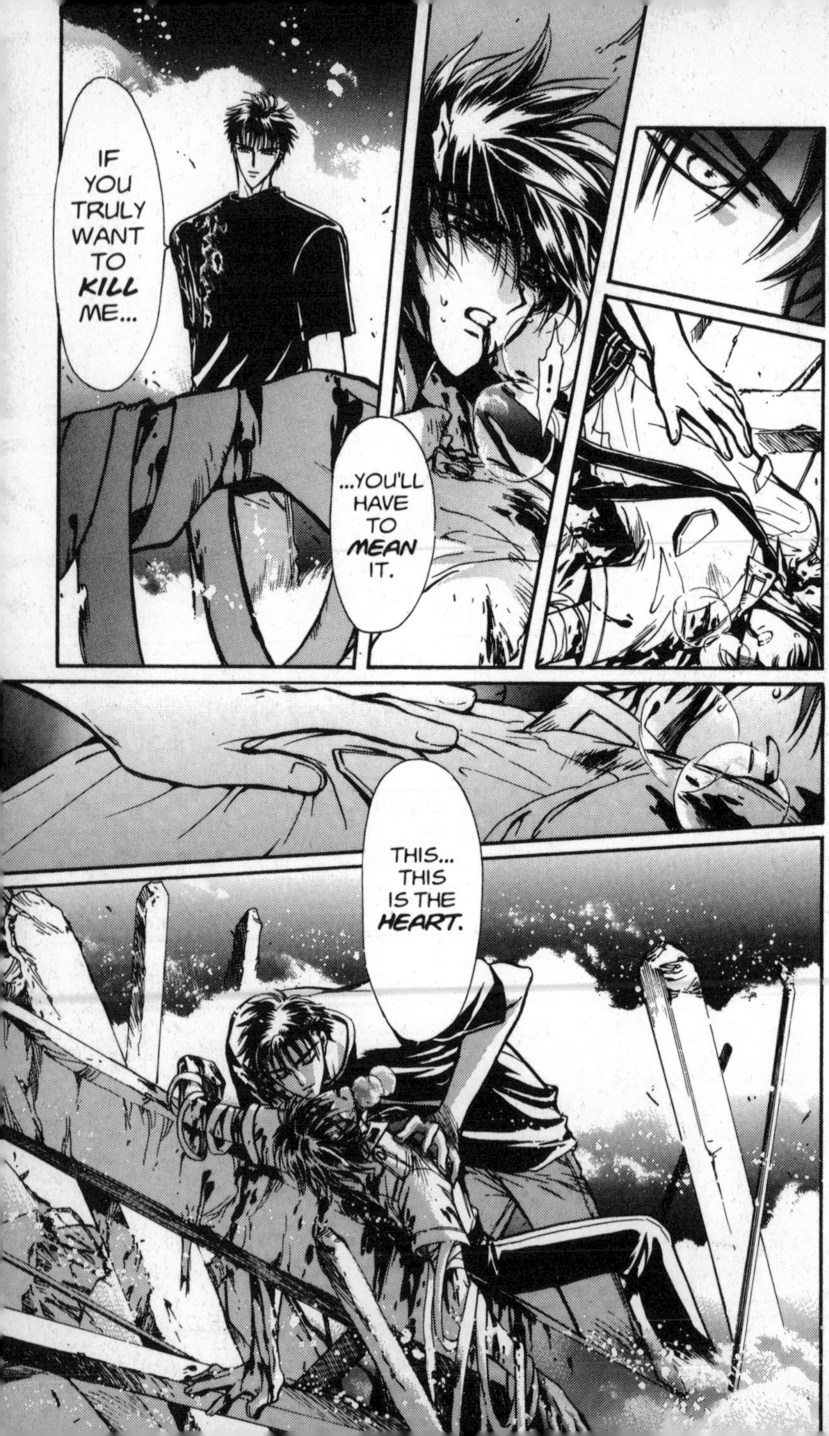
IF YOU TRULY WANT TO KILL ME...
...YOU'LL HAVE TO MEAN IT.
!
THIS... THIS IS THE HEART.

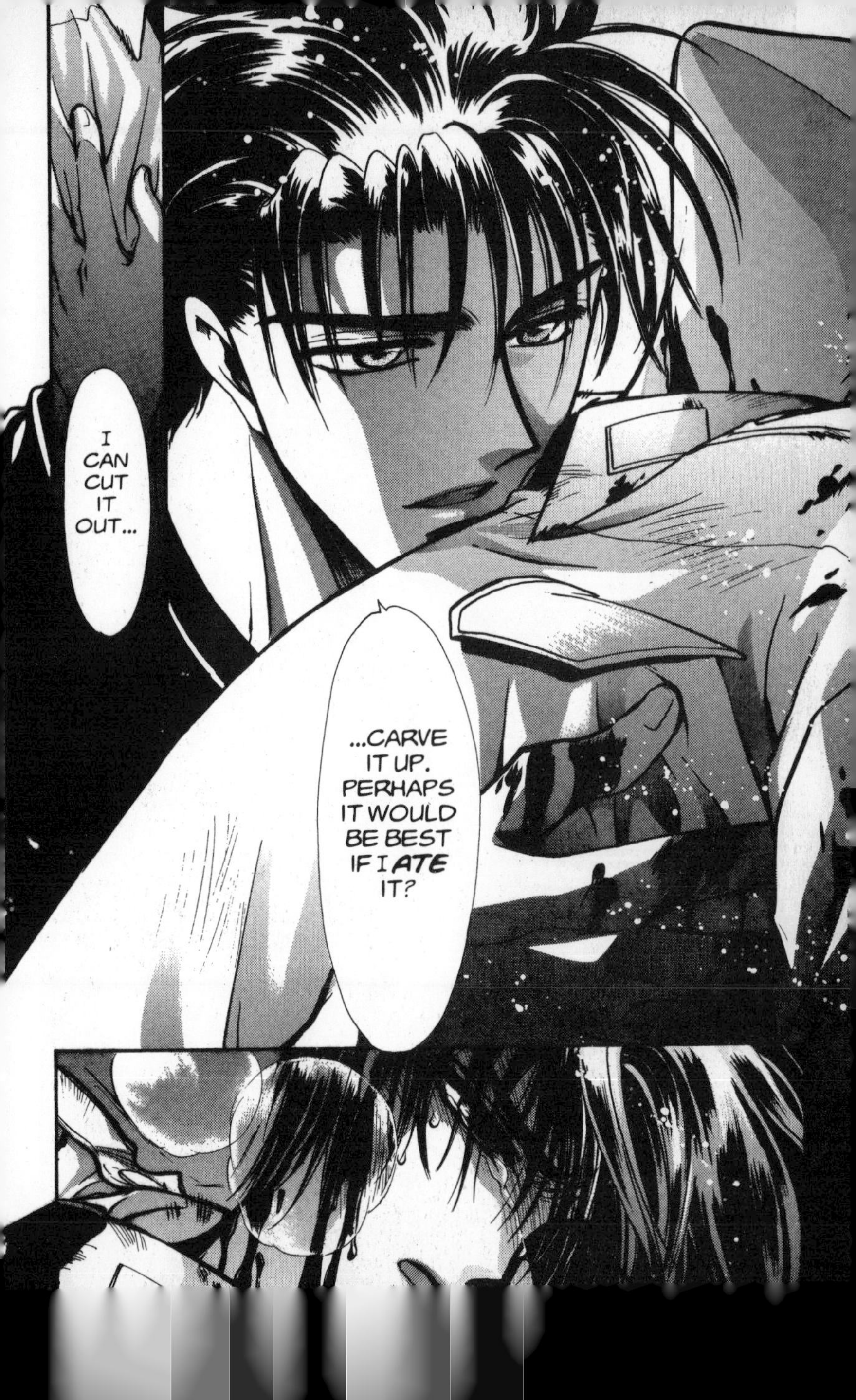
I CAN CUT IT OUT...
...CARVE IT UP. PERHAPS IT WOULD BE BEST IF I ***ATE*** IT?

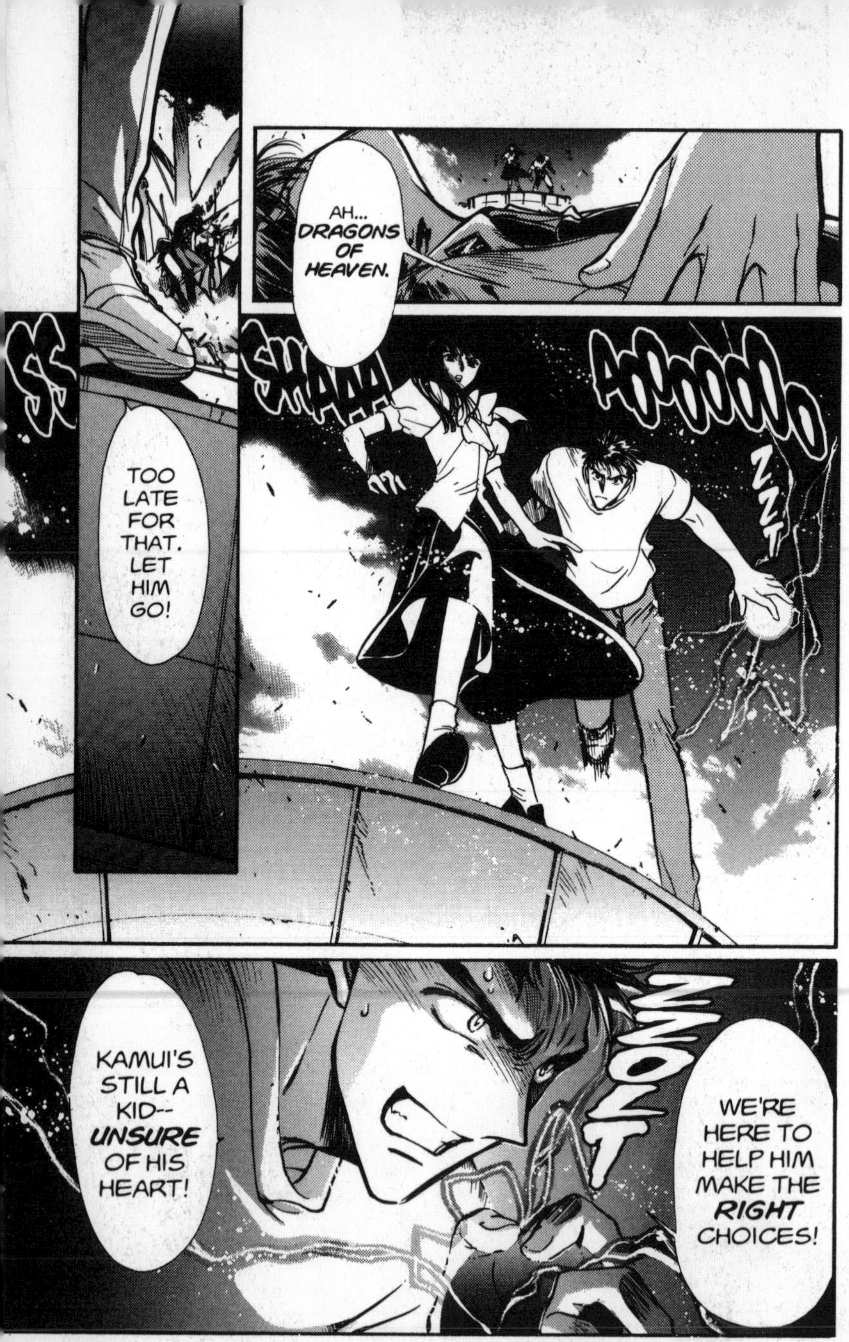
SS
TOO LATE FOR THAT. LET HIM GO!
AH... DRAGONS OF HEAVEN.
SHAAA
AOOOOOO
ZZZT
KAMUI'S STILL A KID-- *UNSURE* OF HIS HEART!
WE'RE HERE TO HELP HIM MAKE THE *RIGHT* CHOICES!

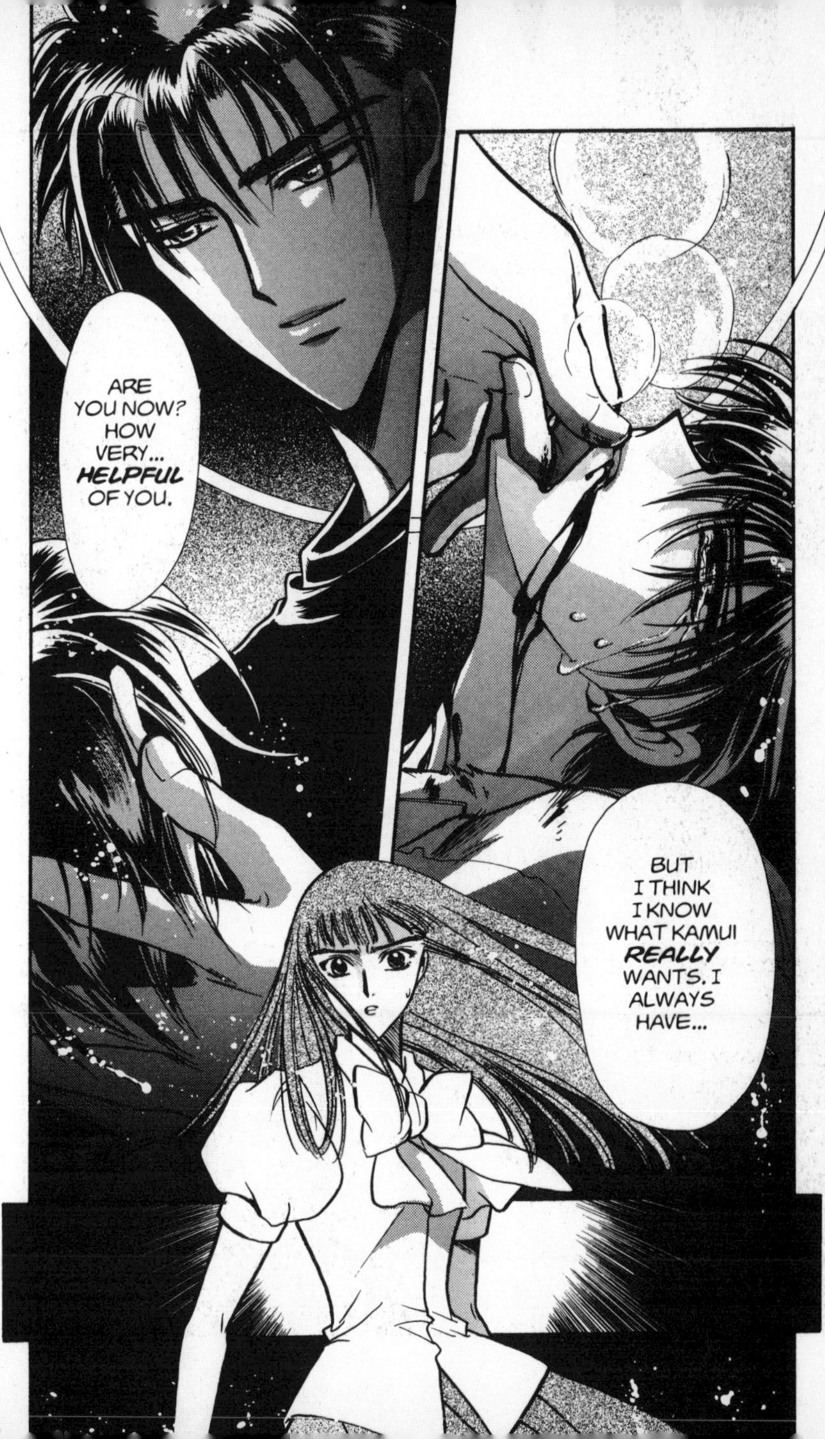
ARE YOU NOW? HOW VERY... **HELPFUL** OF YOU.
BUT I THINK I KNOW WHAT KAMUI **REALLY** WANTS. I ALWAYS HAVE...

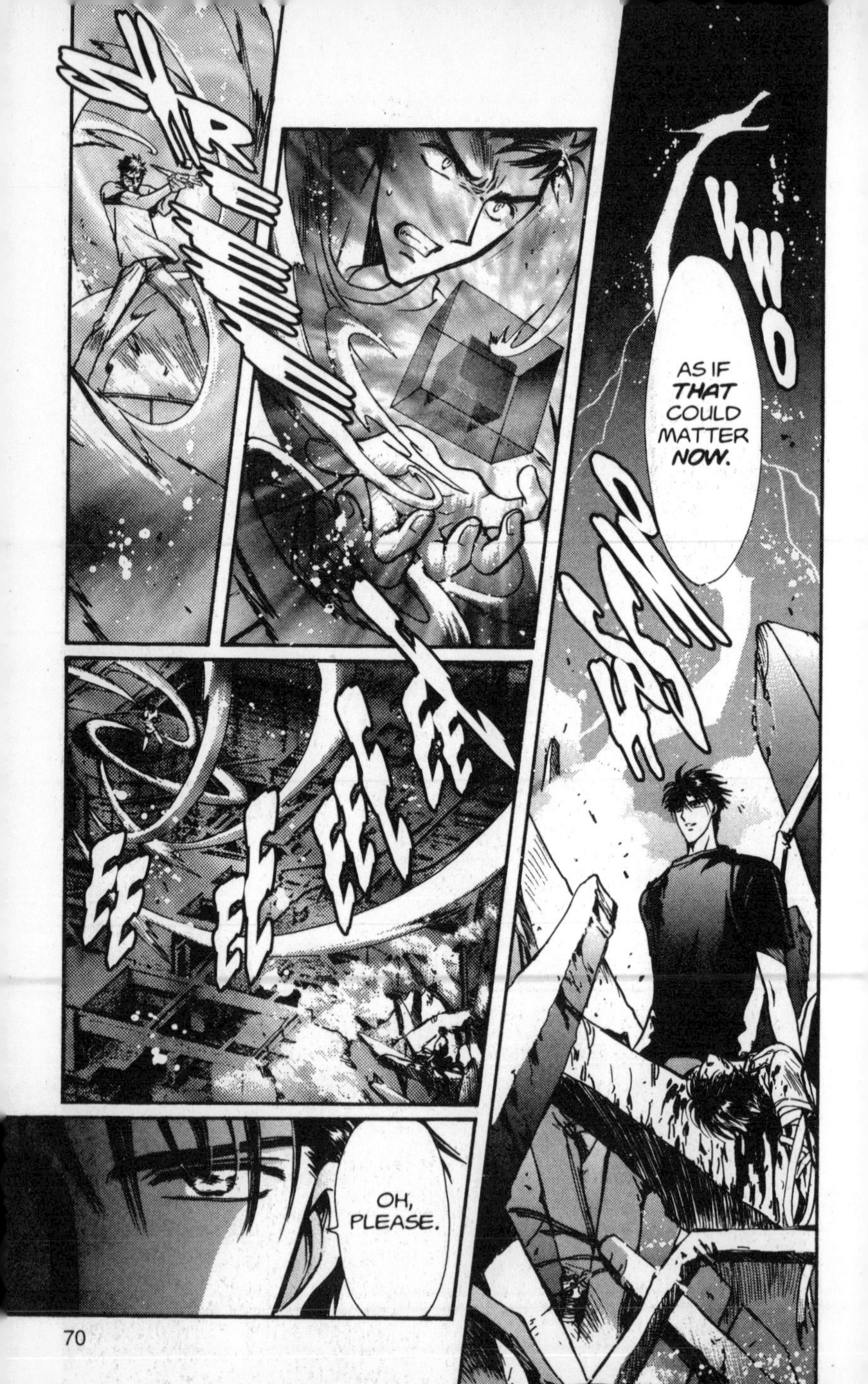
OH, PLEASE.
AS IF THAT COULD MATTER NOW.

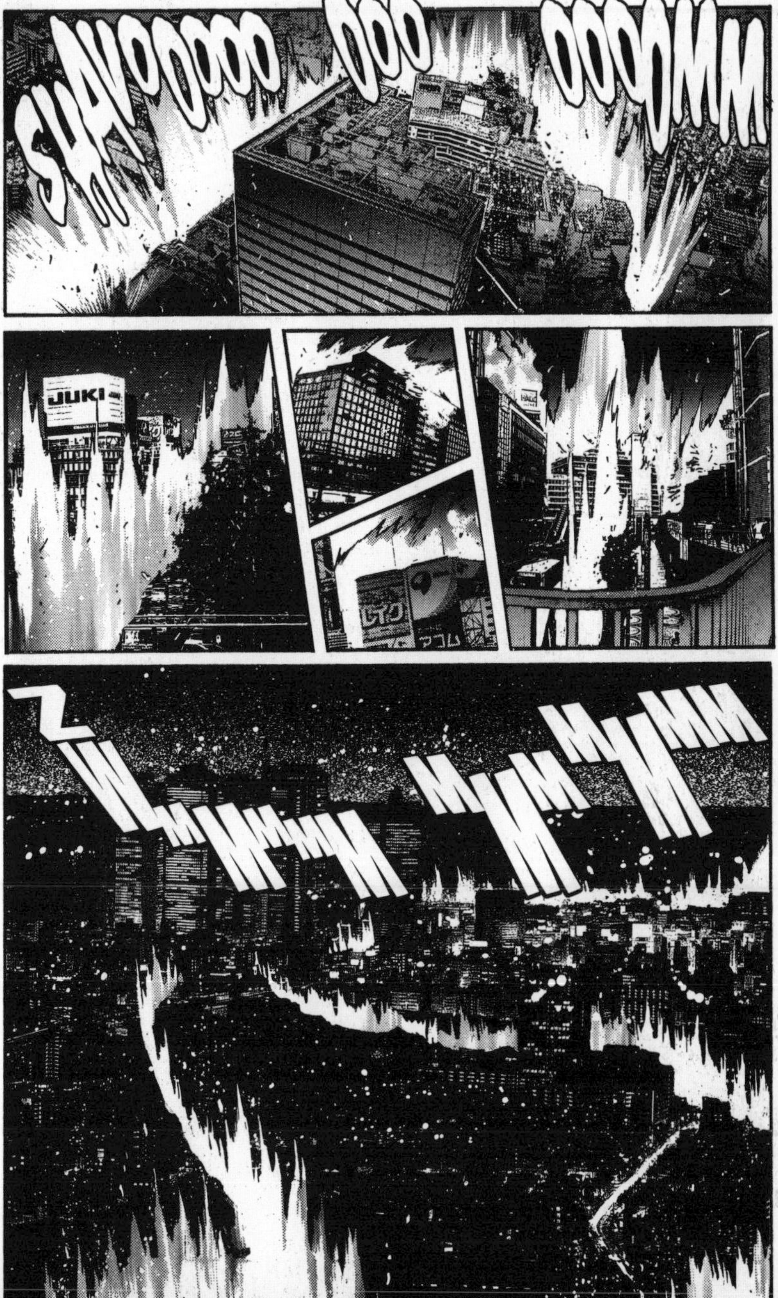
SHVOOOOO OOO OOOOMM
JUKI
レイク
アコム

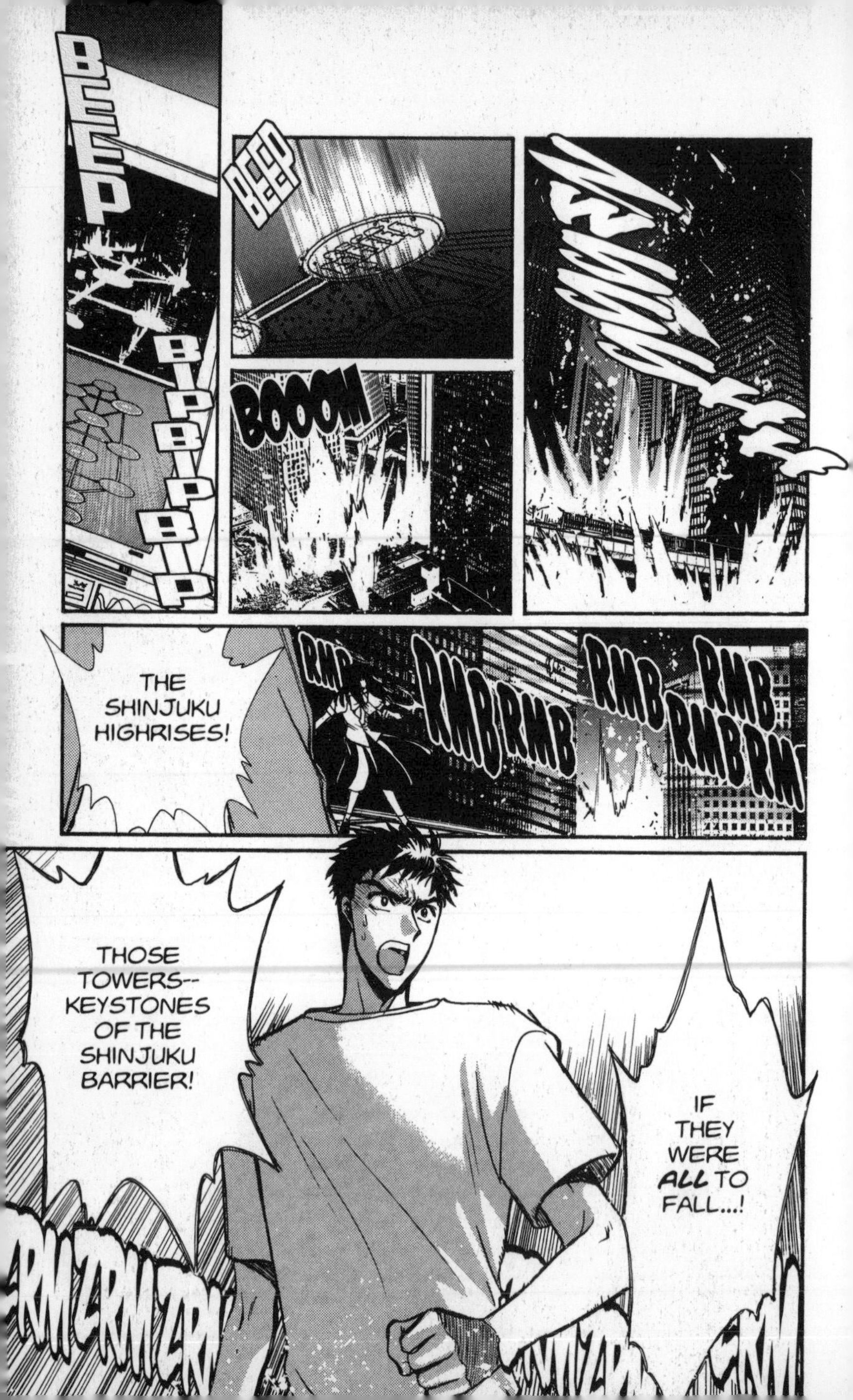
BEEP
BIP BIP BIP
BEEP
BOOOM
RMB
RMB RMB
RMB RMB
THE SHINJUKU HIGHRISES!
THOSE TOWERS--KEYSTONES OF THE SHINJUKU BARRIER!
IF THEY WERE ALL TO FALL...!
ZRM ZRM ZR

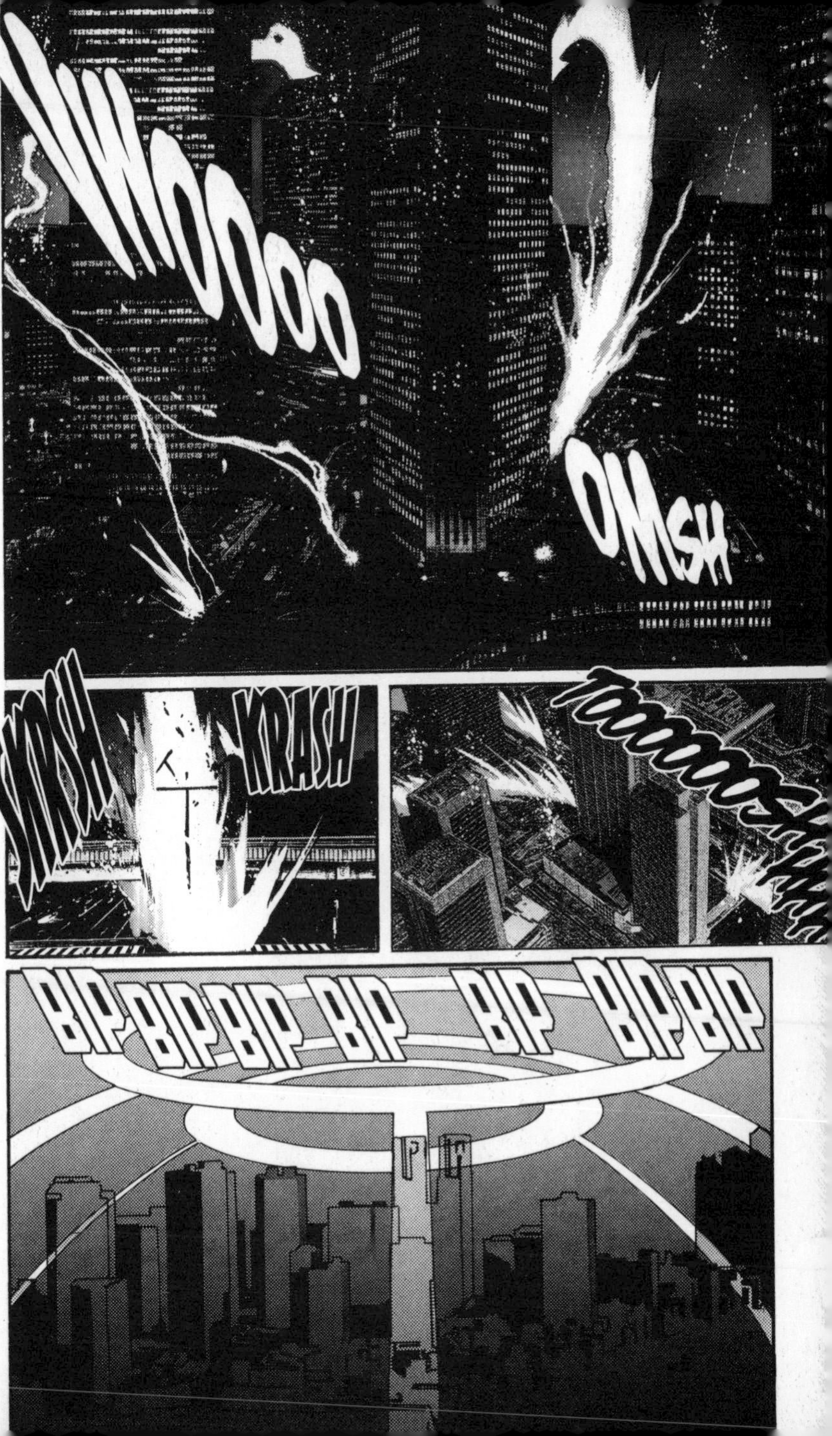
WOOOOO
OMSH
SMASH
KRASH
TOOOOOSH
BIP BIP BIP BIP BIP BIP BIP

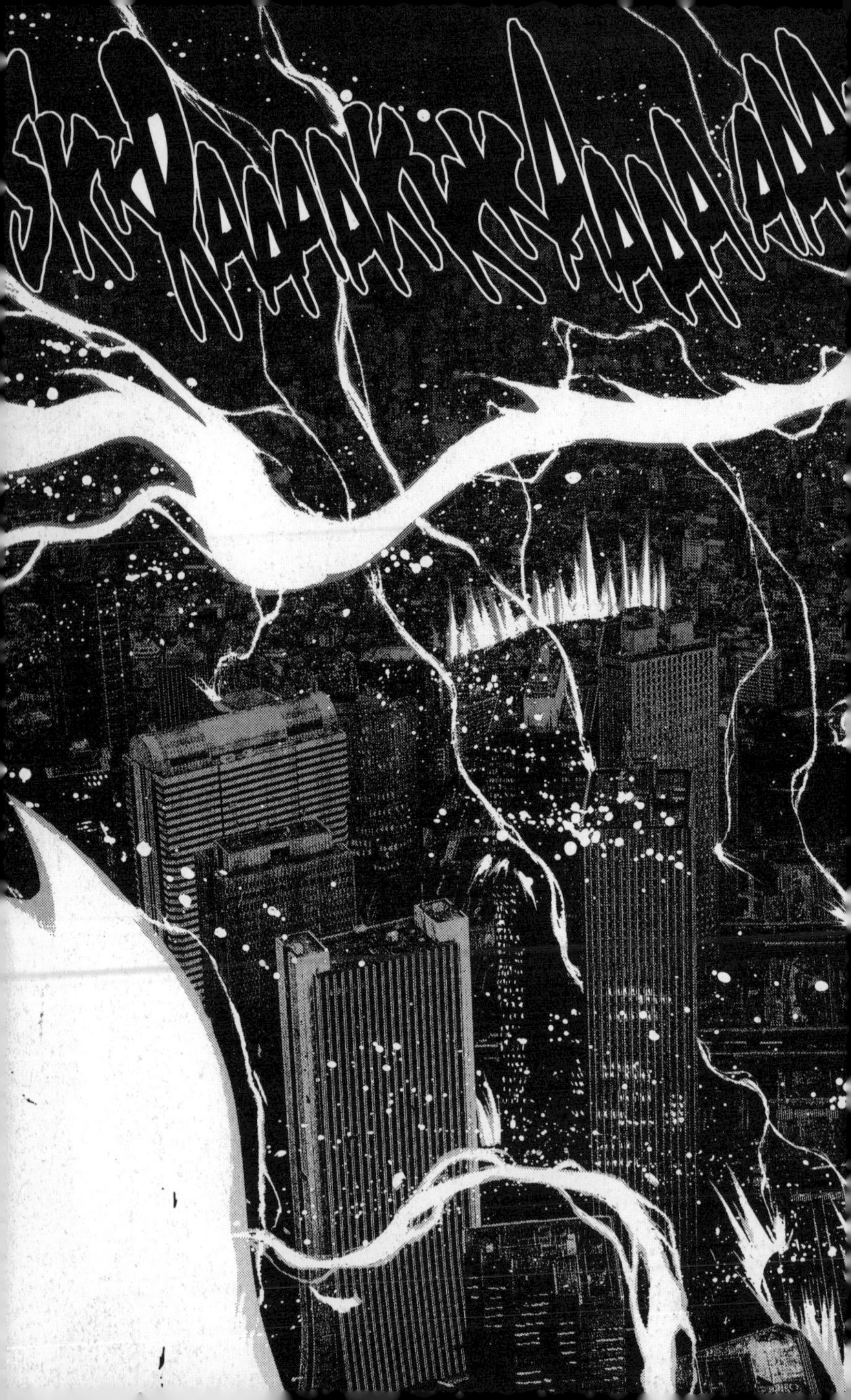
SKRAAAAKKAAAAAAA

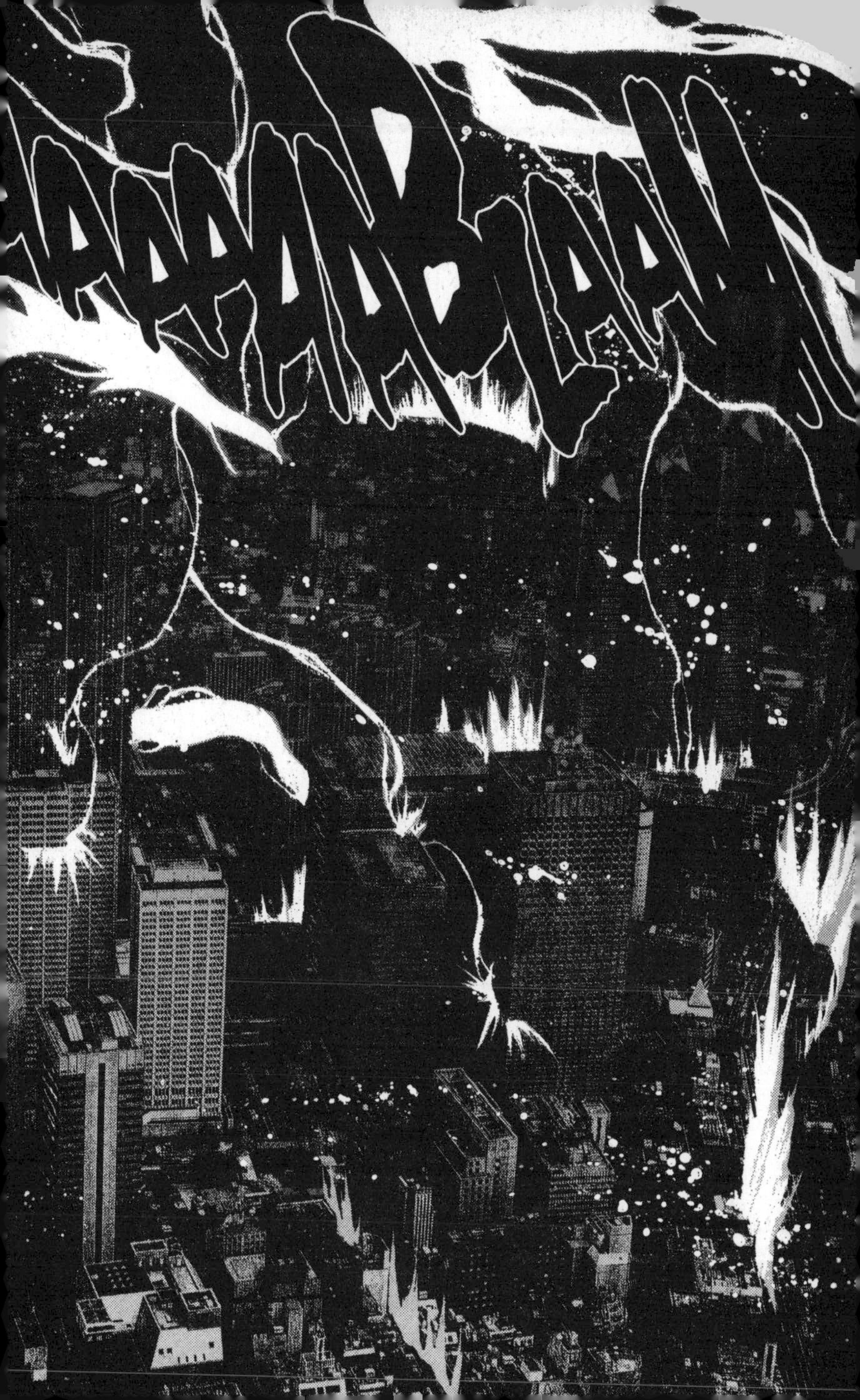

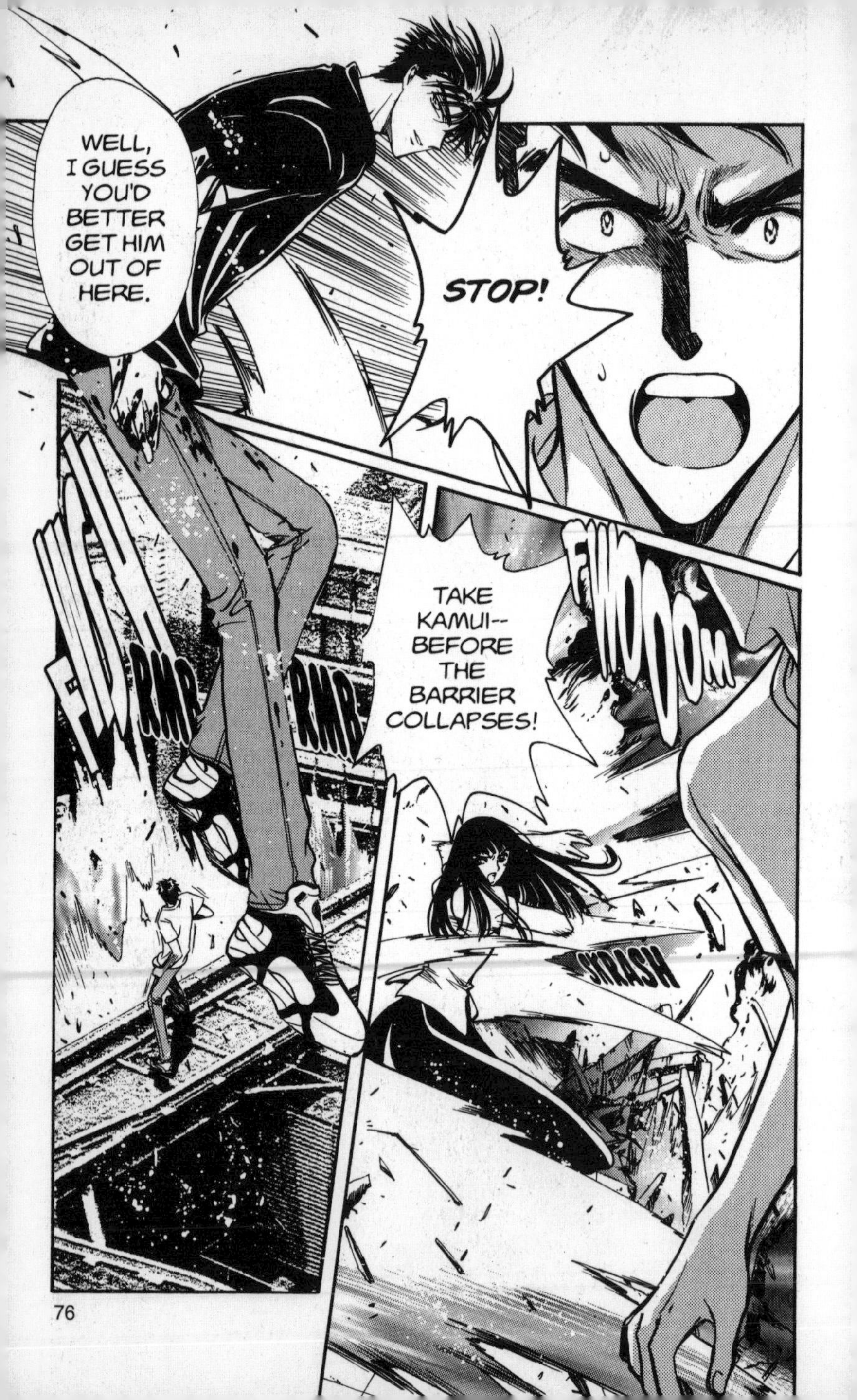
WELL, I GUESS YOU'D BETTER GET HIM OUT OF HERE.
STOP!
RMB
RMB
TAKE KAMUI-- BEFORE THE BARRIER COLLAPSES!
FWOOOM
SKRASH

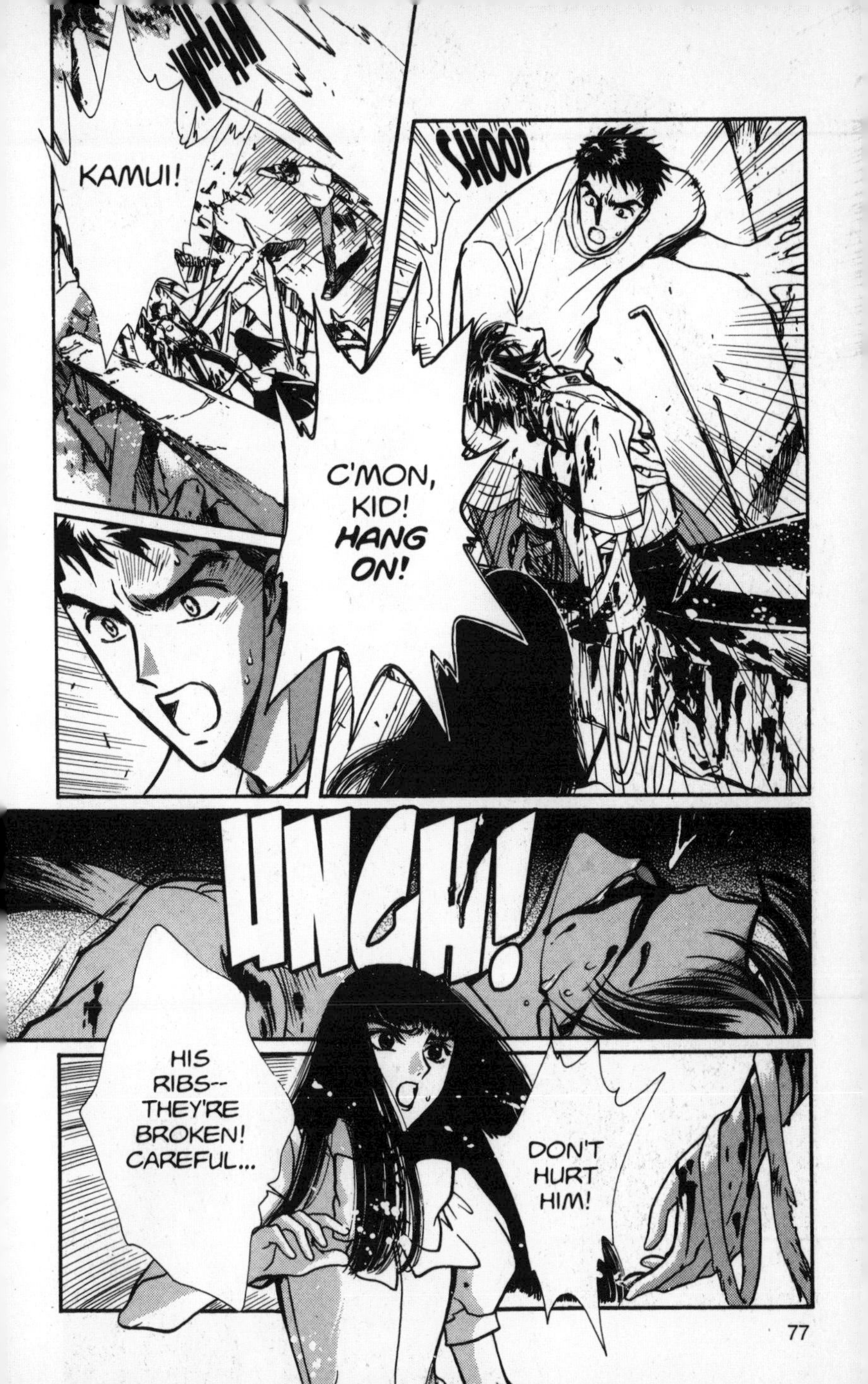
WHAM
KAMUI!
SHOOP
C'MON, KID! HANG ON!
UNCH!
HIS RIBS-- THEY'RE BROKEN! CAREFUL...
DON'T HURT HIM!

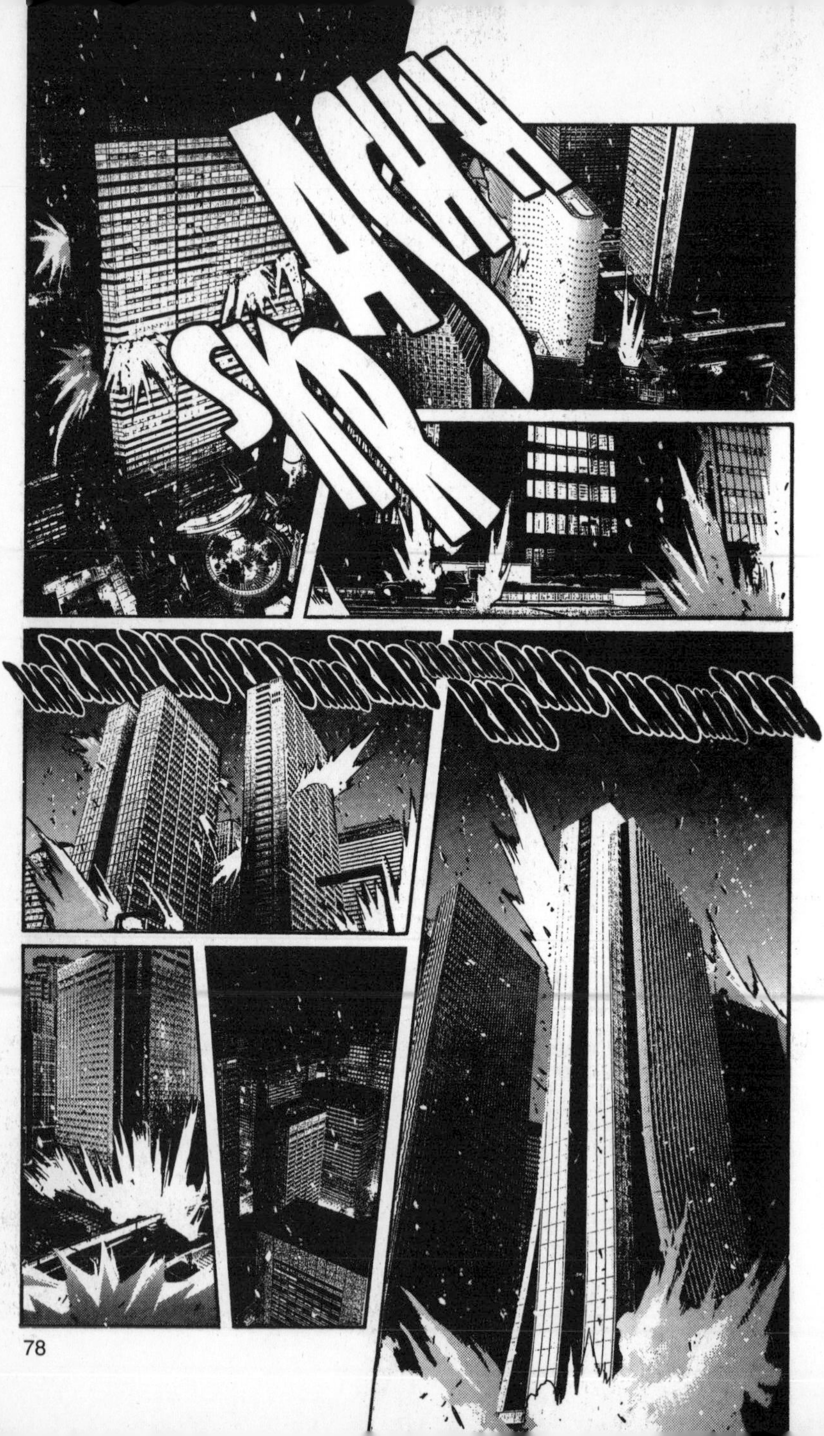

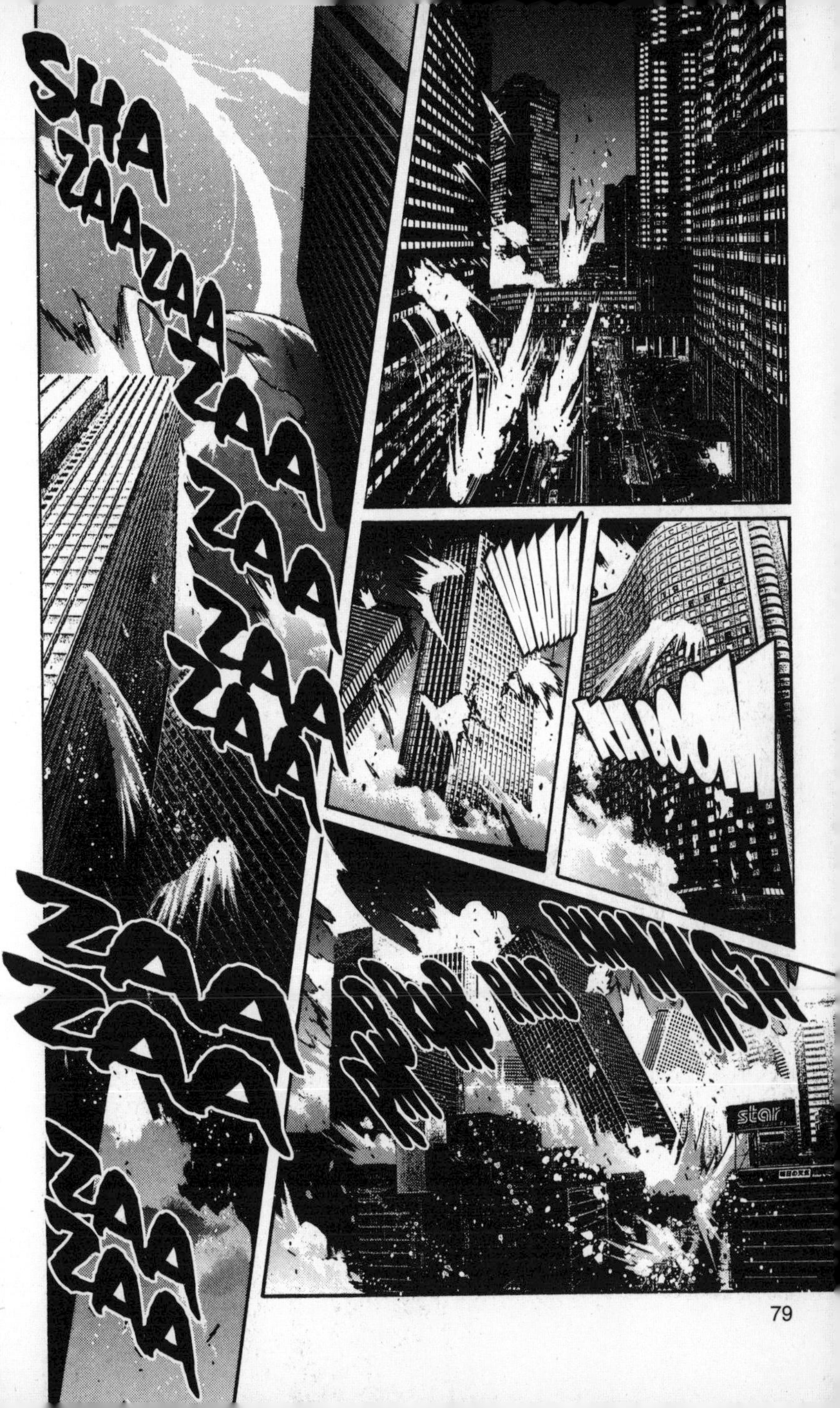
SHA ZAAZAAZAA ZAA ZAA ZAA ZAA
KA BOOM
ZAA ZAA ZAA ZAA ZAA ZAA
star

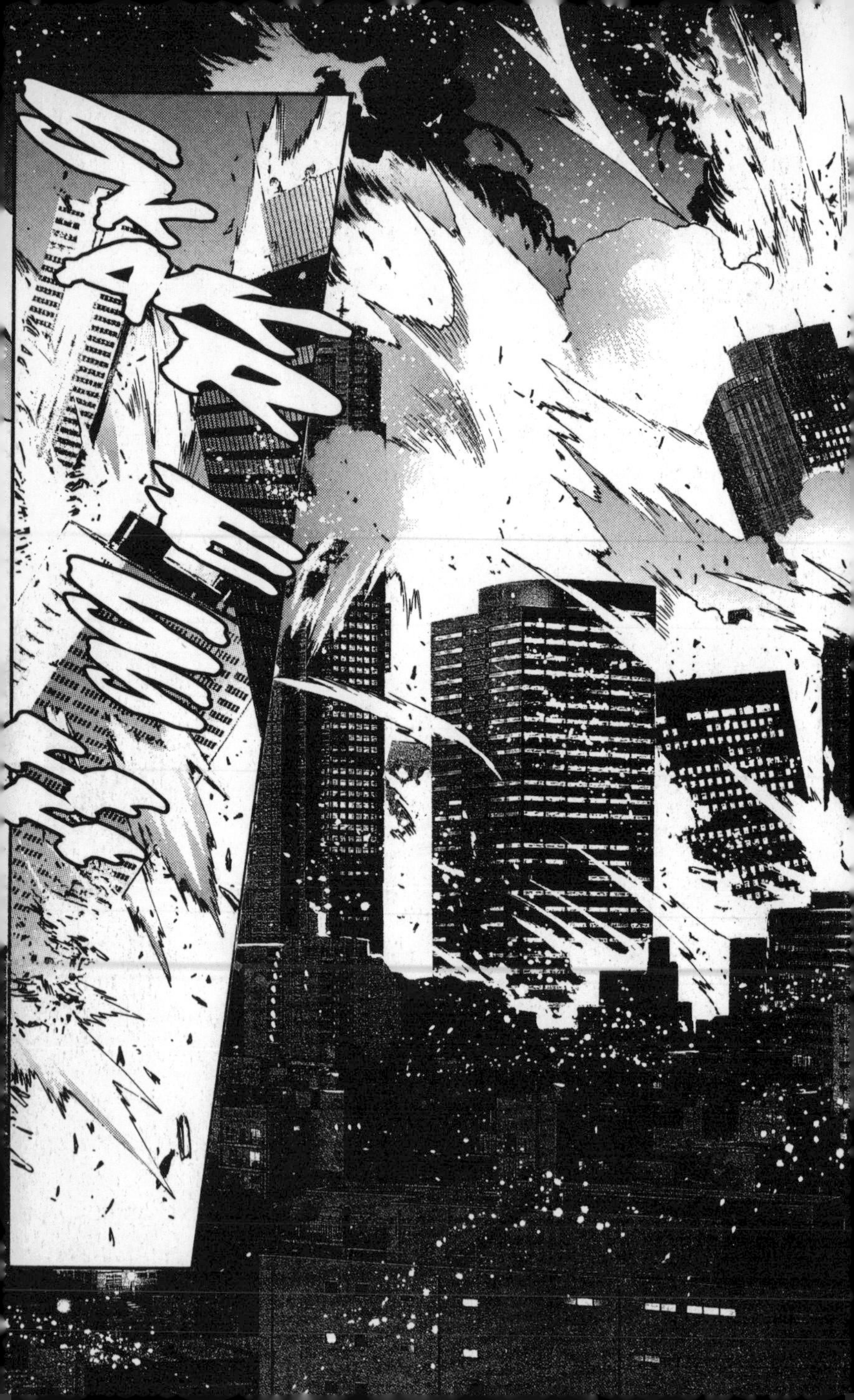

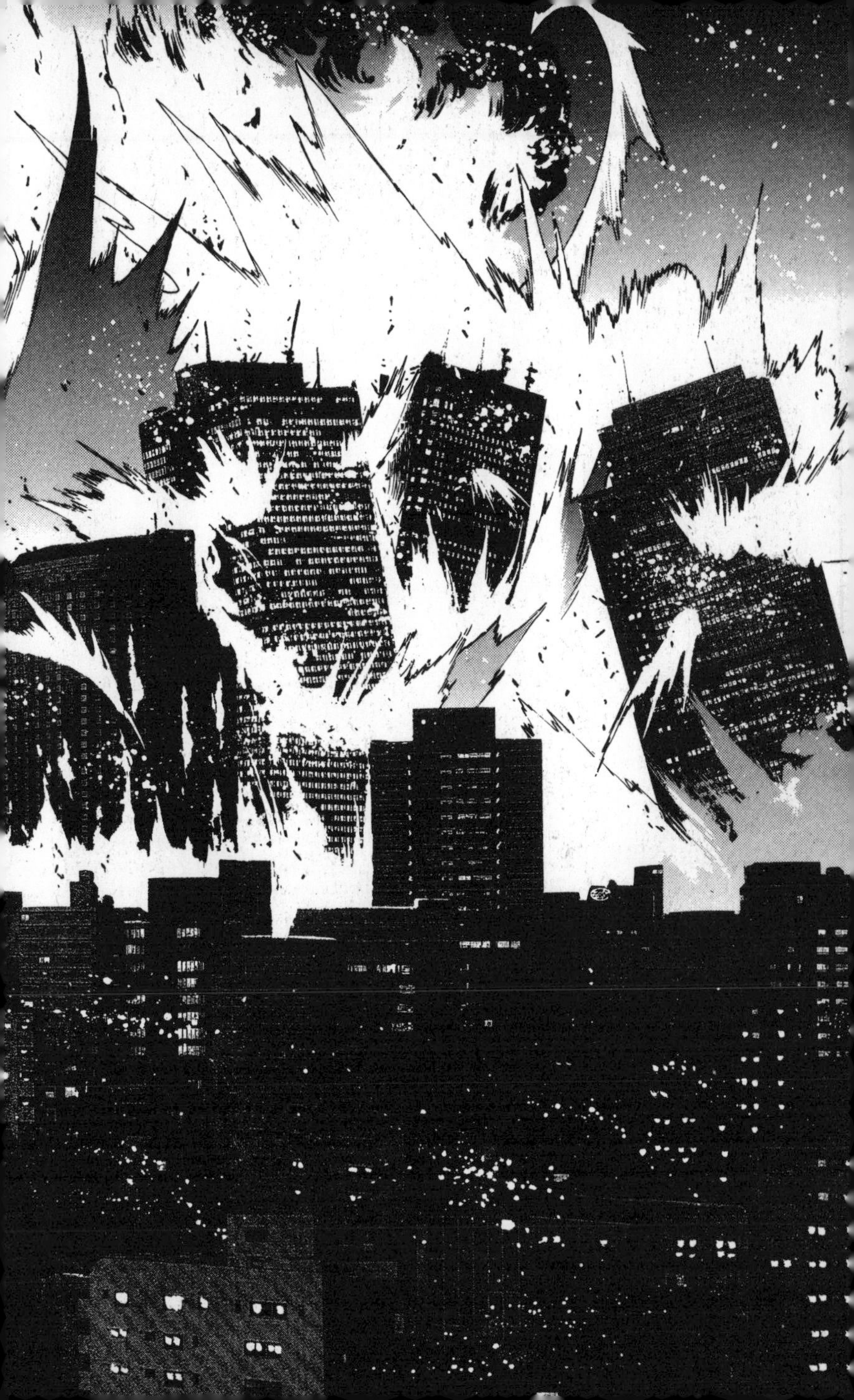

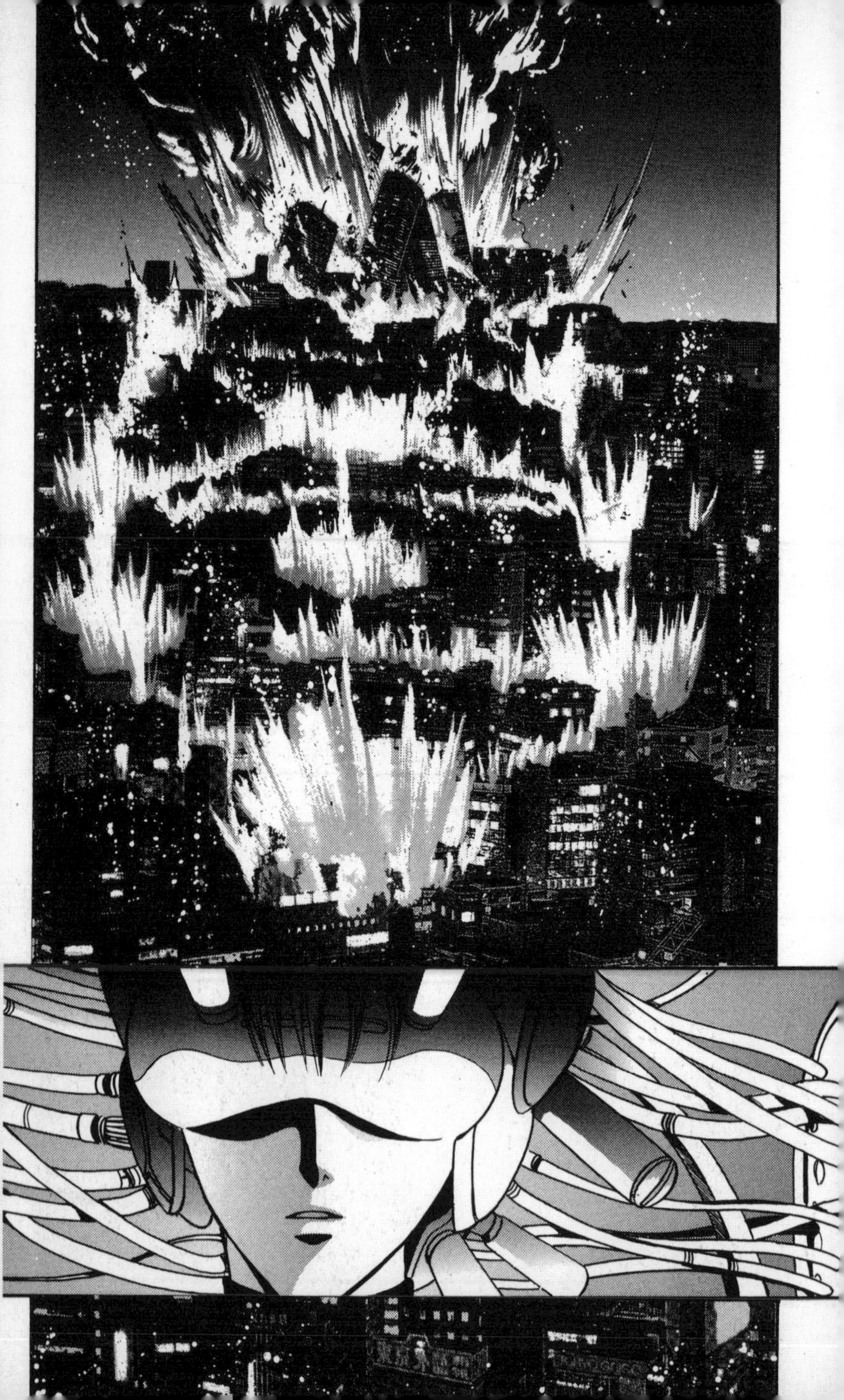

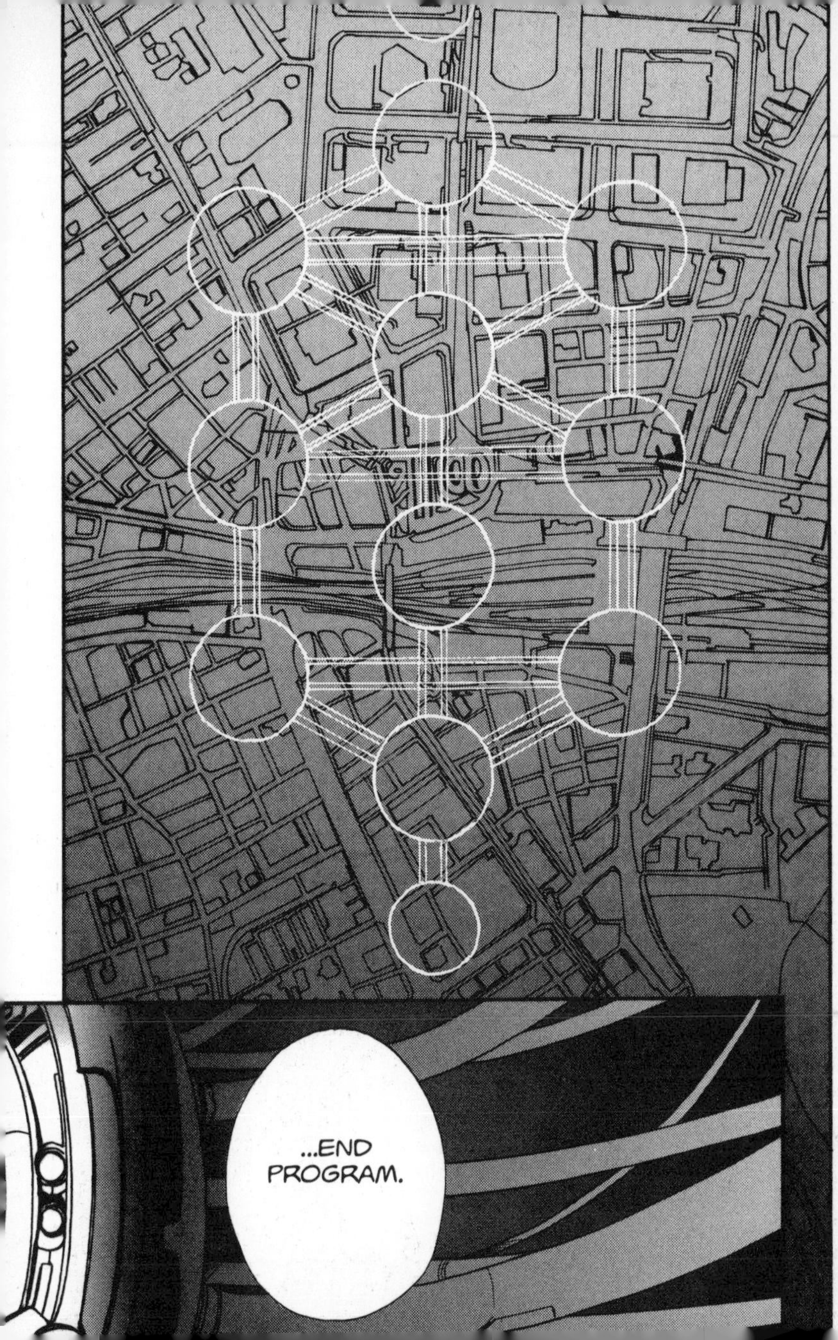
...END
PROGRAM.

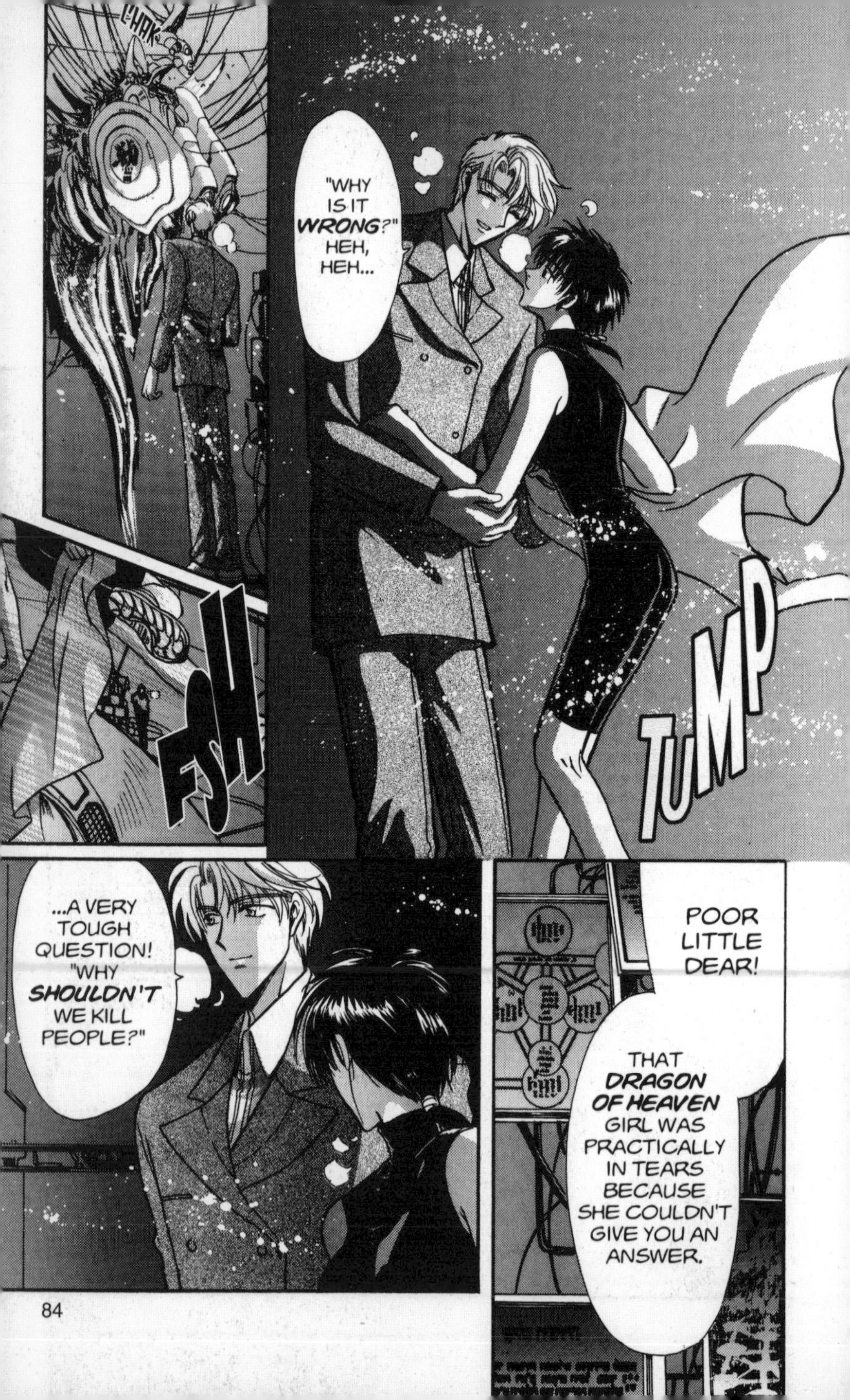
L'HAK
FSH
"WHY IS IT WRONG?" HEH, HEH...
TUMP
...A VERY TOUGH QUESTION! "WHY SHOULDN'T WE KILL PEOPLE?"
POOR LITTLE DEAR!
THAT DRAGON OF HEAVEN GIRL WAS PRACTICALLY IN TEARS BECAUSE SHE COULDN'T GIVE YOU AN ANSWER.

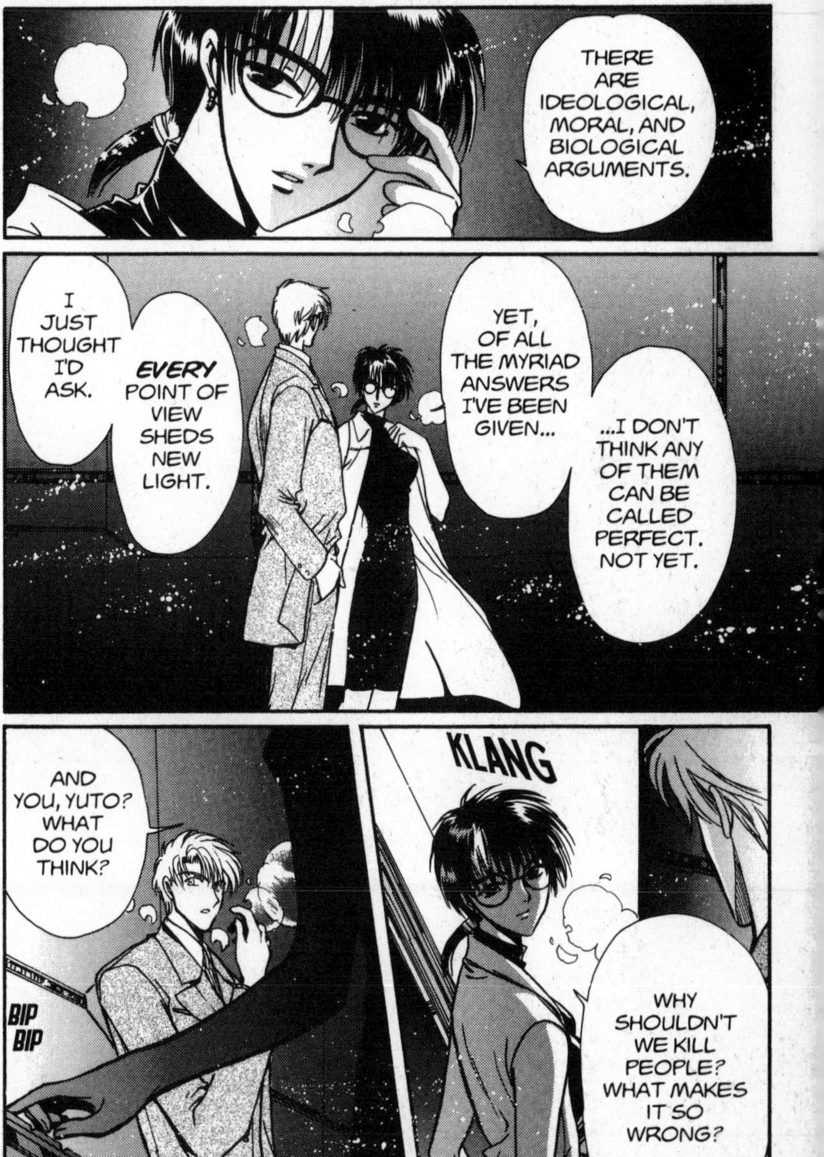
THERE ARE IDEOLOGICAL, MORAL, AND BIOLOGICAL ARGUMENTS.
I JUST THOUGHT I'D ASK.
EVERY POINT OF VIEW SHEDS NEW LIGHT.
YET, OF ALL THE MYRIAD ANSWERS I'VE BEEN GIVEN...
...I DON'T THINK ANY OF THEM CAN BE CALLED PERFECT. NOT YET.
AND YOU, YUTO? WHAT DO YOU THINK?
BIP BIP
KLANG
WHY SHOULDN'T WE KILL PEOPLE? WHAT MAKES IT SO WRONG?

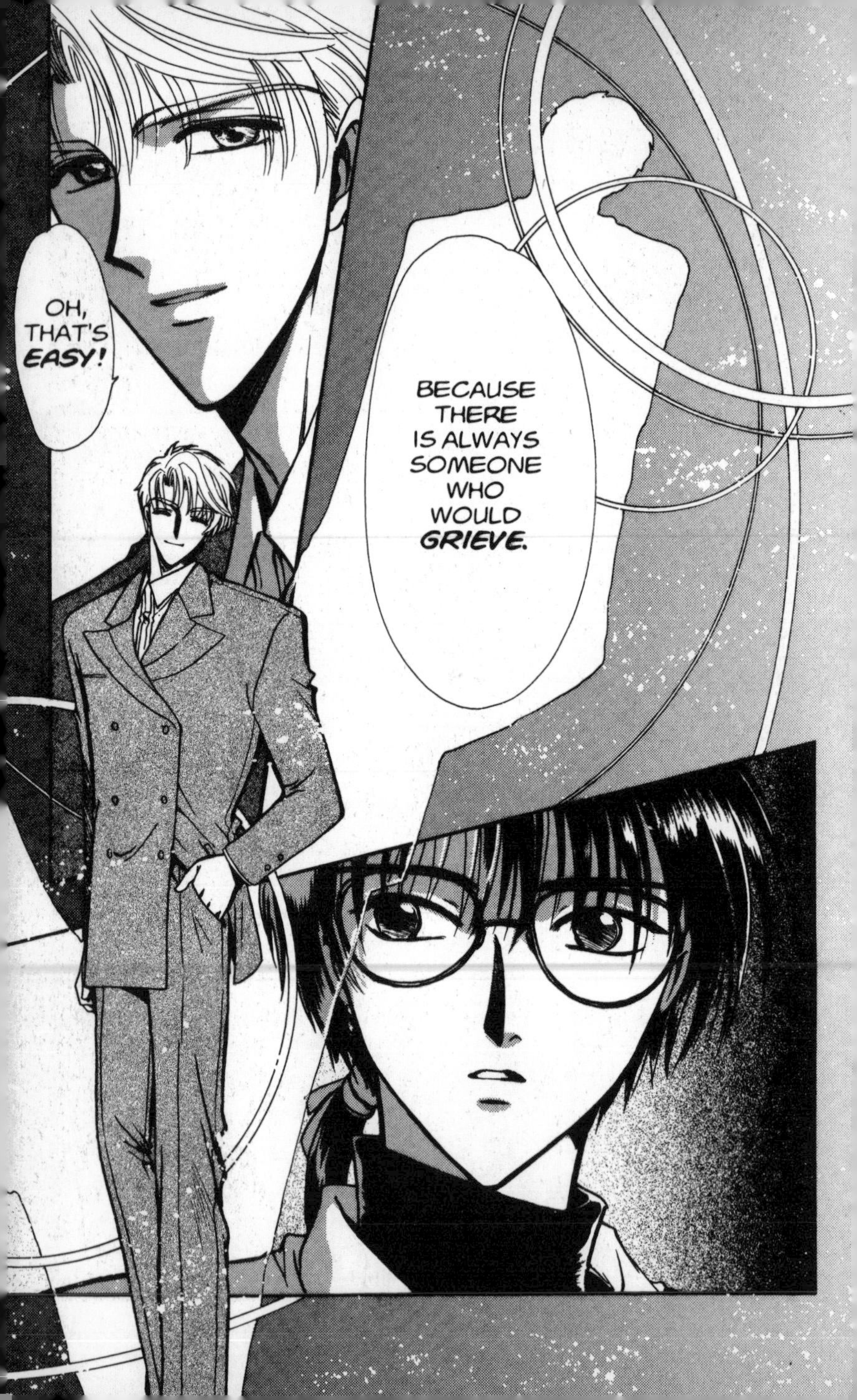
OH, THAT'S EASY!
BECAUSE THERE IS ALWAYS SOMEONE WHO WOULD GRIEVE.

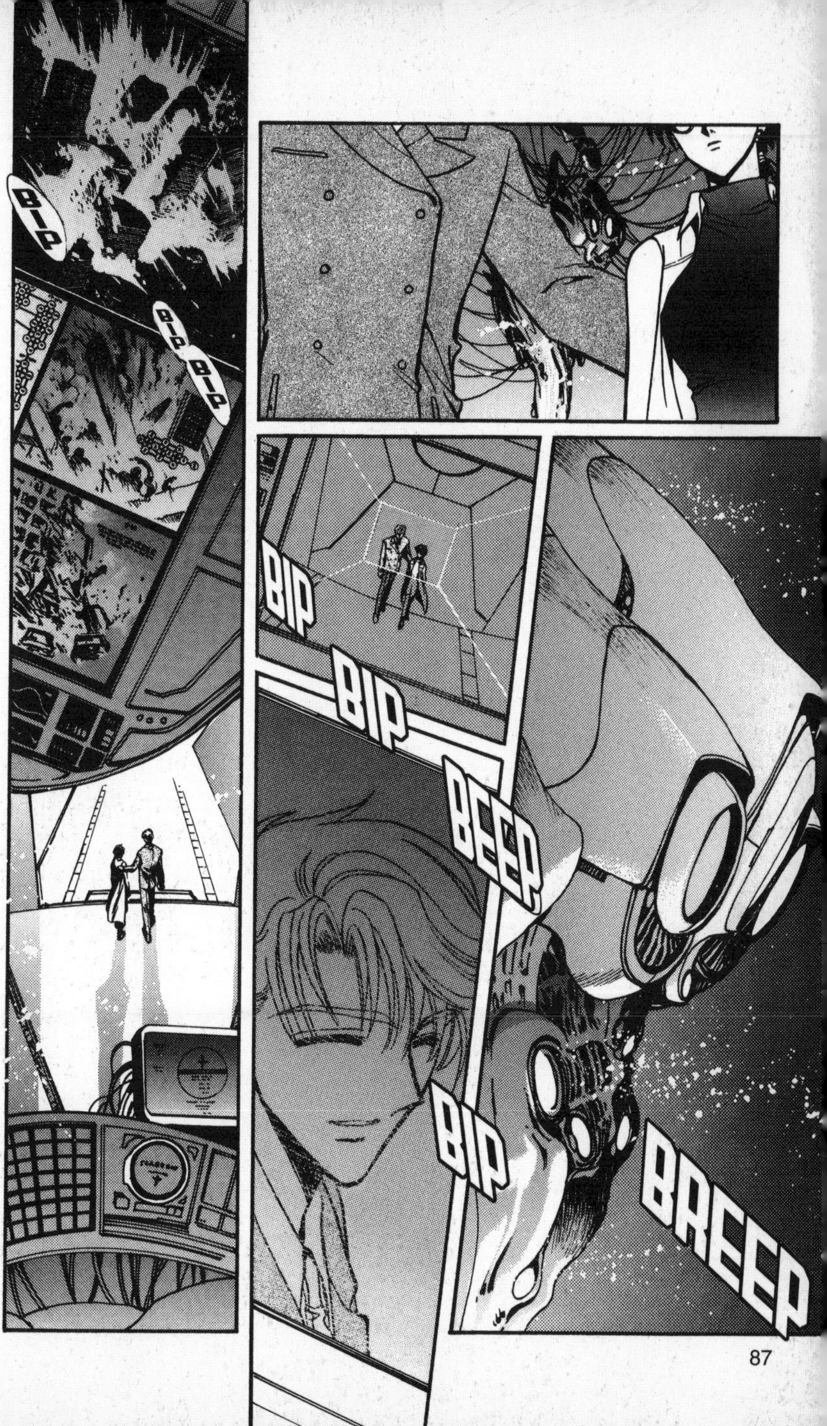
BIP
BIP BIP BIP
BIP
BIP
BEEP
BIP
BREEP

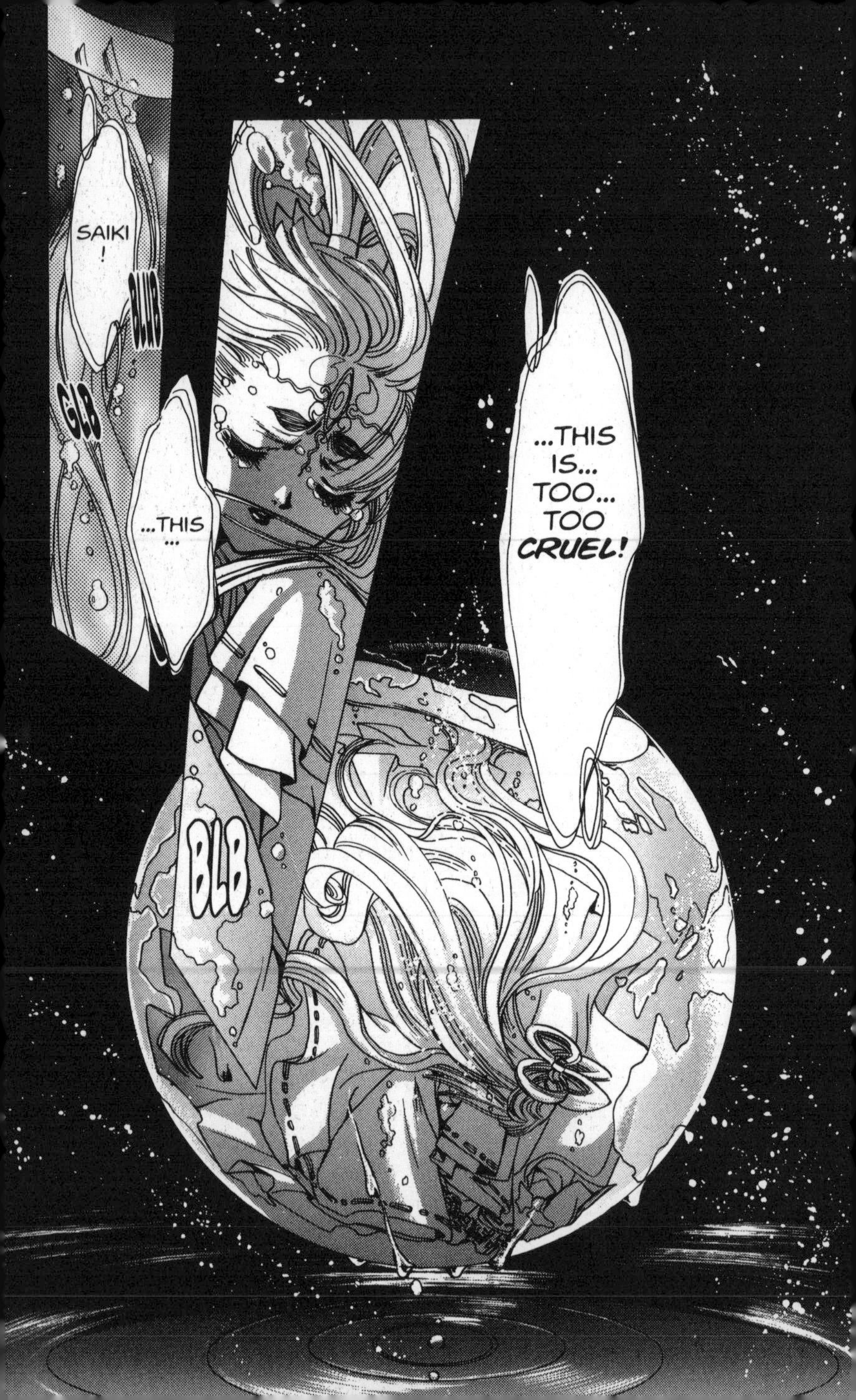
SAIKI!
BLUB
GLB
...THIS...
BLB
...THIS IS... TOO... TOO CRUEL!

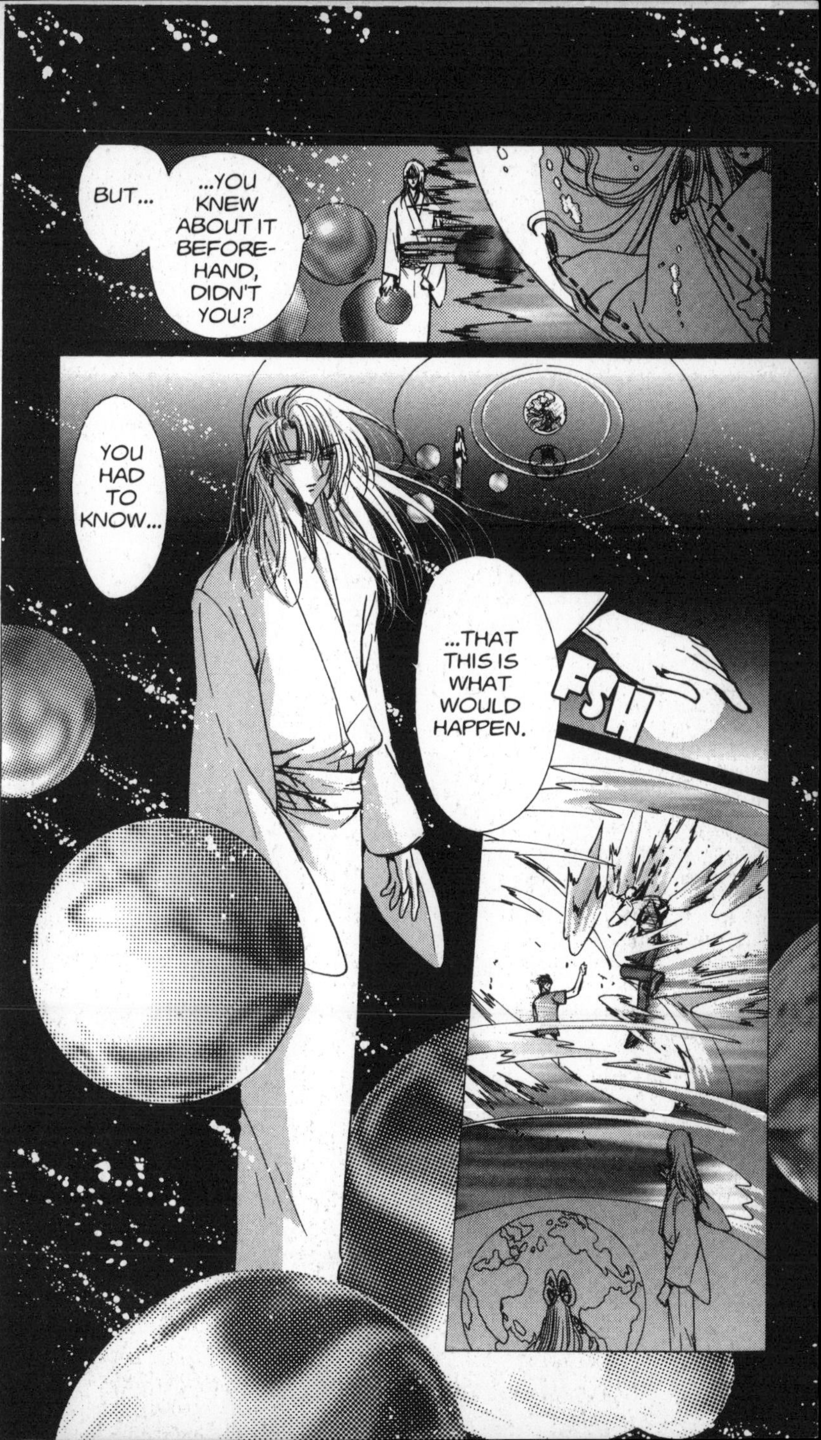
BUT...
...YOU KNEW ABOUT IT BEFORE-HAND, DIDN'T YOU?
YOU HAD TO KNOW...
...THAT THIS IS WHAT WOULD HAPPEN.
FSH

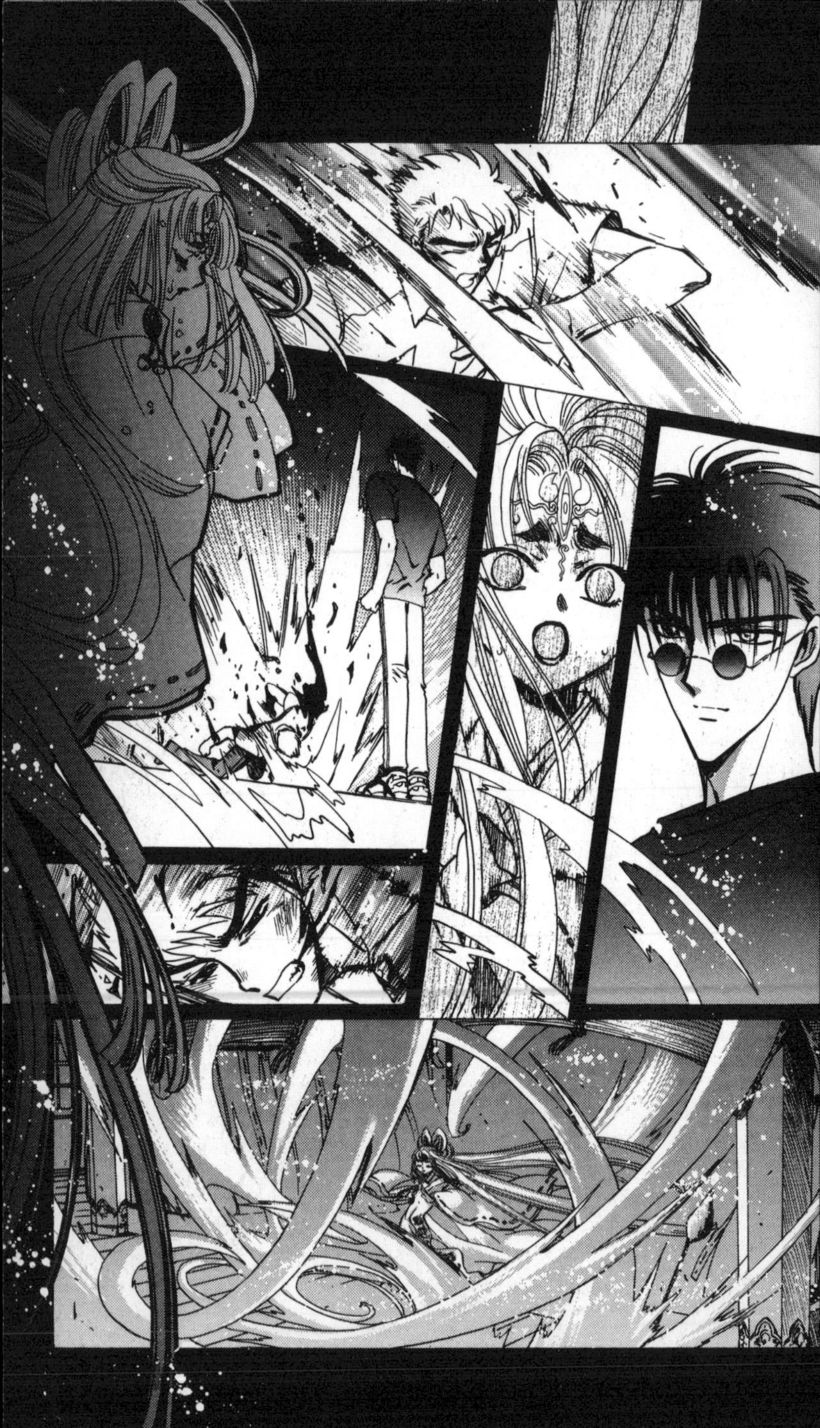

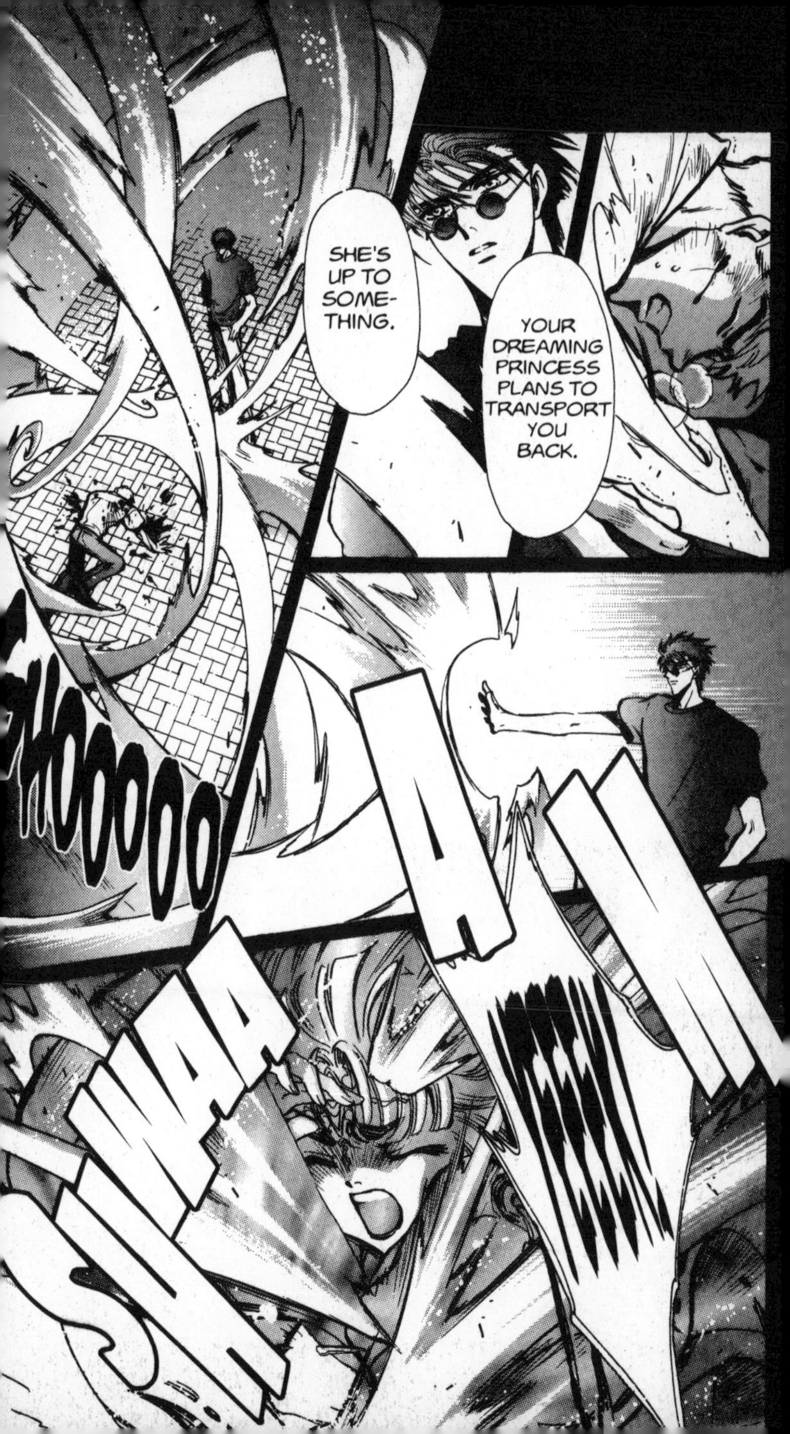

SHE'S UP TO SOME-THING.
YOUR DREAMING PRINCESS PLANS TO TRANSPORT YOU BACK.

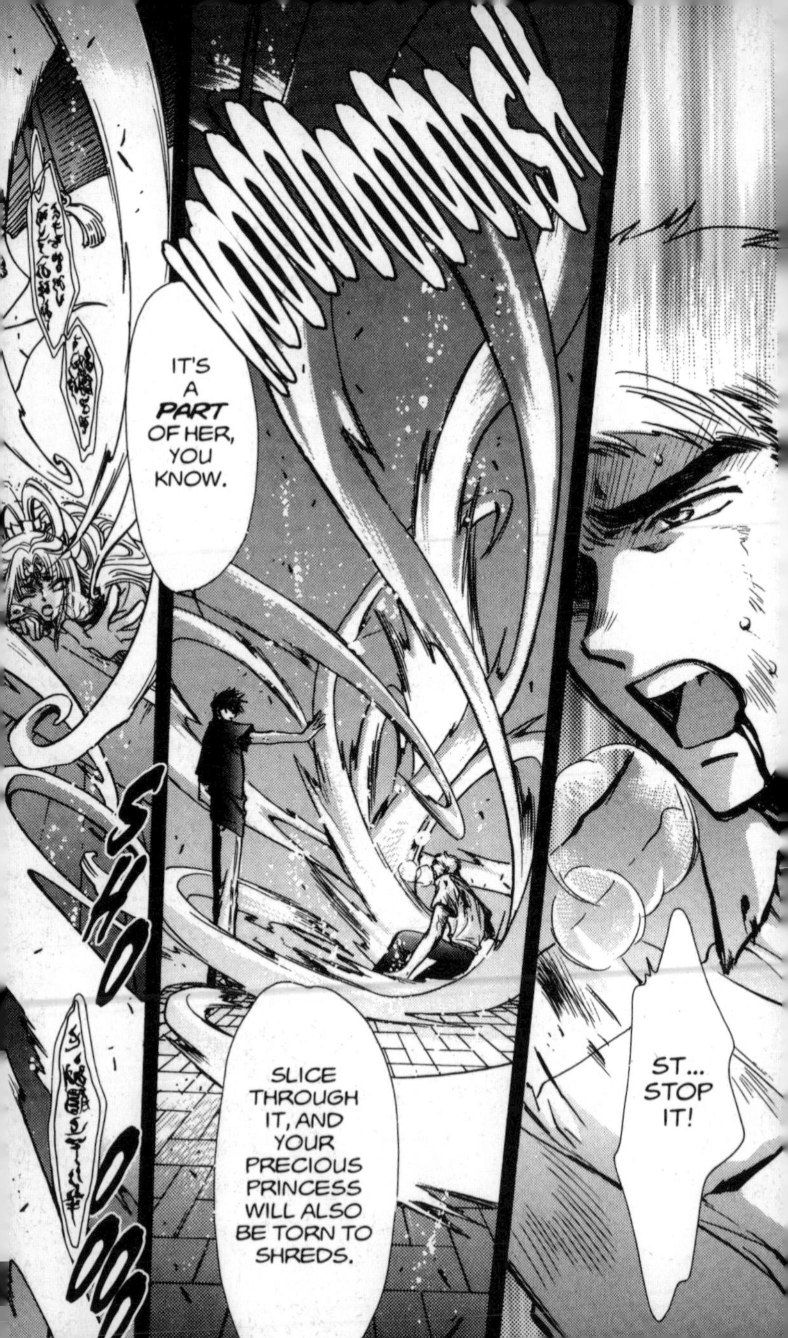
IT'S A PART OF HER, YOU KNOW.
SLICE THROUGH IT, AND YOUR PRECIOUS PRINCESS WILL ALSO BE TORN TO SHREDS.
ST... STOP IT!

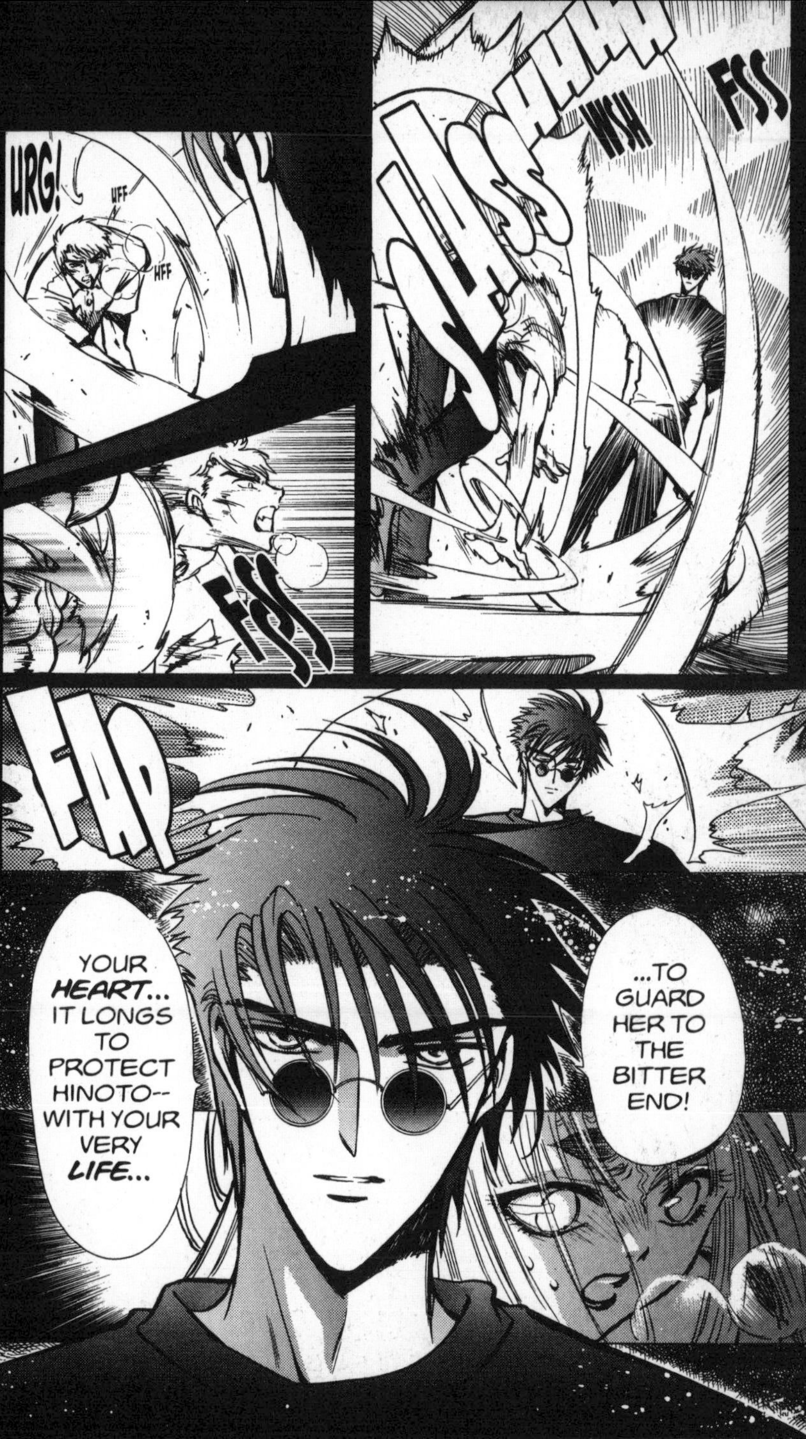
URG!
HFF
HFF
FSS
SHASS--HHHH
WSH
FSS
FAP
YOUR HEART... IT LONGS TO PROTECT HINOTO--WITH YOUR VERY LIFE...
...TO GUARD HER TO THE BITTER END!

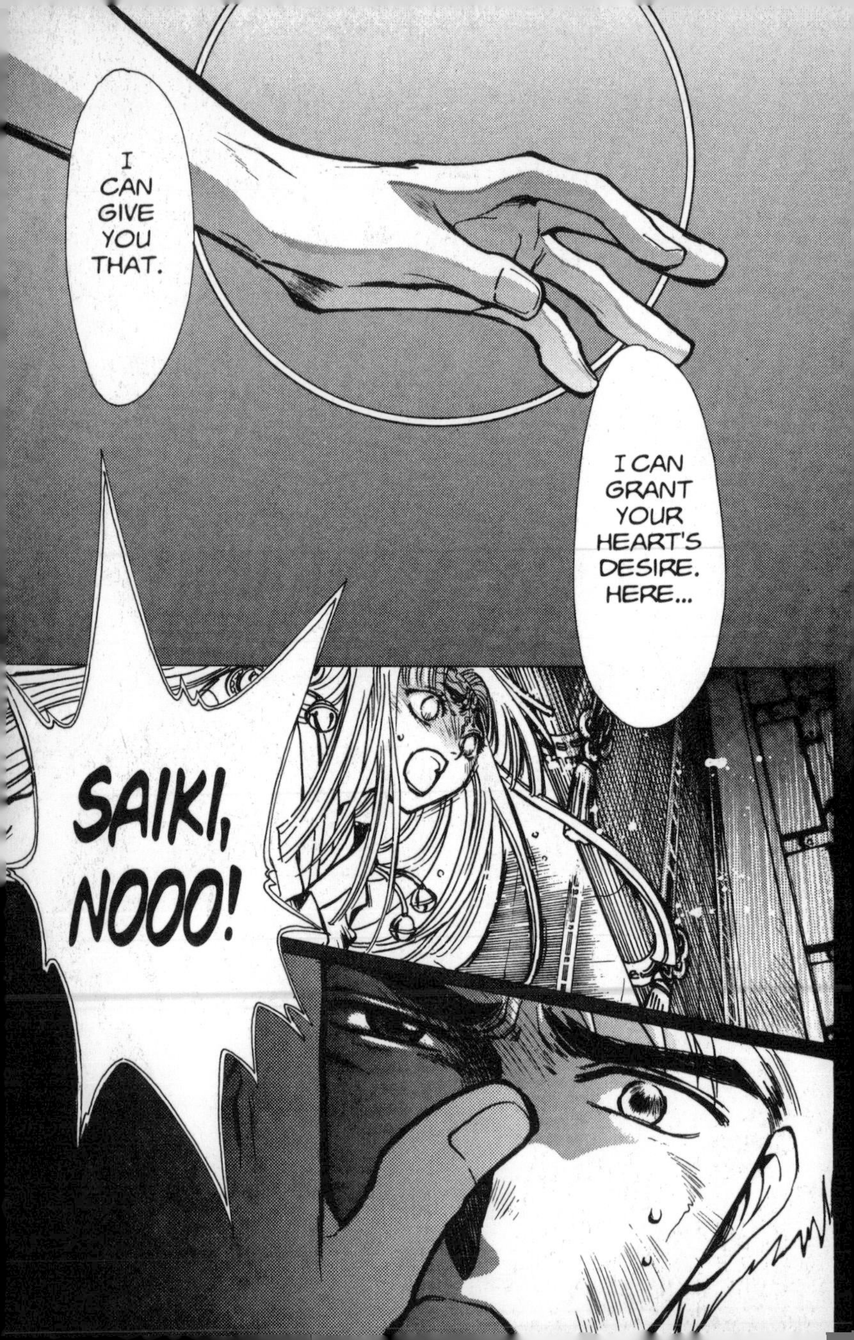
I CAN GIVE YOU THAT.
I CAN GRANT YOUR HEART'S DESIRE. HERE...
SAIKI, NOOO!

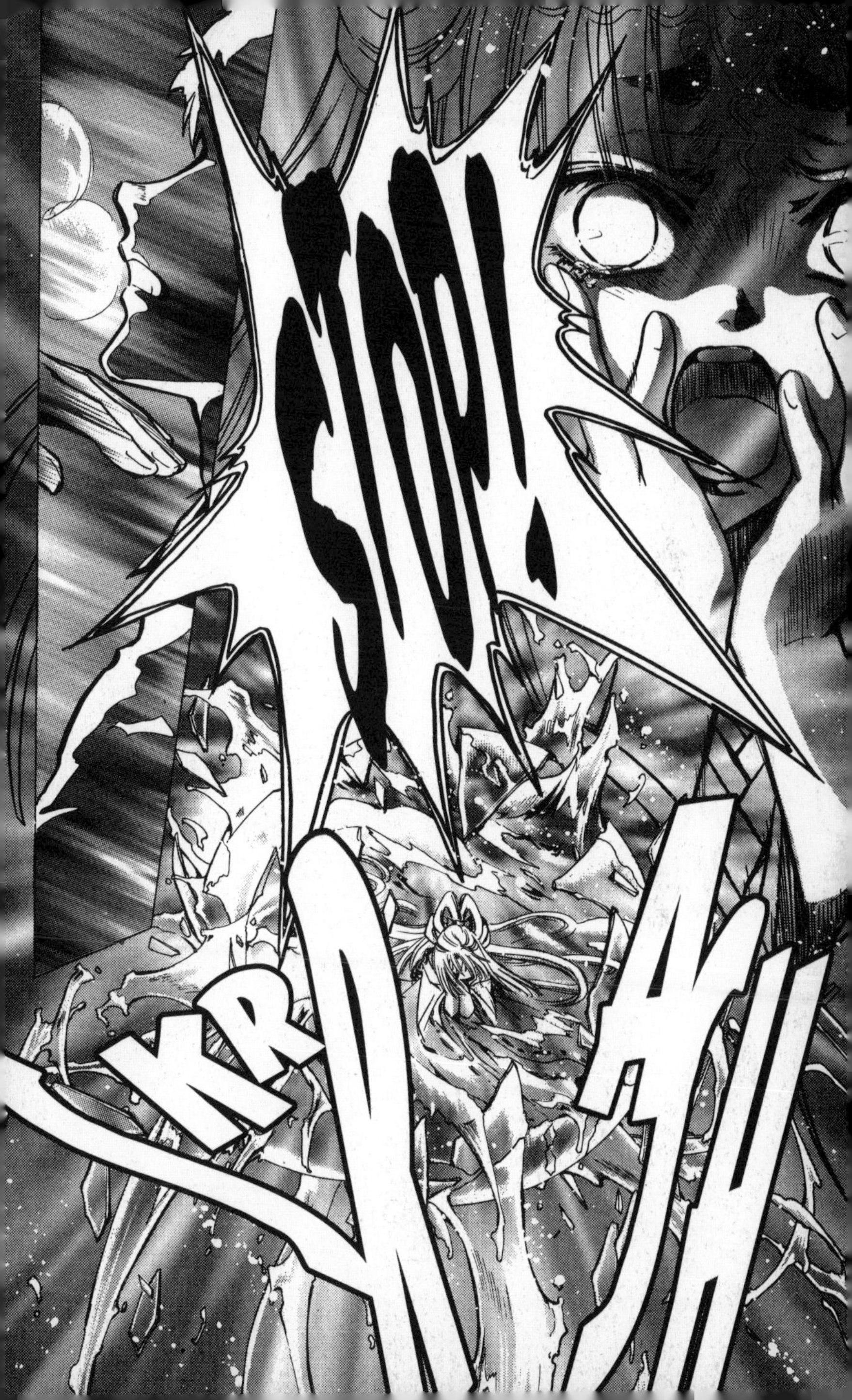
STOP!

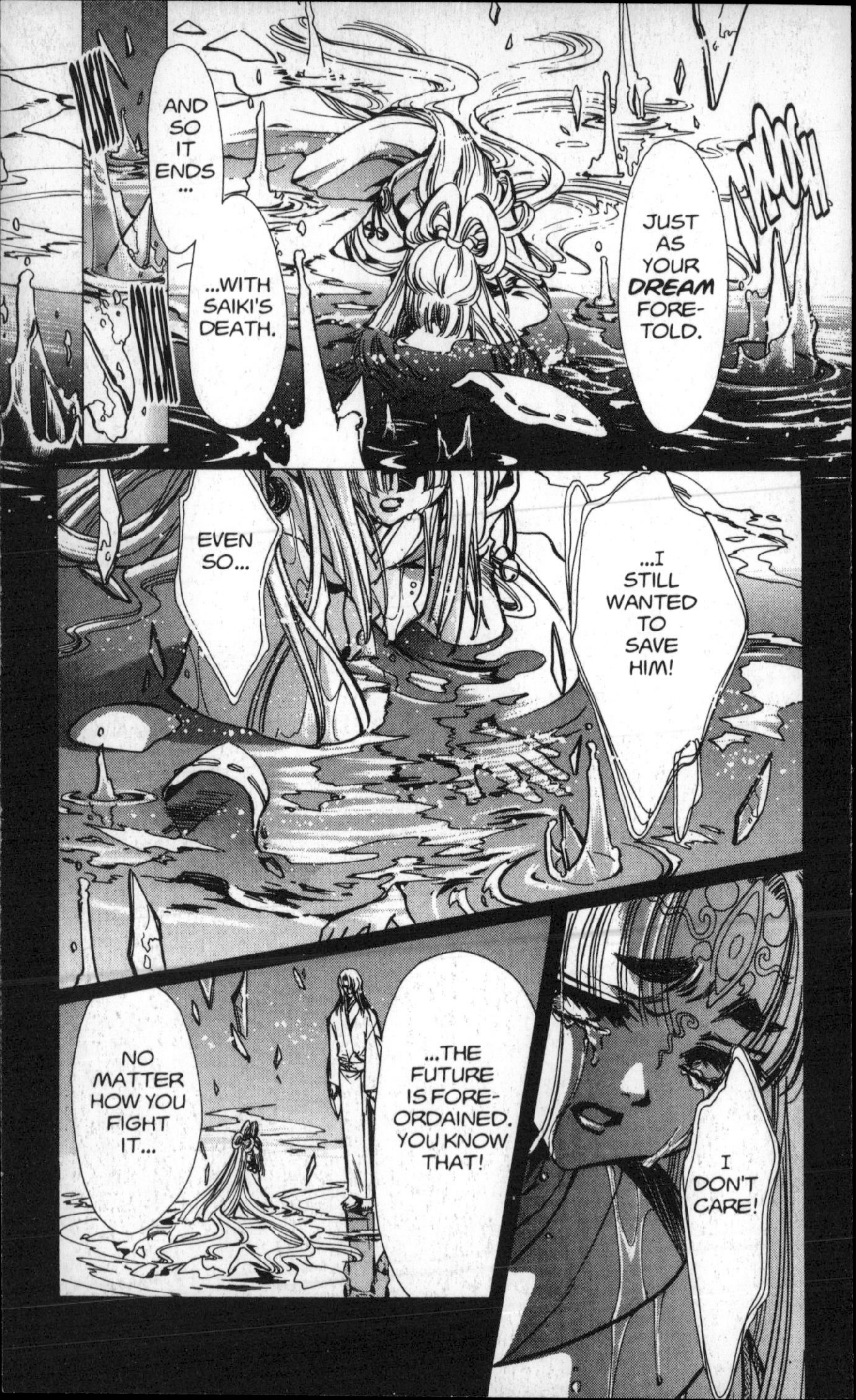
AND SO IT ENDS...
...WITH SAIKI'S DEATH.
JUST AS YOUR DREAM FORE-TOLD.
PLOOSH
EVEN SO...
...I STILL WANTED TO SAVE HIM!
NO MATTER HOW YOU FIGHT IT...
...THE FUTURE IS FORE-ORDAINED. YOU KNOW THAT!
I DON'T CARE!

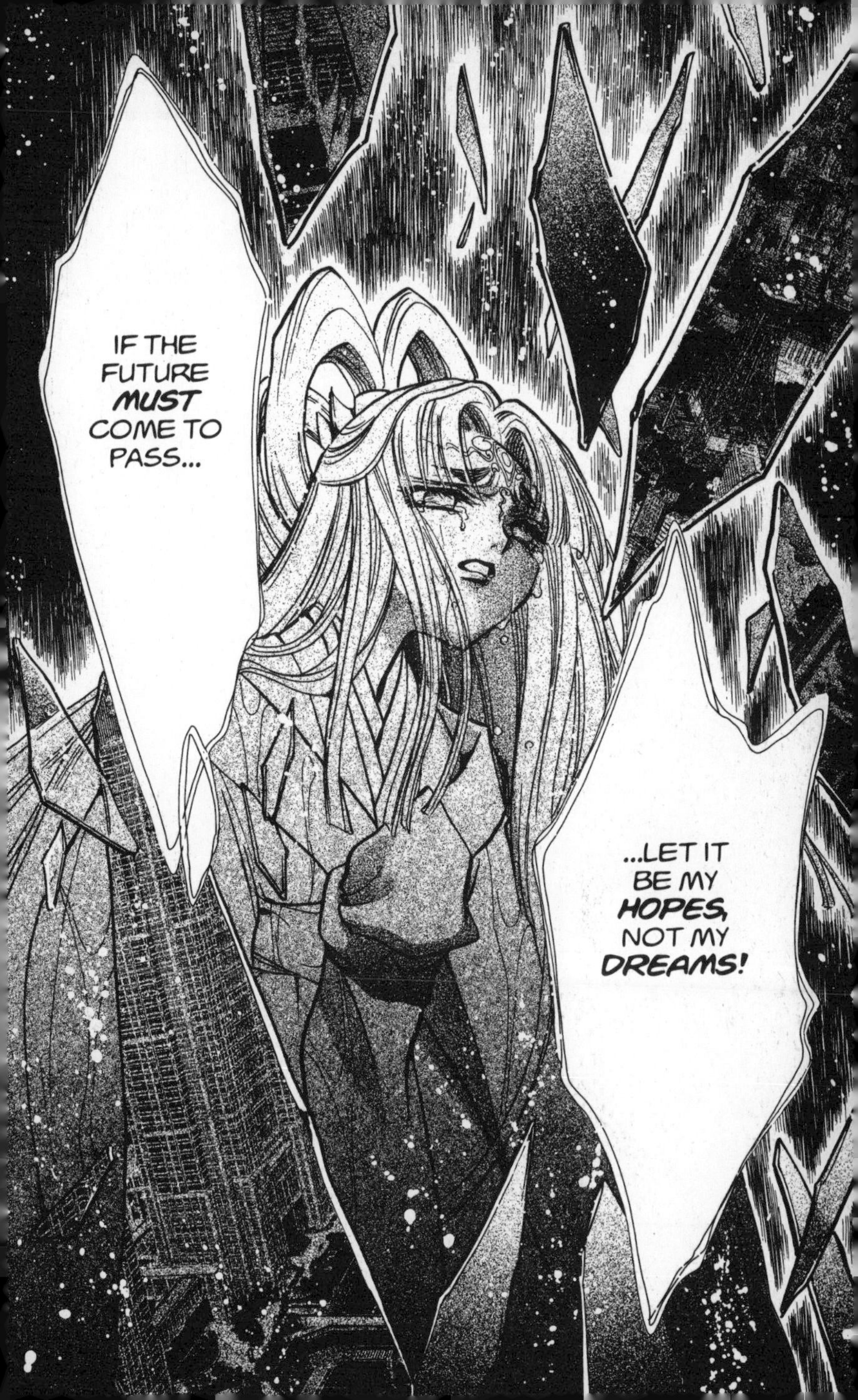
IF THE FUTURE MUST COME TO PASS...
...LET IT BE MY HOPES, NOT MY DREAMS!

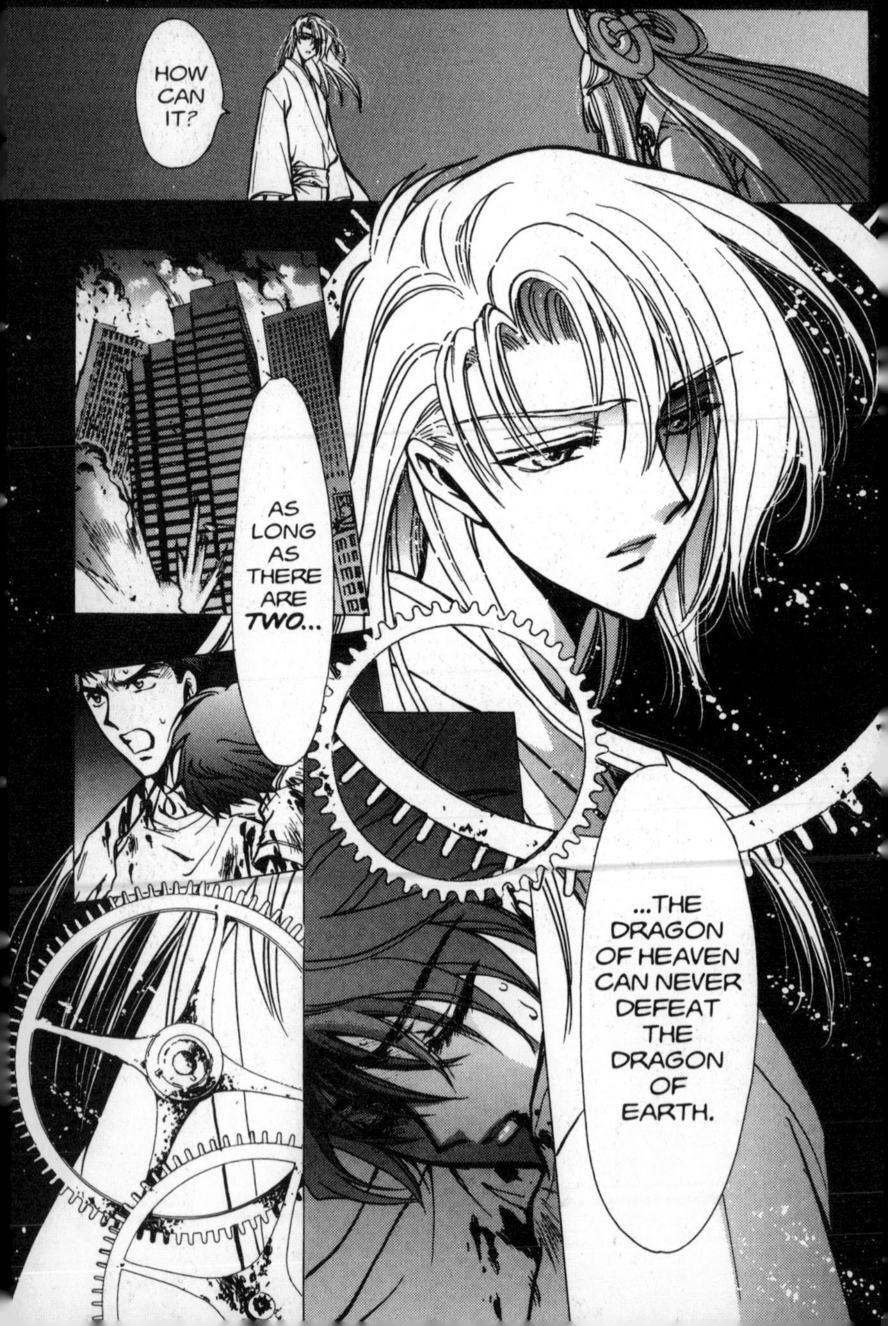
HOW CAN IT?
AS LONG AS THERE ARE TWO...
...THE DRAGON OF HEAVEN CAN NEVER DEFEAT THE DRAGON OF EARTH.

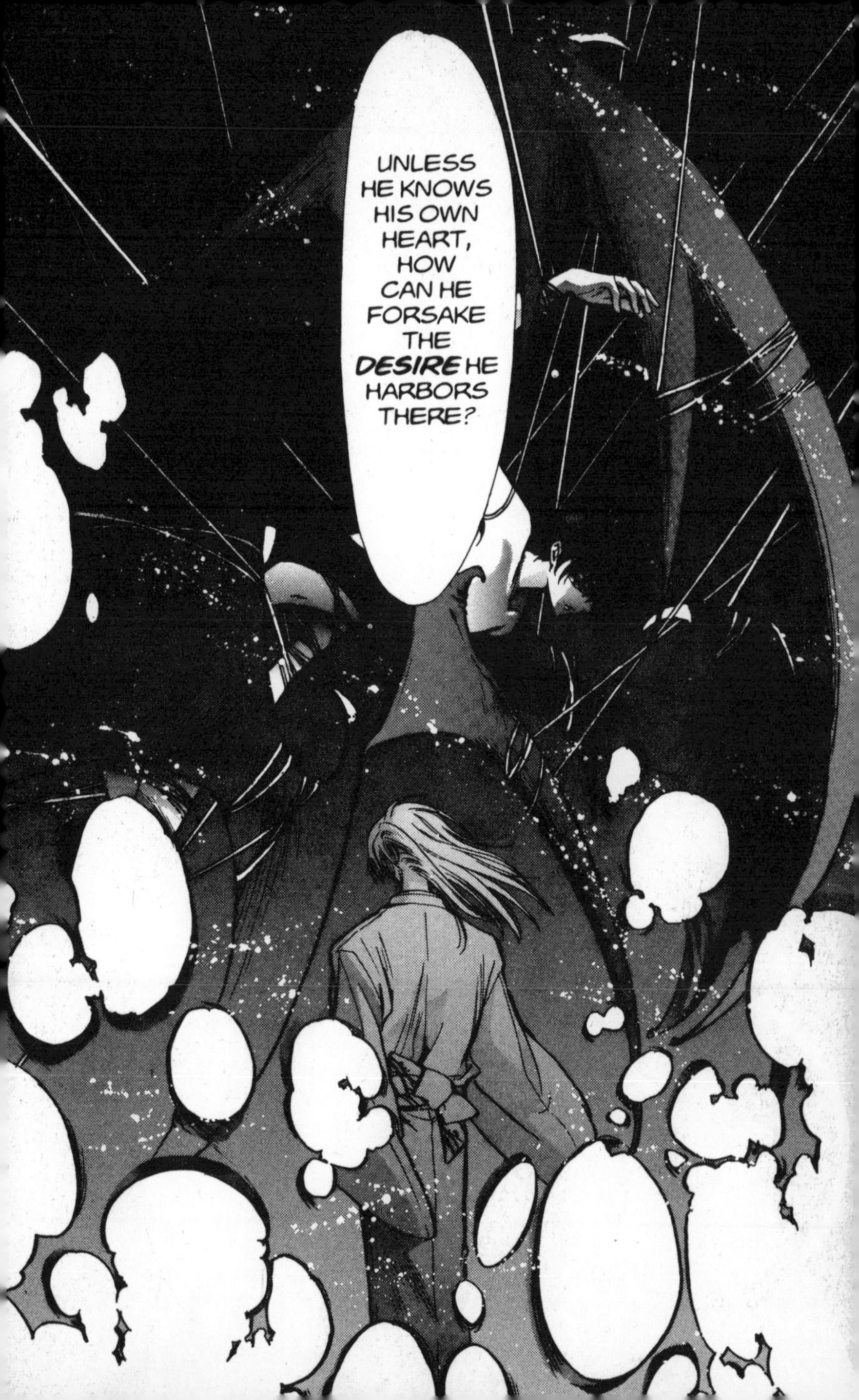
UNLESS HE KNOWS HIS OWN HEART, HOW CAN HE FORSAKE THE ***DESIRE*** HE HARBORS THERE?

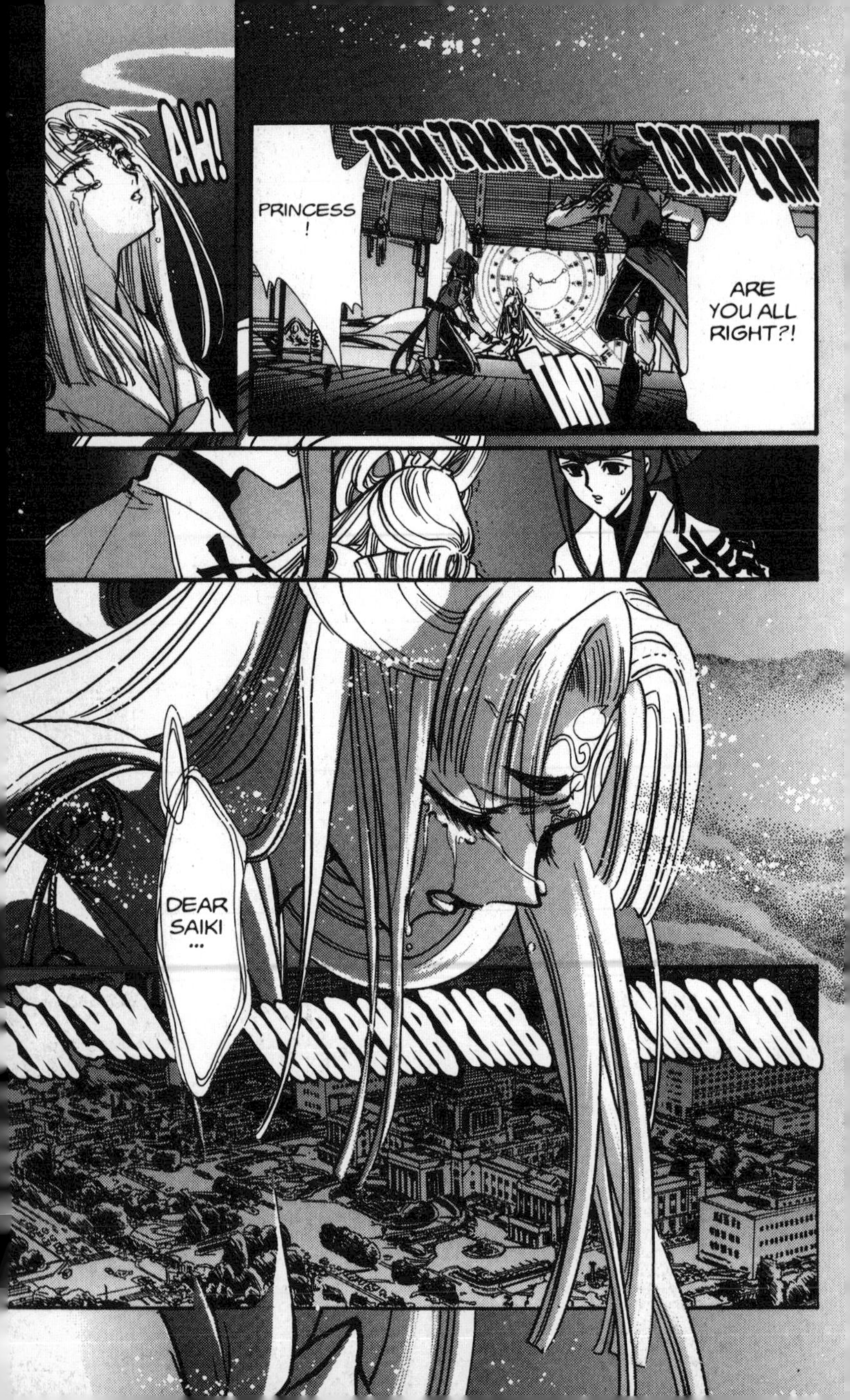
AH!
PRINCESS !
ARE YOU ALL RIGHT?!
TMP
DEAR SAIKI ...

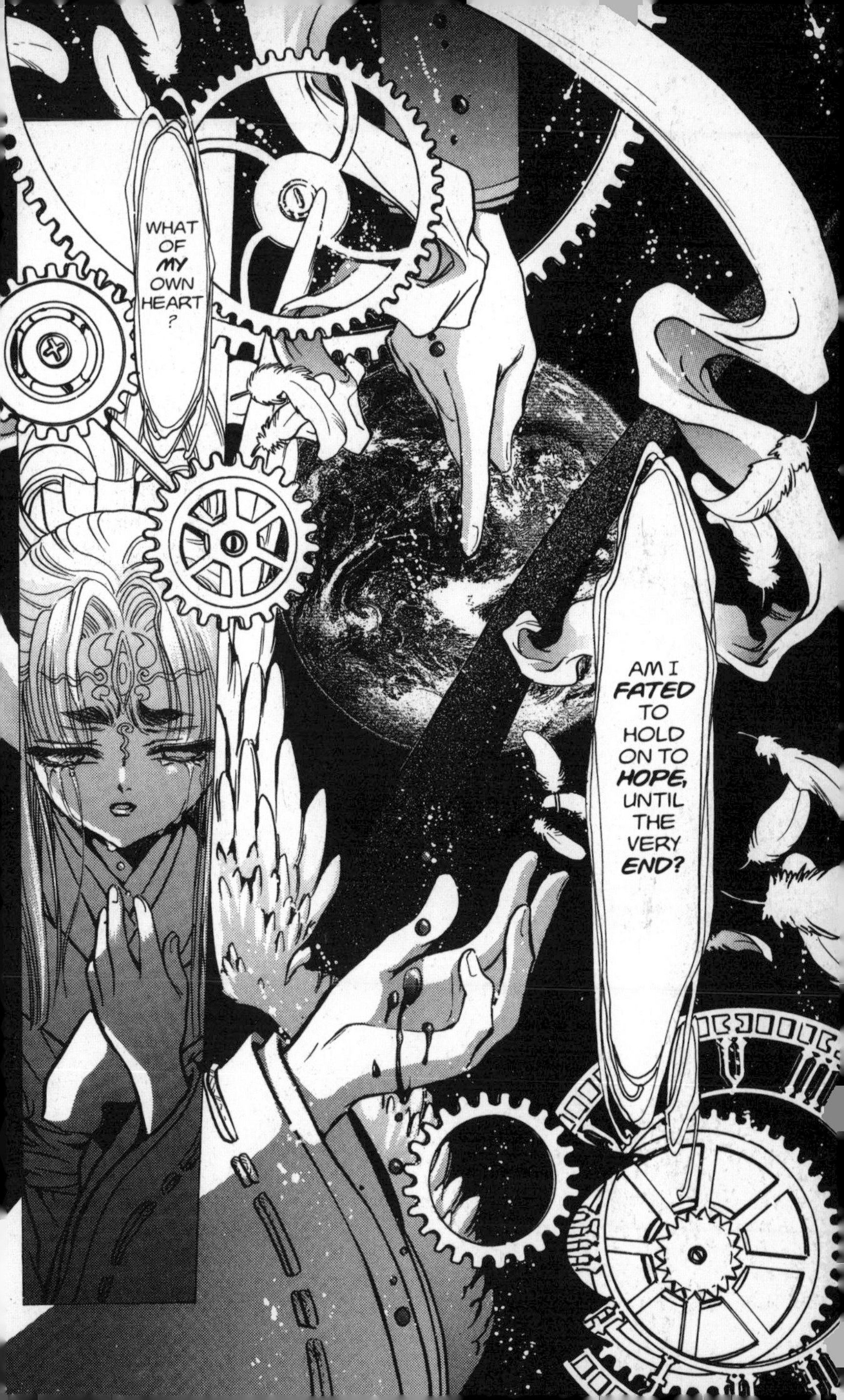
WHAT OF MY OWN HEART ?
AM I FATED TO HOLD ON TO HOPE, UNTIL THE VERY END?

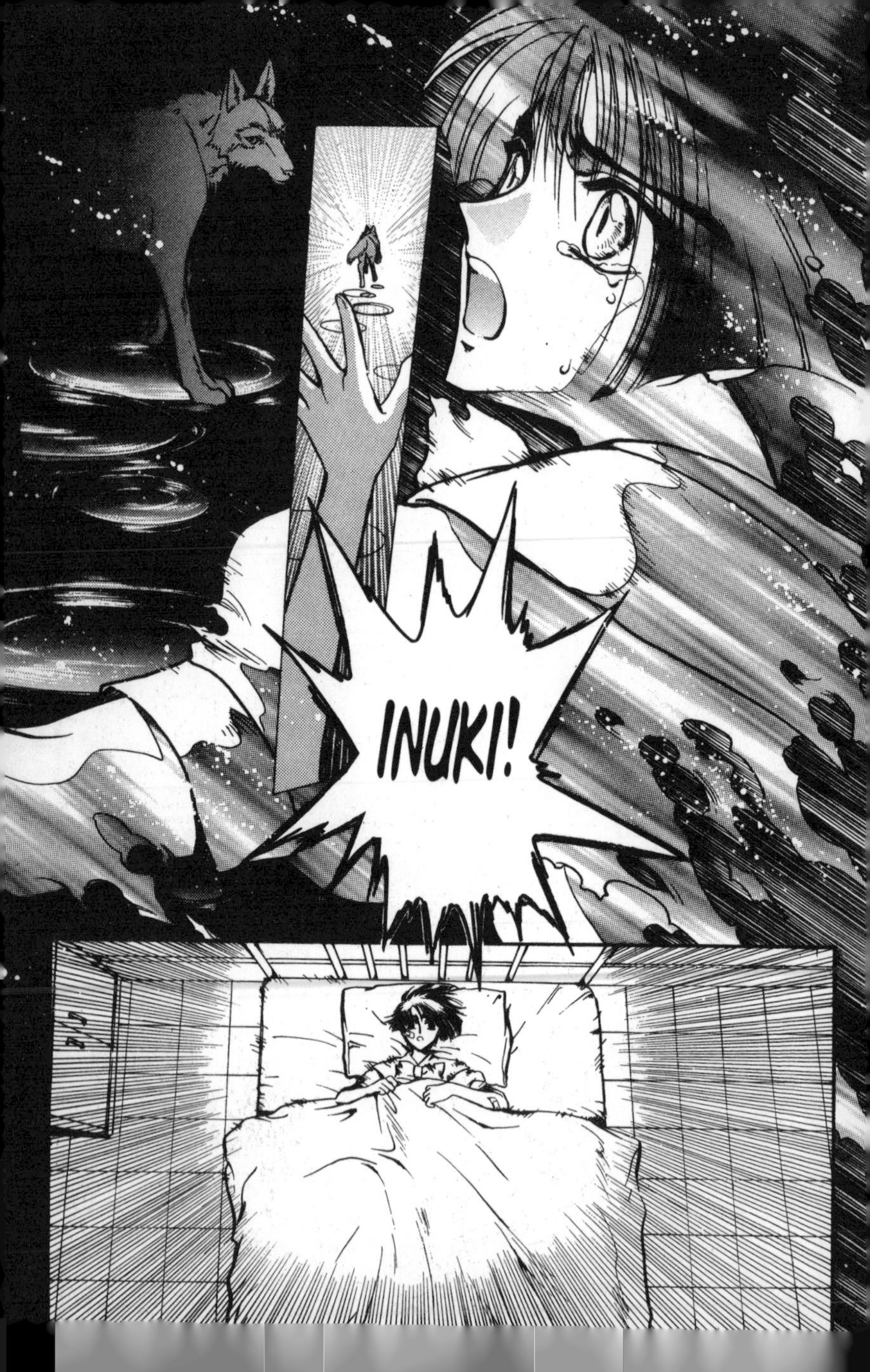
INUKI!

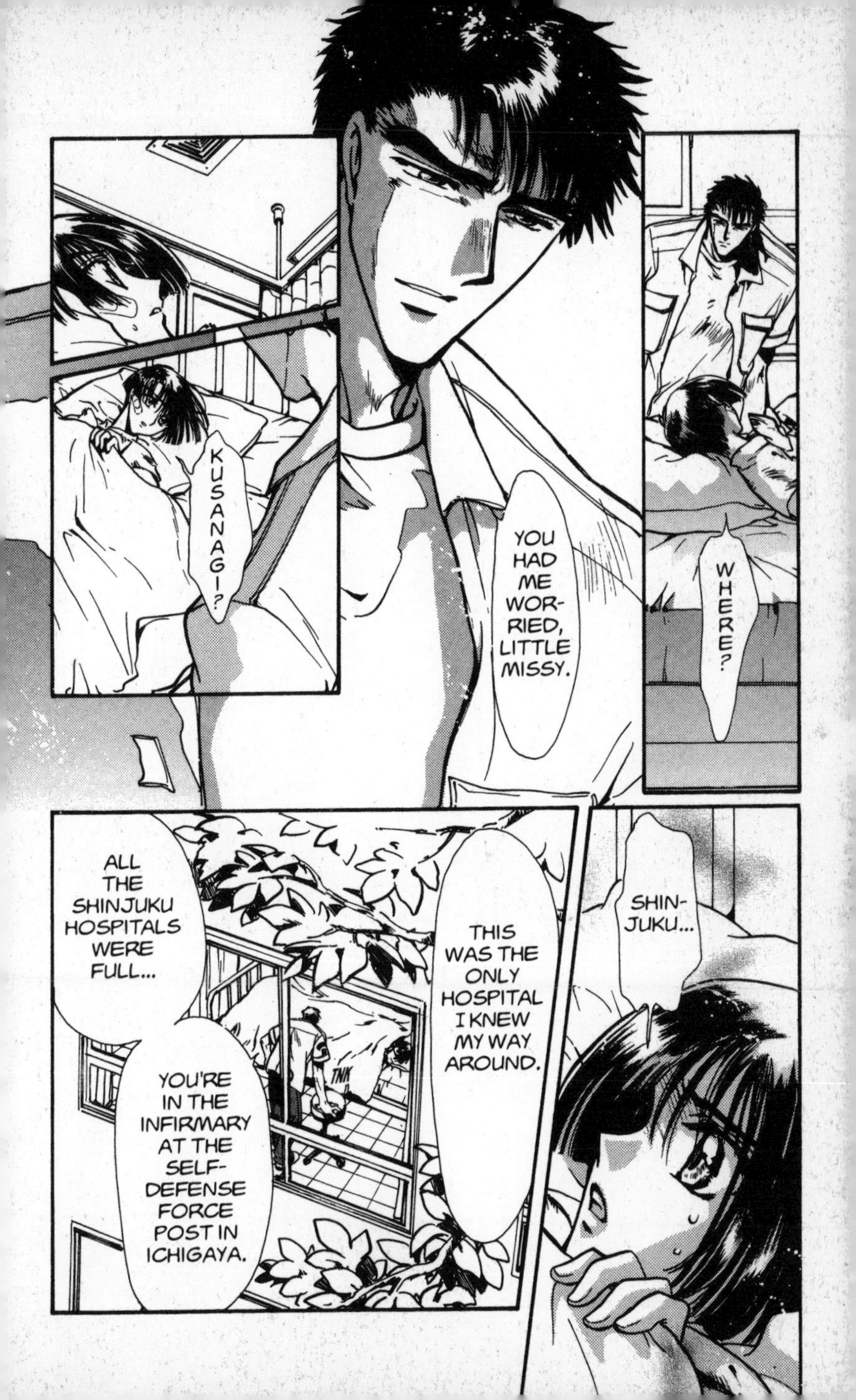
KUSANAGI?
YOU HAD ME WORRIED, LITTLE MISSY.
WHERE?
ALL THE SHINJUKU HOSPITALS WERE FULL...
YOU'RE IN THE INFIRMARY AT THE SELF-DEFENSE FORCE POST IN ICHIGAYA.
THIS WAS THE ONLY HOSPITAL I KNEW MY WAY AROUND.
TNK
SHIN-JUKU...

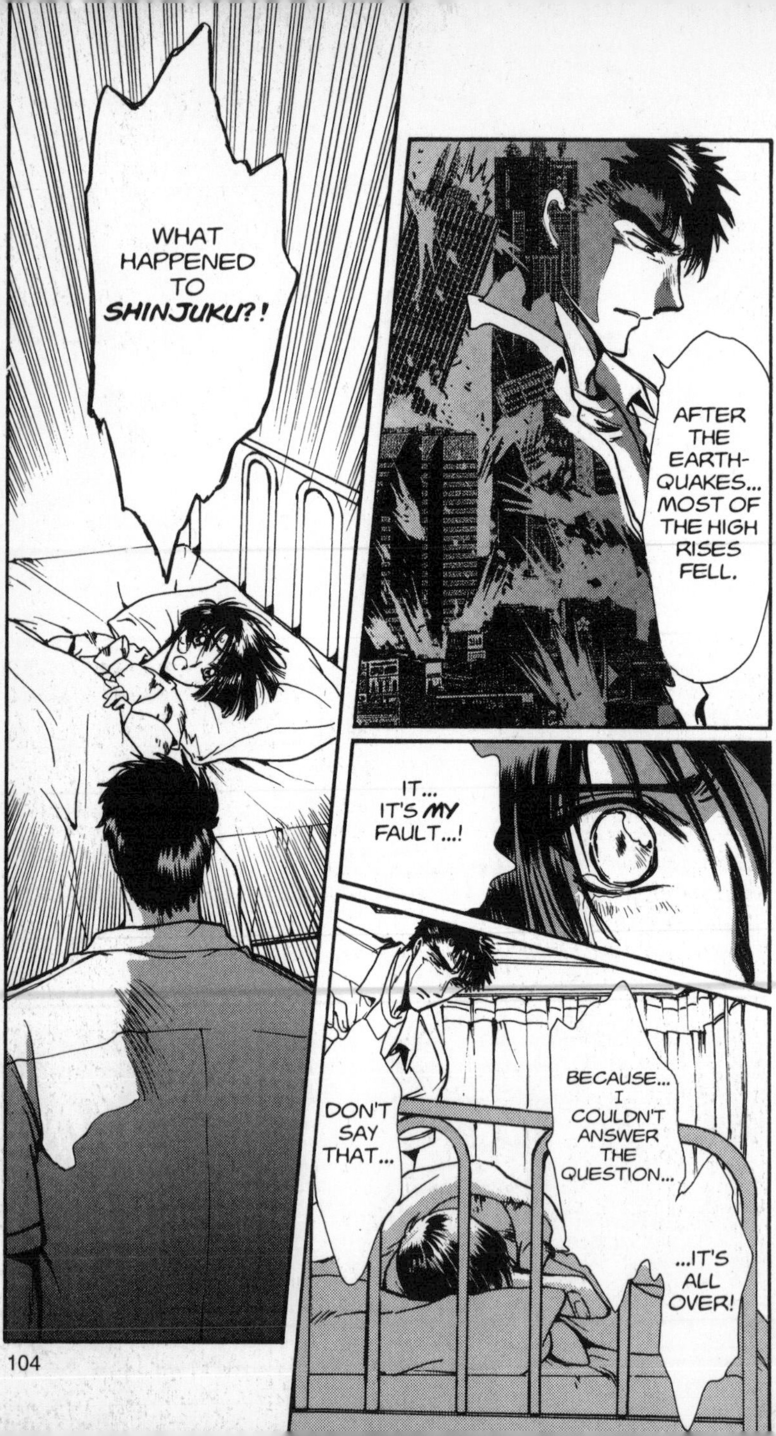

WHAT HAPPENED TO SHINJUKU?!
AFTER THE EARTH-QUAKES... MOST OF THE HIGH RISES FELL.
IT... IT'S MY FAULT...!
DON'T SAY THAT...
BECAUSE... I COULDN'T ANSWER THE QUESTION...
...IT'S ALL OVER!

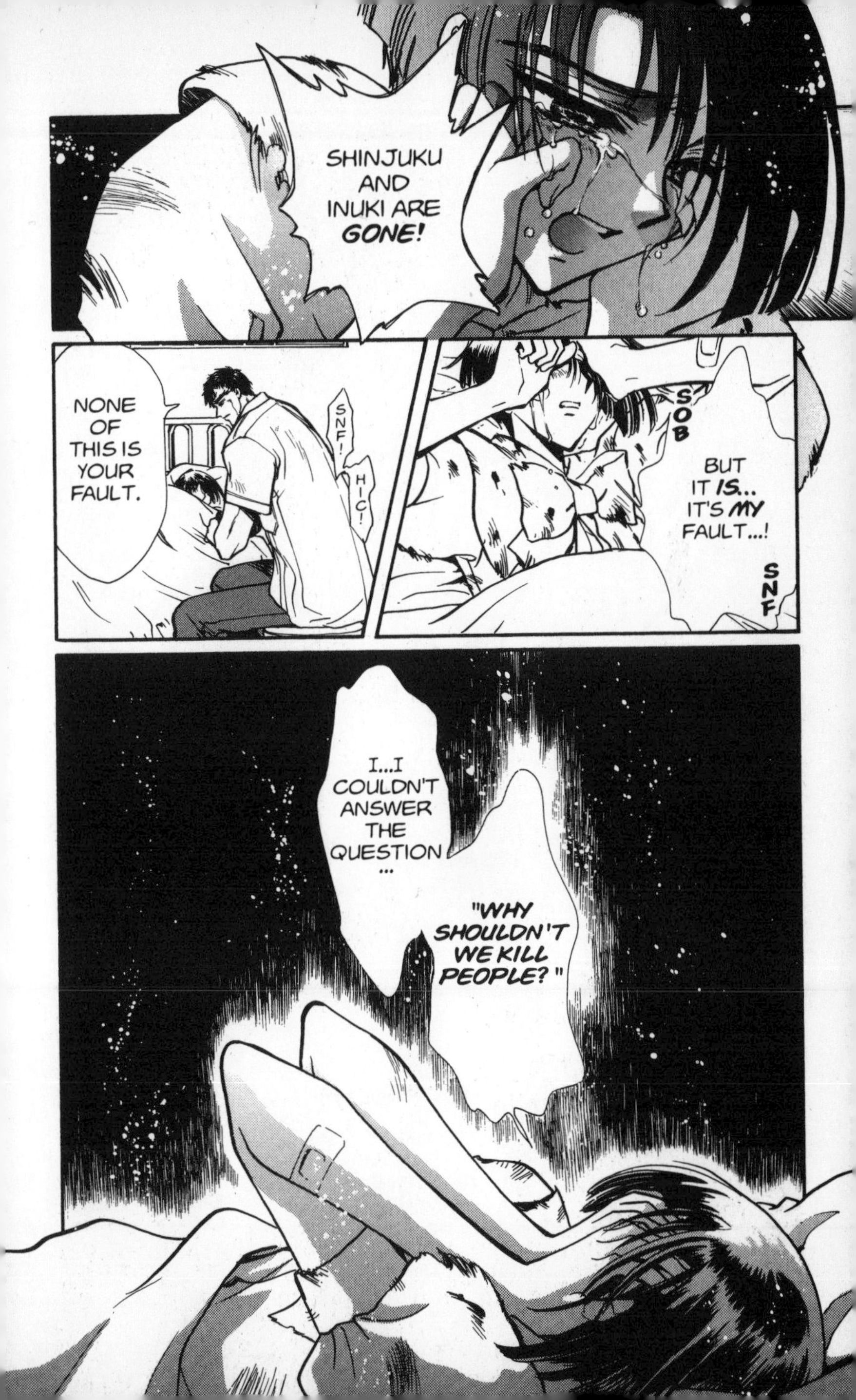
SHINJUKU AND INUKI ARE GONE!
NONE OF THIS IS YOUR FAULT.
SNF!
HIC!
SOB
BUT IT IS... IT'S MY FAULT...!
SNF
I...I COULDN'T ANSWER THE QUESTION ...
"WHY SHOULDN'T WE KILL PEOPLE?"

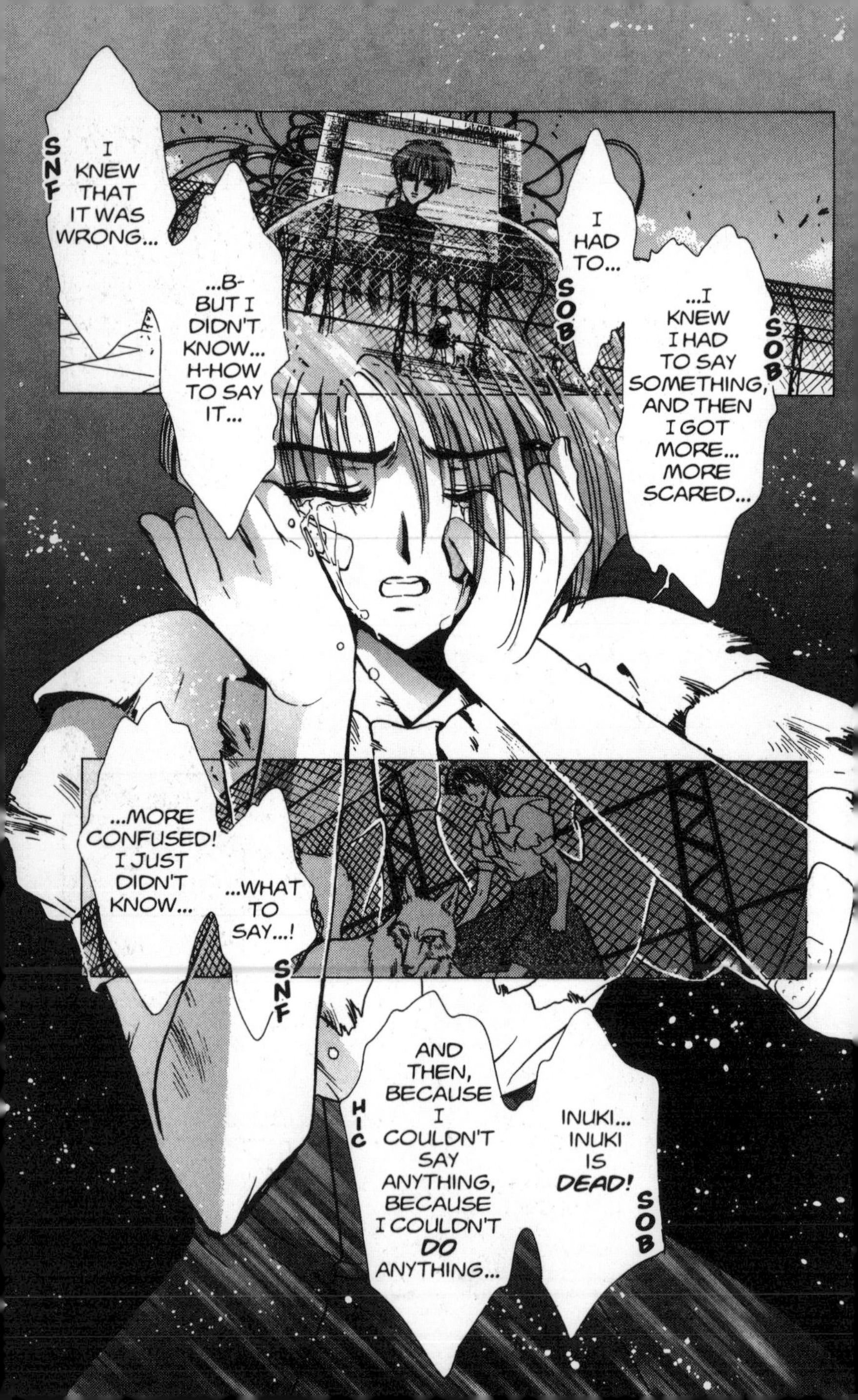
SNF
I KNEW THAT IT WAS WRONG...
...B-BUT I DIDN'T KNOW... H-HOW TO SAY IT...
I HAD TO...
SOB
...I KNEW I HAD TO SAY SOMETHING, AND THEN I GOT MORE... MORE SCARED...
SOB
...MORE CONFUSED! I JUST DIDN'T KNOW...
...WHAT TO SAY...!
SNF
HIC
AND THEN, BECAUSE I COULDN'T SAY ANYTHING, BECAUSE I COULDN'T DO ANYTHING...
INUKI... INUKI IS DEAD!
SOB

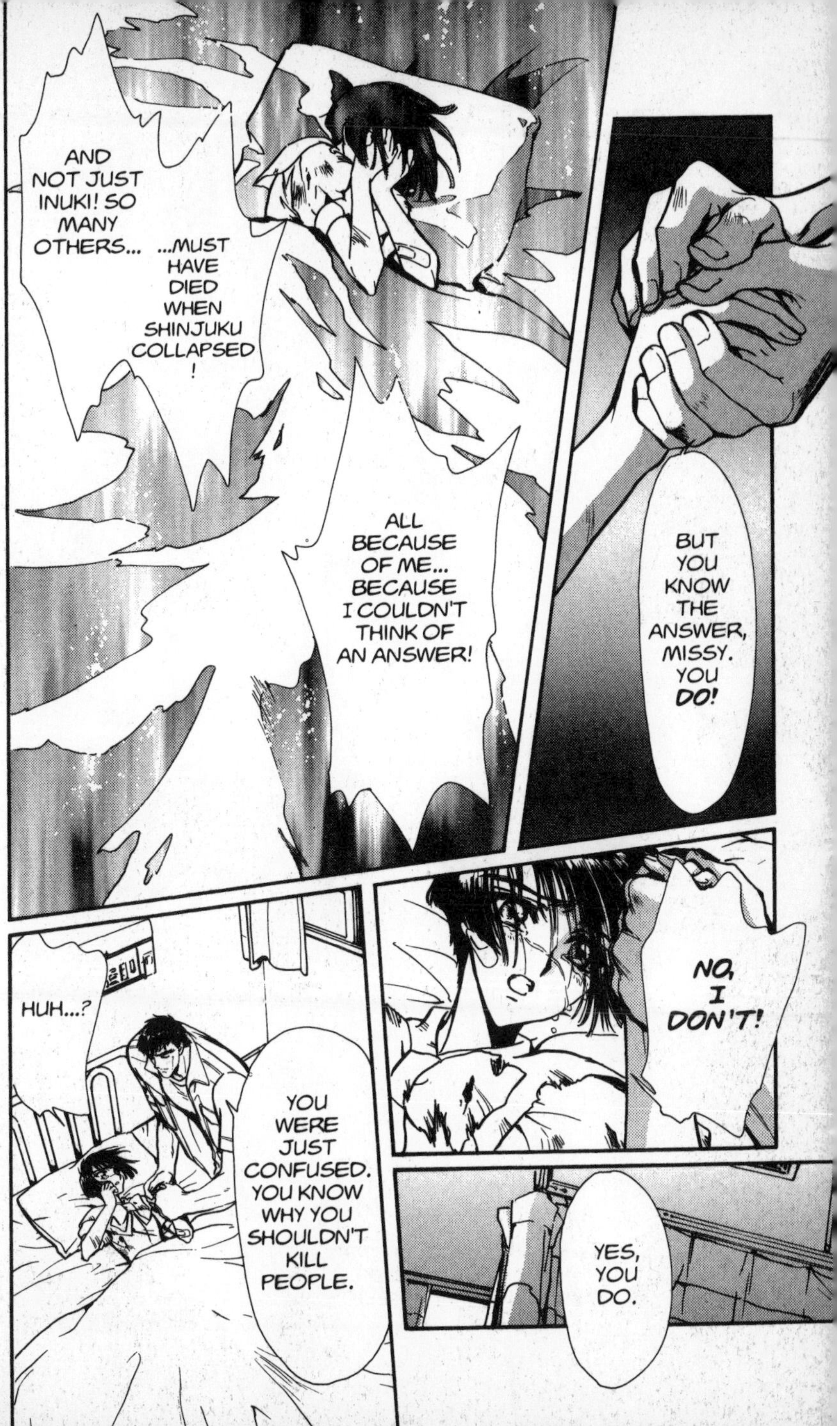
AND NOT JUST INUKI! SO MANY OTHERS...
...MUST HAVE DIED WHEN SHINJUKU COLLAPSED!
ALL BECAUSE OF ME... BECAUSE I COULDN'T THINK OF AN ANSWER!
BUT YOU KNOW THE ANSWER, MISSY. YOU *DO!*
HUH...?
YOU WERE JUST CONFUSED. YOU KNOW WHY YOU SHOULDN'T KILL PEOPLE.
NO, I DON'T!
YES, YOU DO.

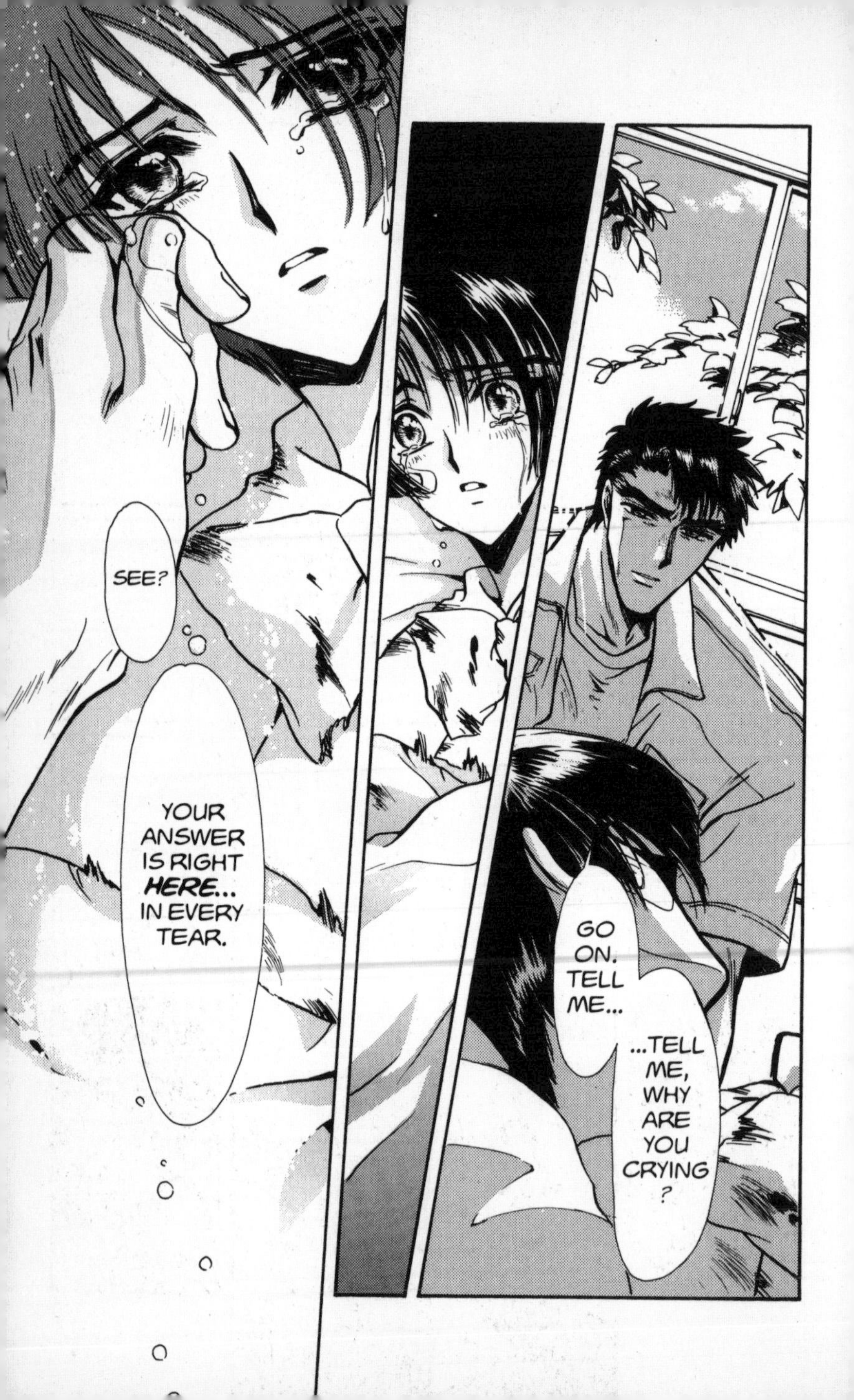
SEE?
YOUR ANSWER IS RIGHT *HERE*... IN EVERY TEAR.
GO ON. TELL ME...
...TELL ME, WHY ARE YOU CRYING?

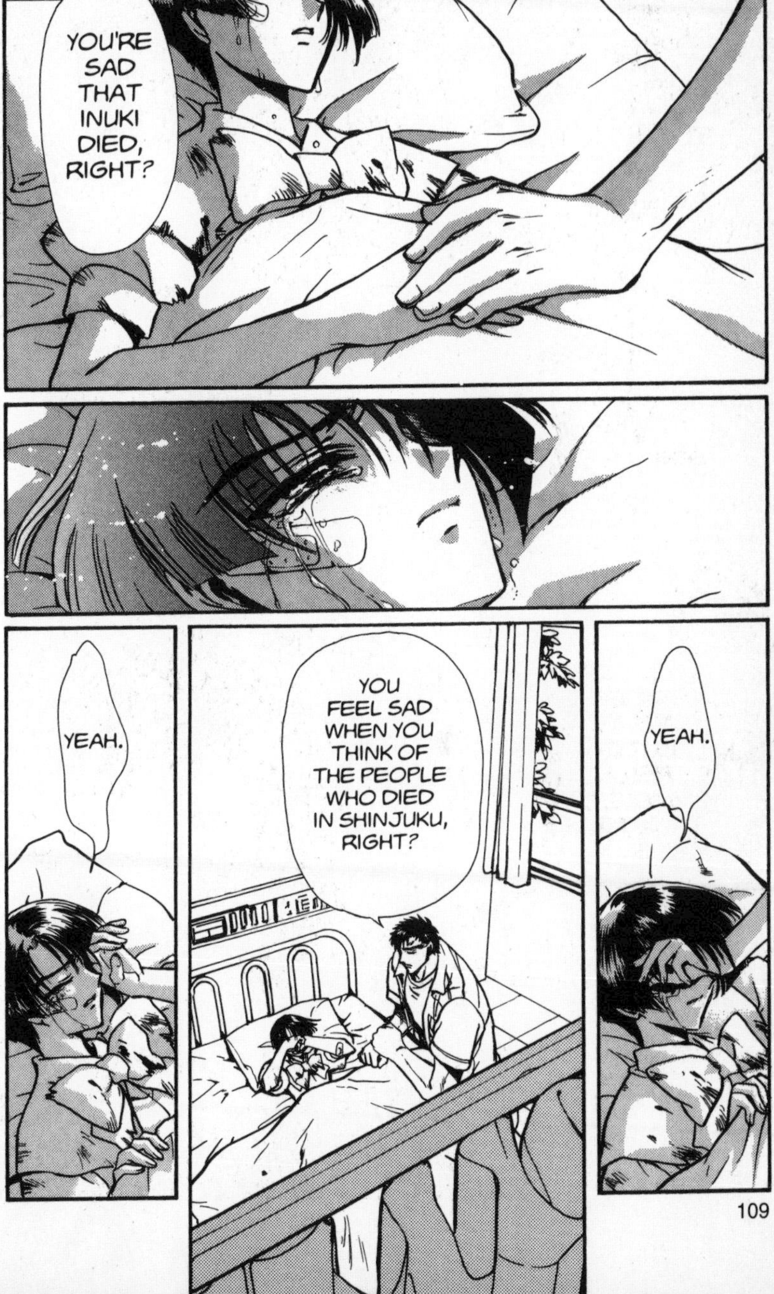
YOU'RE SAD THAT INUKI DIED, RIGHT?
YEAH.
YOU FEEL SAD WHEN YOU THINK OF THE PEOPLE WHO DIED IN SHINJUKU, RIGHT?
YEAH.

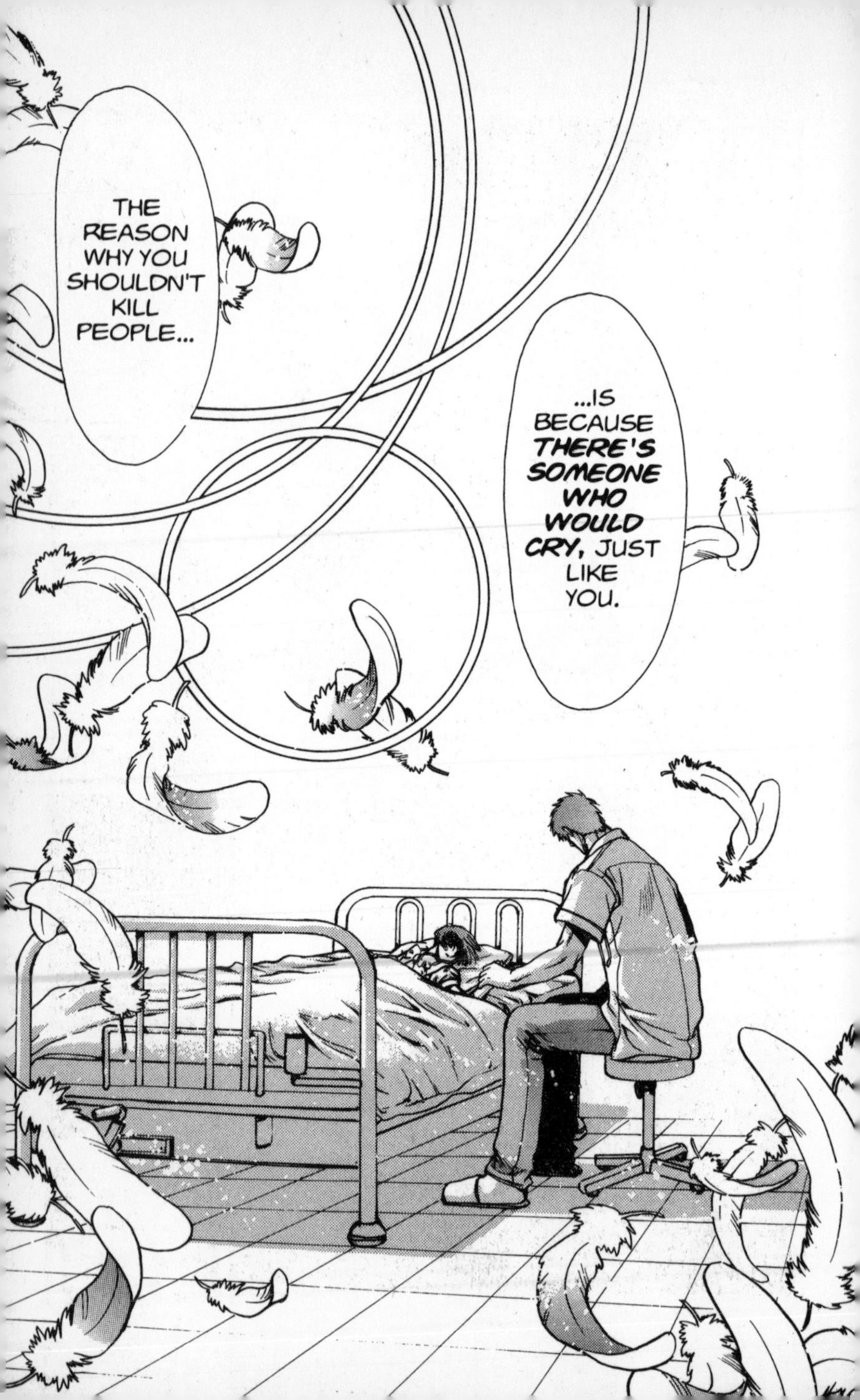
THE REASON WHY YOU SHOULDN'T KILL PEOPLE...
...IS BECAUSE **THERE'S SOMEONE WHO WOULD CRY**, JUST LIKE YOU.

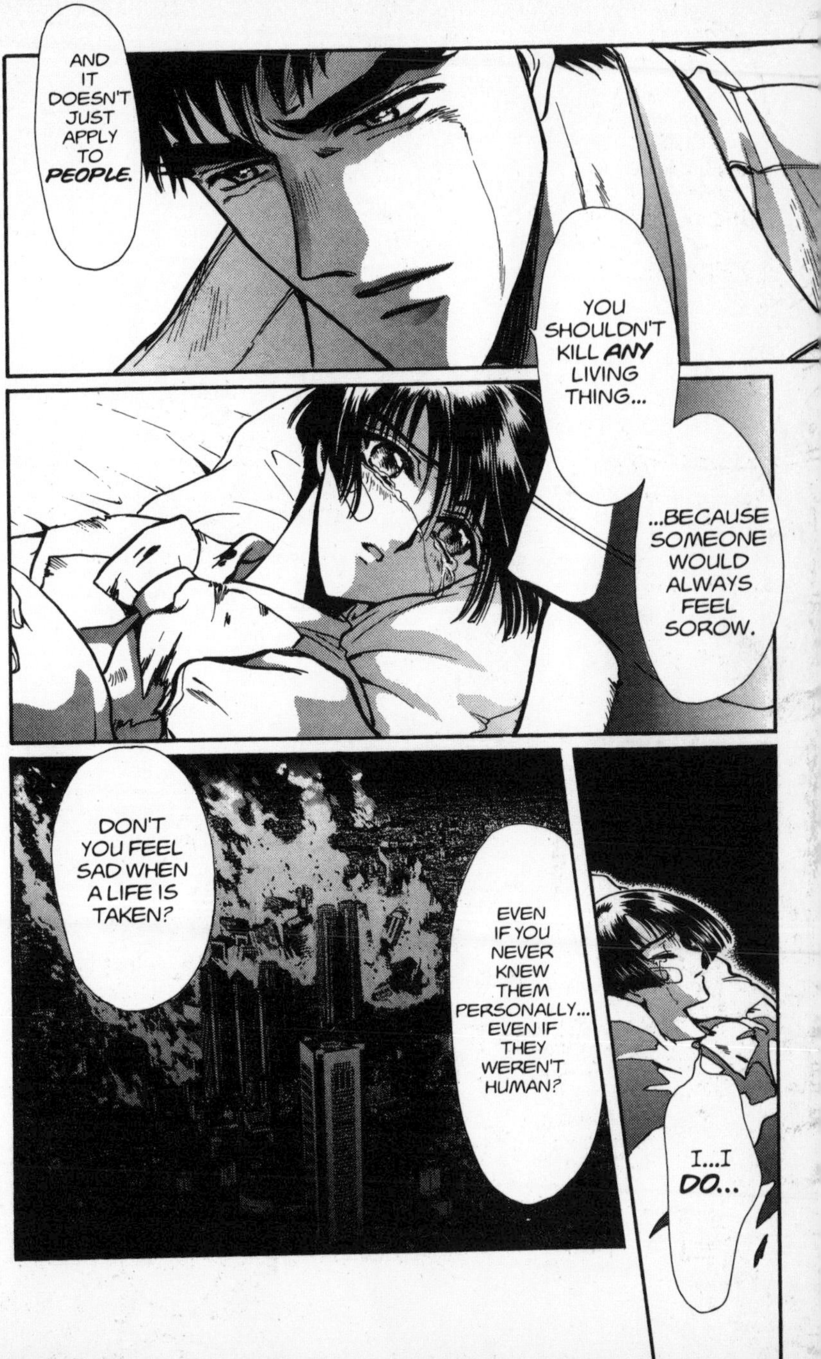
AND IT DOESN'T JUST APPLY TO PEOPLE.
YOU SHOULDN'T KILL ANY LIVING THING...
...BECAUSE SOMEONE WOULD ALWAYS FEEL SOROW.
DON'T YOU FEEL SAD WHEN A LIFE IS TAKEN?
EVEN IF YOU NEVER KNEW THEM PERSONALLY... EVEN IF THEY WEREN'T HUMAN?
I...I DO...

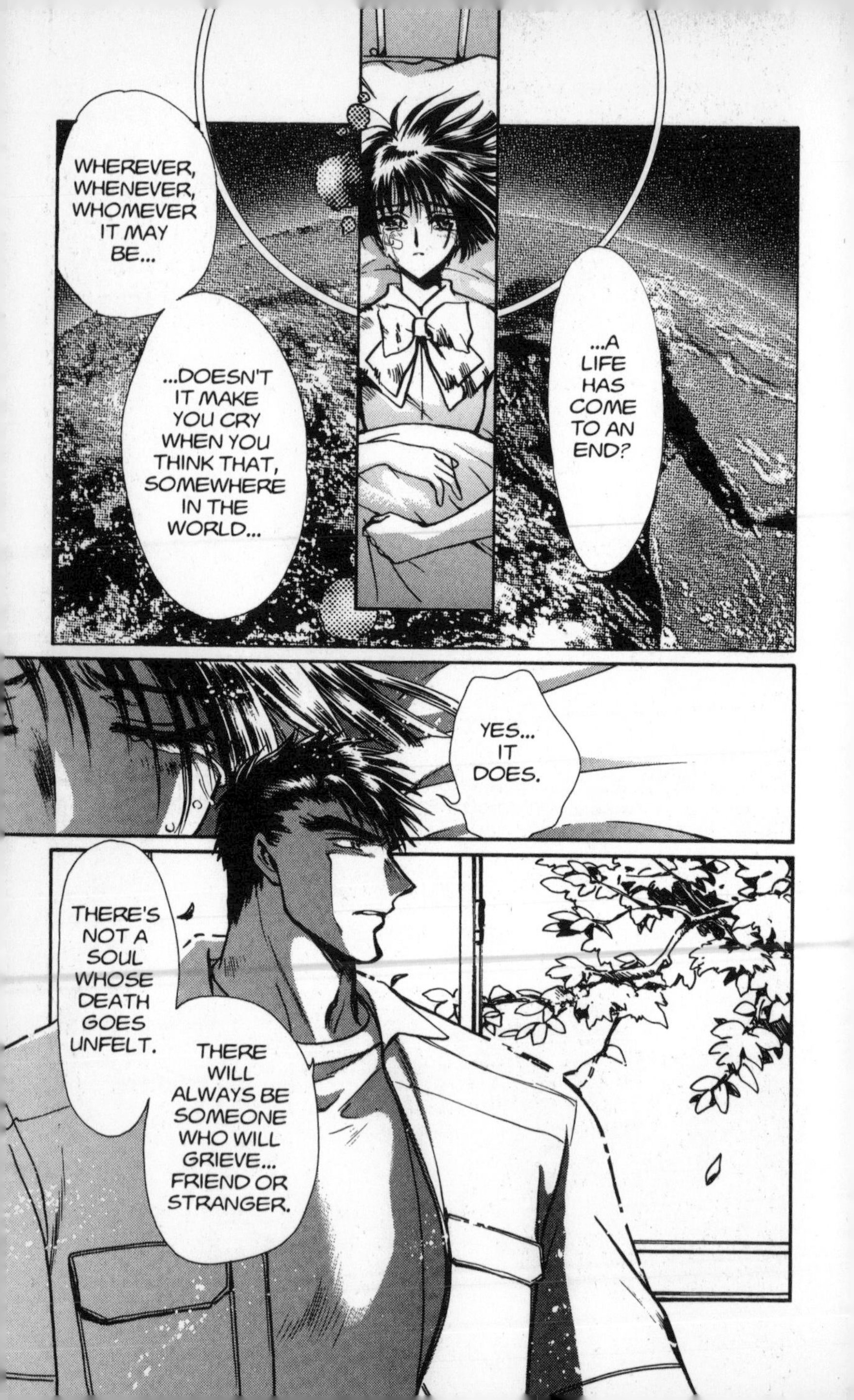
WHEREVER, WHENEVER, WHOMEVER IT MAY BE...
...DOESN'T IT MAKE YOU CRY WHEN YOU THINK THAT, SOMEWHERE IN THE WORLD...
...A LIFE HAS COME TO AN END?
YES... IT DOES.
THERE'S NOT A SOUL WHOSE DEATH GOES UNFELT.
THERE WILL ALWAYS BE SOMEONE WHO WILL GRIEVE... FRIEND OR STRANGER.

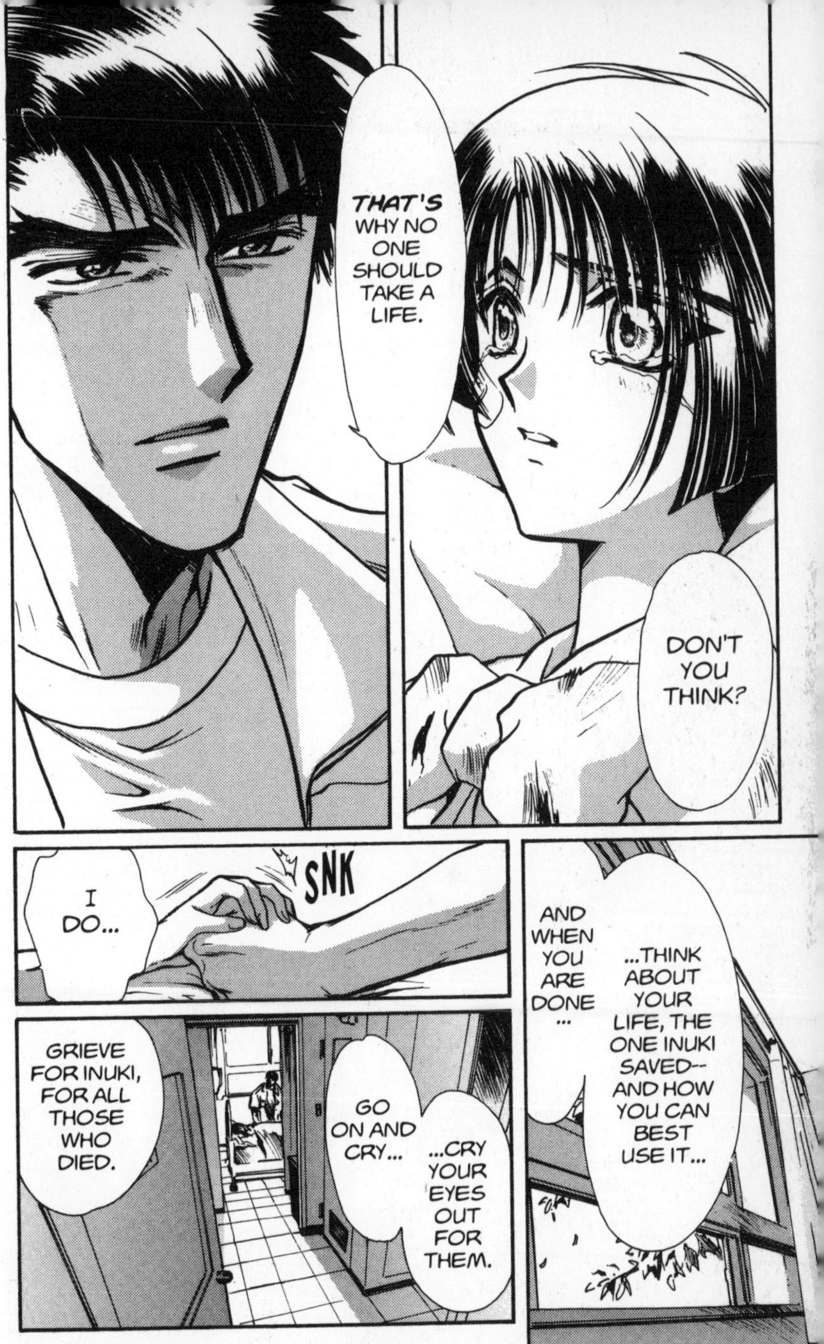
THAT'S WHY NO ONE SHOULD TAKE A LIFE.
DON'T YOU THINK?
I DO...
SNK
GRIEVE FOR INUKI, FOR ALL THOSE WHO DIED.
GO ON AND CRY...
...CRY YOUR EYES OUT FOR THEM.
AND WHEN YOU ARE DONE...
...THINK ABOUT YOUR LIFE, THE ONE INUKI SAVED-- AND HOW YOU CAN BEST USE IT...

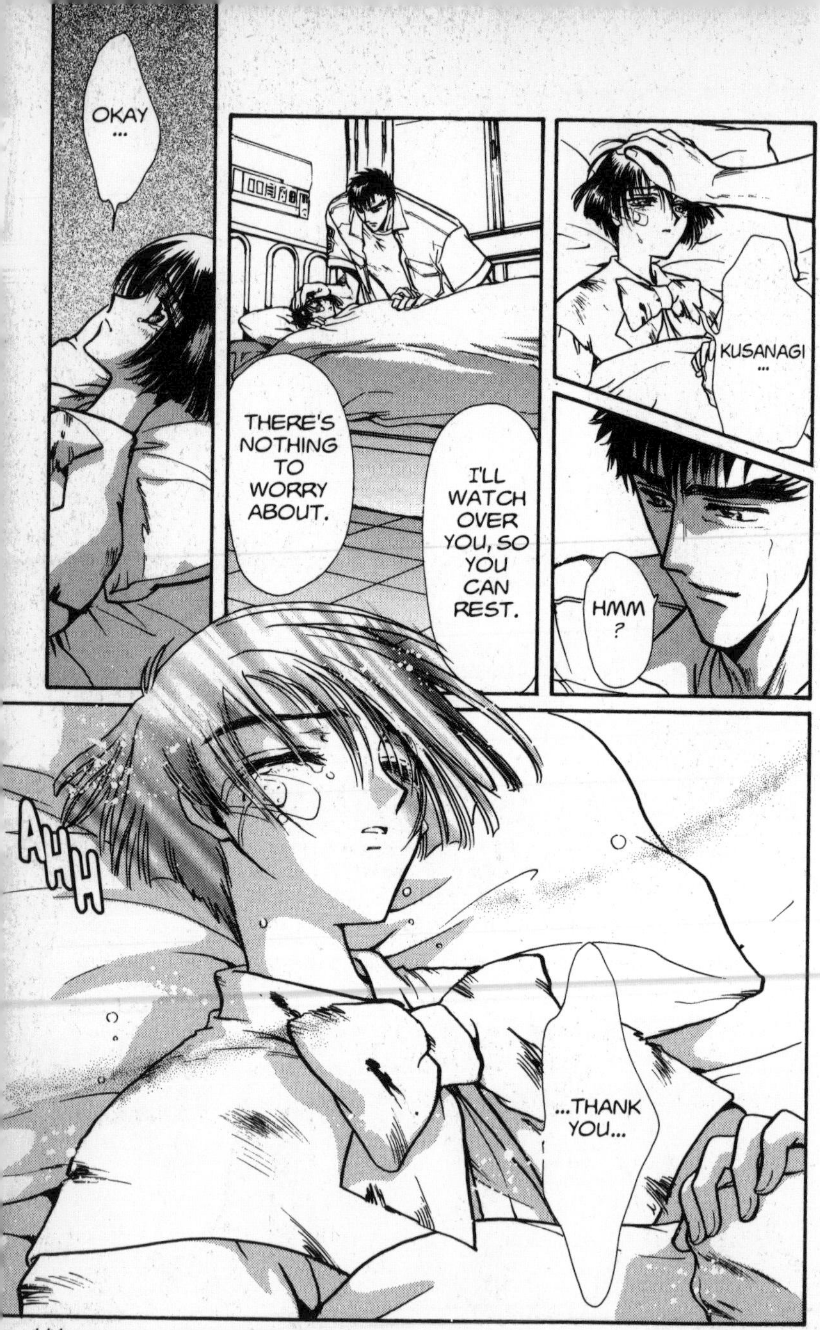
OKAY ...
THERE'S NOTHING TO WORRY ABOUT.
I'LL WATCH OVER YOU, SO YOU CAN REST.
KUSANAGI ...
HMM ?
AHHH
...THANK YOU...

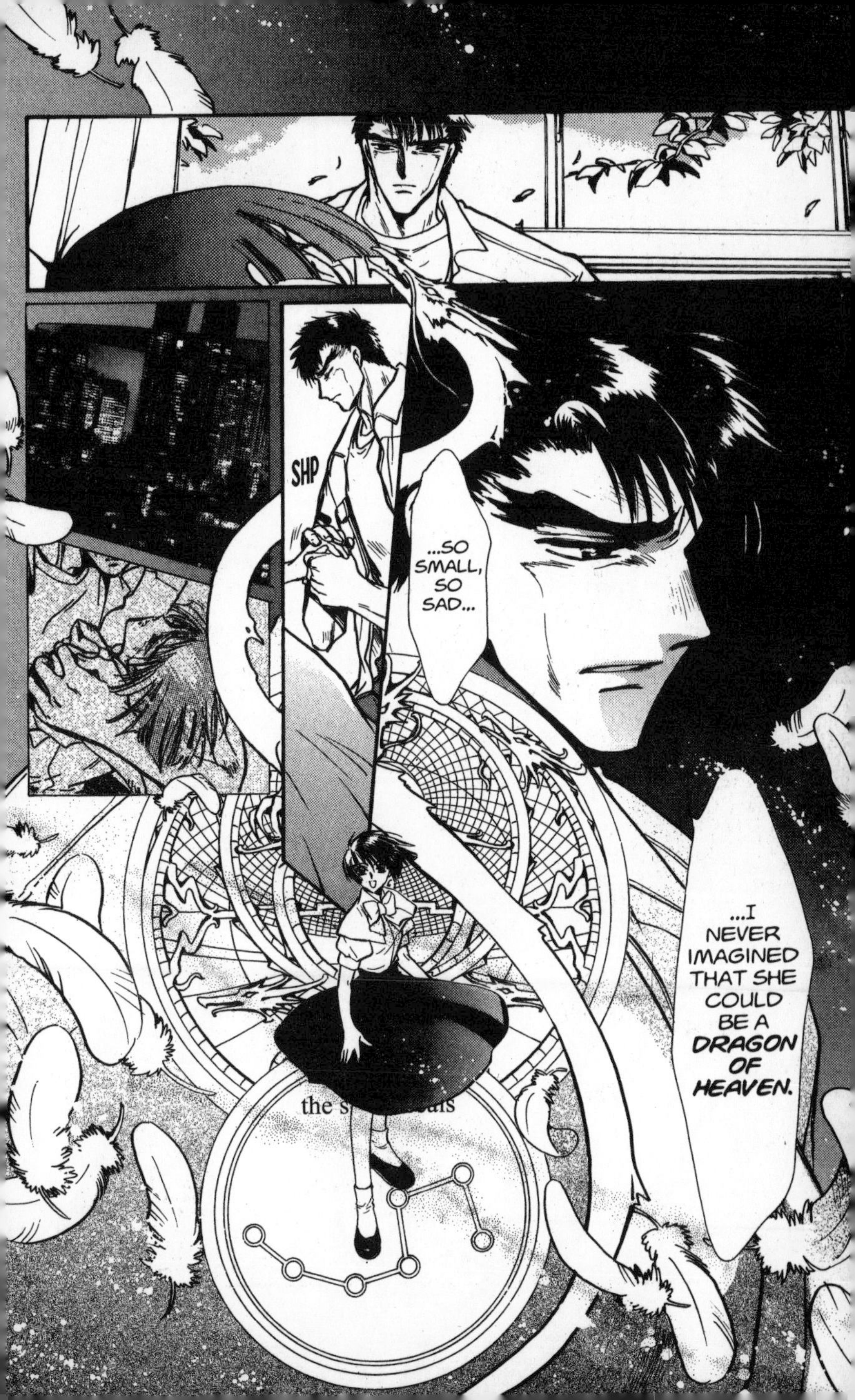
SHP
...SO SMALL, SO SAD...
...I NEVER IMAGINED THAT SHE COULD BE A DRAGON OF HEAVEN.

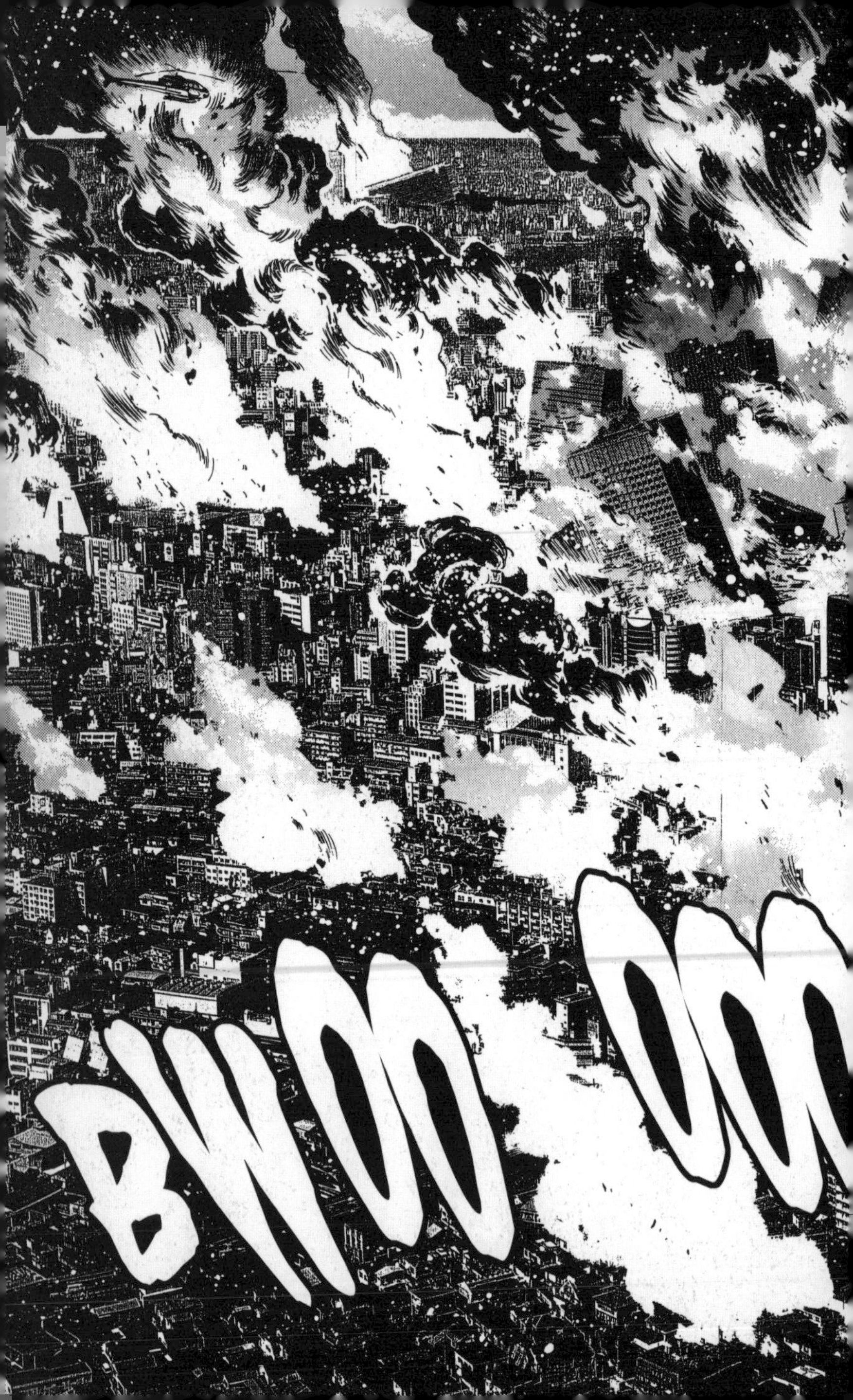
BWOO OOO

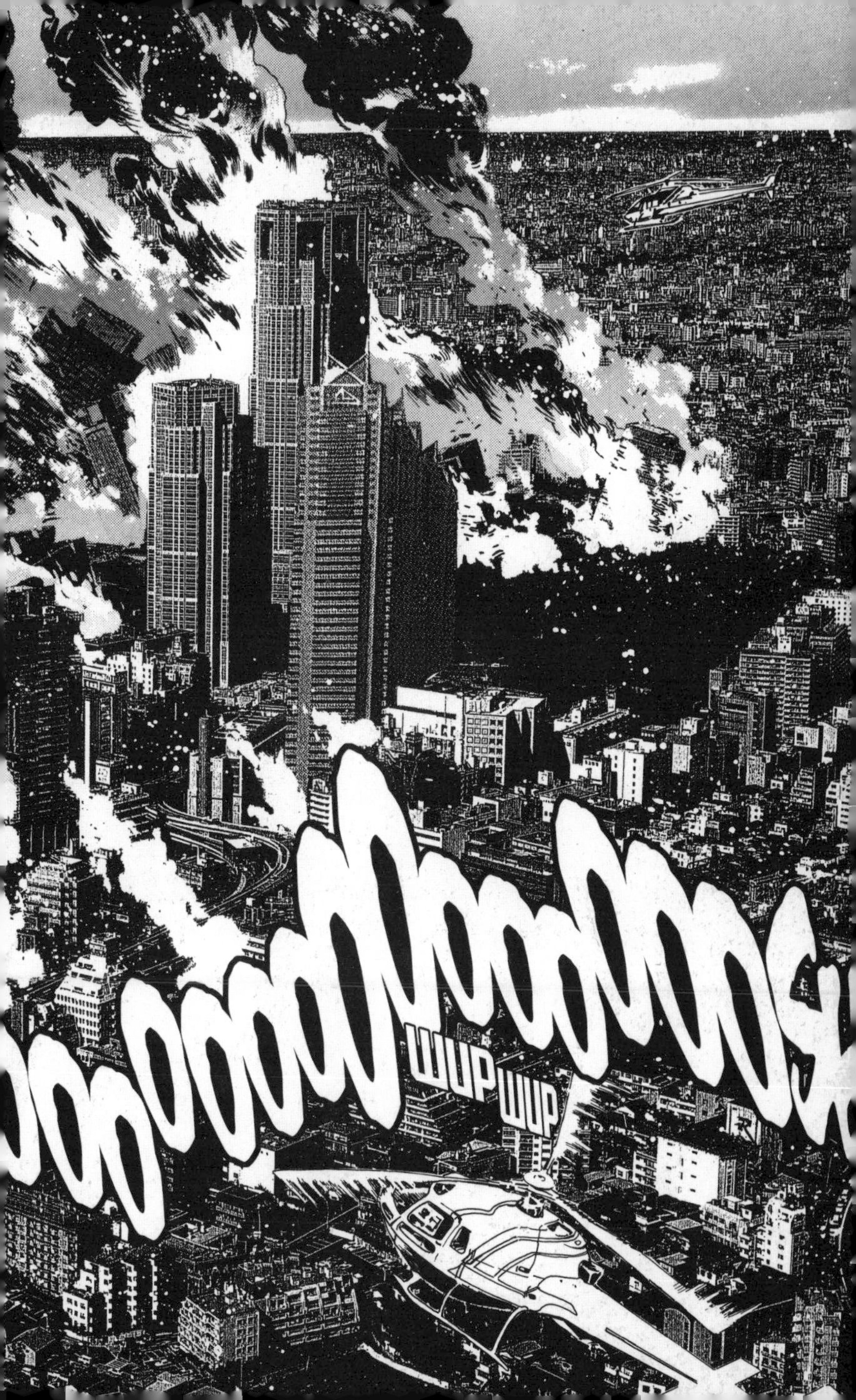
WUP WUP

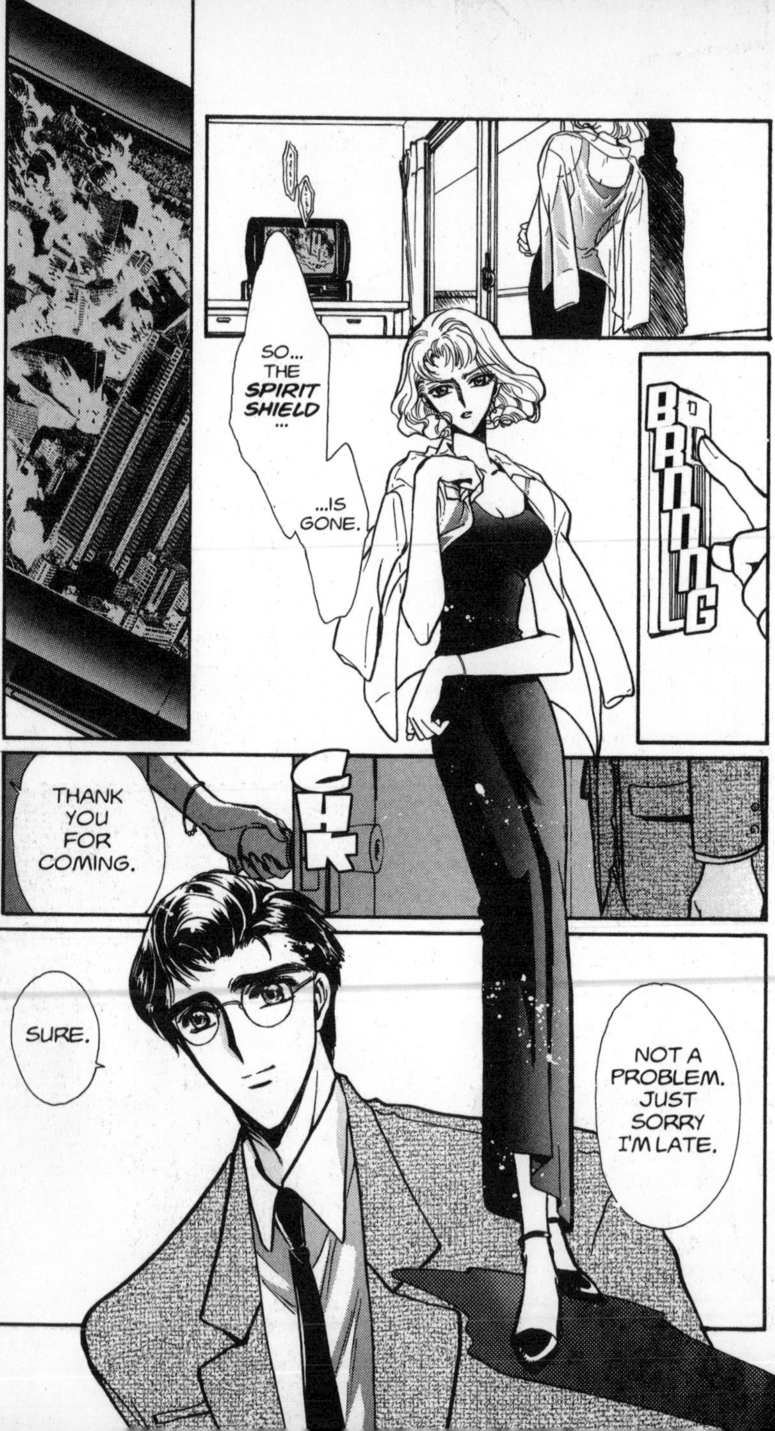
SO... THE SPIRIT SHIELD...
...IS GONE.
THANK YOU FOR COMING.
CHK
SURE.
NOT A PROBLEM. JUST SORRY I'M LATE.

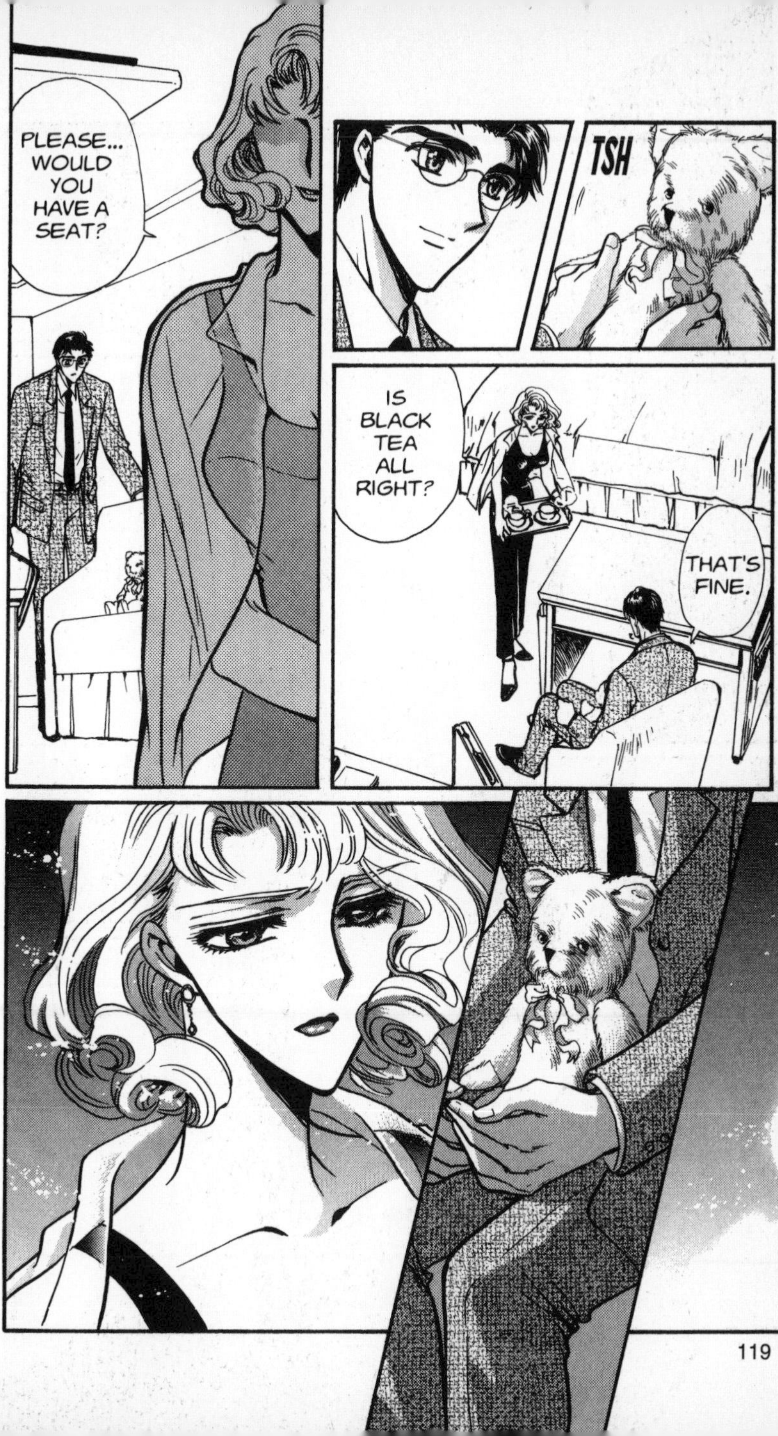
PLEASE... WOULD YOU HAVE A SEAT?
TSH
IS BLACK TEA ALL RIGHT?
THAT'S FINE.

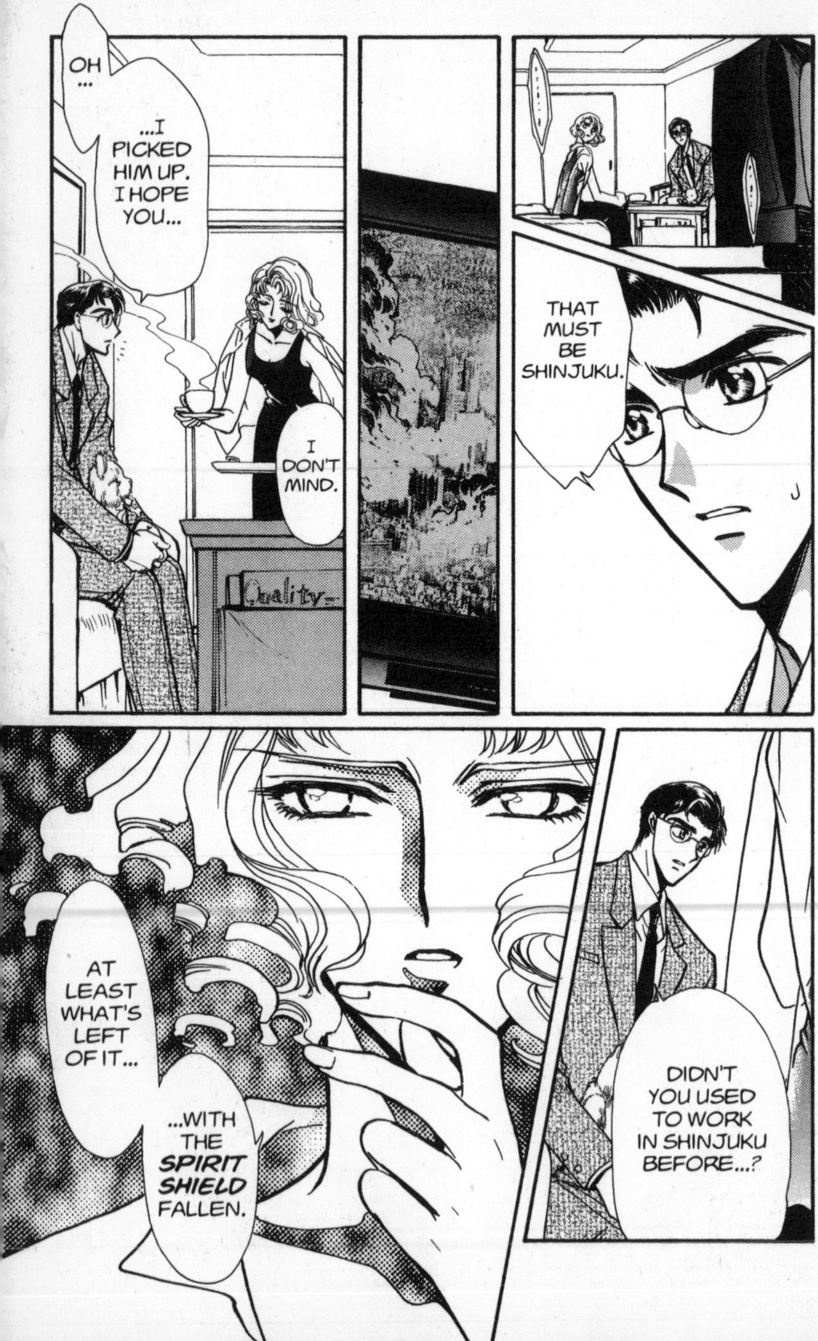
OH ...
...I PICKED HIM UP. I HOPE YOU...
I DON'T MIND.
Quality
THAT MUST BE SHINJUKU.
AT LEAST WHAT'S LEFT OF IT...
...WITH THE *SPIRIT SHIELD* FALLEN.
DIDN'T YOU USED TO WORK IN SHINJUKU BEFORE...?

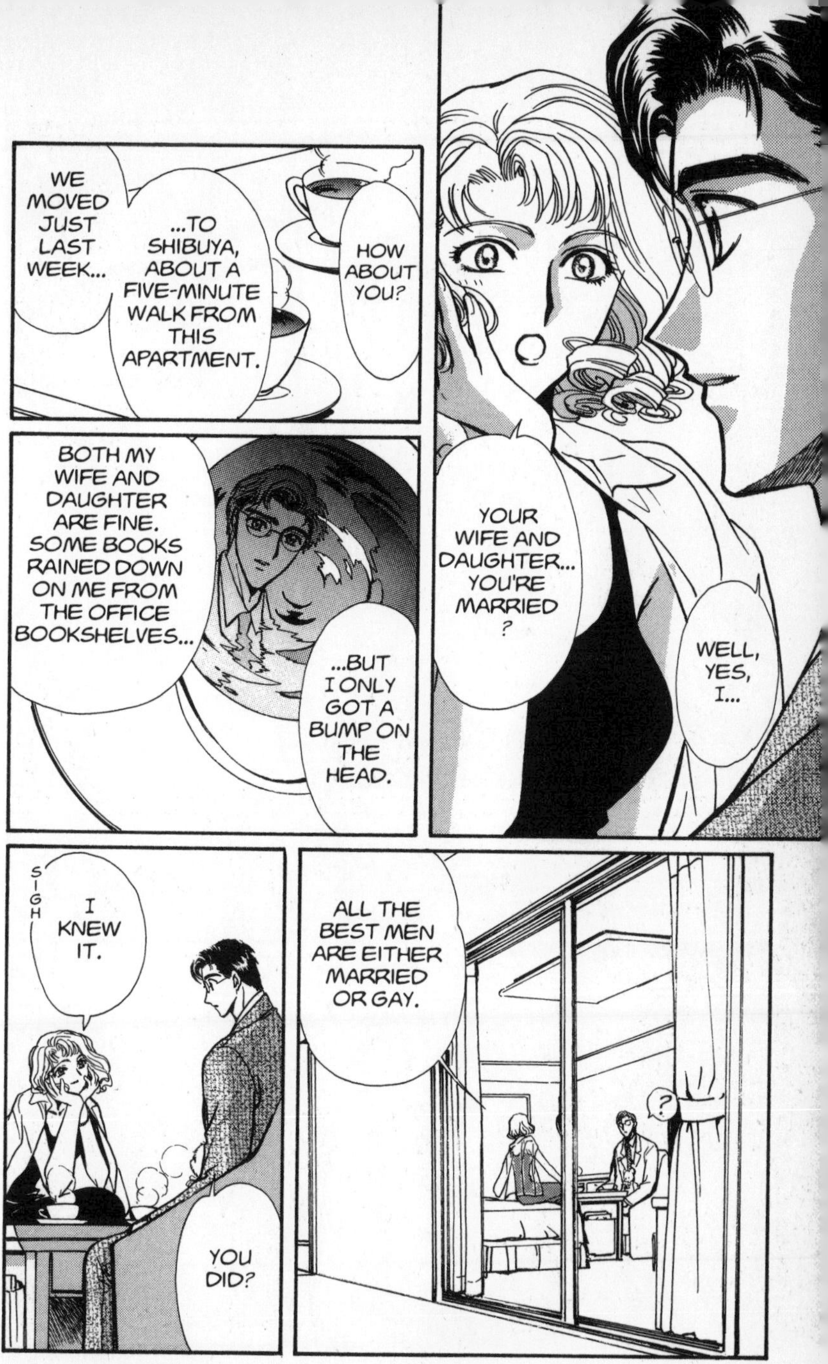
WE MOVED JUST LAST WEEK...
...TO SHIBUYA, ABOUT A FIVE-MINUTE WALK FROM THIS APARTMENT.
HOW ABOUT YOU?
BOTH MY WIFE AND DAUGHTER ARE FINE. SOME BOOKS RAINED DOWN ON ME FROM THE OFFICE BOOKSHELVES...
...BUT I ONLY GOT A BUMP ON THE HEAD.
YOUR WIFE AND DAUGHTER... YOU'RE MARRIED ?
WELL, YES, I...
SIGH
I KNEW IT.
YOU DID?
ALL THE BEST MEN ARE EITHER MARRIED OR GAY.
?

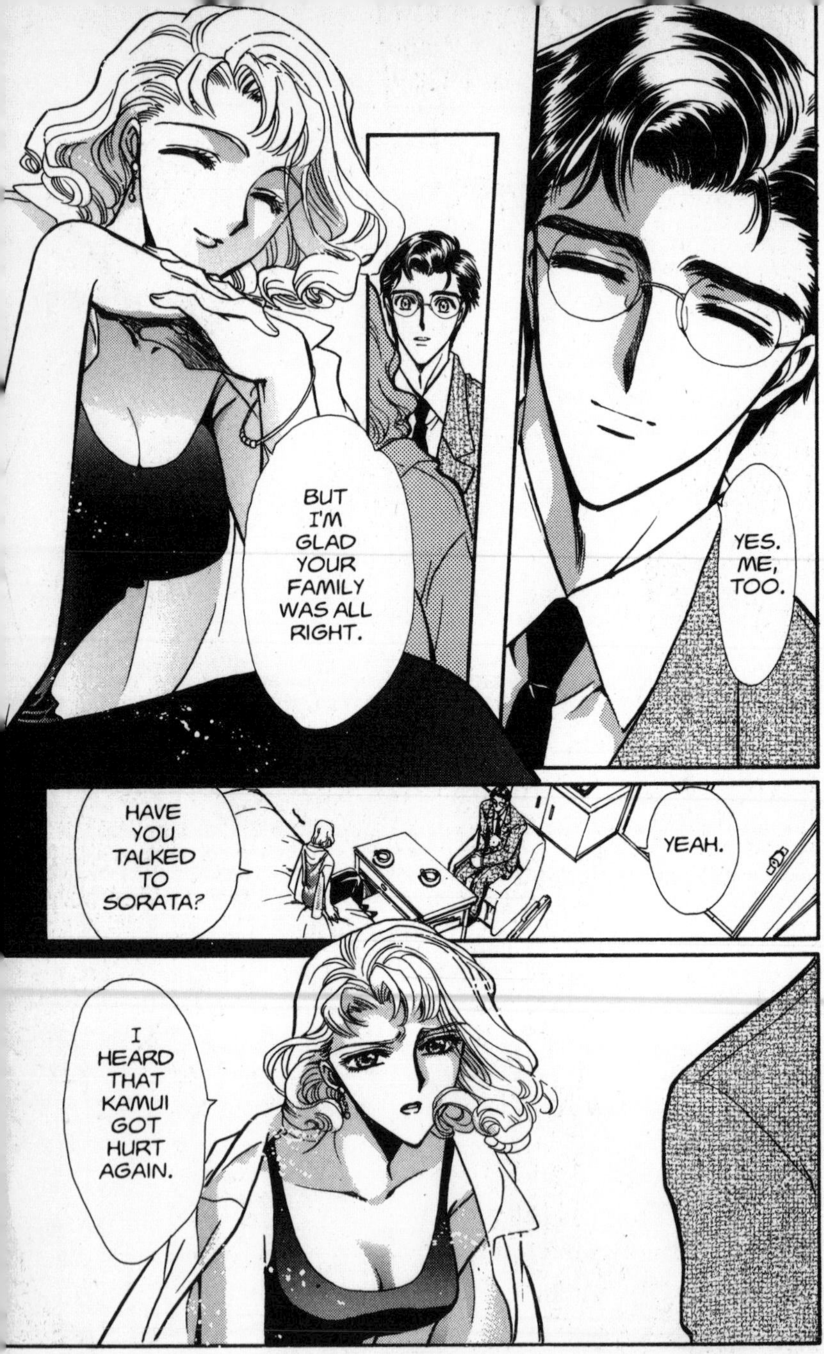
BUT I'M GLAD YOUR FAMILY WAS ALL RIGHT.
YES. ME, TOO.
HAVE YOU TALKED TO SORATA?
YEAH.
I HEARD THAT KAMUI GOT HURT AGAIN.

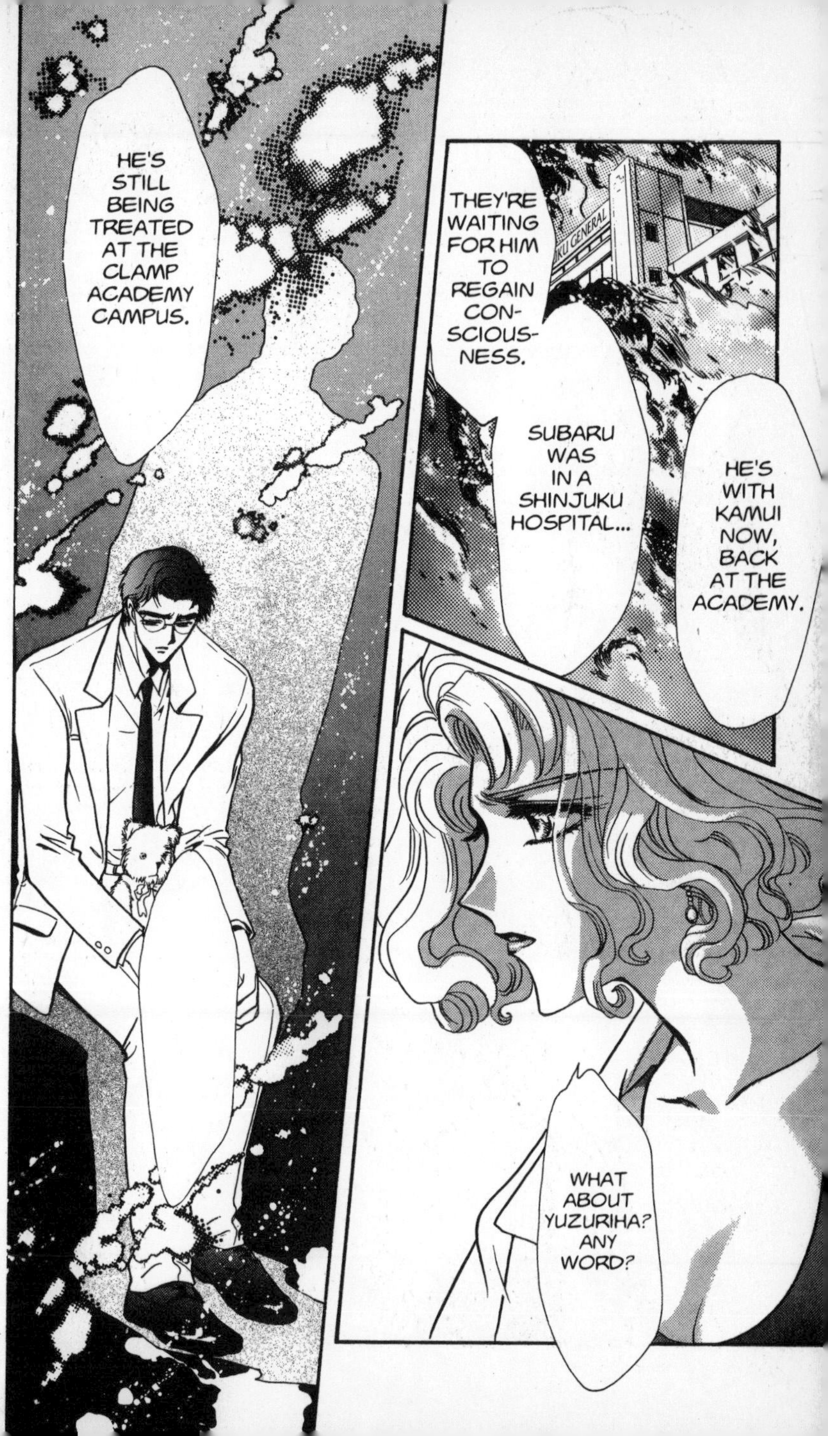
HE'S STILL BEING TREATED AT THE CLAMP ACADEMY CAMPUS.
THEY'RE WAITING FOR HIM TO REGAIN CON-SCIOUS-NESS.
SUBARU WAS IN A SHINJUKU HOSPITAL...
HE'S WITH KAMUI NOW, BACK AT THE ACADEMY.
WHAT ABOUT YUZURIHA? ANY WORD?

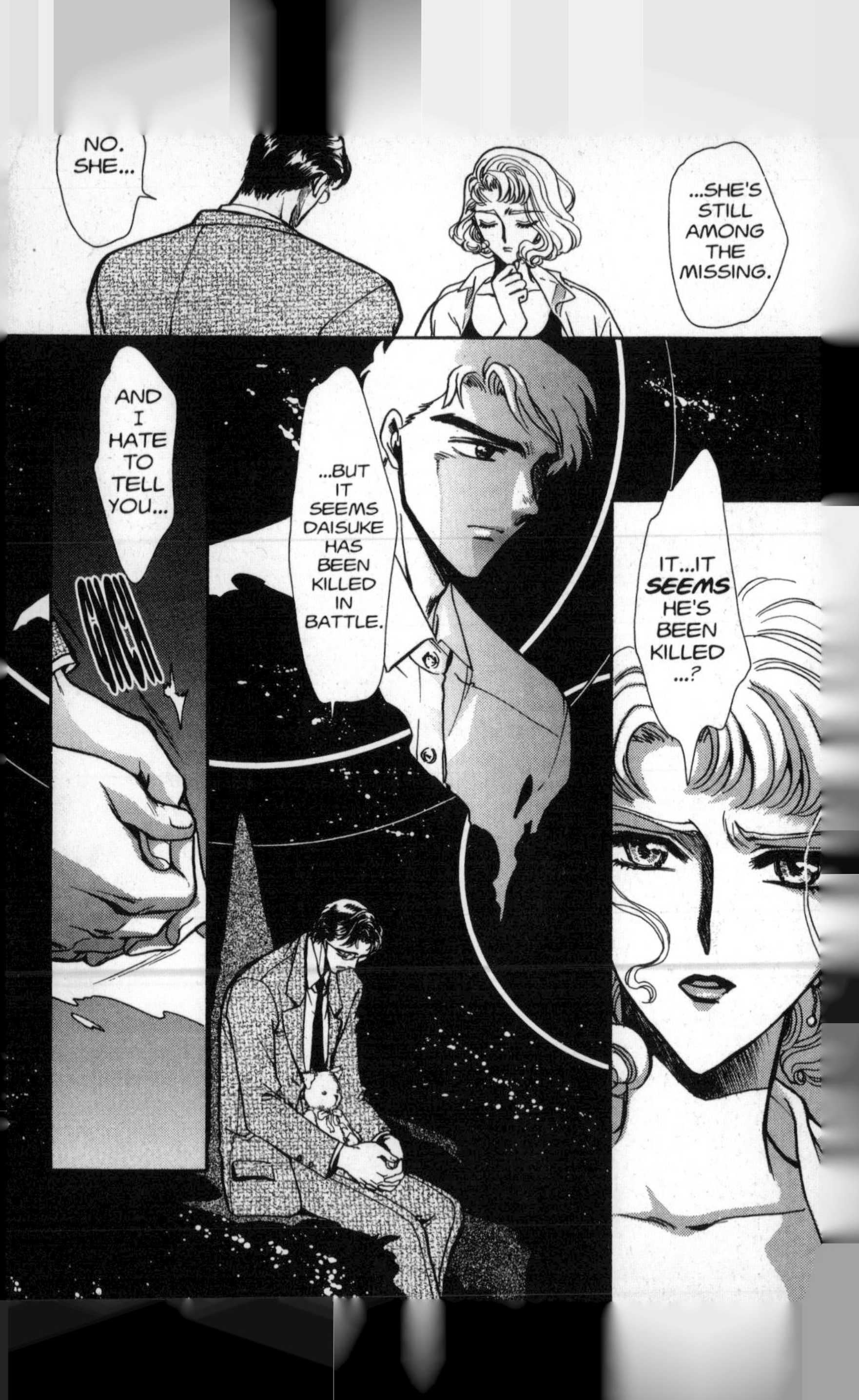
NO. SHE...
...SHE'S STILL AMONG THE MISSING.
AND I HATE TO TELL YOU...
...BUT IT SEEMS DAISUKE HAS BEEN KILLED IN BATTLE.
IT...IT SEEMS HE'S BEEN KILLED...?

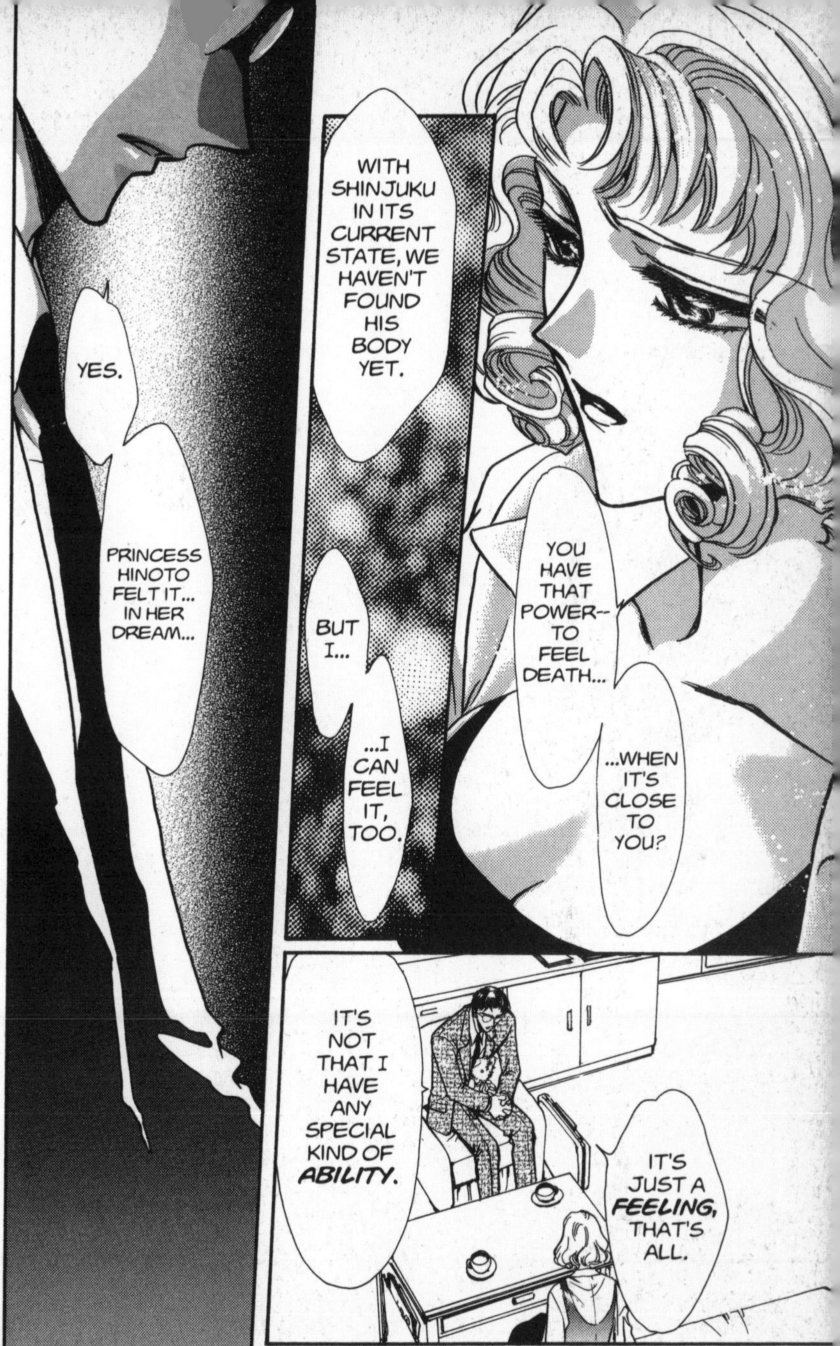
YES.
PRINCESS HINOTO FELT IT... IN HER DREAM...
WITH SHINJUKU IN ITS CURRENT STATE, WE HAVEN'T FOUND HIS BODY YET.
BUT I...
...I CAN FEEL IT, TOO.
YOU HAVE THAT POWER-- TO FEEL DEATH...
...WHEN IT'S CLOSE TO YOU?
IT'S NOT THAT I HAVE ANY SPECIAL KIND OF **ABILITY**.
IT'S JUST A **FEELING**, THAT'S ALL.

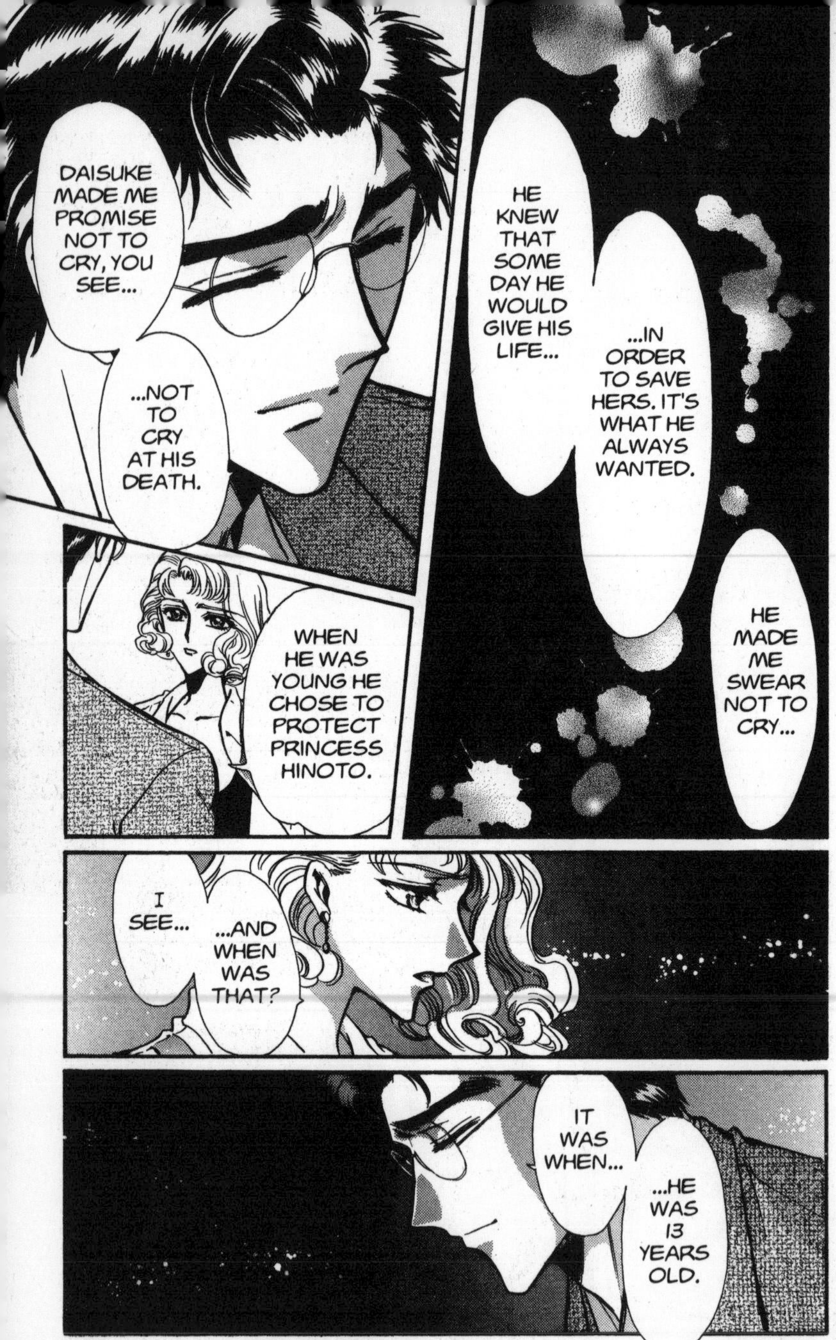
DAISUKE MADE ME PROMISE NOT TO CRY, YOU SEE...
...NOT TO CRY AT HIS DEATH.
WHEN HE WAS YOUNG HE CHOSE TO PROTECT PRINCESS HINOTO.
HE KNEW THAT SOME DAY HE WOULD GIVE HIS LIFE...
...IN ORDER TO SAVE HERS. IT'S WHAT HE ALWAYS WANTED.
HE MADE ME SWEAR NOT TO CRY...
I SEE...
...AND WHEN WAS THAT?
IT WAS WHEN...
...HE WAS 13 YEARS OLD.

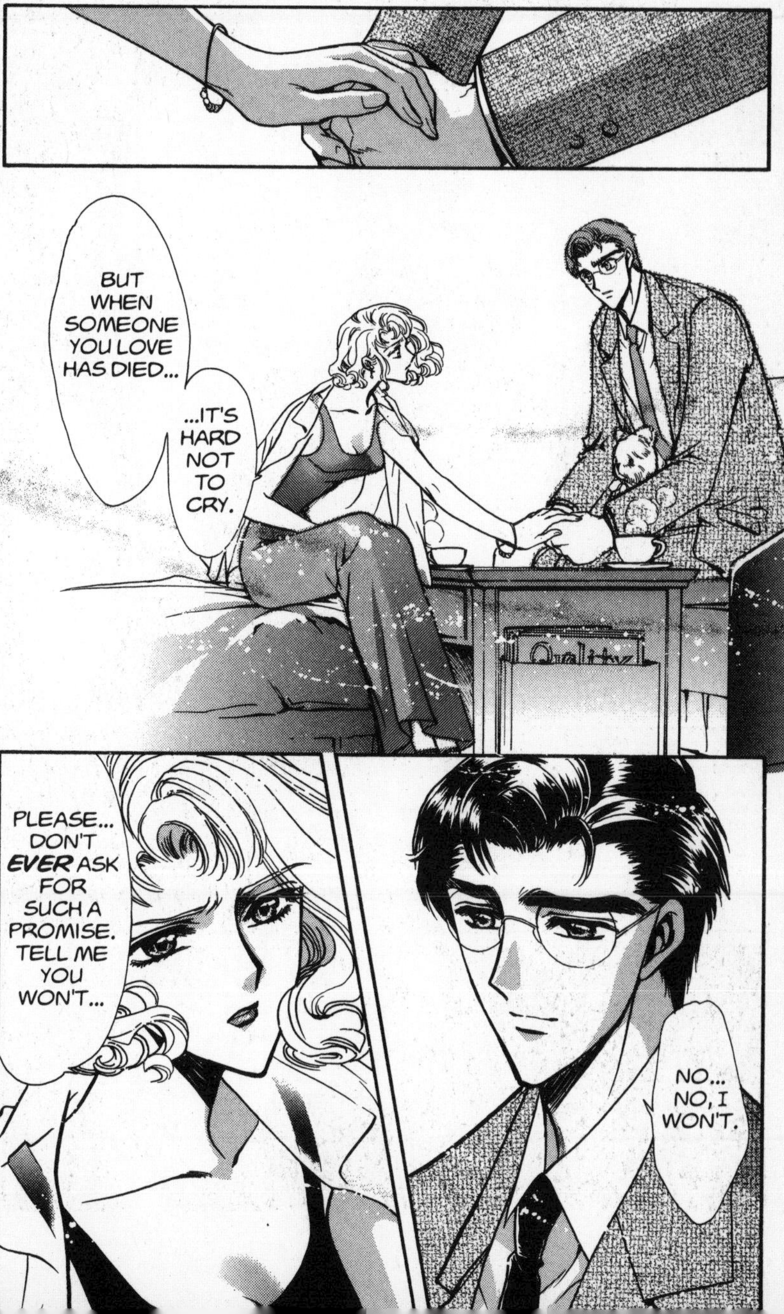
BUT WHEN SOMEONE YOU LOVE HAS DIED...
...IT'S HARD NOT TO CRY.
PLEASE... DON'T **EVER** ASK FOR SUCH A PROMISE. TELL ME YOU WON'T...
NO... NO, I WON'T.

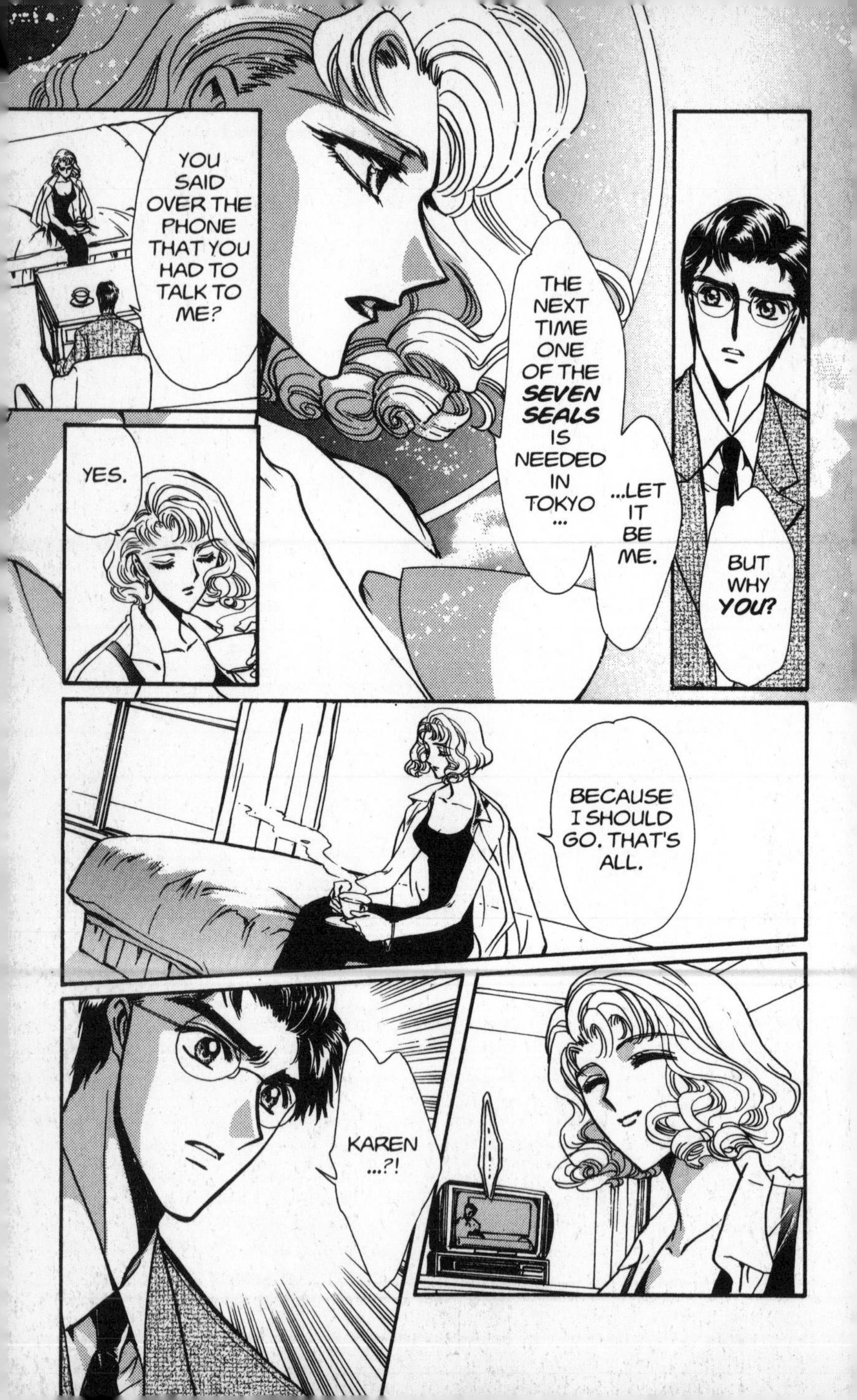
YOU SAID OVER THE PHONE THAT YOU HAD TO TALK TO ME?
YES.
THE NEXT TIME ONE OF THE SEVEN SEALS IS NEEDED IN TOKYO ...
...LET IT BE ME.
BUT WHY YOU?
BECAUSE I SHOULD GO. THAT'S ALL.
KAREN ...?!

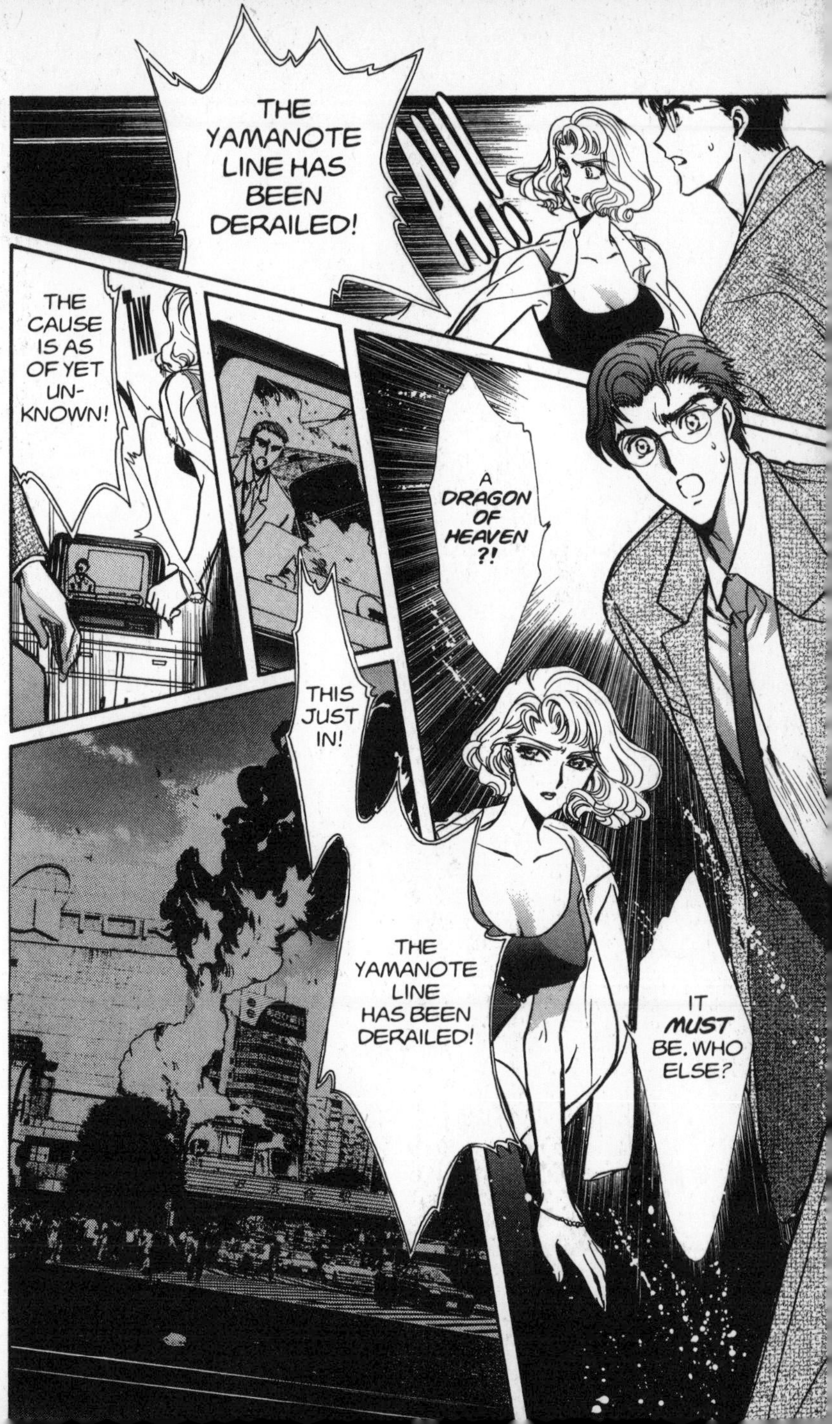
THE YAMANOTE LINE HAS BEEN DERAILED!
AH!!
THE CAUSE IS AS OF YET UN-KNOWN!
TMK
A *DRAGON OF HEAVEN* ?!
THIS JUST IN!
THE YAMANOTE LINE HAS BEEN DERAILED!
IT *MUST* BE. WHO ELSE?

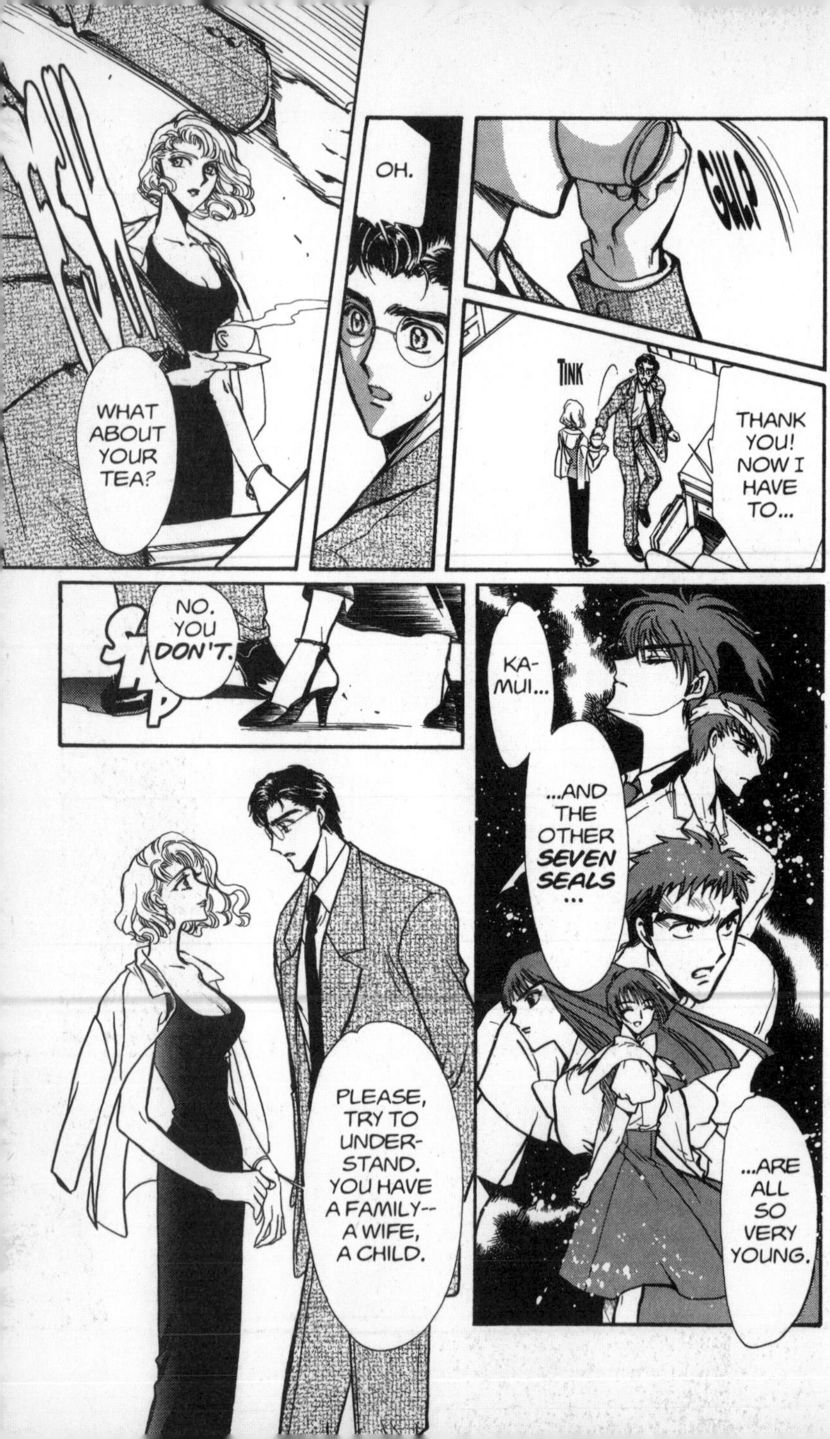
WHAT ABOUT YOUR TEA?
OH.
GULP
TINK
THANK YOU! NOW I HAVE TO...
NO. YOU *DON'T.*
PLEASE, TRY TO UNDER-STAND. YOU HAVE A FAMILY-- A WIFE, A CHILD.
KA-MUI...
...AND THE OTHER *SEVEN SEALS* ...
...ARE ALL SO VERY YOUNG.

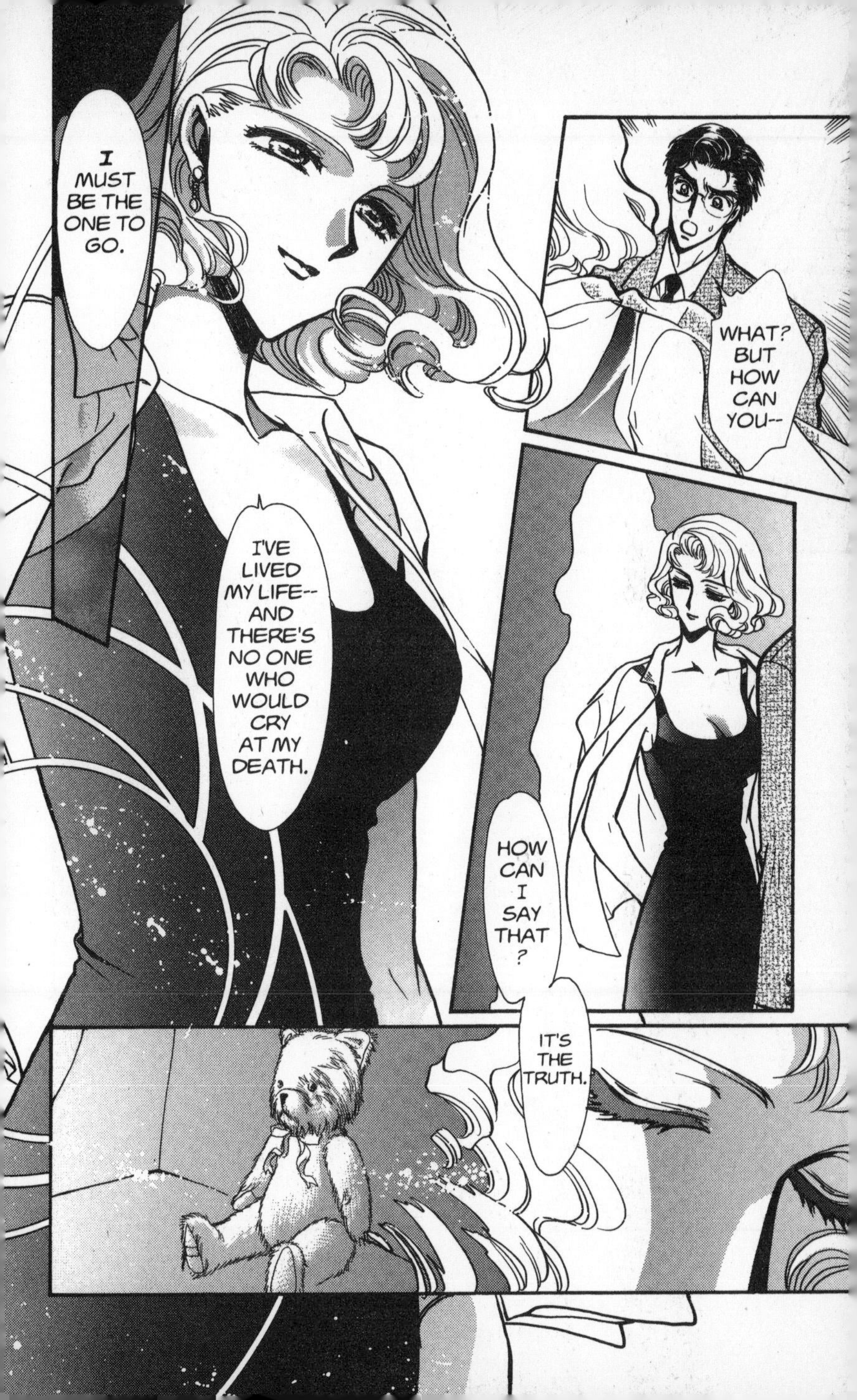
I MUST BE THE ONE TO GO.
I'VE LIVED MY LIFE-- AND THERE'S NO ONE WHO WOULD CRY AT MY DEATH.
WHAT? BUT HOW CAN YOU--
HOW CAN I SAY THAT?
IT'S THE TRUTH.

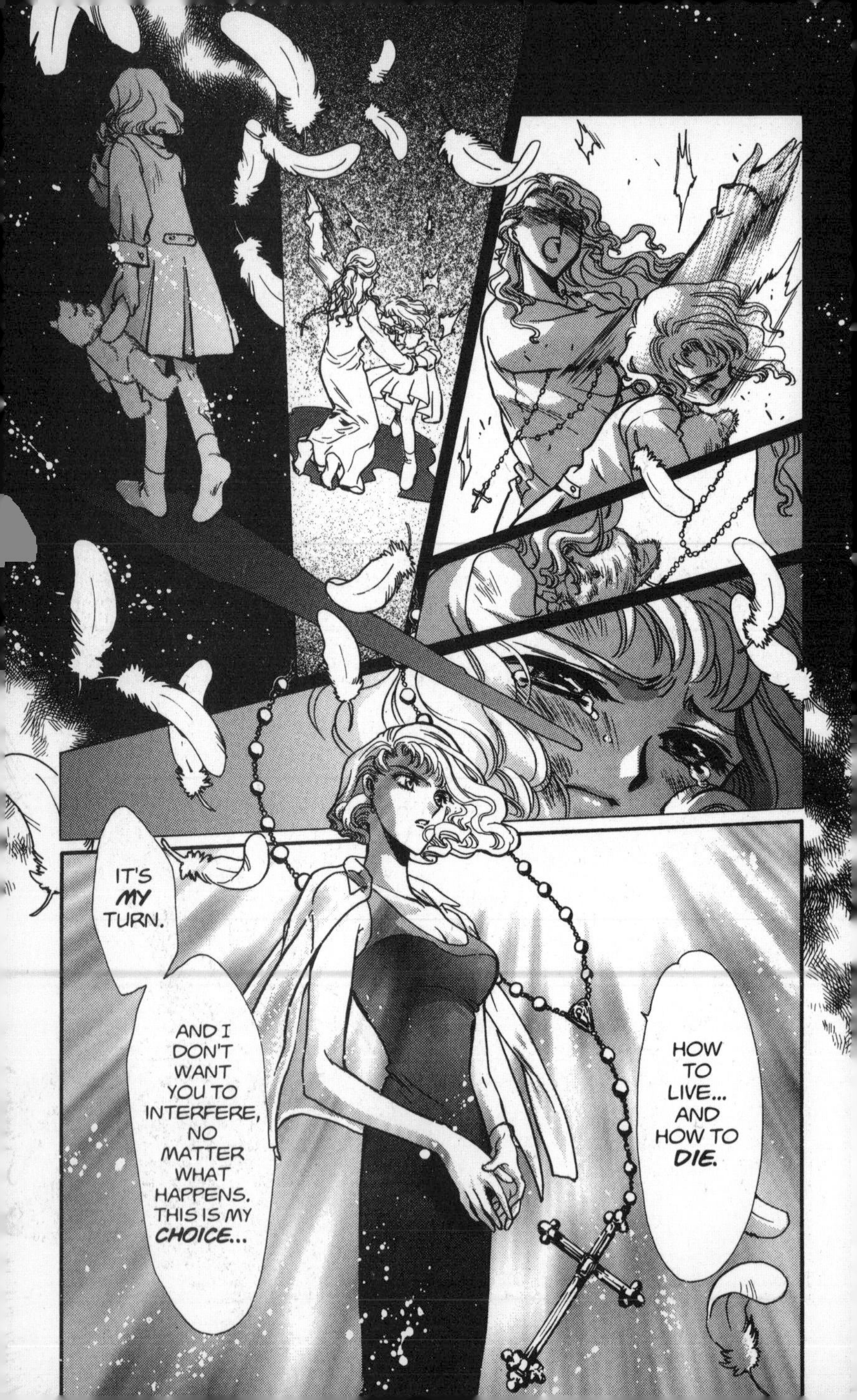
IT'S **MY** TURN.
AND I DON'T WANT YOU TO INTERFERE, NO MATTER WHAT HAPPENS. THIS IS MY **CHOICE...**
HOW TO LIVE... AND HOW TO **DIE.**

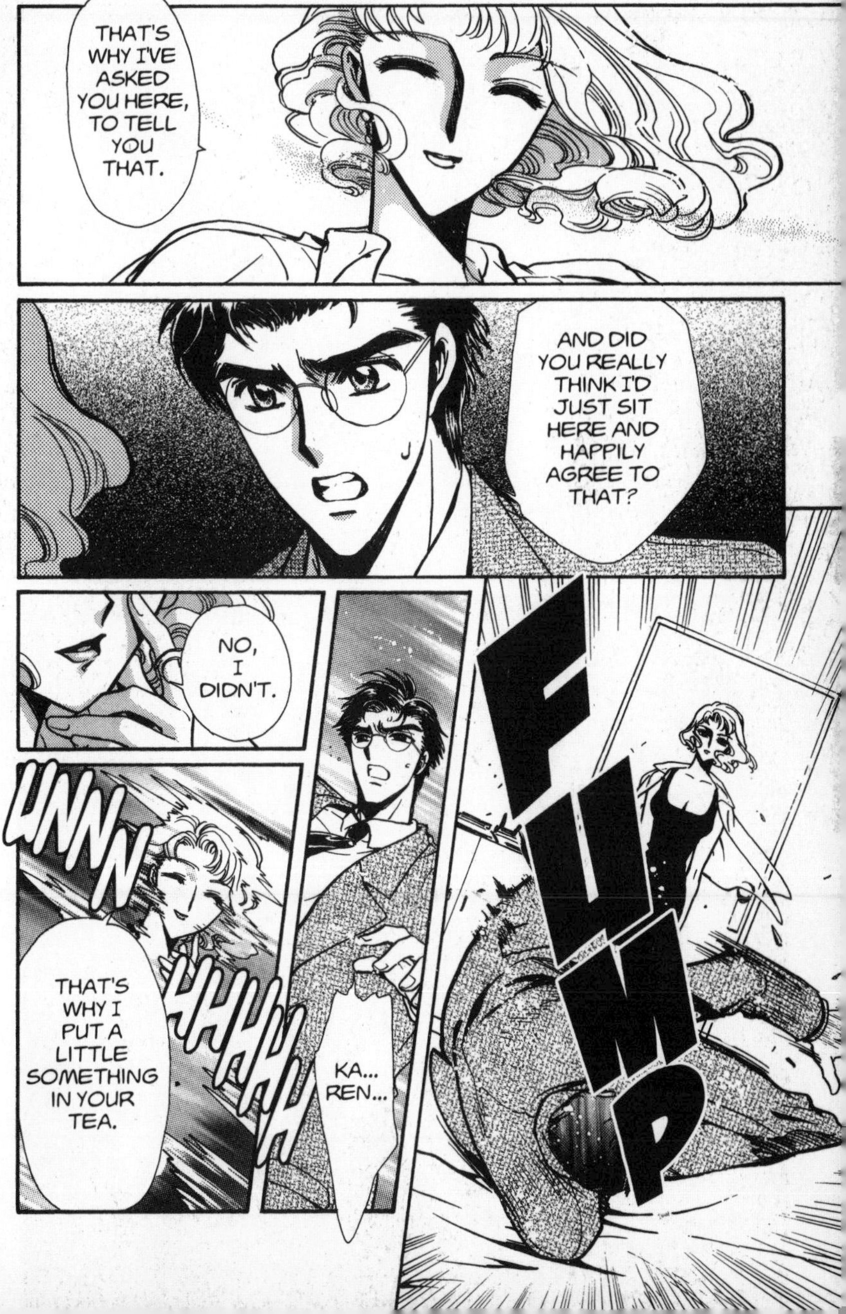
THAT'S WHY I'VE ASKED YOU HERE, TO TELL YOU THAT.
AND DID YOU REALLY THINK I'D JUST SIT HERE AND HAPPILY AGREE TO THAT?
NO, I DIDN'T.
UNNNHHHHH
THAT'S WHY I PUT A LITTLE SOMETHING IN YOUR TEA.
KA... REN...
FUMP

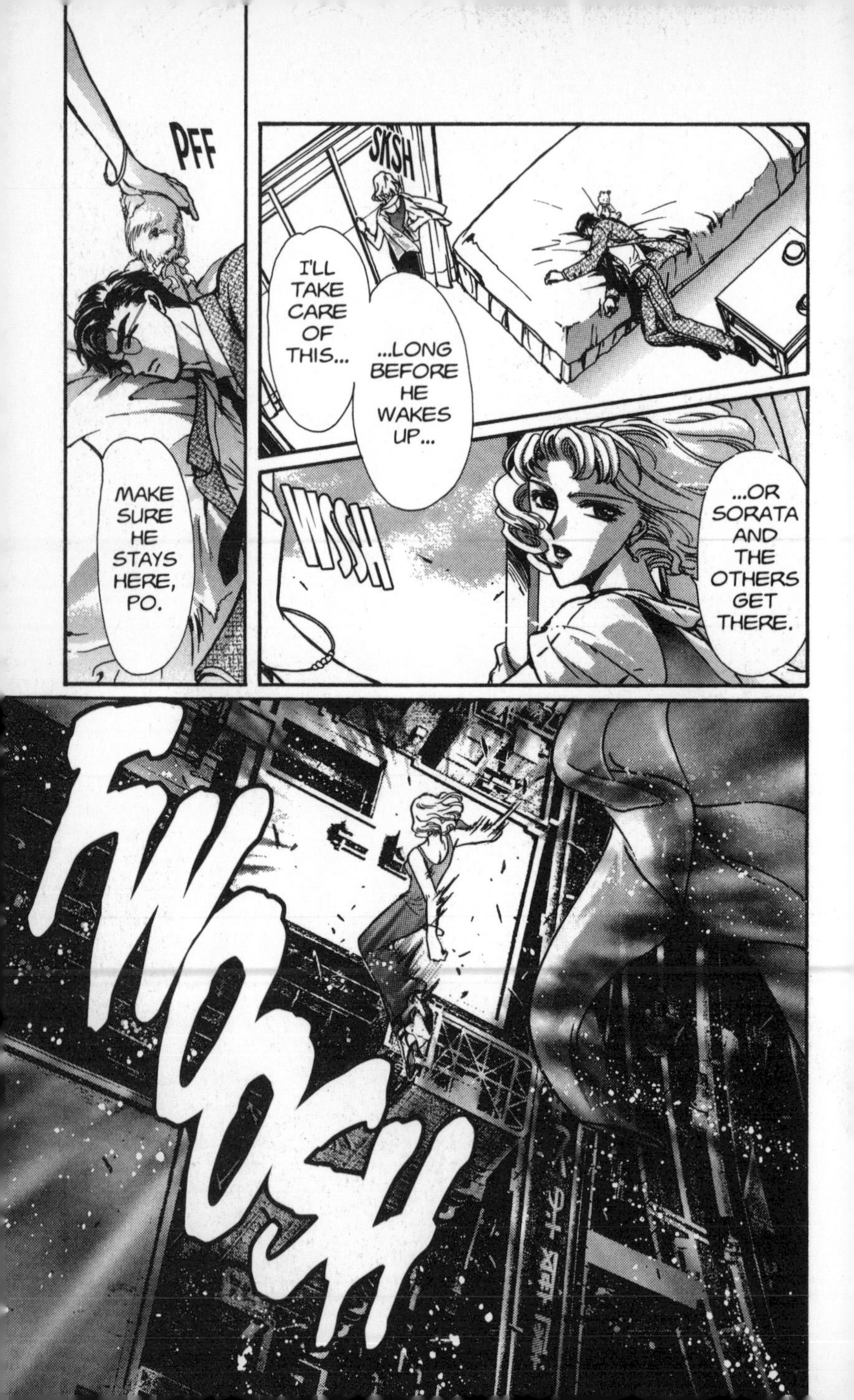
PFF
MAKE SURE HE STAYS HERE, PO.
SKSH
I'LL TAKE CARE OF THIS...
...LONG BEFORE HE WAKES UP...
WSSH
...OR SORATA AND THE OTHERS GET THERE.
FWOOSH

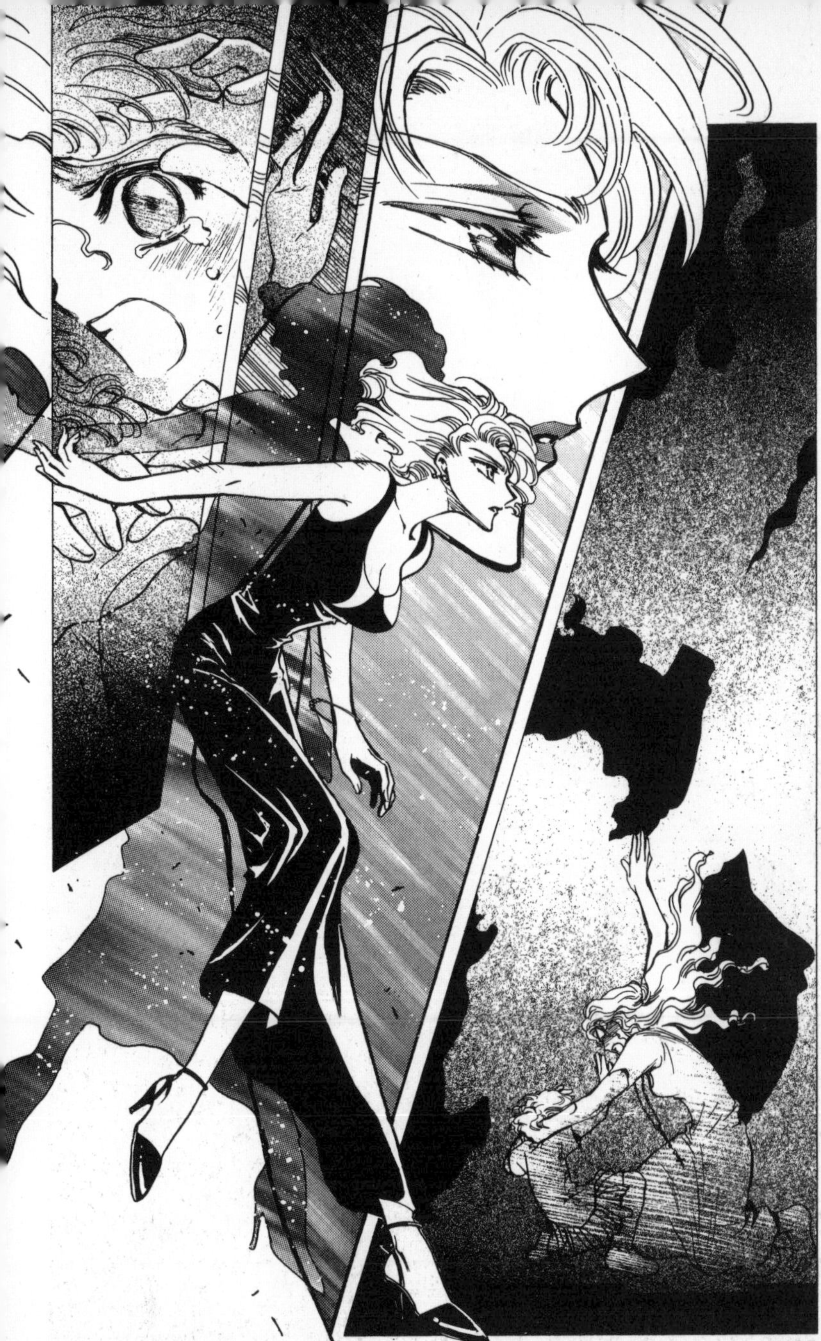

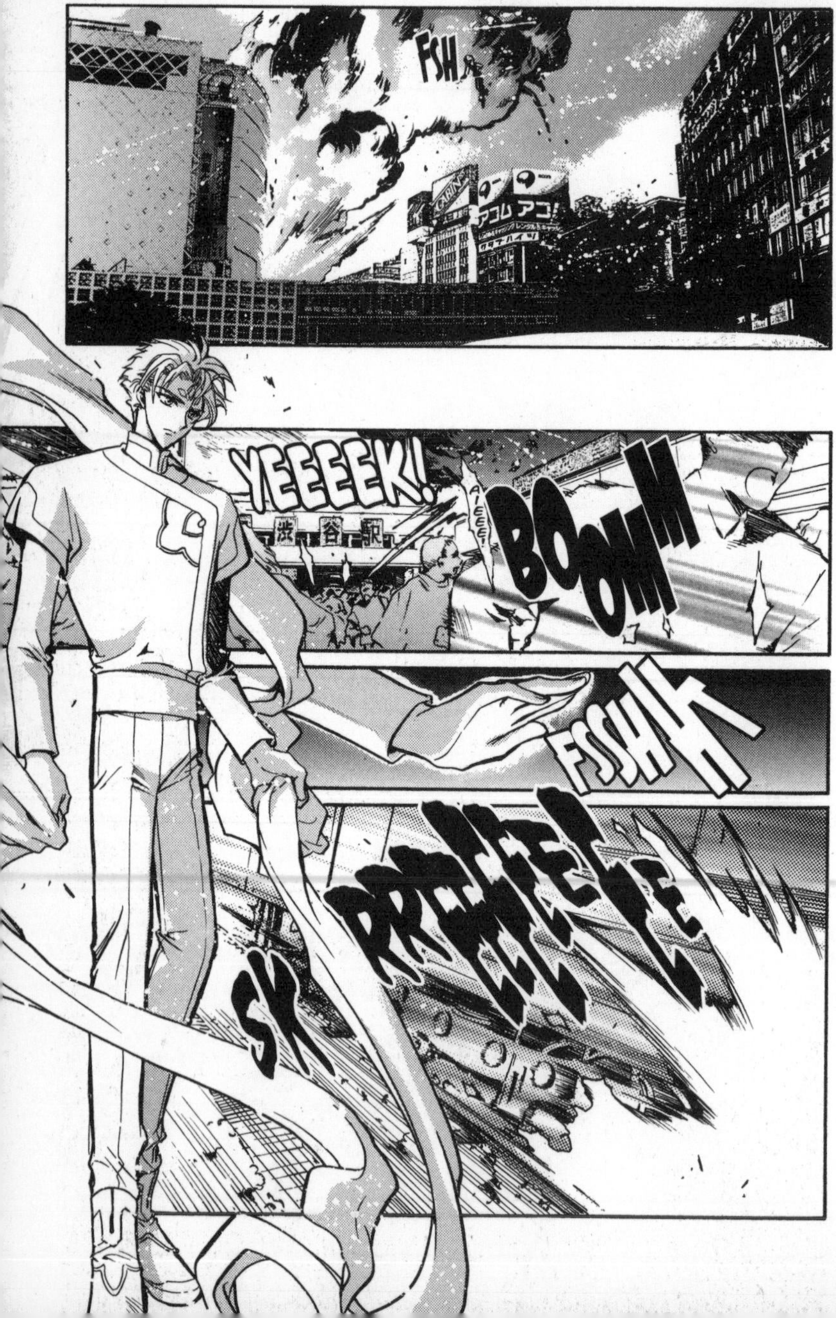
FSH
CABIN
アコム アコ!
YEEEEK!
渋谷駅
AIEEE!
BOOMMM
FSSHH

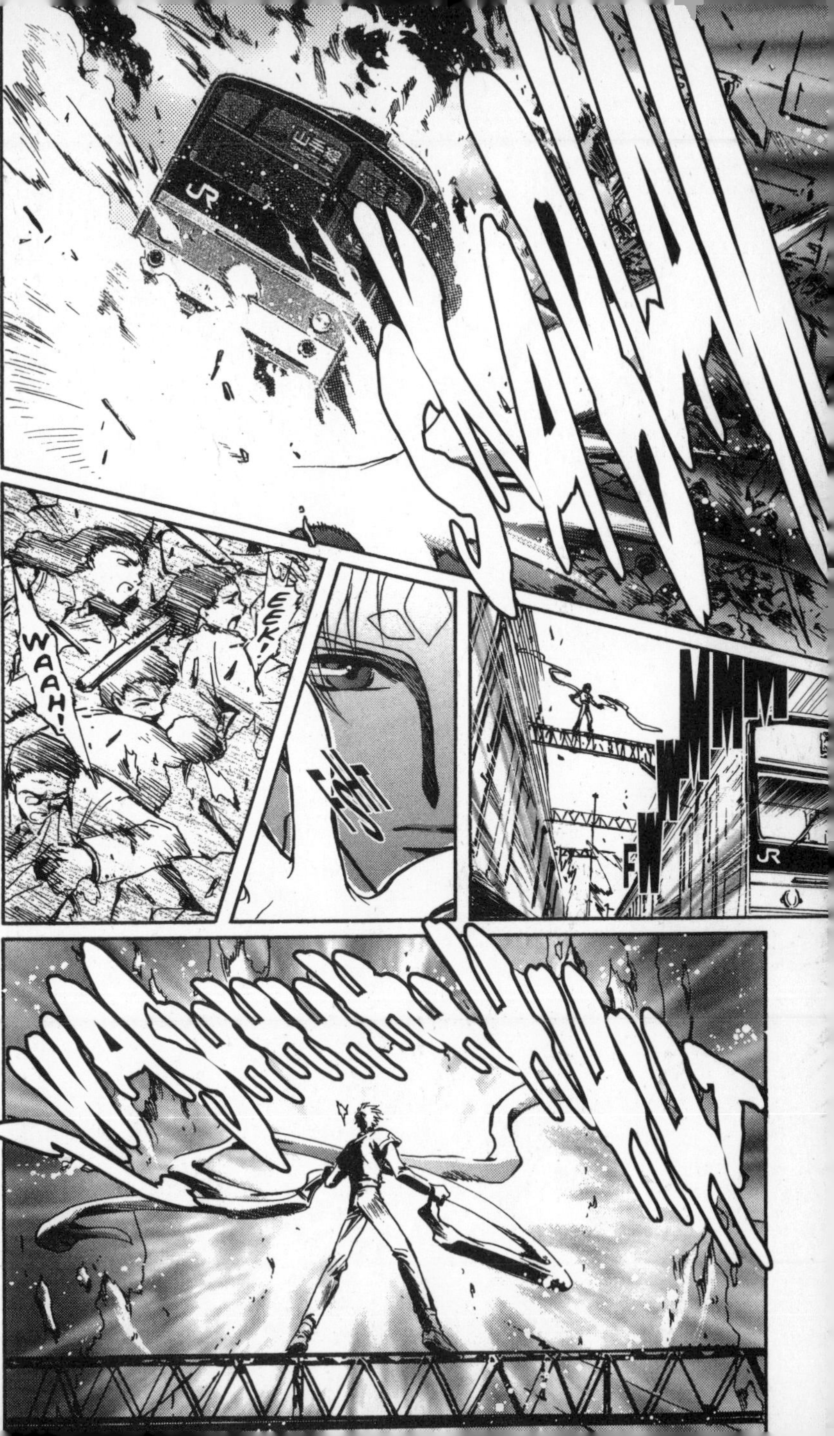
JR
WAAH!
EEK!
FWMMM
JR

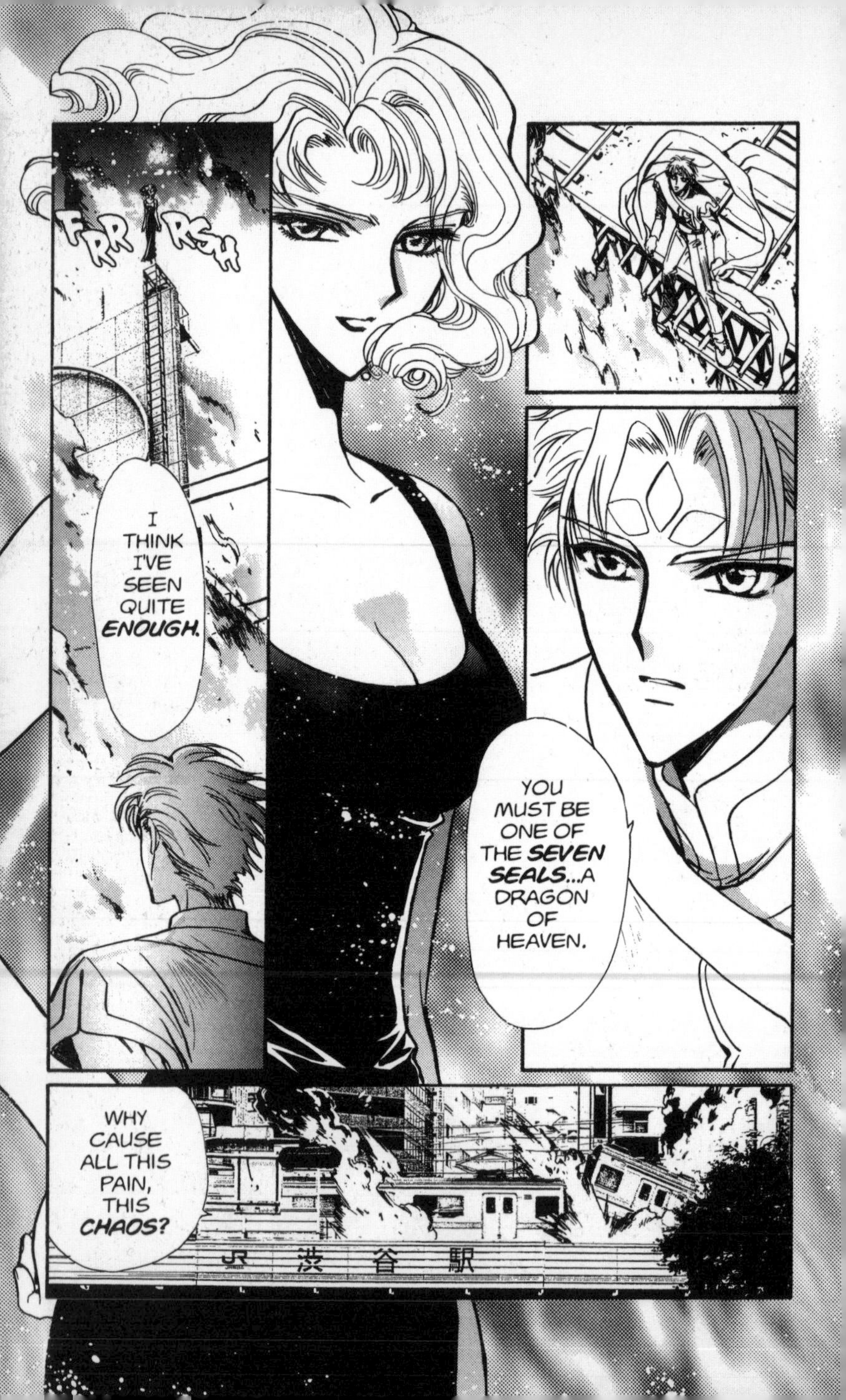
FRR RSH
I THINK I'VE SEEN QUITE ENOUGH.
YOU MUST BE ONE OF THE SEVEN SEALS...A DRAGON OF HEAVEN.
WHY CAUSE ALL THIS PAIN, THIS CHAOS?
JR 渋谷駅

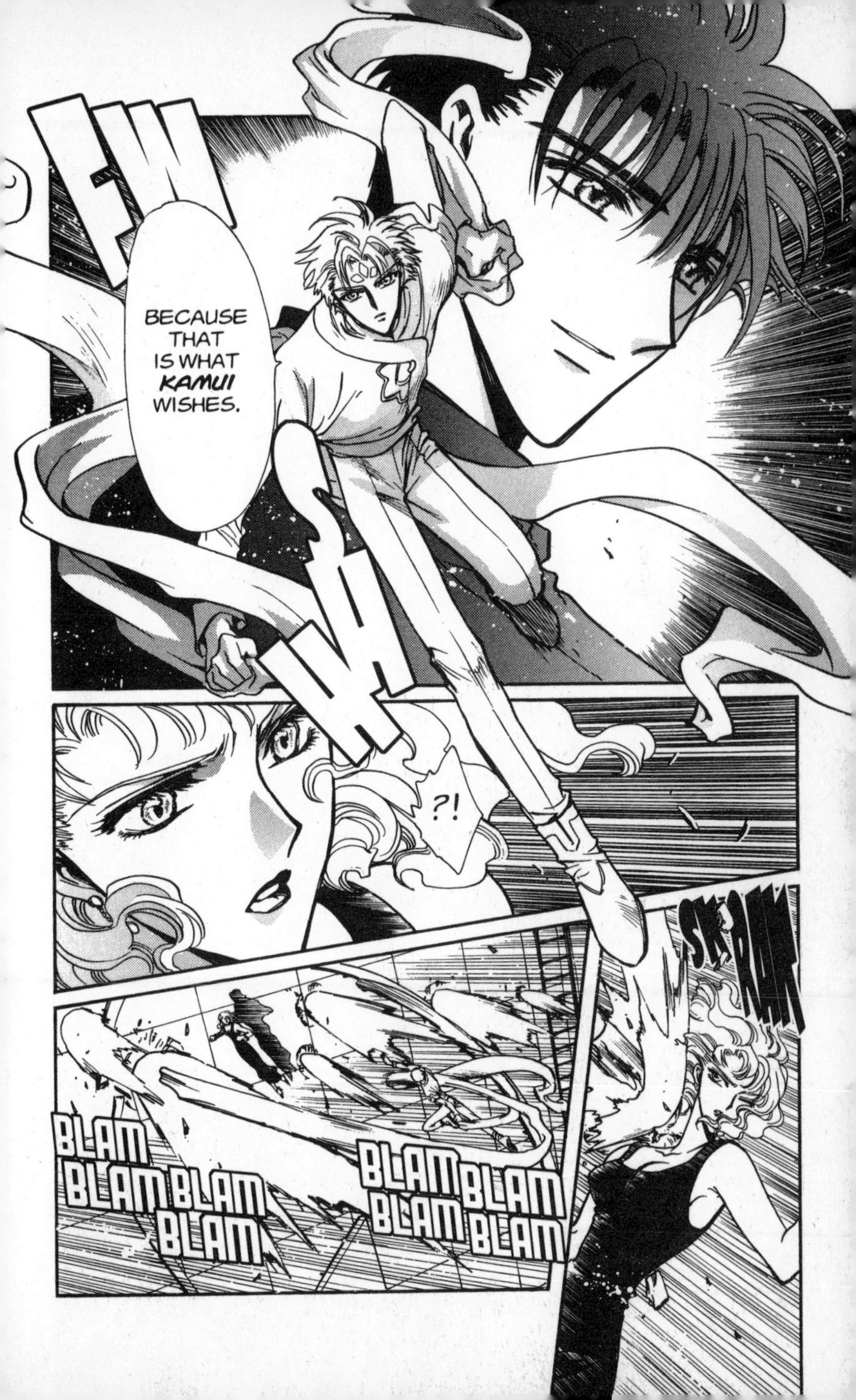
BECAUSE THAT IS WHAT *KAMUI* WISHES.
?!
BLAM BLAM BLAM BLAM
BLAM BLAM BLAM BLAM

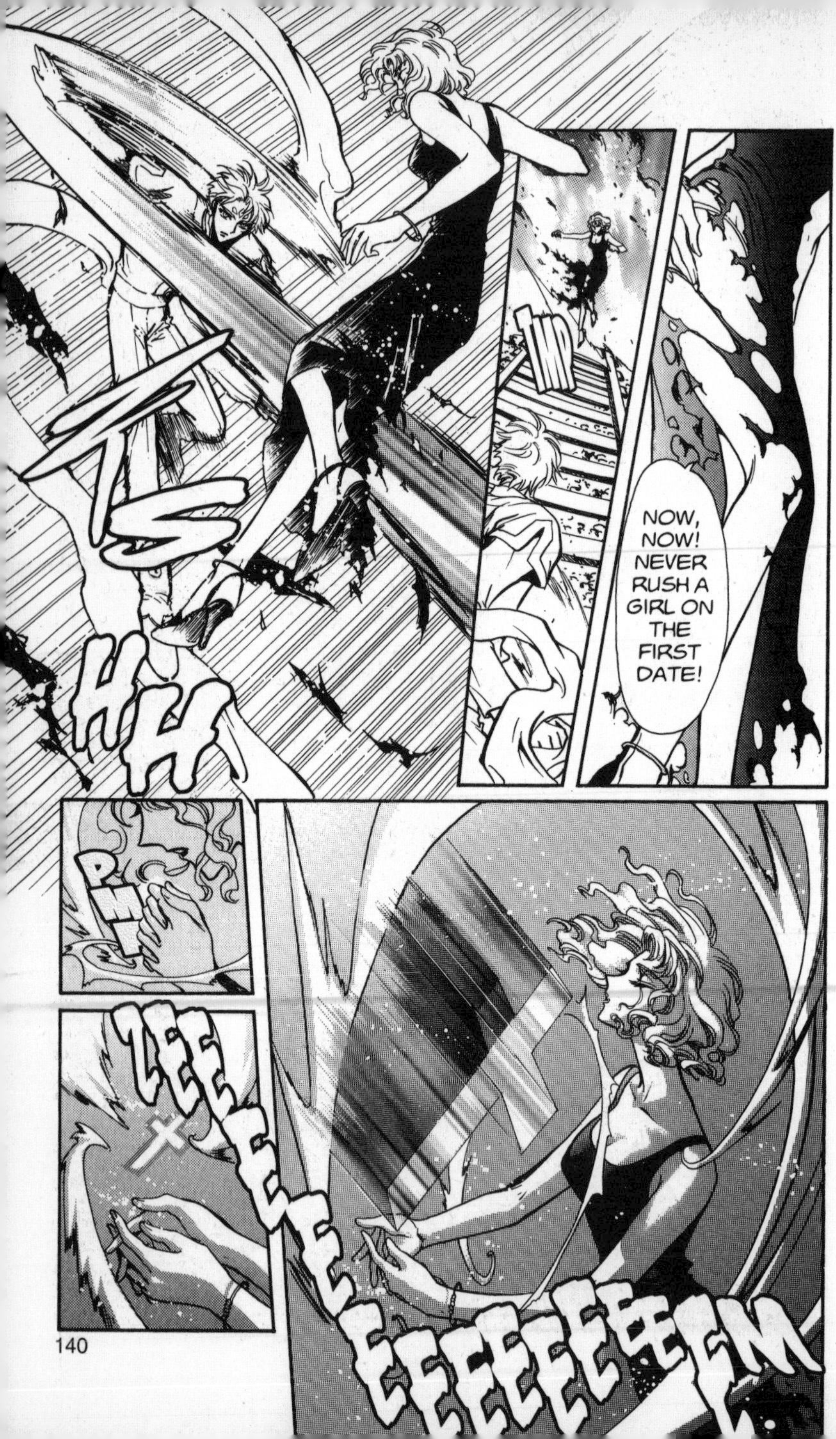
ZSHH
NOW, NOW! NEVER RUSH A GIRL ON THE FIRST DATE!
PHT
ZEEEEEEEEEEEEEEEEEM

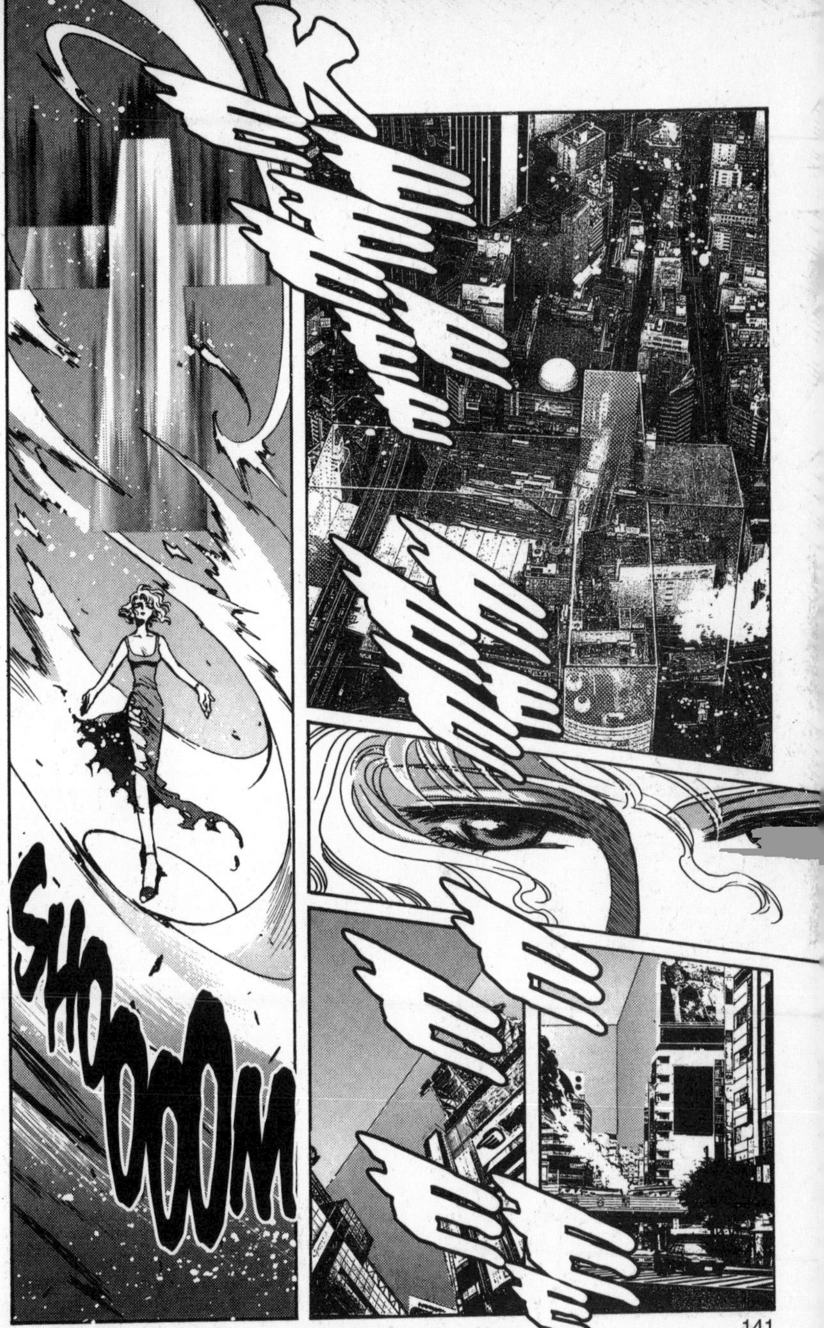
KEEEEEEEEEEEEEEE
SHOOOOM

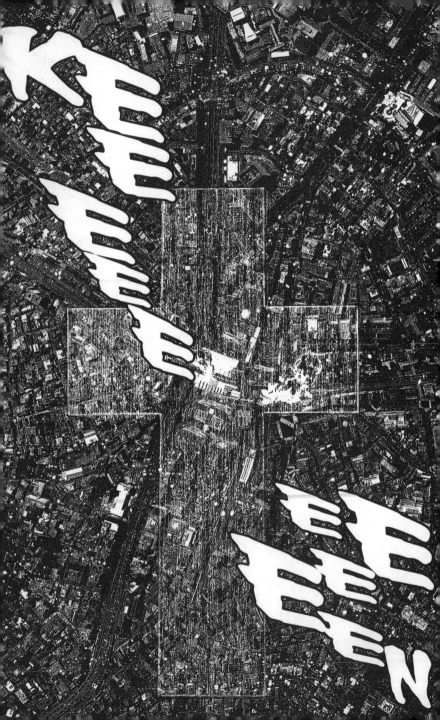

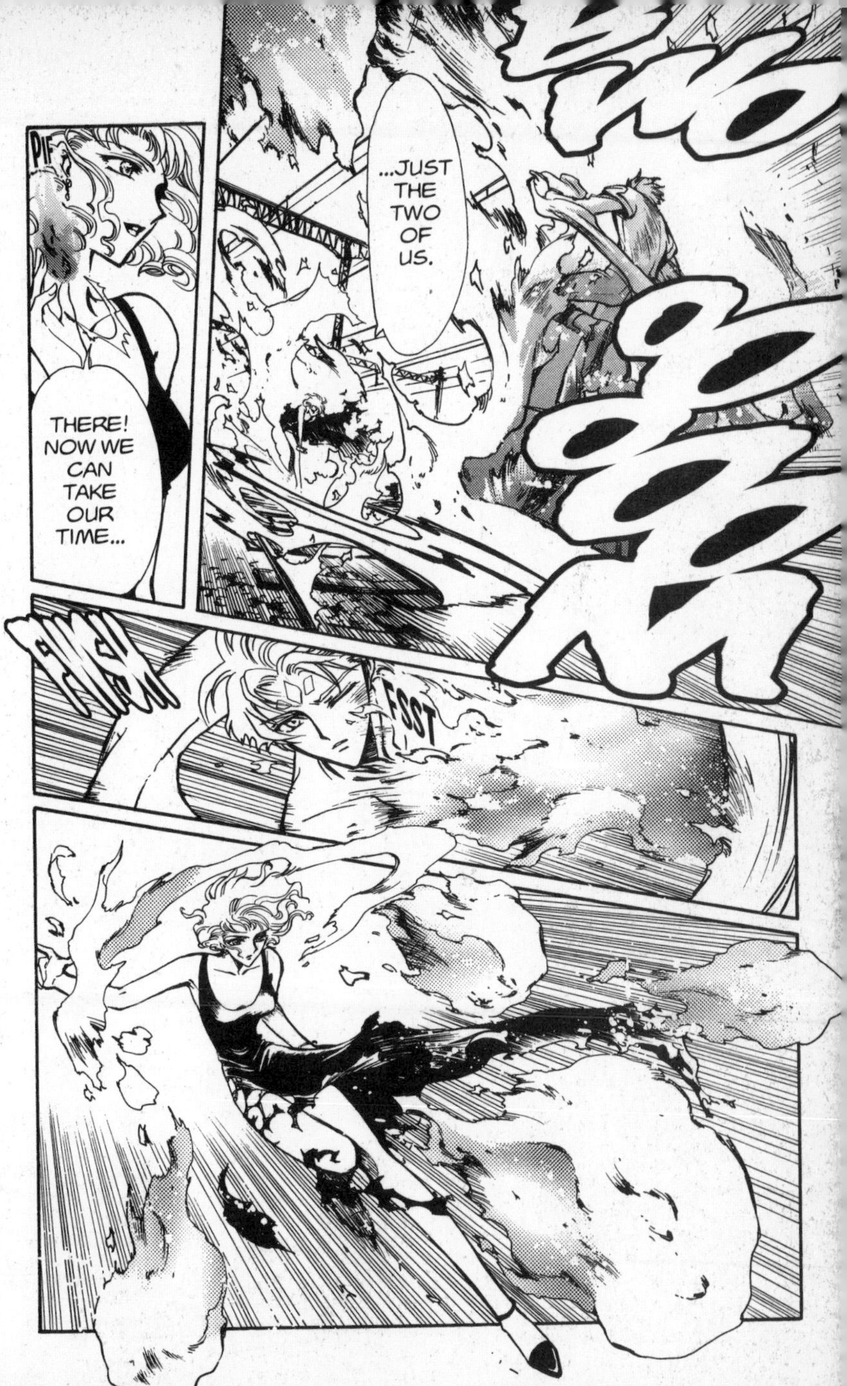
PIF
THERE! NOW WE CAN TAKE OUR TIME...
...JUST THE TWO OF US.
FSST

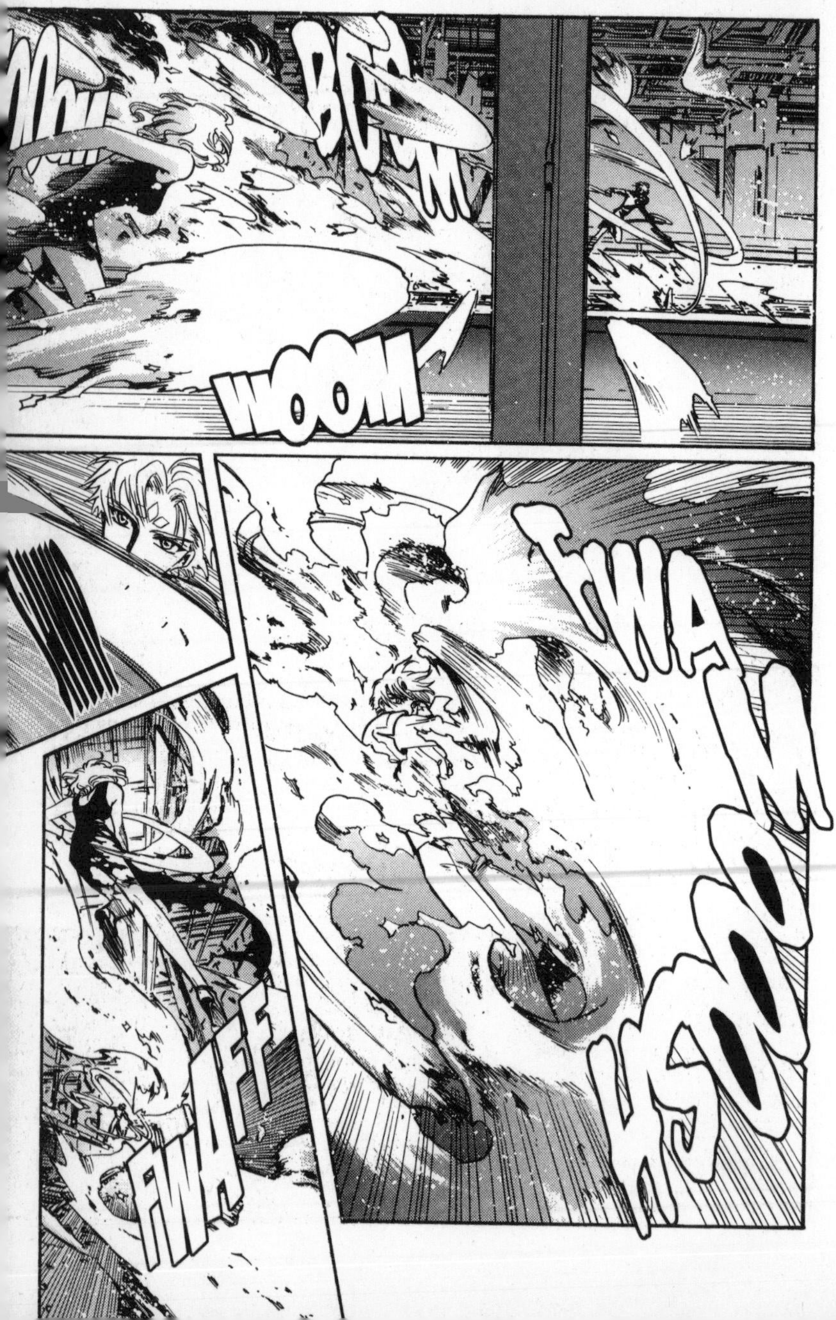
BOOM
WOOM
FWAFF
FWA

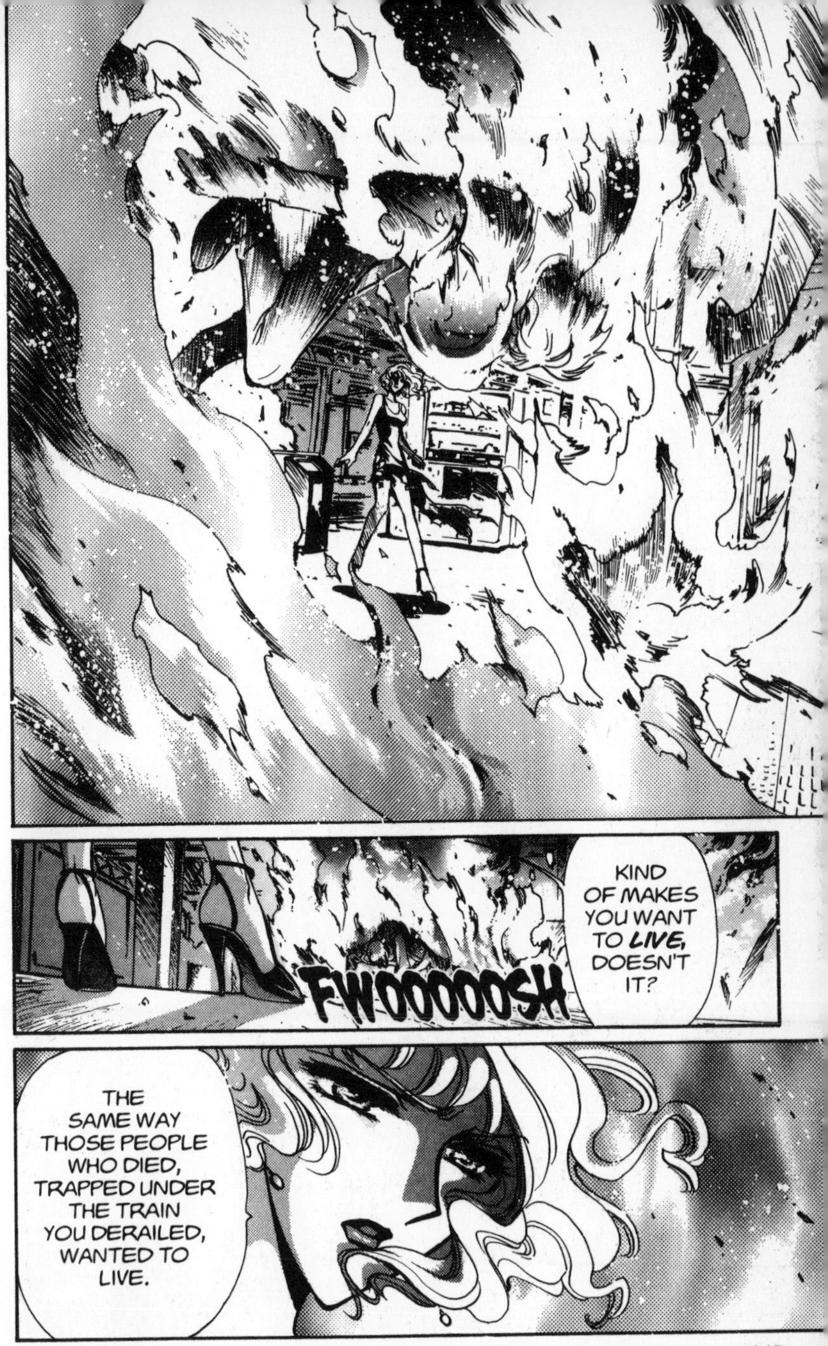
FWOOOOOSH
KIND OF MAKES YOU WANT TO *LIVE,* DOESN'T IT?
THE SAME WAY THOSE PEOPLE WHO DIED, TRAPPED UNDER THE TRAIN YOU DERAILED, WANTED TO LIVE.

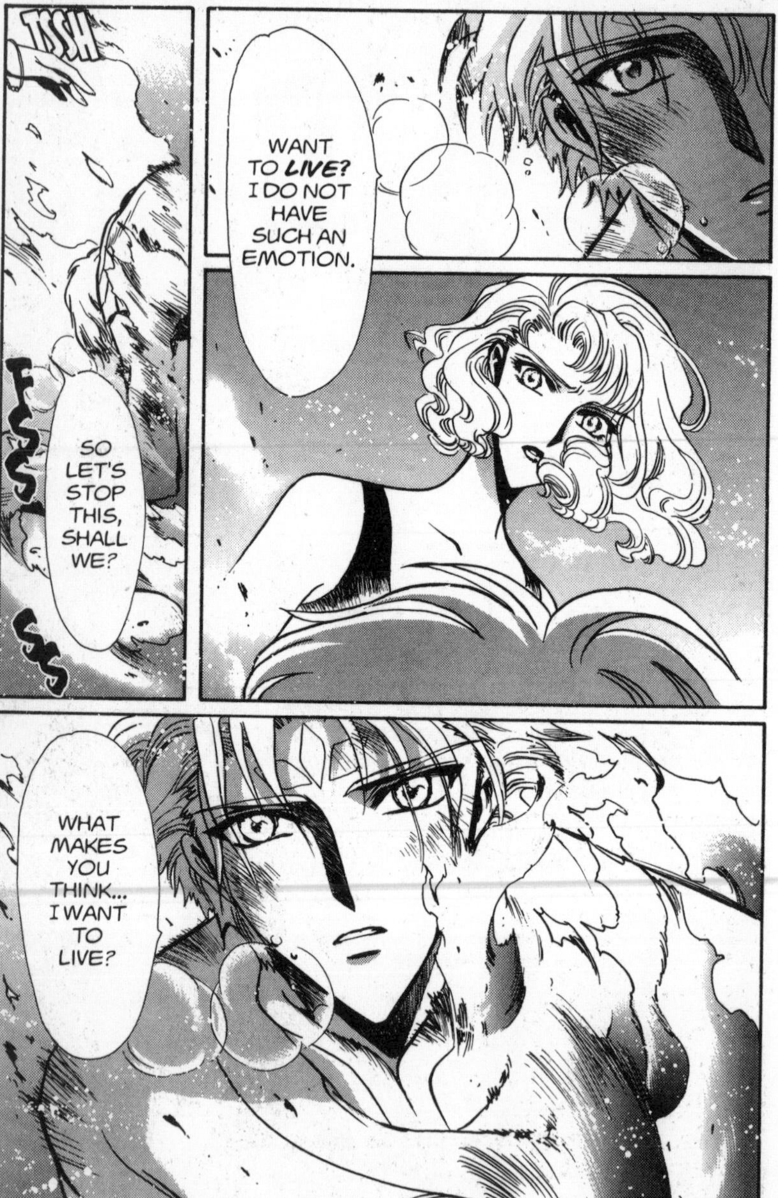
TSSH
FSSS
SO LET'S STOP THIS, SHALL WE?
SSS
WANT TO **LIVE?** I DO NOT HAVE SUCH AN EMOTION.
WHAT MAKES YOU THINK... I WANT TO LIVE?

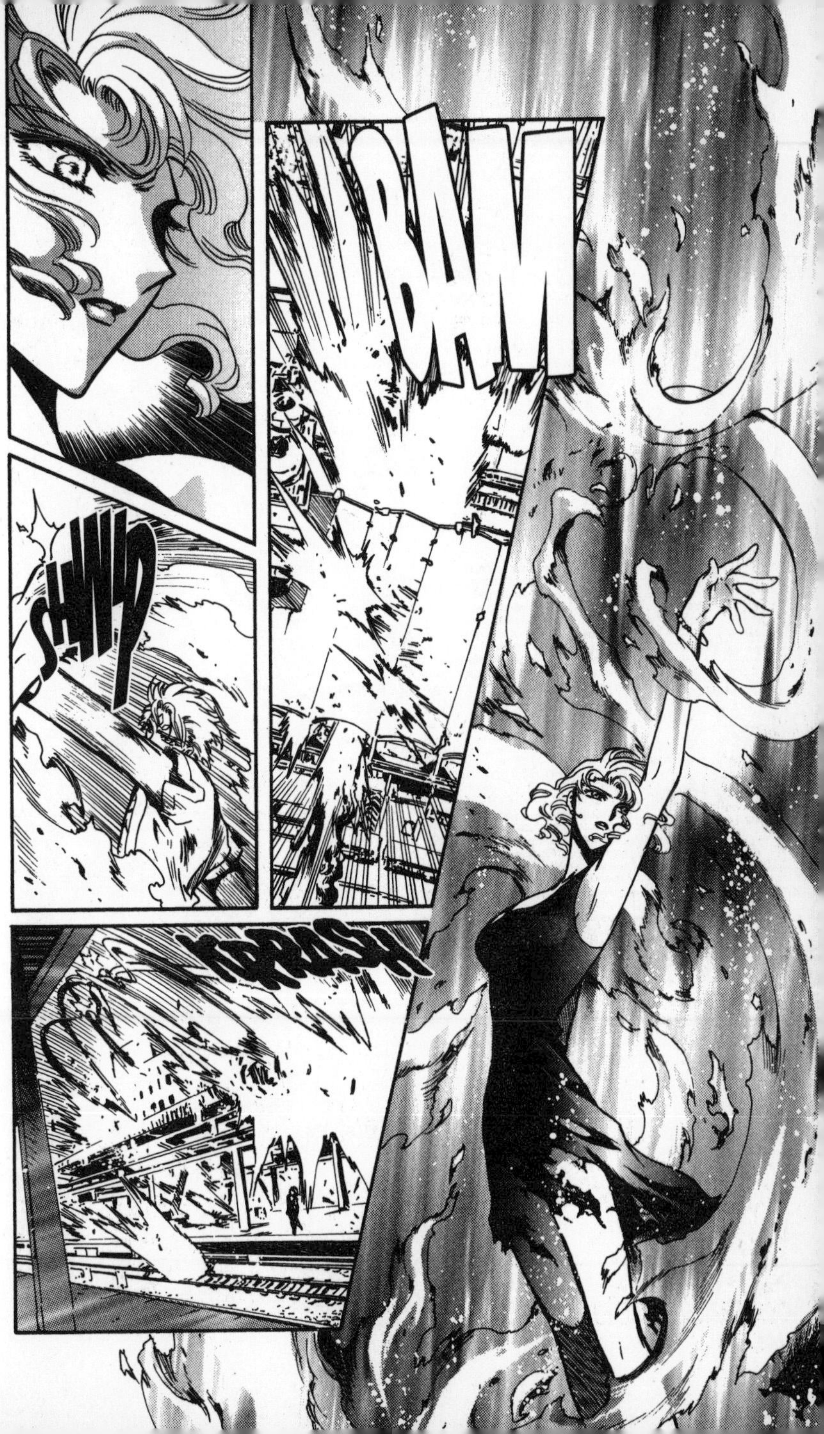
SHWP
VRAM
KRASH

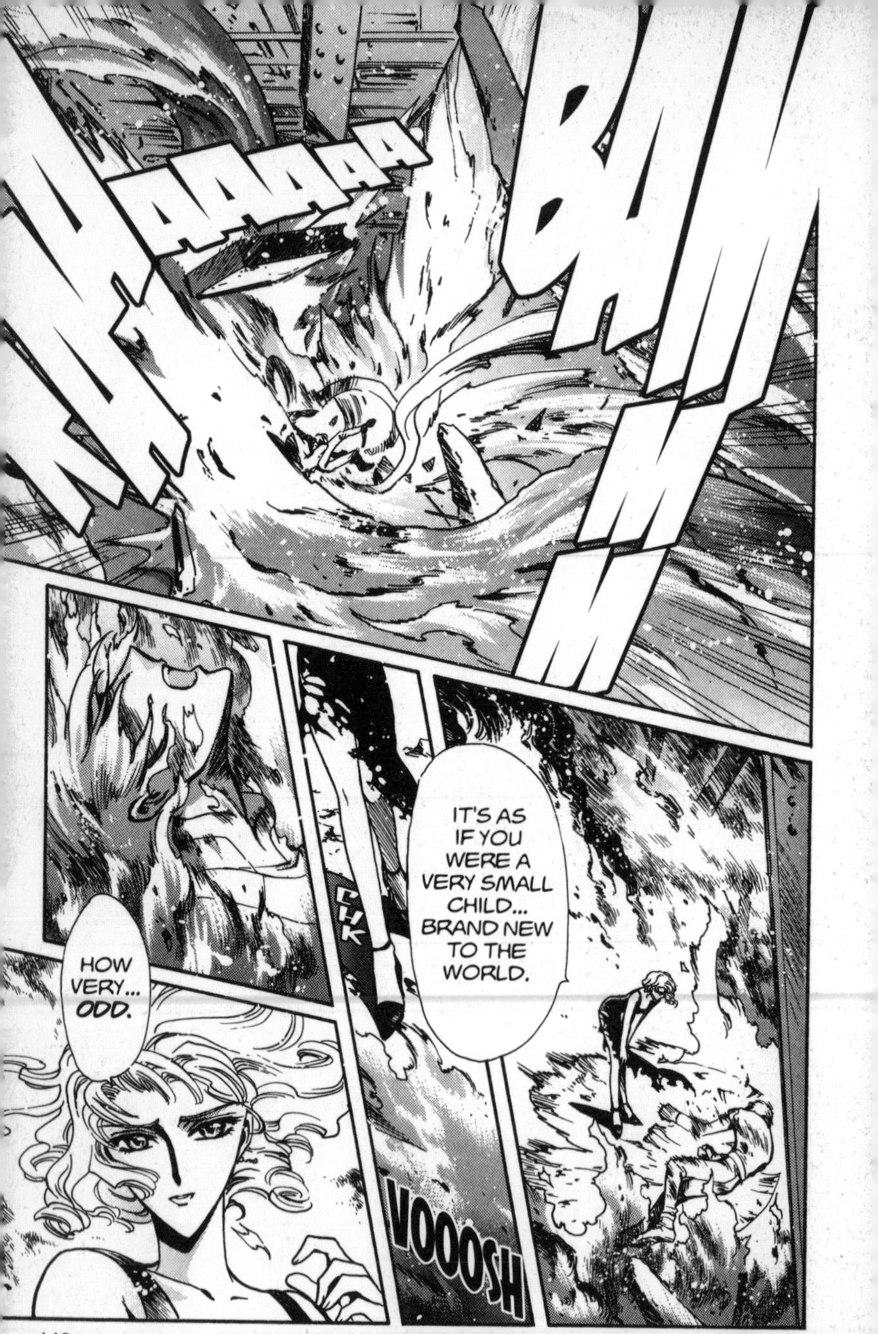
WHAAAAA
BAMMM
HOW VERY... ODD.
IT'S AS IF YOU WERE A VERY SMALL CHILD... BRAND NEW TO THE WORLD.
CHK
VOOOSH

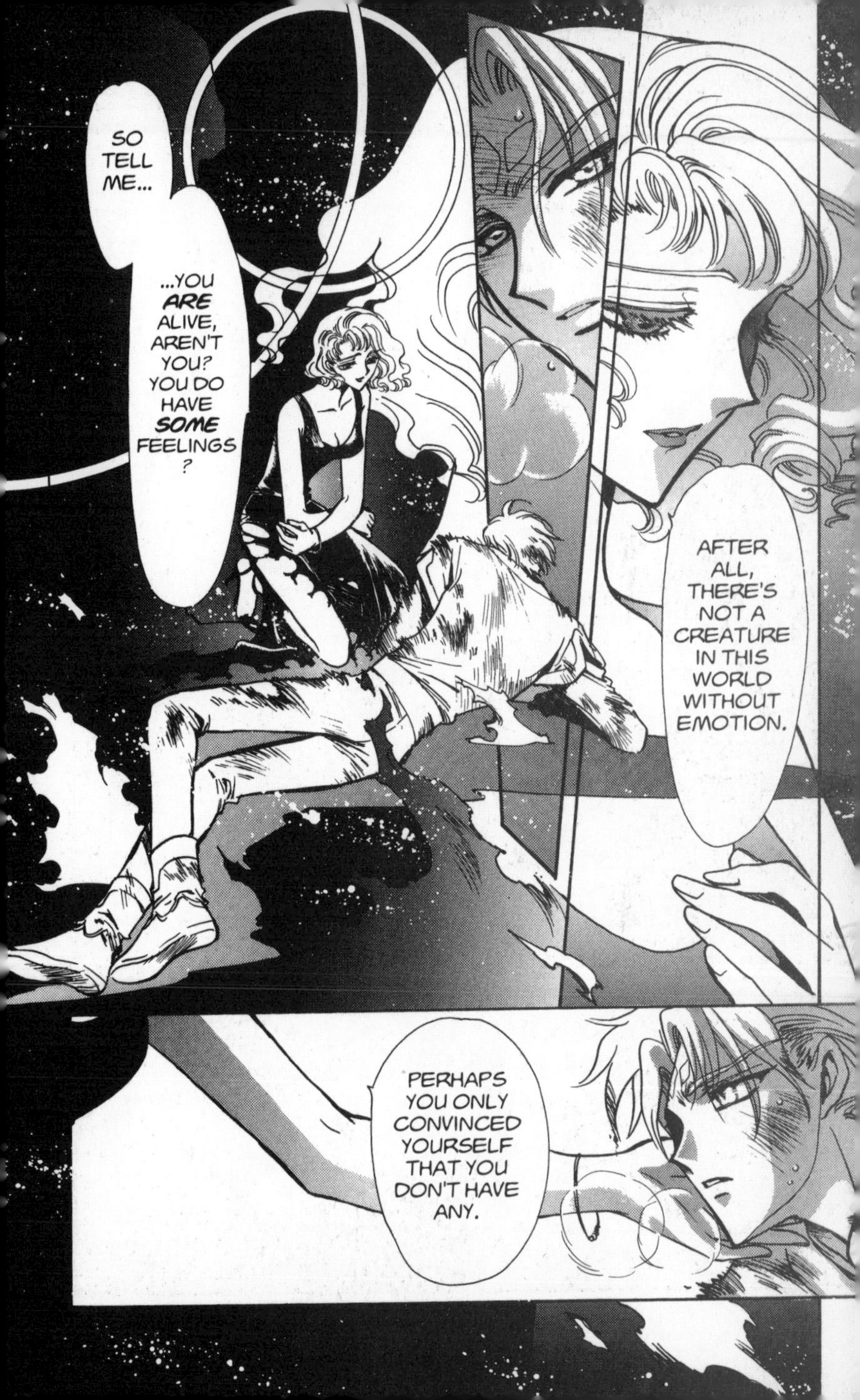
SO TELL ME...
...YOU ARE ALIVE, AREN'T YOU? YOU DO HAVE SOME FEELINGS?
AFTER ALL, THERE'S NOT A CREATURE IN THIS WORLD WITHOUT EMOTION.
PERHAPS YOU ONLY CONVINCED YOURSELF THAT YOU DON'T HAVE ANY.

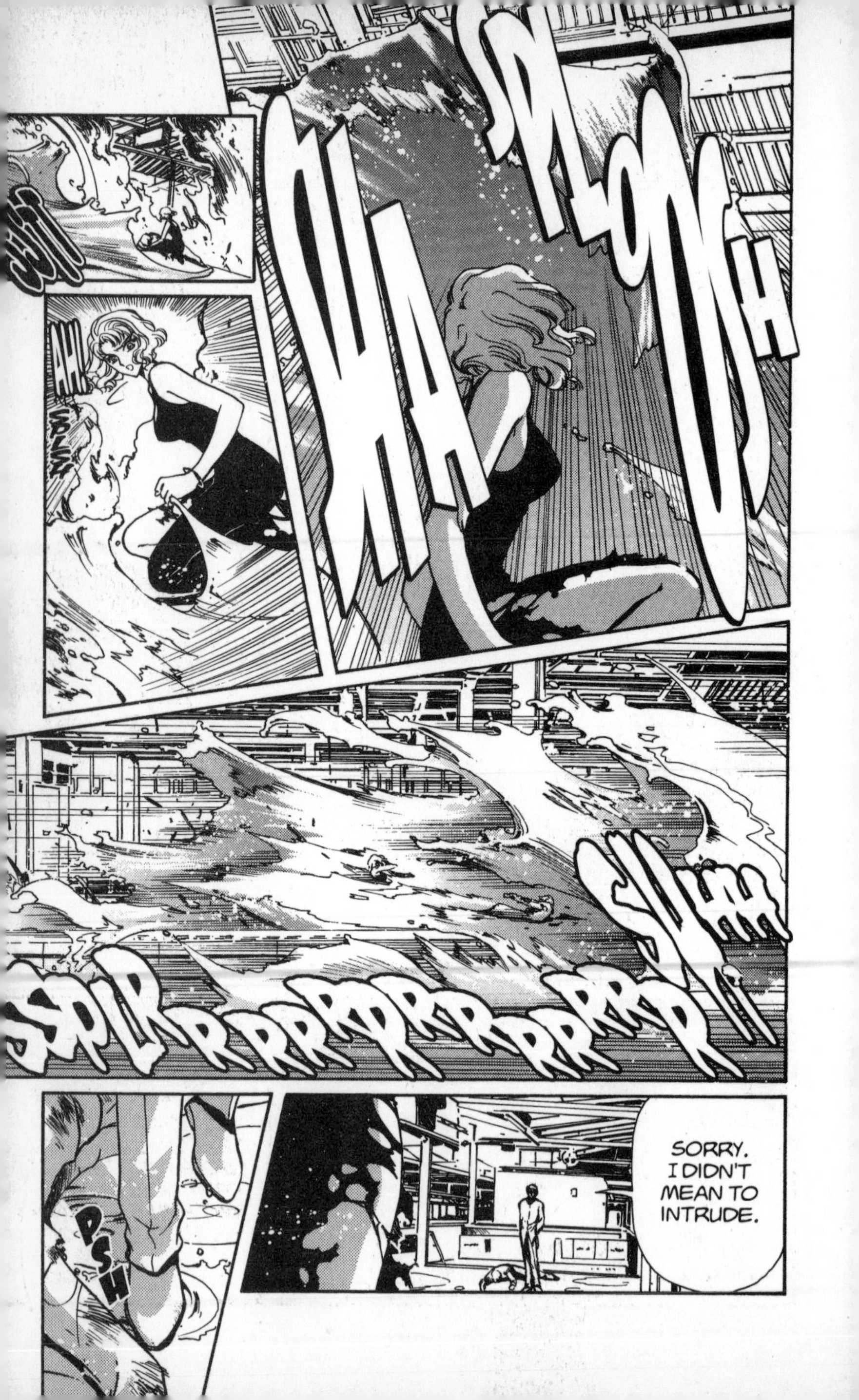
AHH
PSH
SORRY. I DIDN'T MEAN TO INTRUDE.

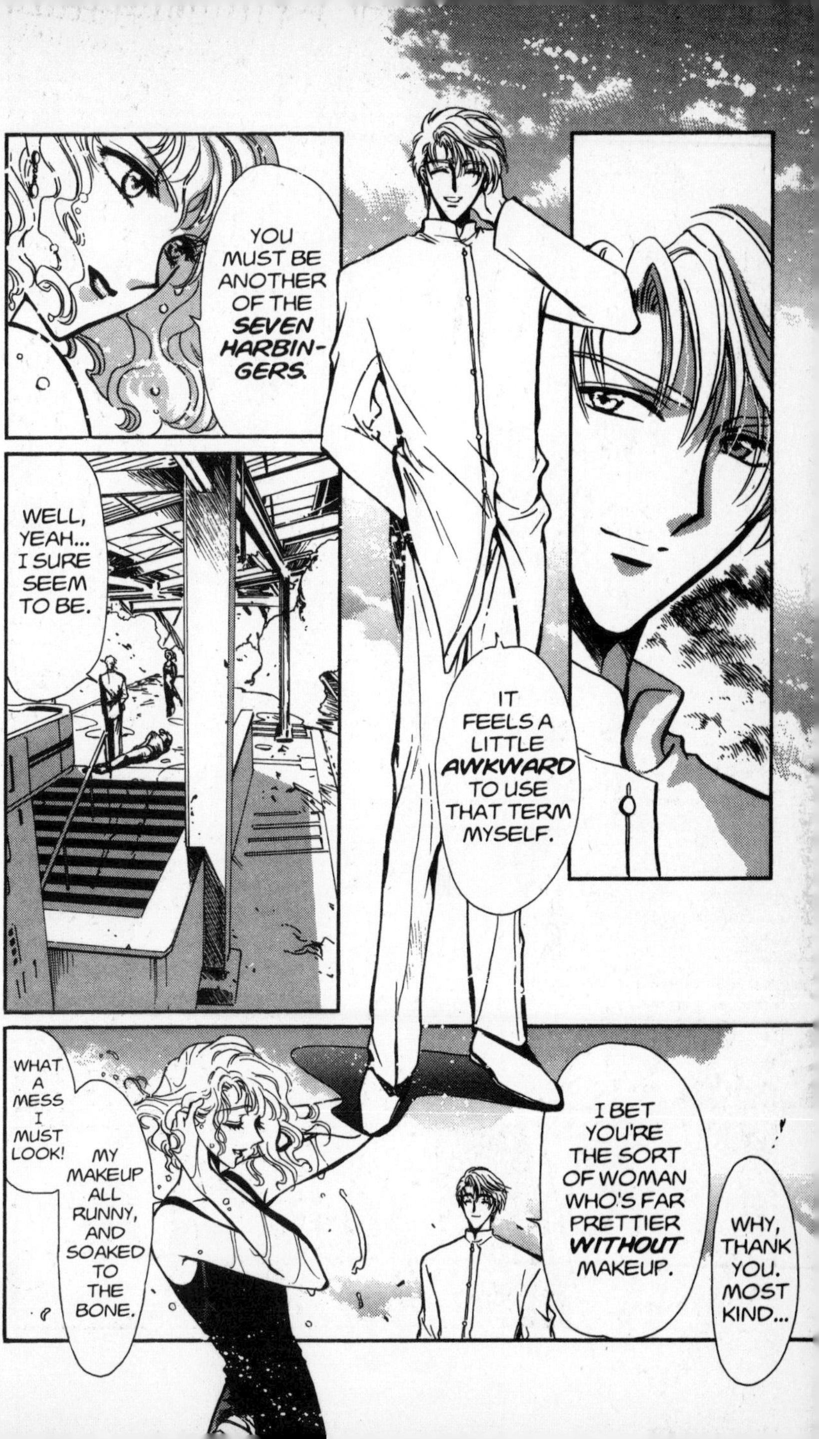
YOU MUST BE ANOTHER OF THE SEVEN HARBINGERS.
WELL, YEAH... I SURE SEEM TO BE.
IT FEELS A LITTLE AWKWARD TO USE THAT TERM MYSELF.
WHAT A MESS I MUST LOOK!
MY MAKEUP ALL RUNNY, AND SOAKED TO THE BONE.
I BET YOU'RE THE SORT OF WOMAN WHO'S FAR PRETTIER WITHOUT MAKEUP.
WHY, THANK YOU. MOST KIND...

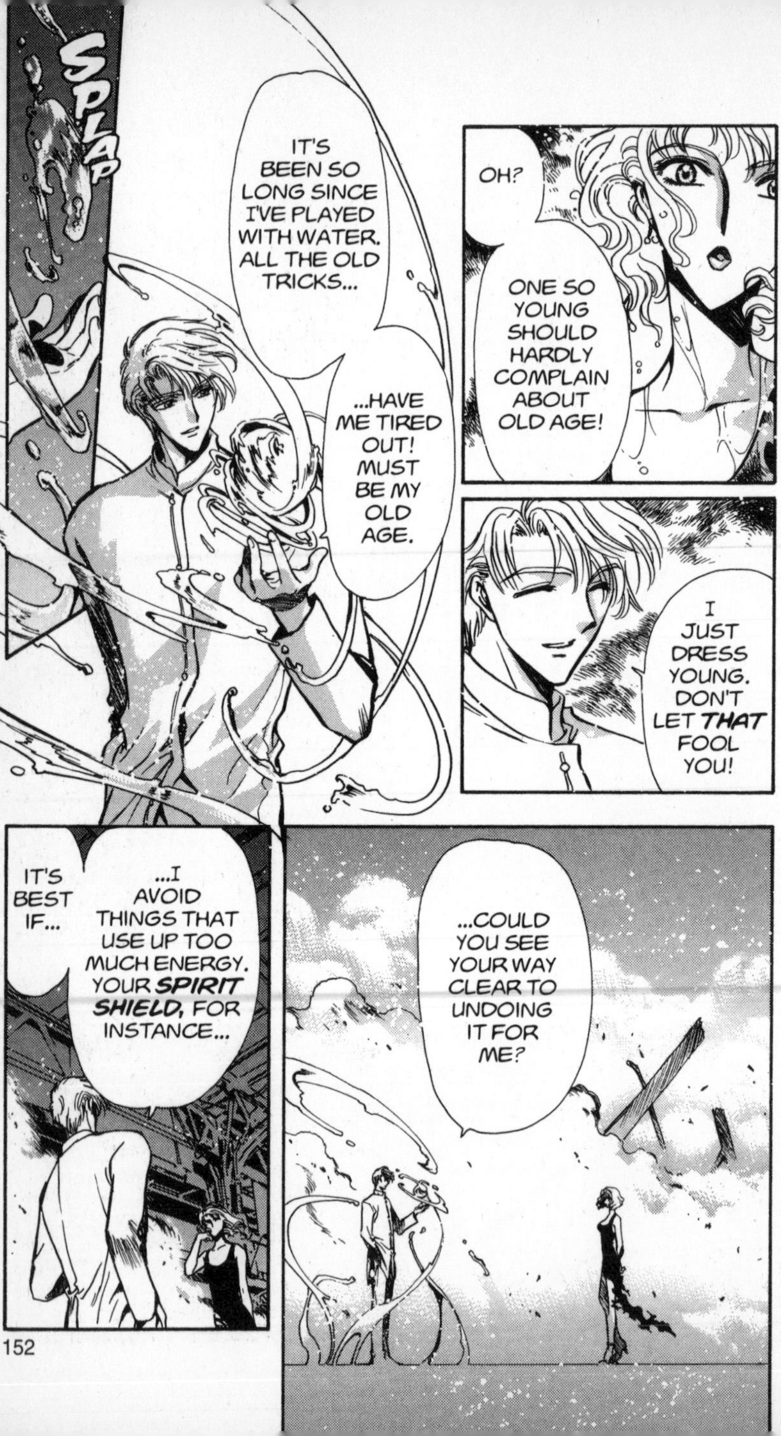
SPLAP
IT'S BEEN SO LONG SINCE I'VE PLAYED WITH WATER. ALL THE OLD TRICKS...
...HAVE ME TIRED OUT! MUST BE MY OLD AGE.
OH?
ONE SO YOUNG SHOULD HARDLY COMPLAIN ABOUT OLD AGE!
I JUST DRESS YOUNG. DON'T LET ***THAT*** FOOL YOU!
IT'S BEST IF...
...I AVOID THINGS THAT USE UP TOO MUCH ENERGY. YOUR ***SPIRIT SHIELD,*** FOR INSTANCE...
...COULD YOU SEE YOUR WAY CLEAR TO UNDOING IT FOR ME?

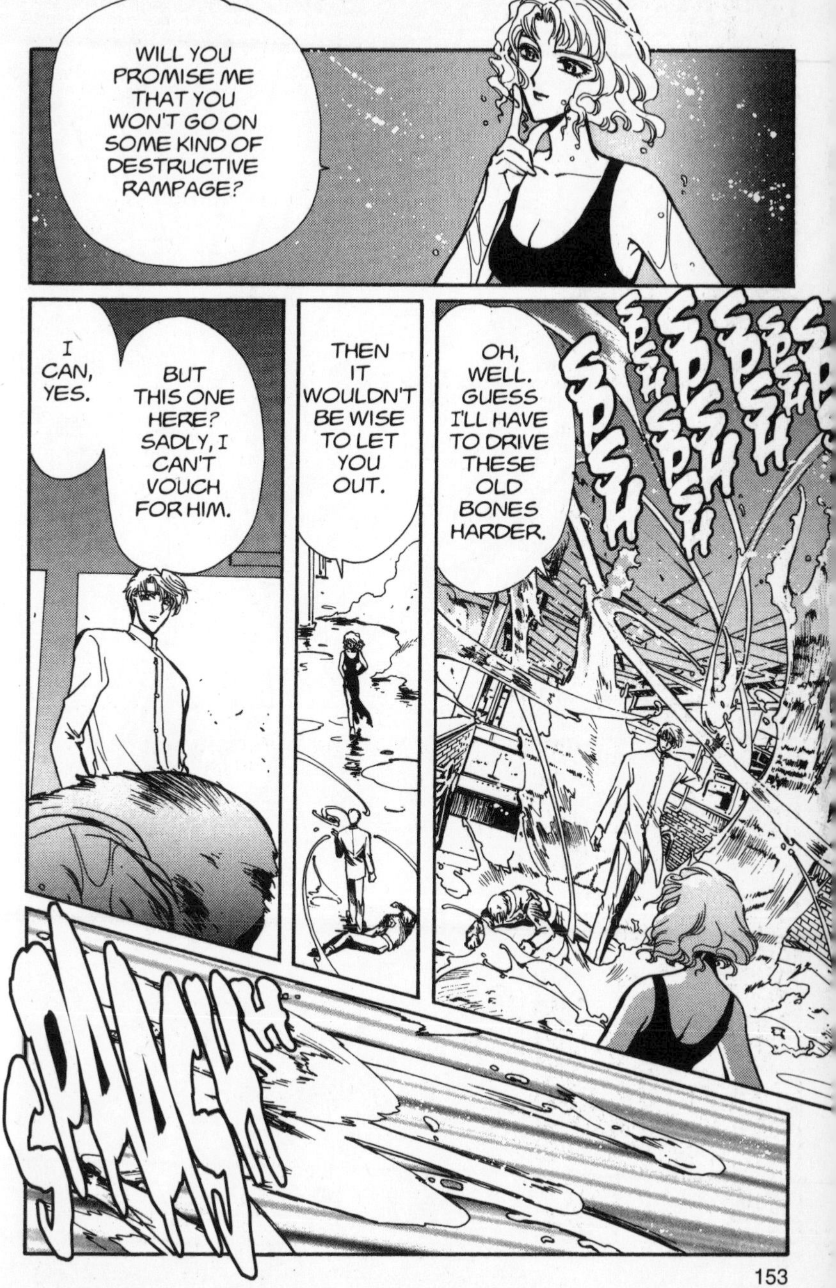
WILL YOU PROMISE ME THAT YOU WON'T GO ON SOME KIND OF DESTRUCTIVE RAMPAGE?
I CAN, YES.
BUT THIS ONE HERE? SADLY, I CAN'T VOUCH FOR HIM.
THEN IT WOULDN'T BE WISE TO LET YOU OUT.
OH, WELL. GUESS I'LL HAVE TO DRIVE THESE OLD BONES HARDER.
SPSH SPSH SPSH SPSH SPSH SPSH

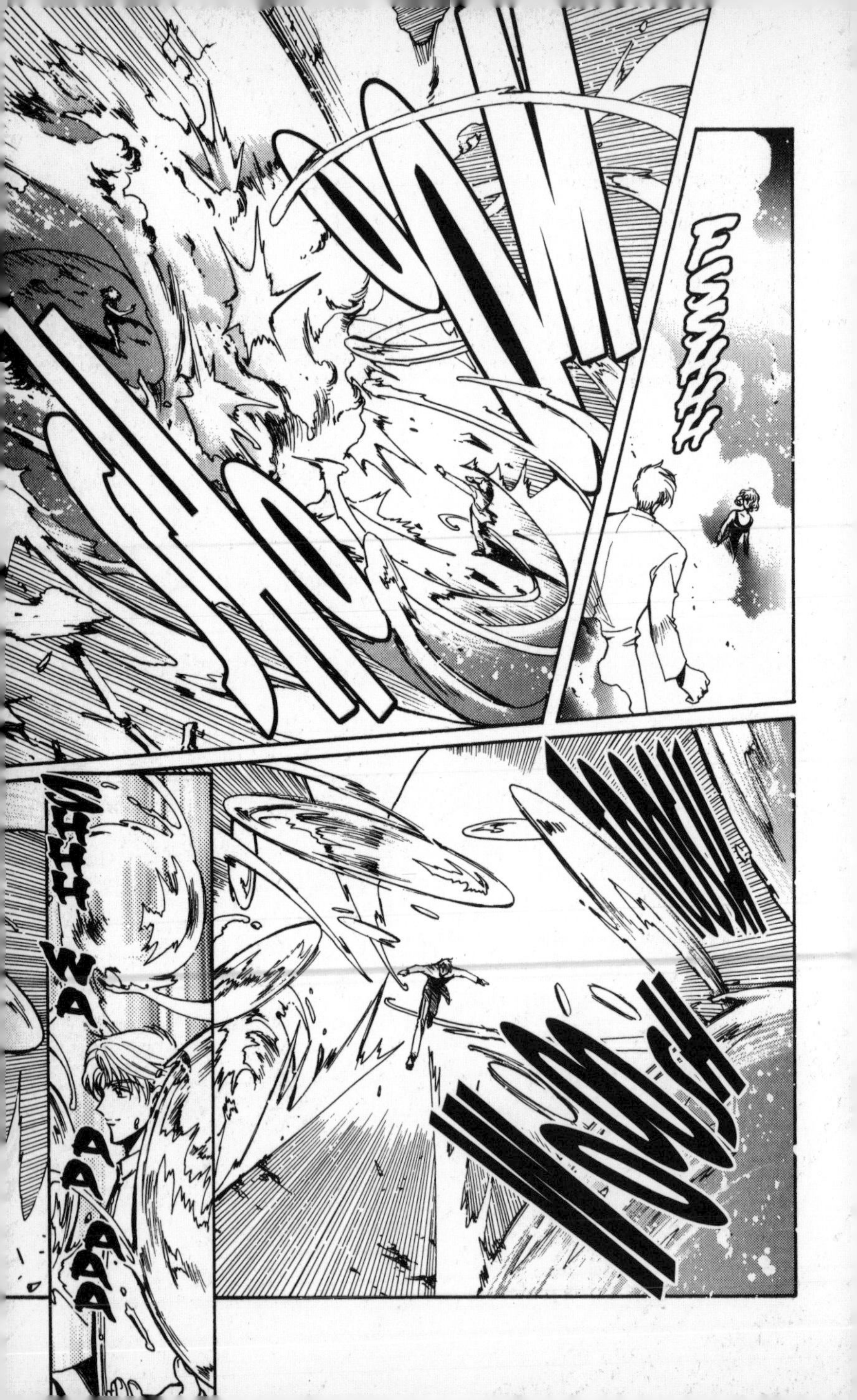
FWSHHH
WHOOSH

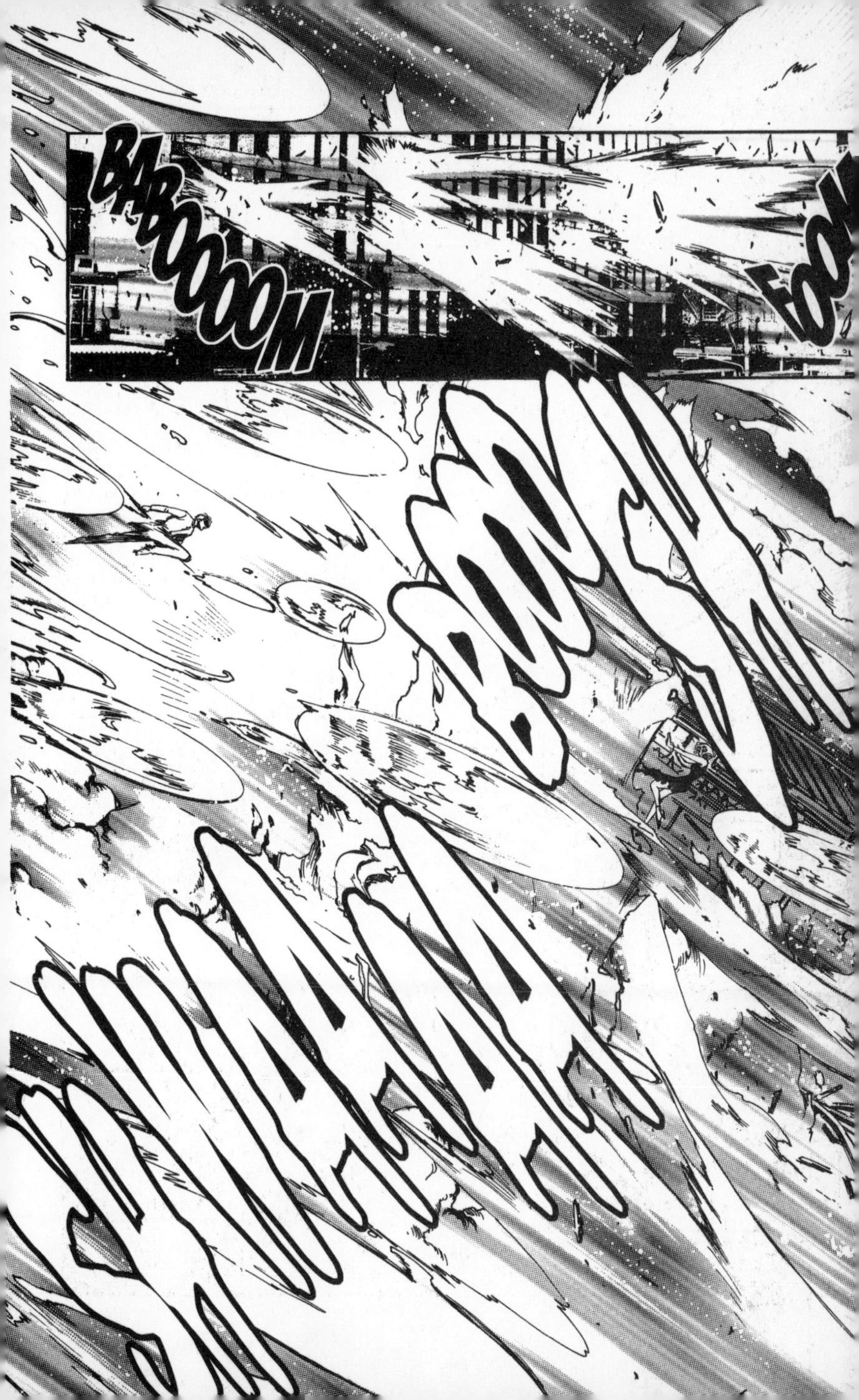
BABOOOOM

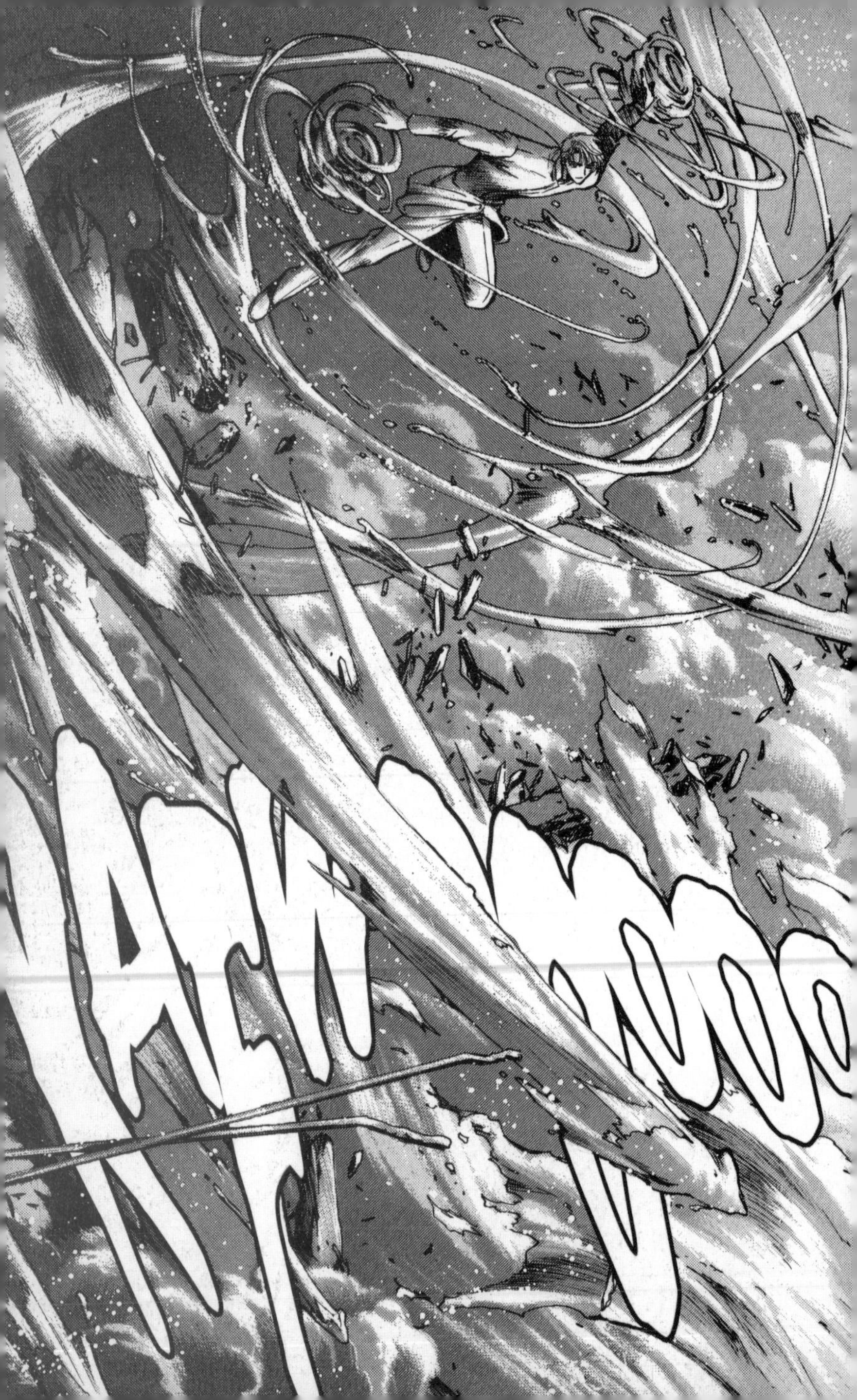

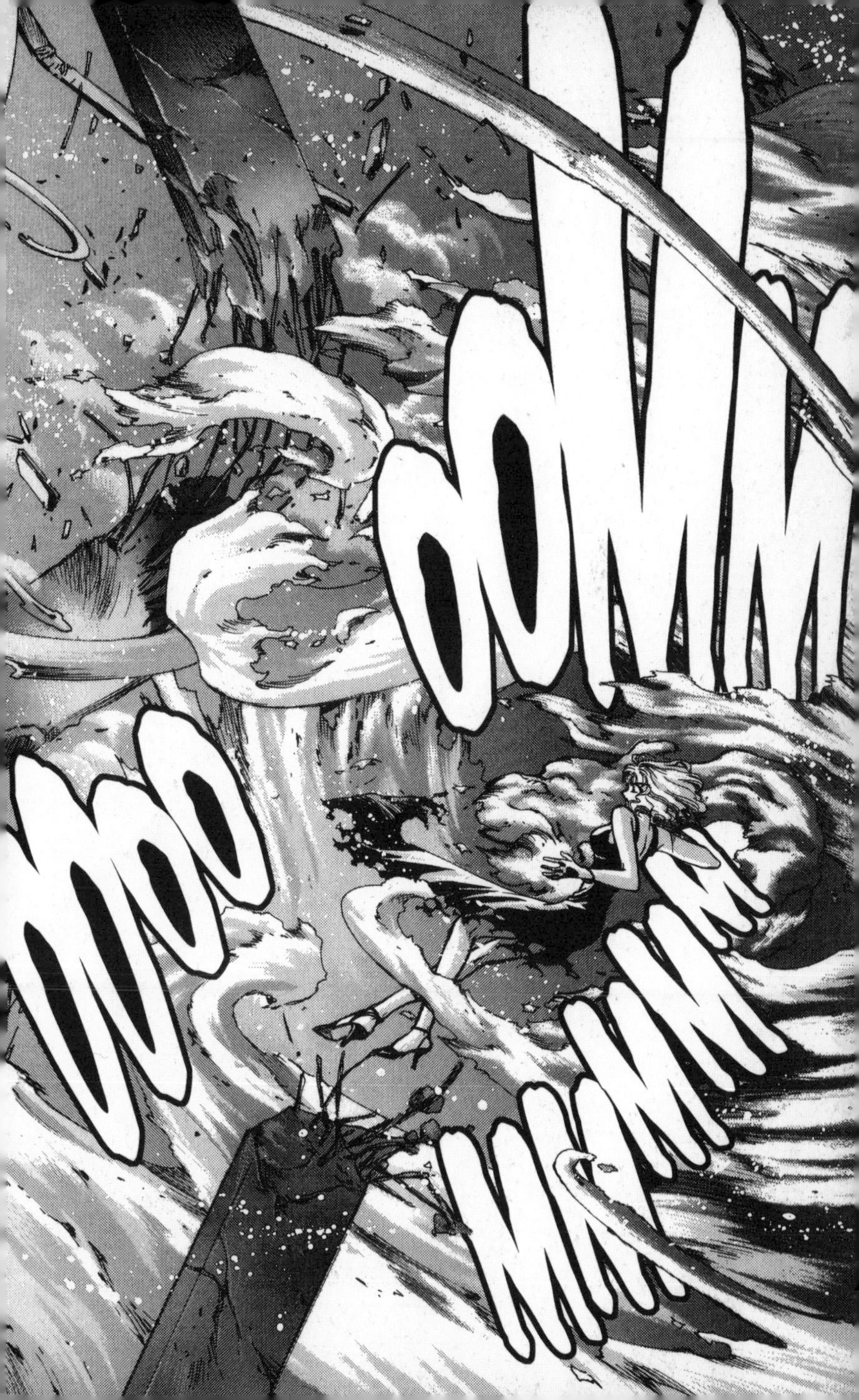

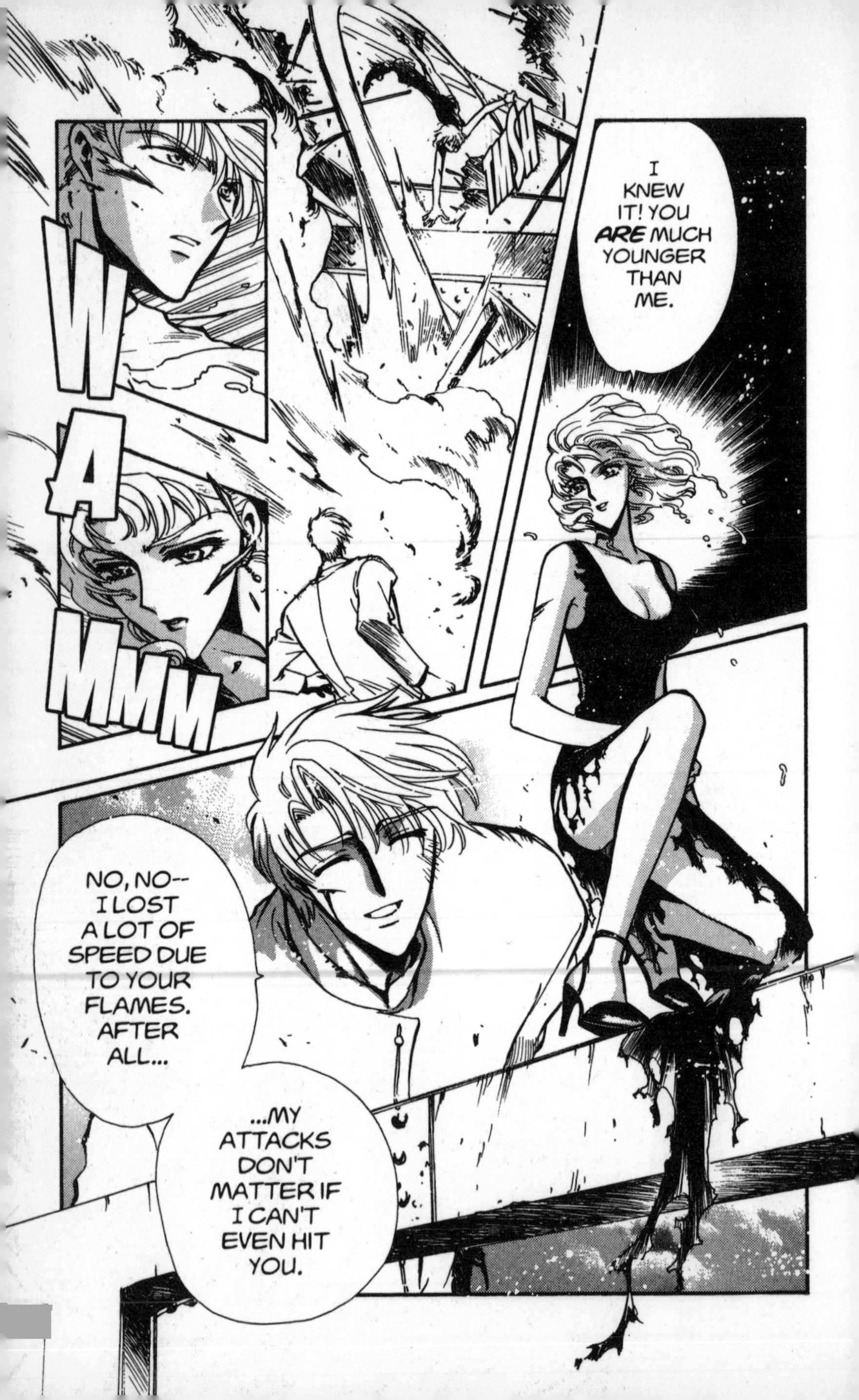

WAMMM
I KNEW IT! YOU ARE MUCH YOUNGER THAN ME.
NO, NO-- I LOST A LOT OF SPEED DUE TO YOUR FLAMES. AFTER ALL...
...MY ATTACKS DON'T MATTER IF I CAN'T EVEN HIT YOU.

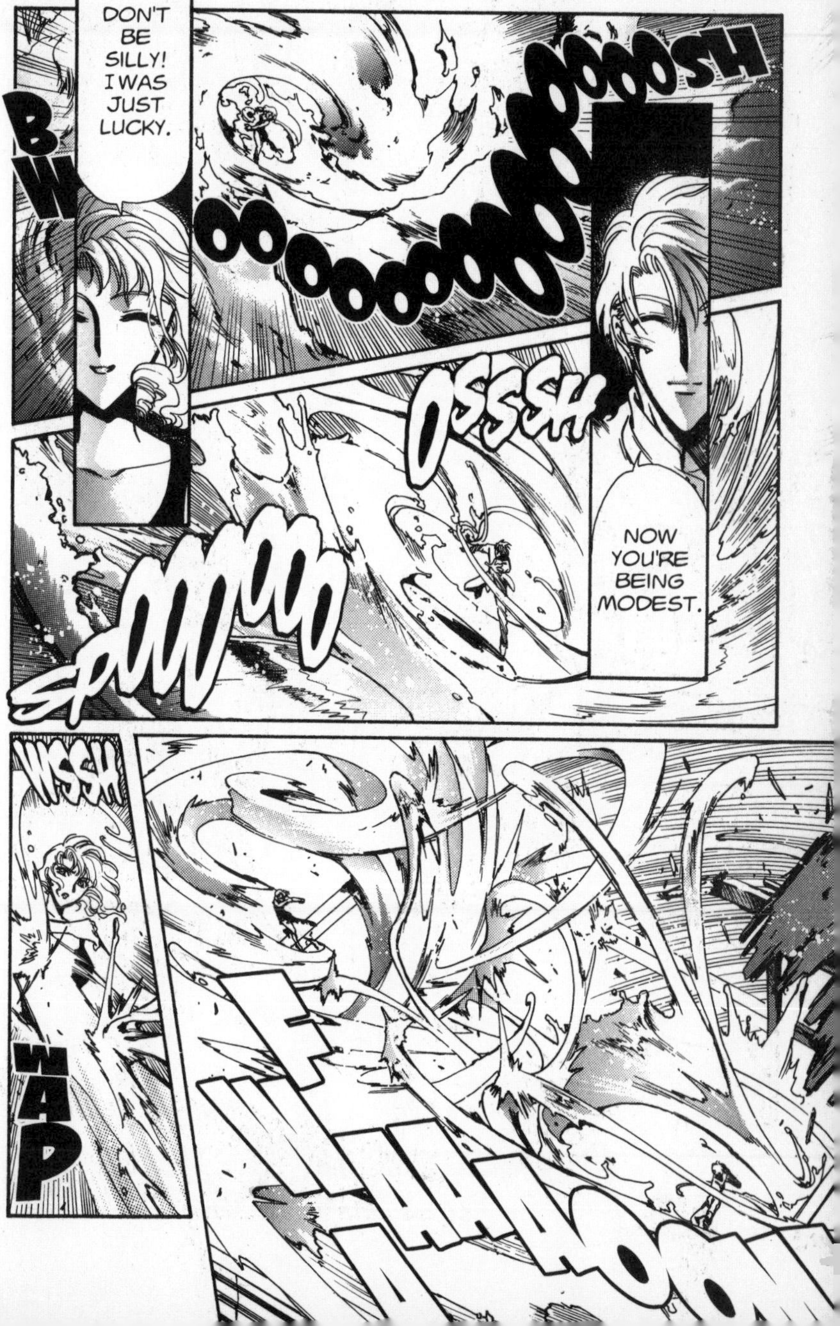
DON'T BE SILLY! I WAS JUST LUCKY.
NOW YOU'RE BEING MODEST.
OSSSH
WSSH
WAP

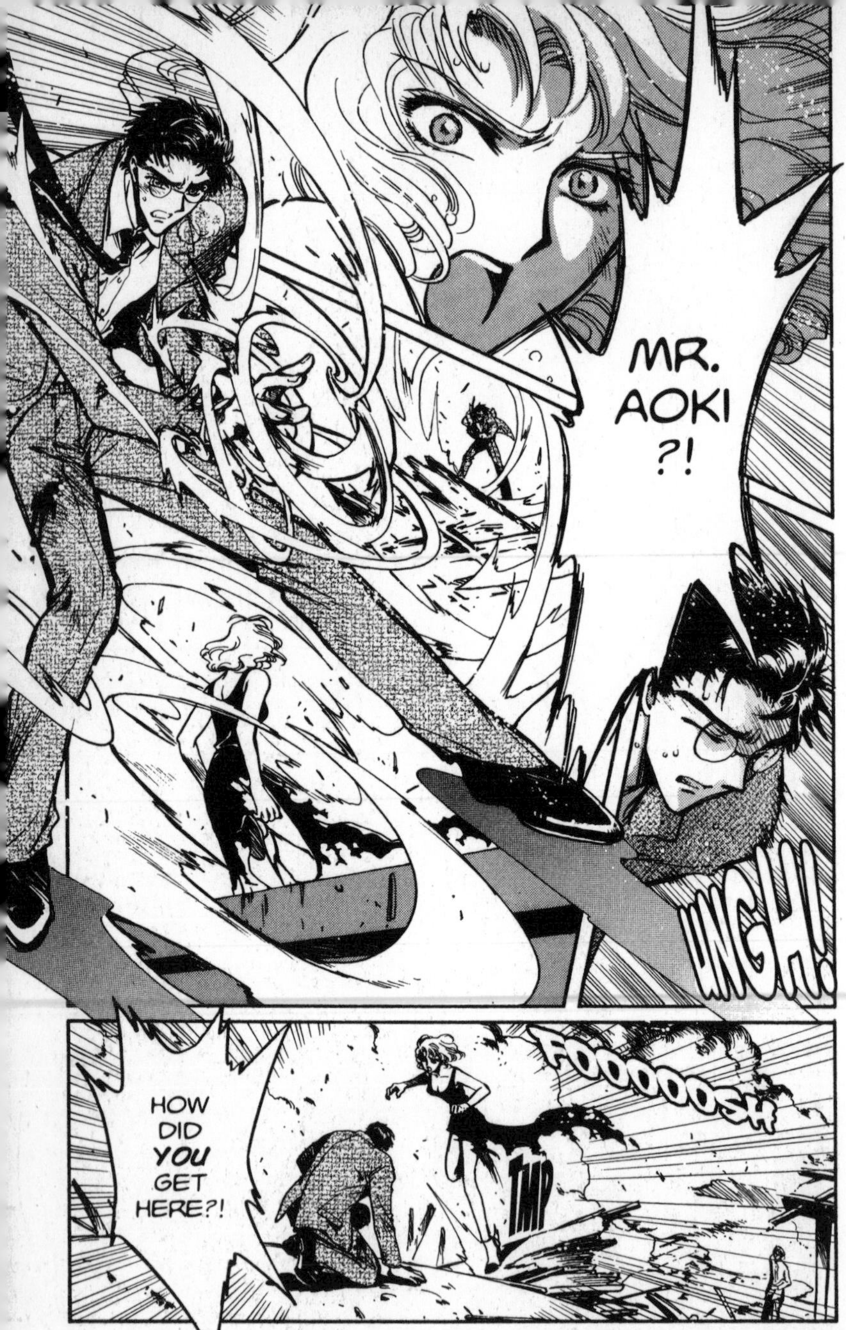
MR. AOKI ?!
UNGH!!
HOW DID *YOU* GET HERE?!
FOOOOOSH
TMP

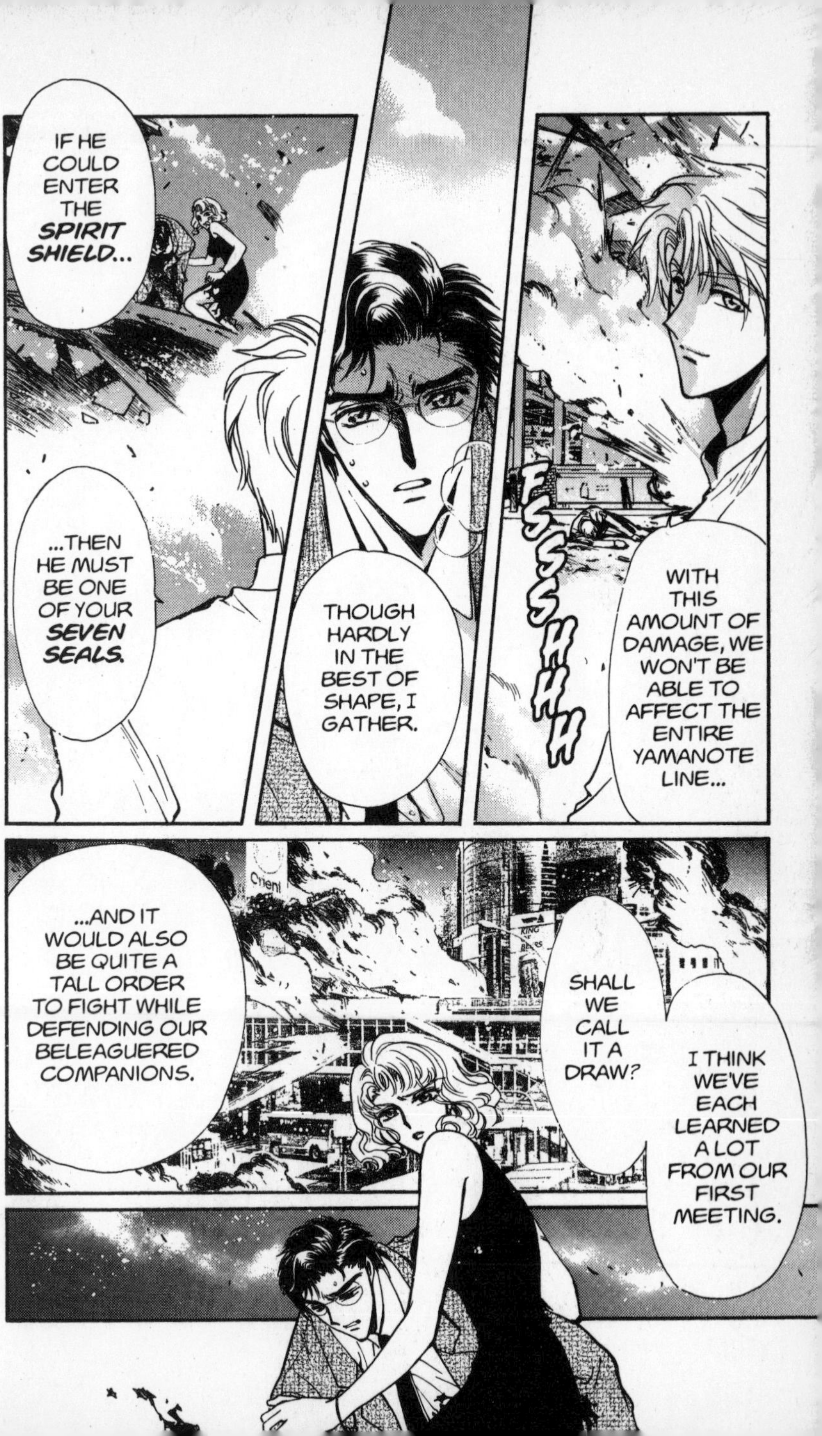
IF HE COULD ENTER THE SPIRIT SHIELD...
...THEN HE MUST BE ONE OF YOUR SEVEN SEALS.
THOUGH HARDLY IN THE BEST OF SHAPE, I GATHER.
FSSSHHH
WITH THIS AMOUNT OF DAMAGE, WE WON'T BE ABLE TO AFFECT THE ENTIRE YAMANOTE LINE...
...AND IT WOULD ALSO BE QUITE A TALL ORDER TO FIGHT WHILE DEFENDING OUR BELEAGUERED COMPANIONS.
SHALL WE CALL IT A DRAW?
I THINK WE'VE EACH LEARNED A LOT FROM OUR FIRST MEETING.

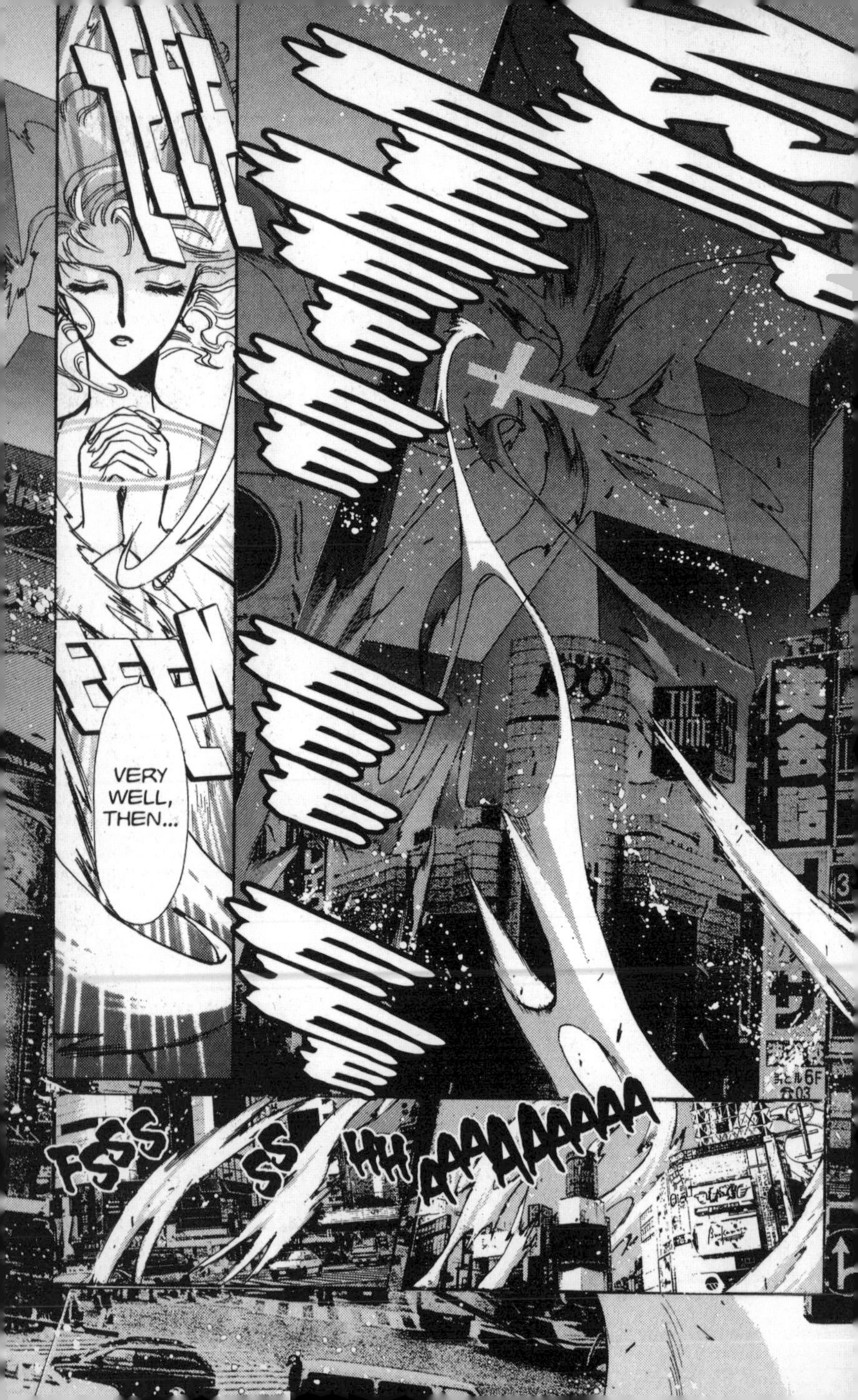
VERY WELL, THEN...
FSSS SS HH AAAAAAAAAA

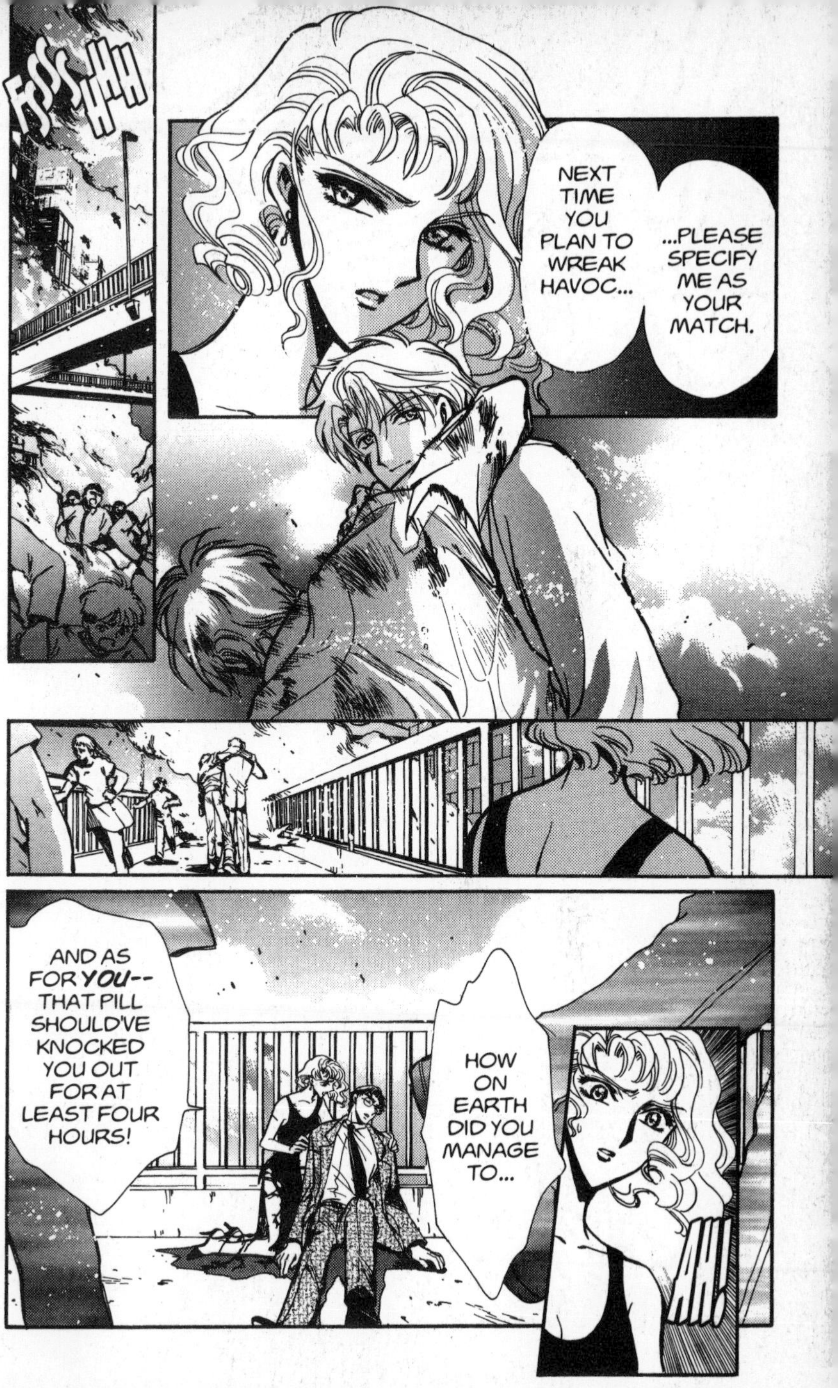
FSSSHHH
NEXT TIME YOU PLAN TO WREAK HAVOC...
...PLEASE SPECIFY ME AS YOUR MATCH.
AND AS FOR *YOU*-- THAT PILL SHOULD'VE KNOCKED YOU OUT FOR AT LEAST FOUR HOURS!
HOW ON EARTH DID YOU MANAGE TO...
AH!

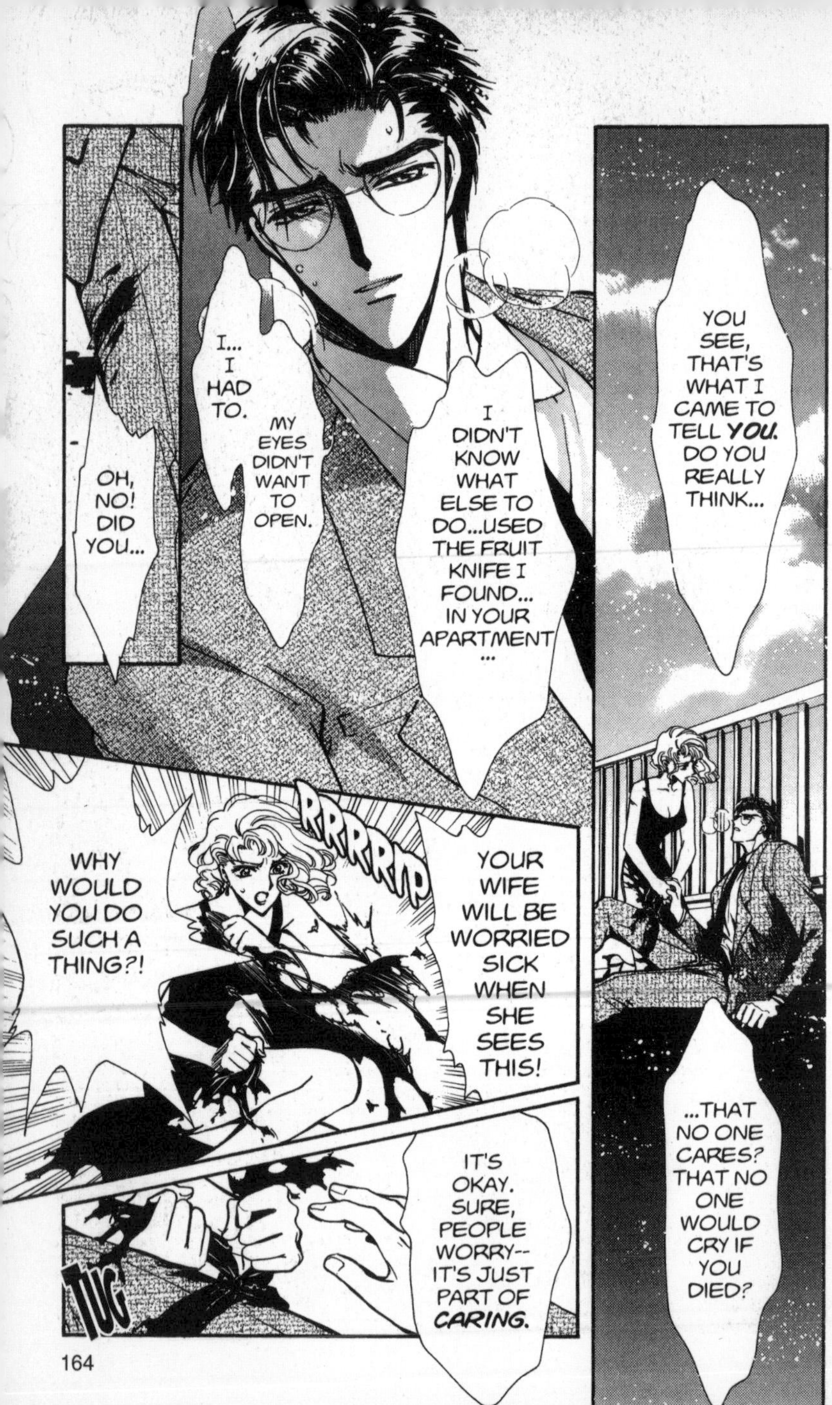
OH, NO! DID YOU...
I... I HAD TO.
MY EYES DIDN'T WANT TO OPEN.
I DIDN'T KNOW WHAT ELSE TO DO...USED THE FRUIT KNIFE I FOUND... IN YOUR APARTMENT...
WHY WOULD YOU DO SUCH A THING?!
RRRRRIP
YOUR WIFE WILL BE WORRIED SICK WHEN SHE SEES THIS!
TUG
IT'S OKAY. SURE, PEOPLE WORRY-- IT'S JUST PART OF ***CARING.***
YOU SEE, THAT'S WHAT I CAME TO TELL ***YOU.*** DO YOU REALLY THINK...
...THAT NO ONE CARES? THAT NO ONE WOULD CRY IF YOU DIED?

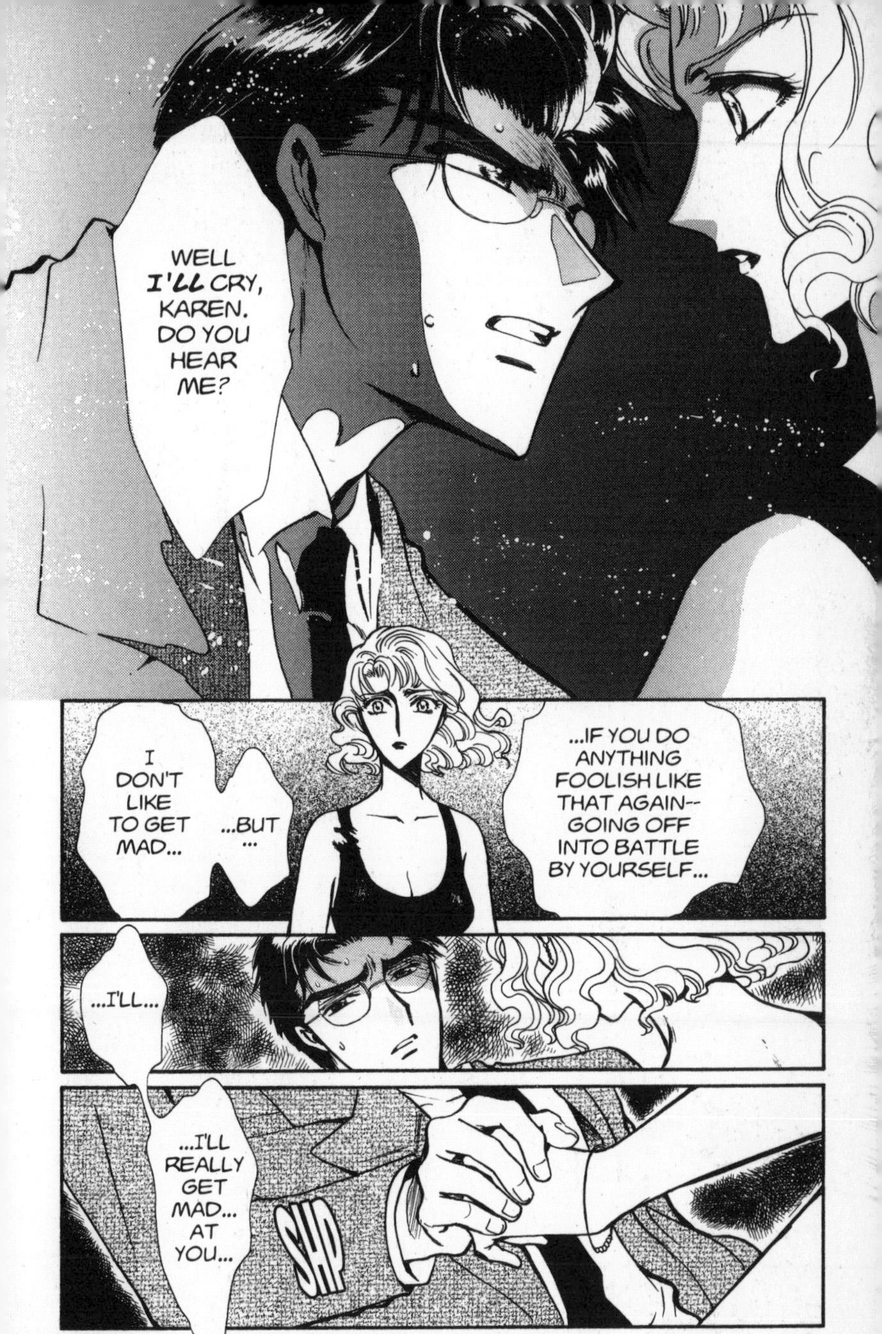
WELL I'LL CRY, KAREN. DO YOU HEAR ME?
I DON'T LIKE TO GET MAD...
...BUT ...
...IF YOU DO ANYTHING FOOLISH LIKE THAT AGAIN-- GOING OFF INTO BATTLE BY YOURSELF...
...I'LL...
...I'LL REALLY GET MAD... AT YOU...
SHP

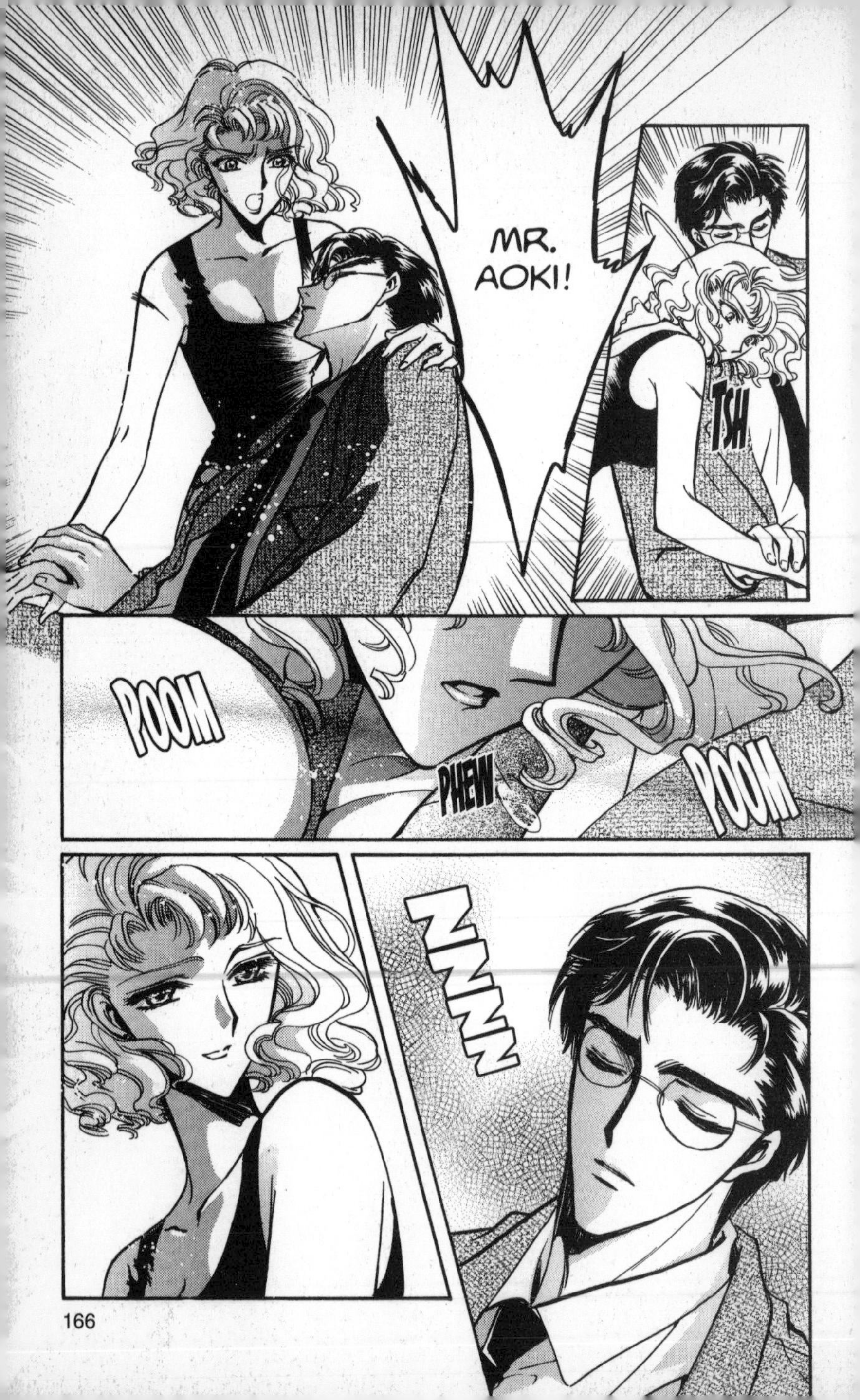
MR. AOKI!
TSH
POOM
PHEW
POOM
NNNN

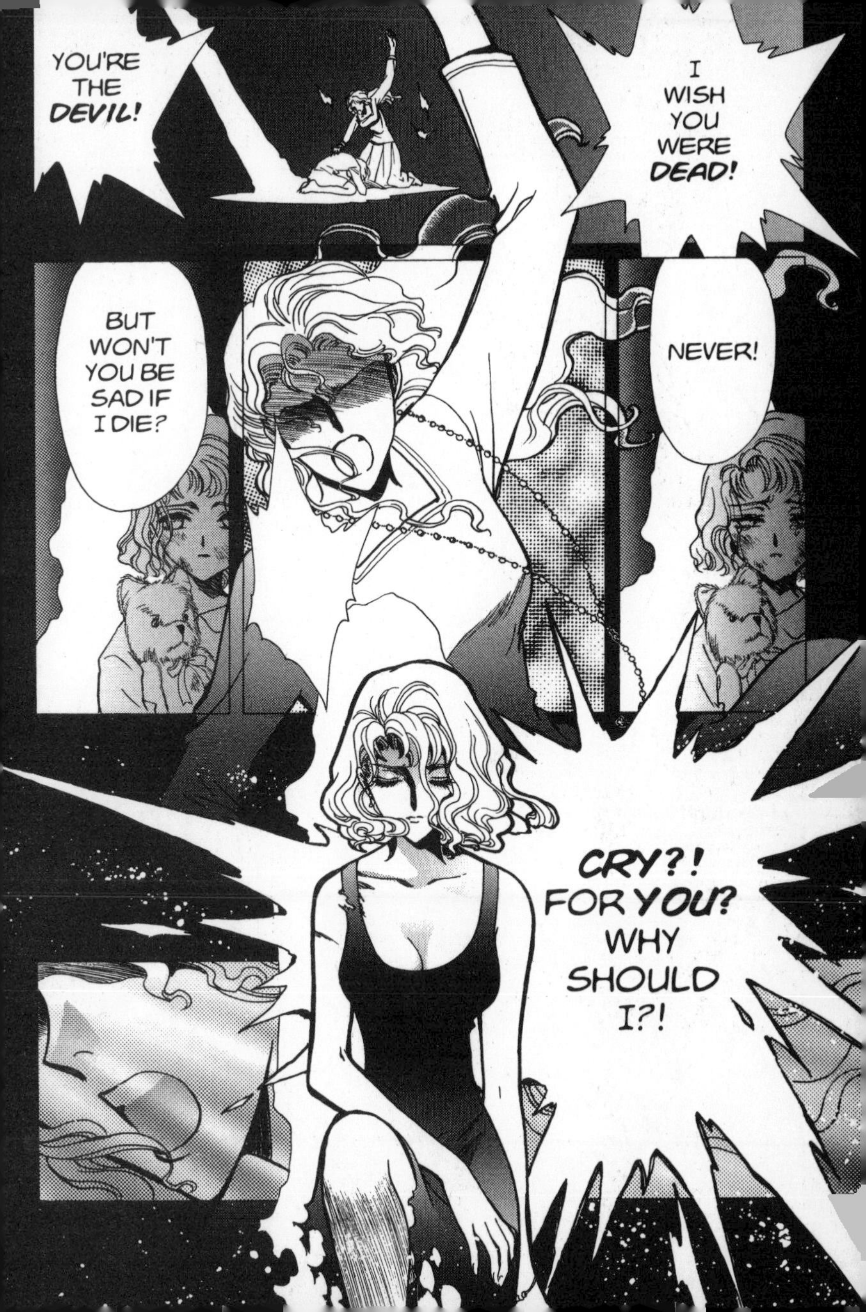
YOU'RE THE DEVIL!
I WISH YOU WERE DEAD!
BUT WON'T YOU BE SAD IF I DIE?
NEVER!
CRY?! FOR YOU? WHY SHOULD I?!

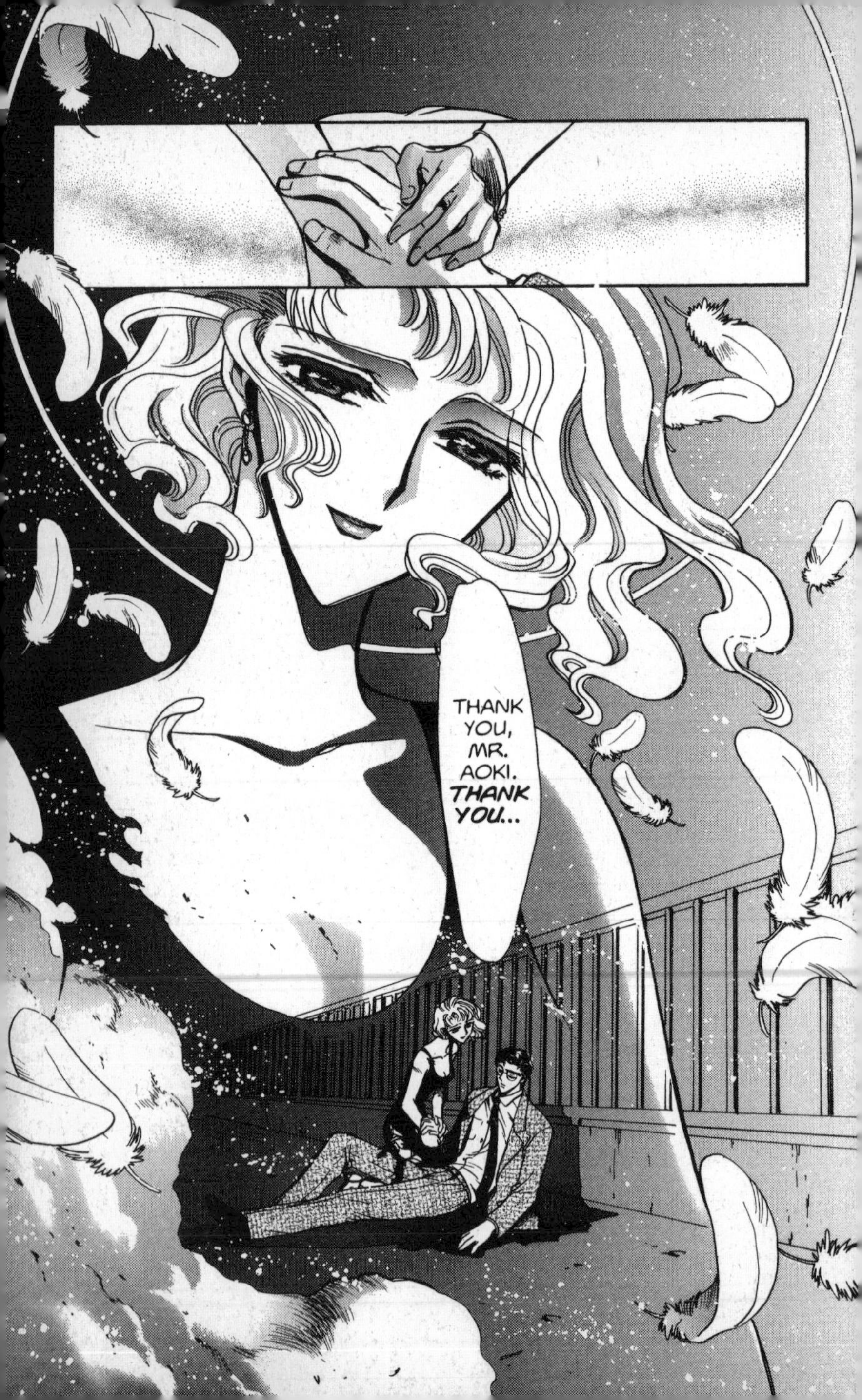
THANK YOU, MR. AOKI. *THANK YOU...*

X/1999™

X

KAREN KASUMI

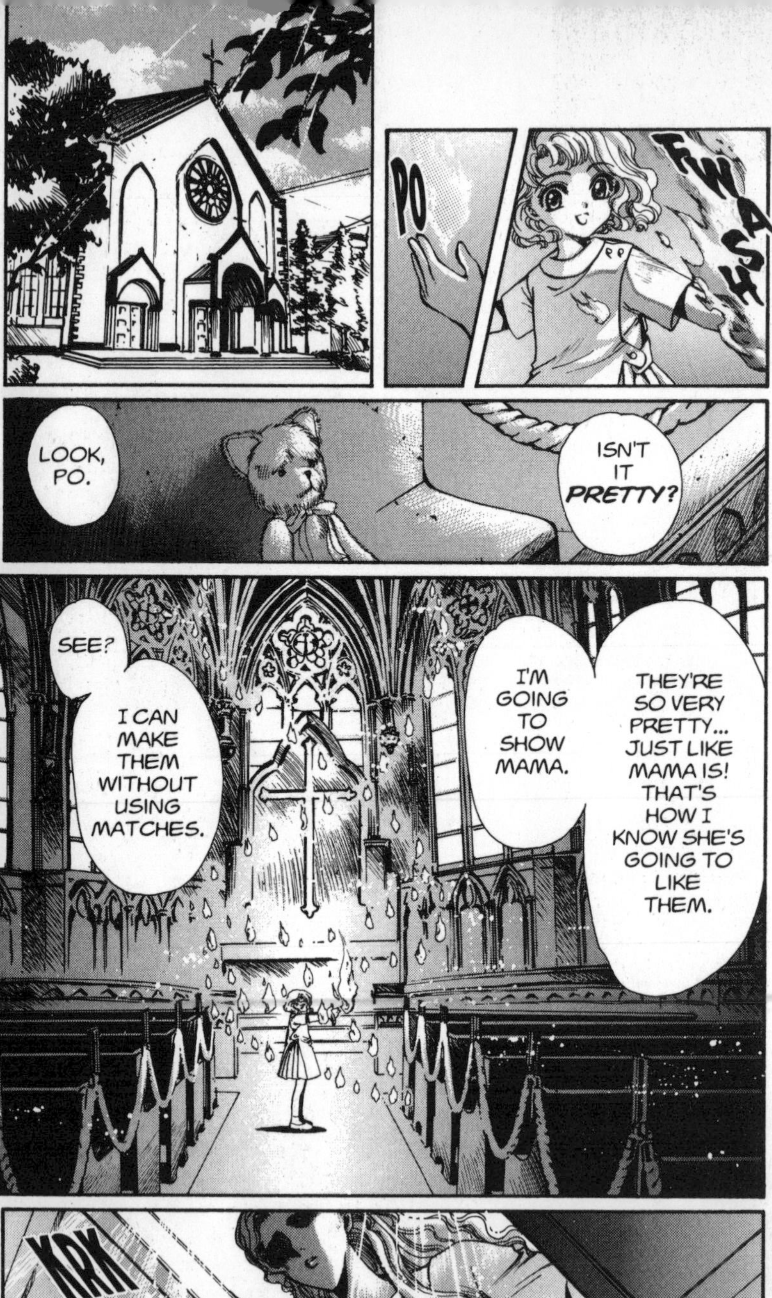
PO
FWASH
LOOK, PO.
ISN'T IT *PRETTY?*
SEE?
I CAN MAKE THEM WITHOUT USING MATCHES.
I'M GOING TO SHOW MAMA.
THEY'RE SO VERY PRETTY... JUST LIKE MAMA IS! THAT'S HOW I KNOW SHE'S GOING TO LIKE THEM.
KRK

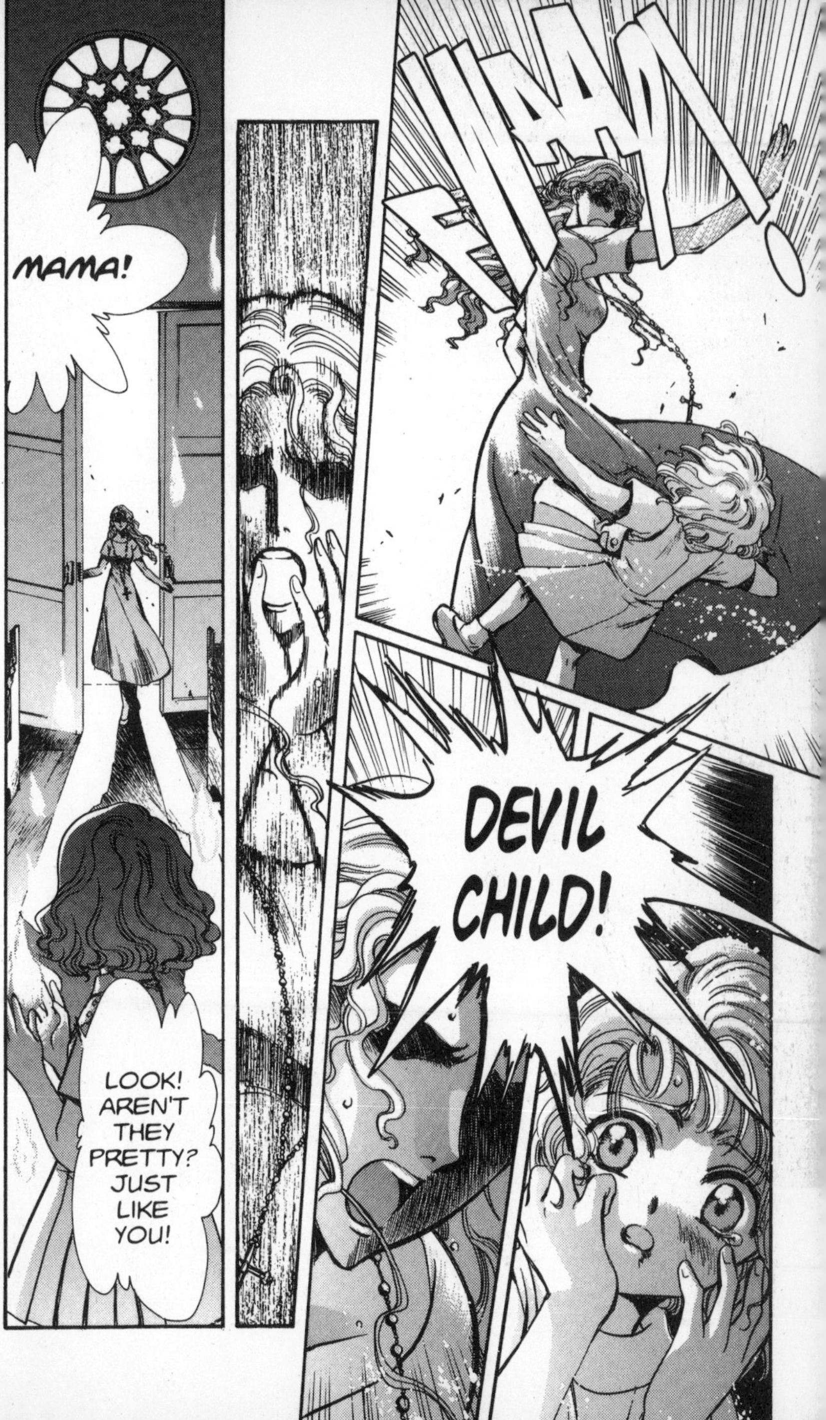
MAMA!
LOOK! AREN'T THEY PRETTY? JUST LIKE YOU!
WHAP!
DEVIL CHILD!

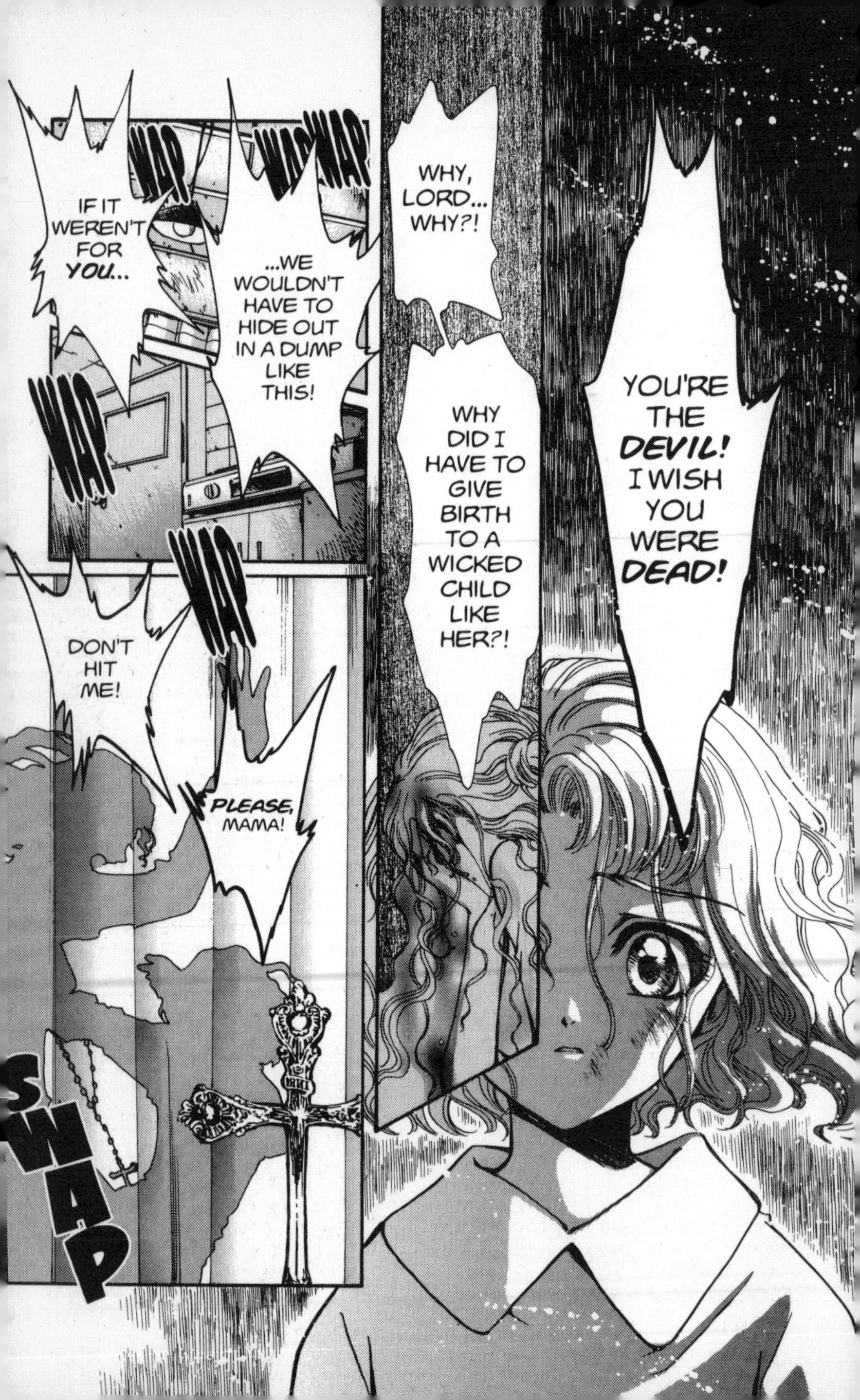

IF IT WEREN'T FOR YOU...
WAP
WAP WAP
...WE WOULDN'T HAVE TO HIDE OUT IN A DUMP LIKE THIS!
WAP
WAP
DON'T HIT ME!
PLEASE, MAMA!
SWAP
WHY, LORD... WHY?!
WHY DID I HAVE TO GIVE BIRTH TO A WICKED CHILD LIKE HER?!
YOU'RE THE DEVIL! I WISH YOU WERE DEAD!

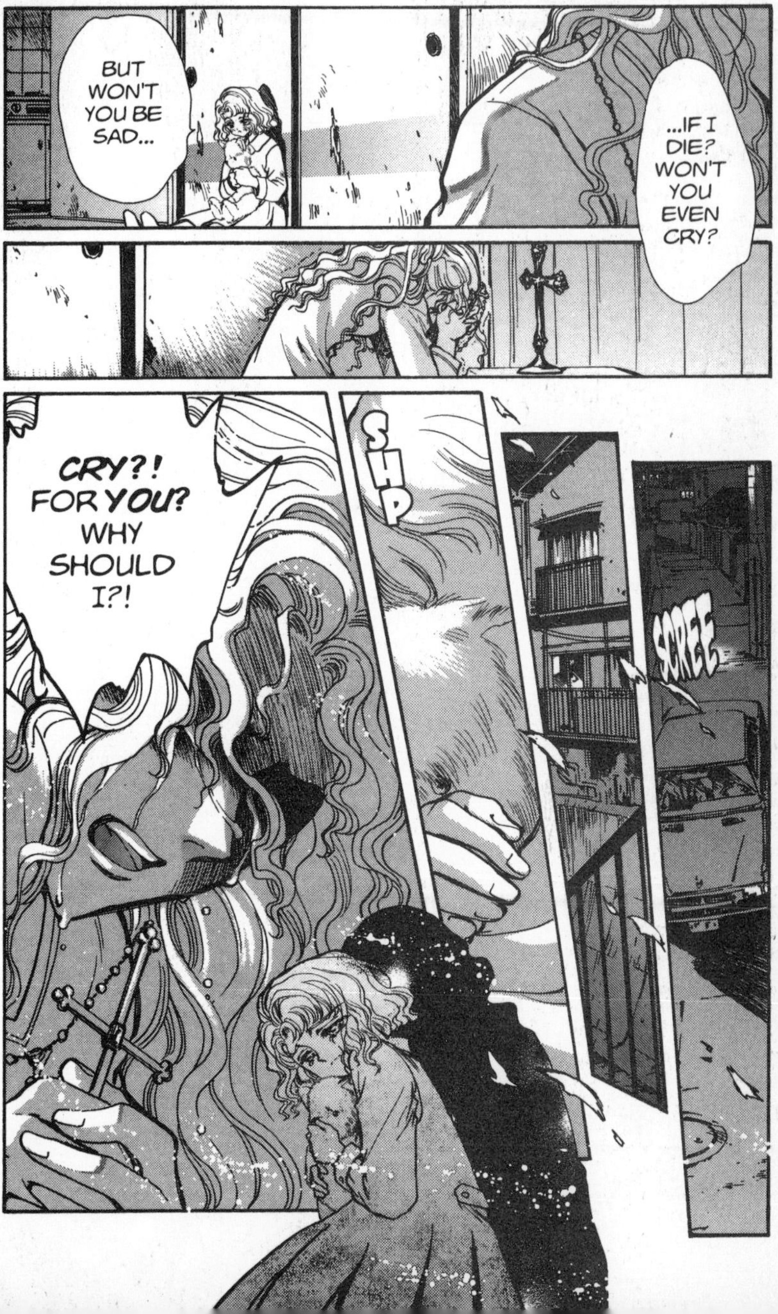
BUT WON'T YOU BE SAD...
...IF I DIE? WON'T YOU EVEN CRY?
CRY?! FOR YOU? WHY SHOULD I?!
SHP
SCREE

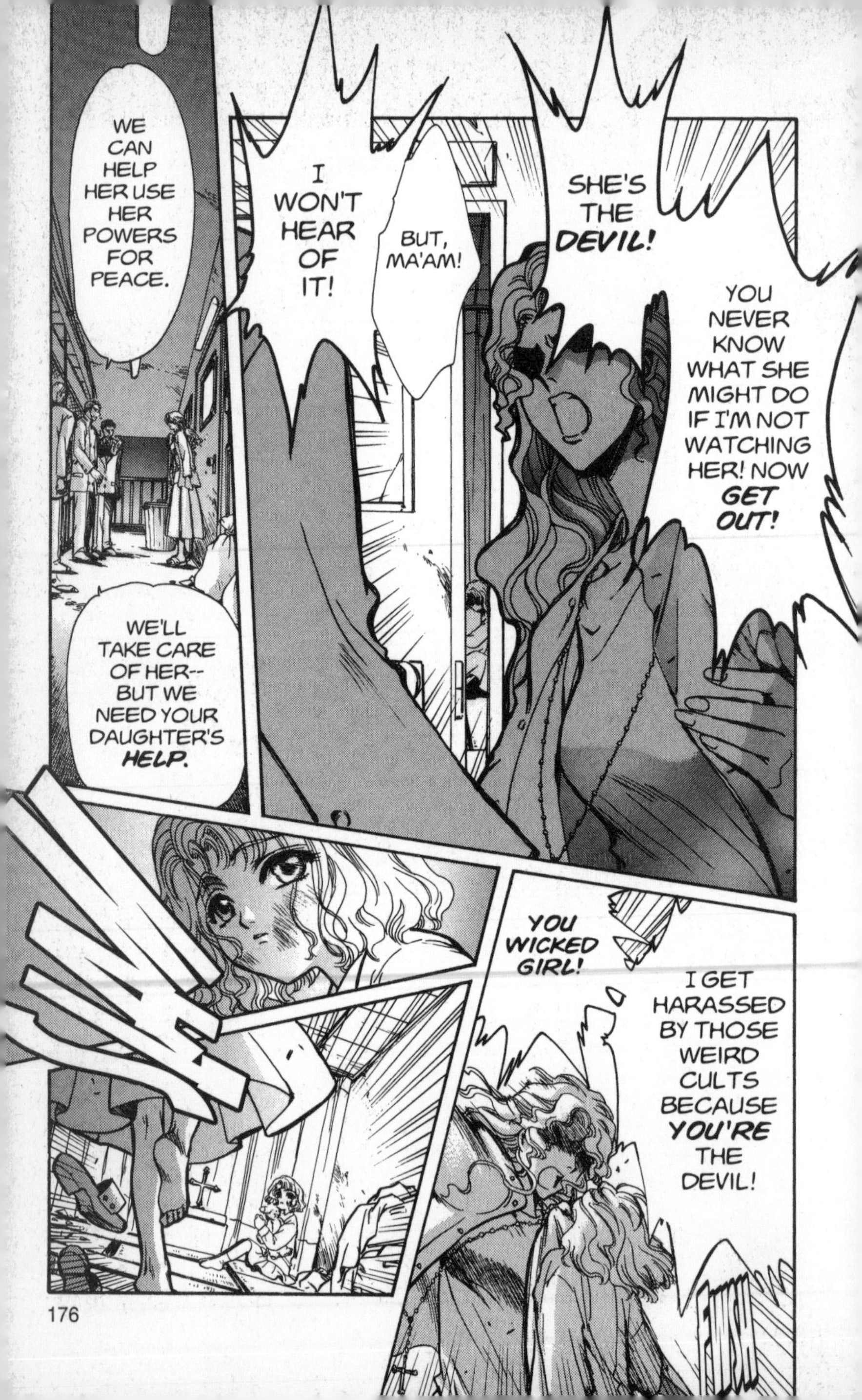
WE CAN HELP HER USE HER POWERS FOR PEACE.
WE'LL TAKE CARE OF HER-- BUT WE NEED YOUR DAUGHTER'S *HELP*.
I WON'T HEAR OF IT!
BUT, MA'AM!
SHE'S THE *DEVIL!*
YOU NEVER KNOW WHAT SHE MIGHT DO IF I'M NOT WATCHING HER! NOW *GET OUT!*
YOU WICKED GIRL!
I GET HARASSED BY THOSE WEIRD CULTS BECAUSE *YOU'RE* THE DEVIL!
FWISH

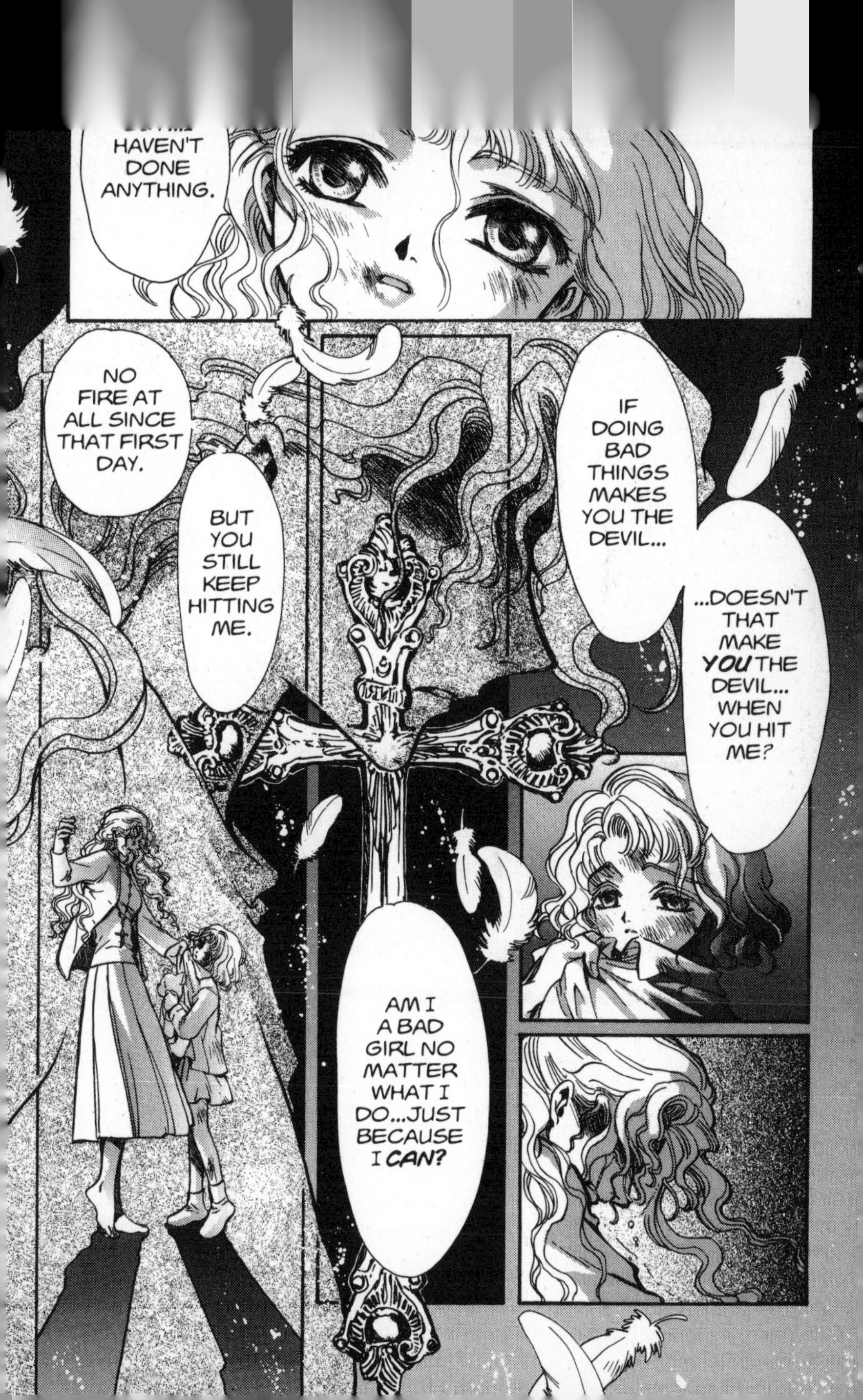
HAVEN'T DONE ANYTHING.
NO FIRE AT ALL SINCE THAT FIRST DAY.
BUT YOU STILL KEEP HITTING ME.
IF DOING BAD THINGS MAKES YOU THE DEVIL...
...DOESN'T THAT MAKE YOU THE DEVIL... WHEN YOU HIT ME?
AM I A BAD GIRL NO MATTER WHAT I DO...JUST BECAUSE I CAN?

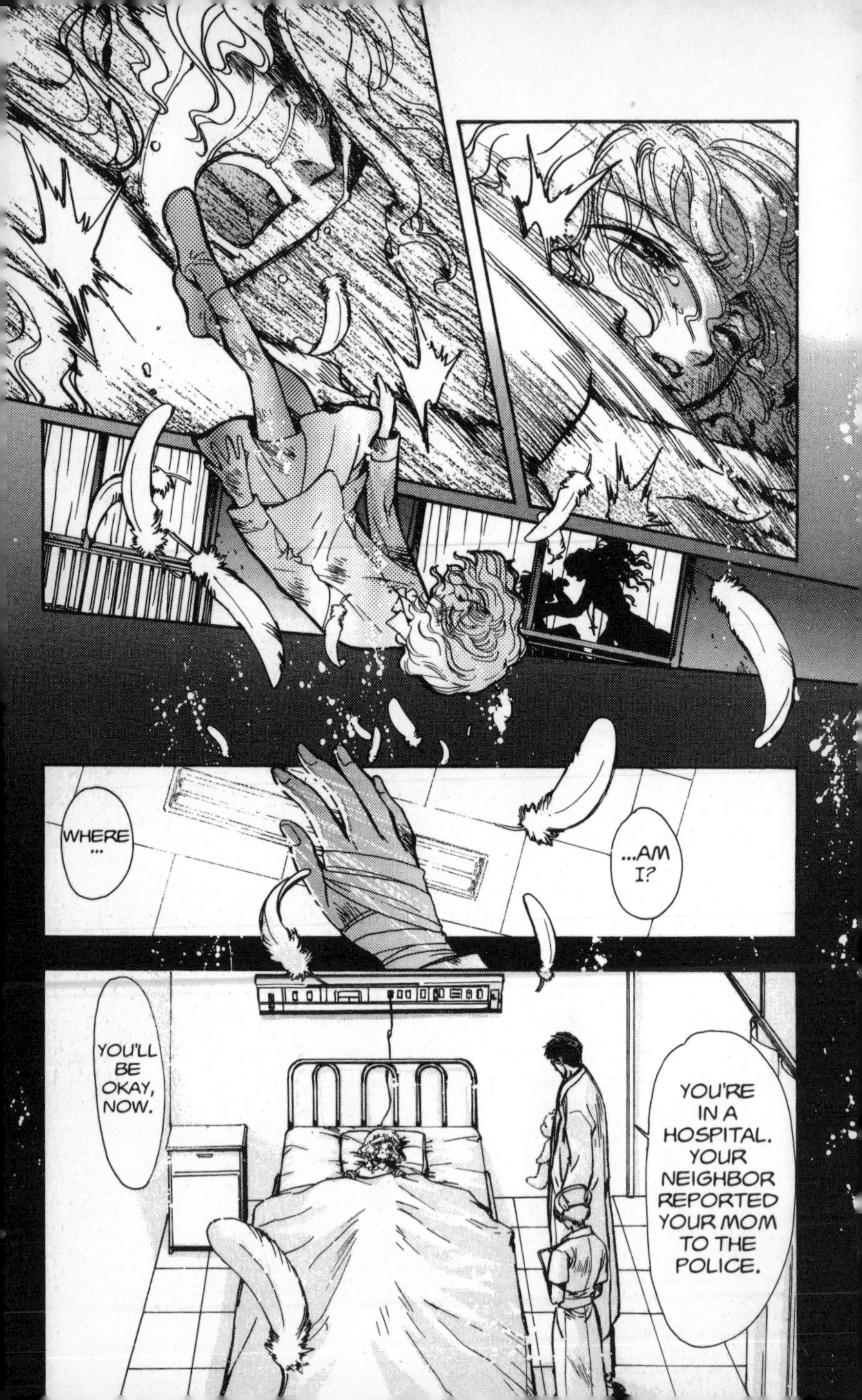
WHERE ...
...AM I?
YOU'LL BE OKAY, NOW.
YOU'RE IN A HOSPITAL. YOUR NEIGHBOR REPORTED YOUR MOM TO THE POLICE.

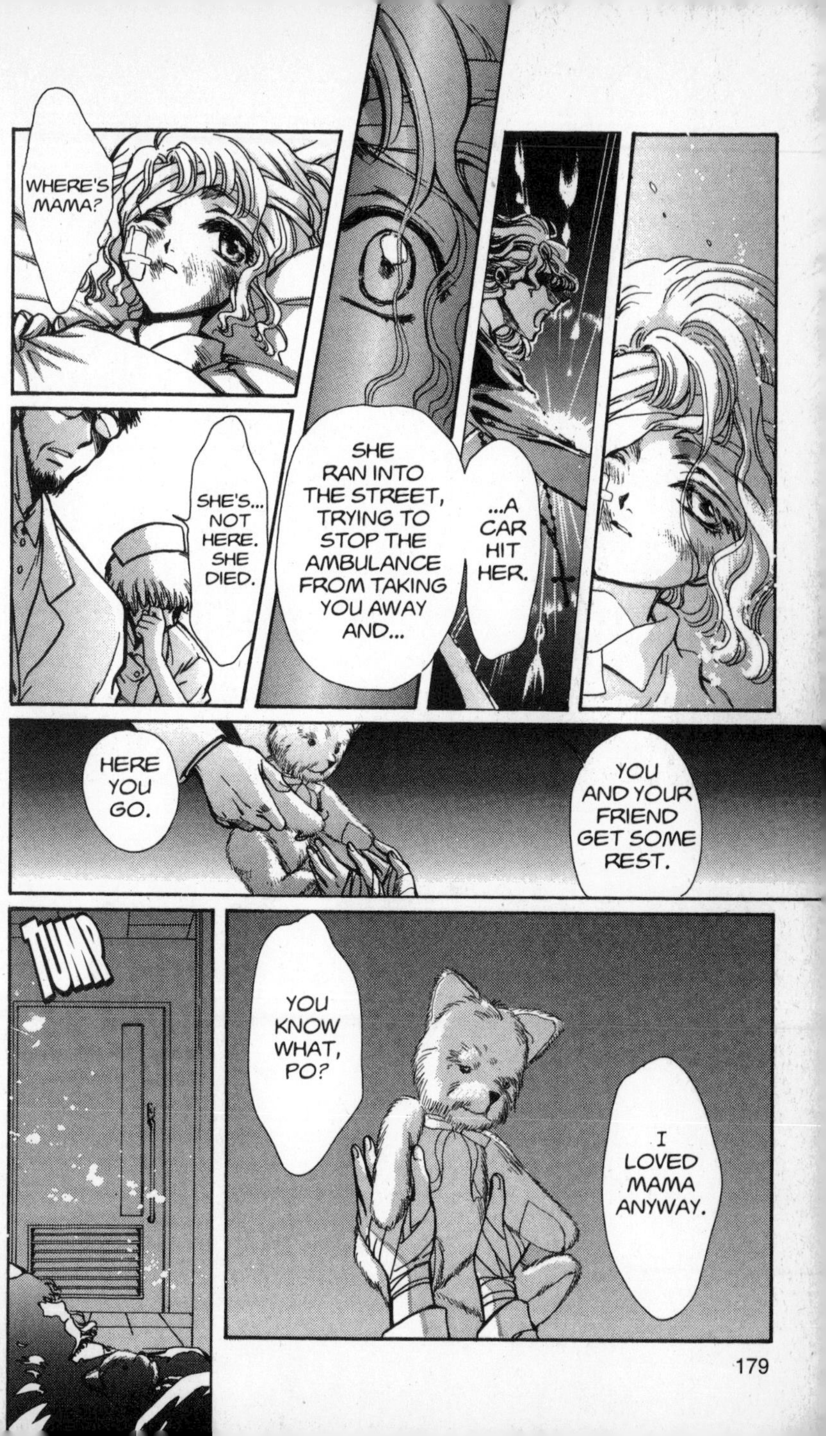
WHERE'S MAMA?
SHE'S... NOT HERE. SHE DIED.
SHE RAN INTO THE STREET, TRYING TO STOP THE AMBULANCE FROM TAKING YOU AWAY AND...
...A CAR HIT HER.
HERE YOU GO.
YOU AND YOUR FRIEND GET SOME REST.
TUMP
YOU KNOW WHAT, PO?
I LOVED MAMA ANYWAY.

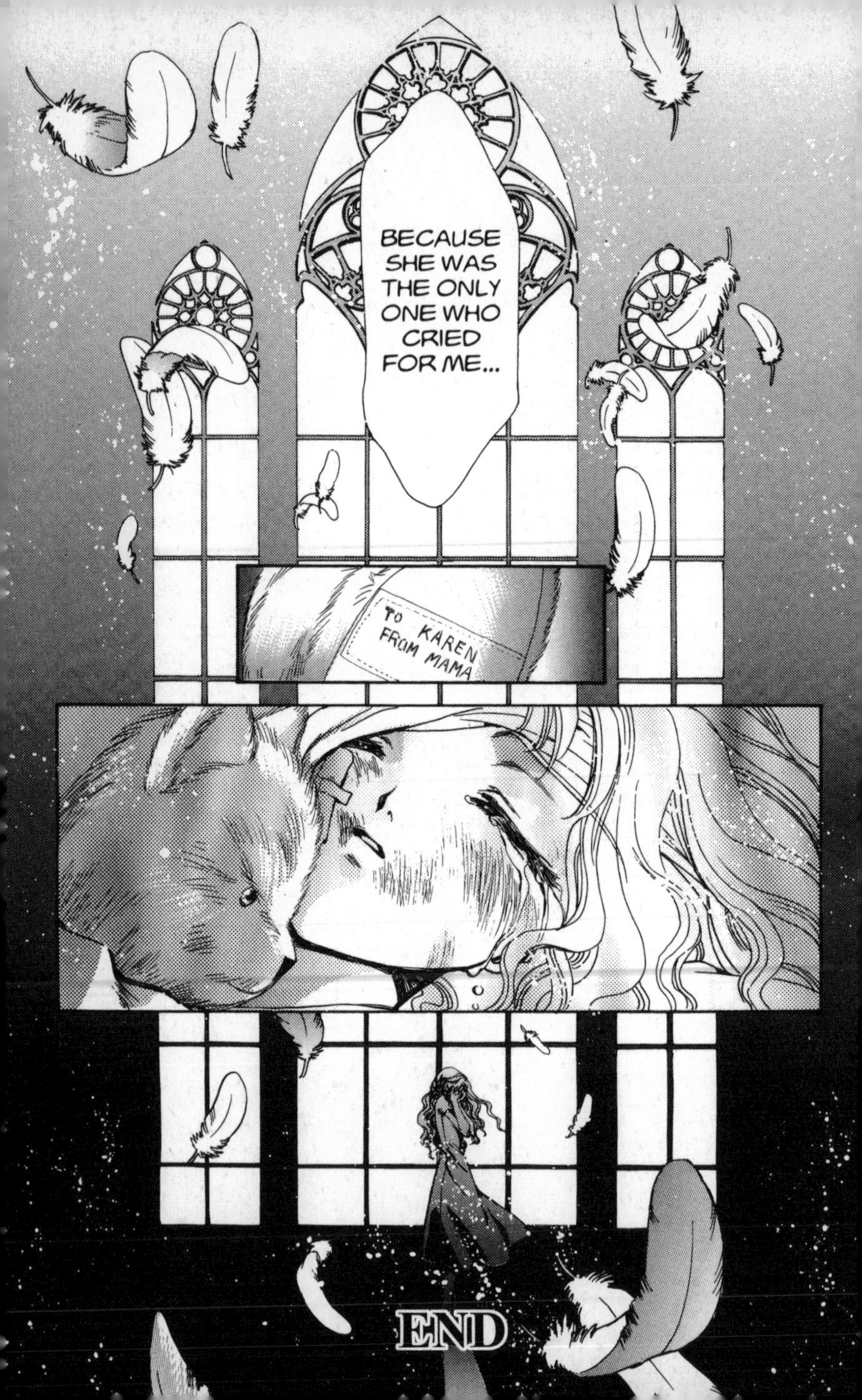

BECAUSE SHE WAS THE ONLY ONE WHO CRIED FOR ME...
TO KAREN FROM MAMA
END

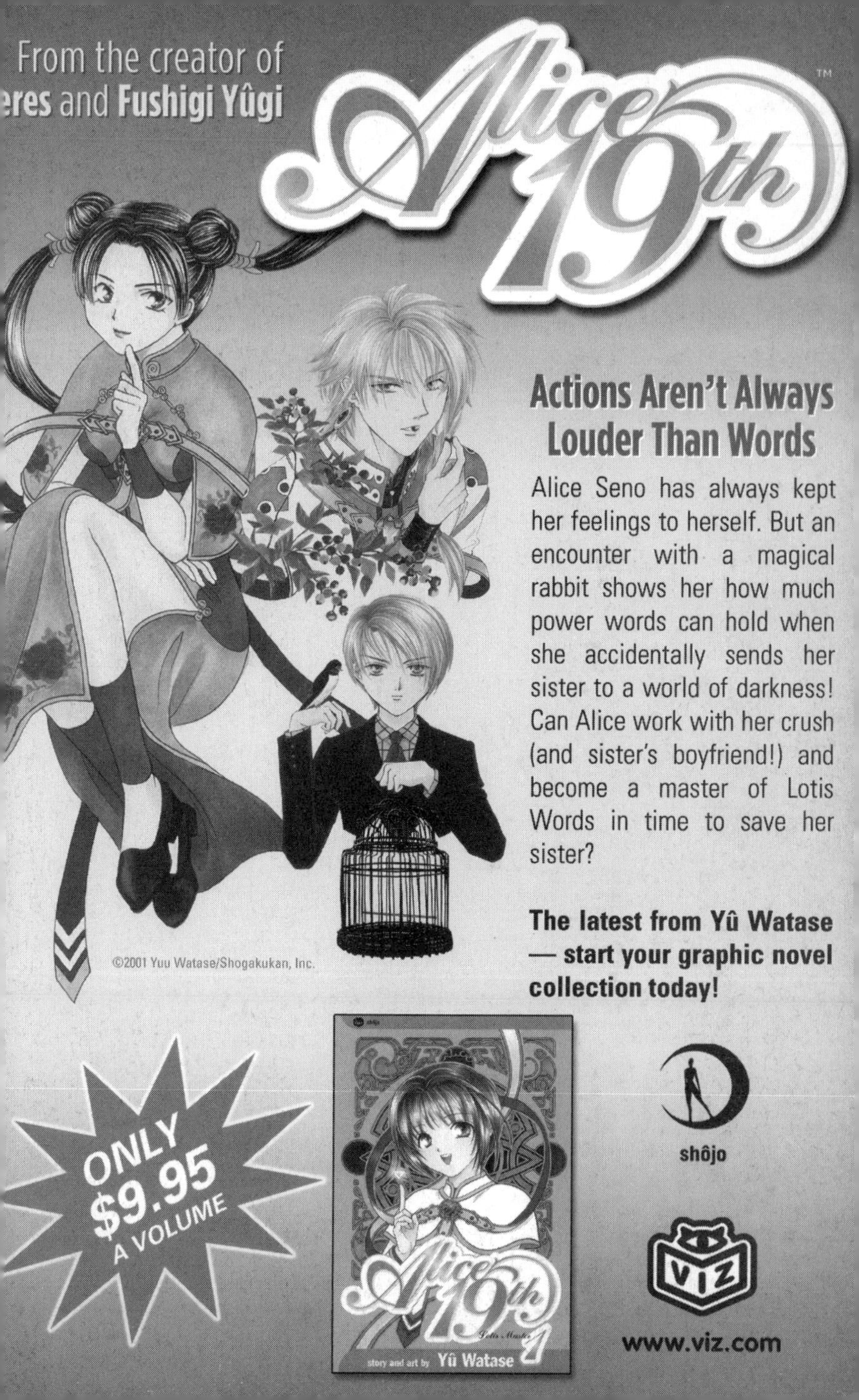
From the creator of
eres and Fushigi Yûgi
Alice 19th™
Actions Aren't Always Louder Than Words
Alice Seno has always kept her feelings to herself. But an encounter with a magical rabbit shows her how much power words can hold when she accidentally sends her sister to a world of darkness! Can Alice work with her crush (and sister's boyfriend!) and become a master of Lotis Words in time to save her sister?
The latest from Yû Watase — start your graphic novel collection today!
©2001 Yuu Watase/Shogakukan, Inc.
ONLY $9.95 A VOLUME
Alice 19th
story and art by Yû Watase
shôjo
VIZ
www.viz.com

COMPLETE OUR SURVEY AND LET US KNOW WHAT YOU THINK!

☐ Please do NOT send me information about VIZ products, news and events, special offers, or other information.

☐ Please do NOT send me information from VIZ's trusted business partners.

Name: _____

Address: _____

City: _____ **State:** _____ **Zip:** _____

E-mail: _____

☐ Male ☐ Female   **Date of Birth** (mm/dd/yyyy): ___ / ___ / ___   (Under 13? Parental consent required)

What race/ethnicity do you consider yourself? (please check one)

☐ Asian/Pacific Islander   ☐ Black/African American   ☐ Hispanic/Latino

☐ Native American/Alaskan Native ☐ White/Caucasian   ☐ Other: _____

What VIZ product did you purchase? (check all that apply and indicate title purchased)

☐ DVD/VHS _____

☐ Graphic Novel _____

☐ Magazines _____

☐ Merchandise _____

Reason for purchase: (check all that apply)

☐ Special offer   ☐ Favorite title   ☐ Gift

☐ Recommendation   ☐ Other _____

Where did you make your purchase? (please check one)

☐ Comic store   ☐ Bookstore   ☐ Mass/Grocery Store

☐ Newsstand   ☐ Video/Video Game Store ☐ Other: _____

☐ Online (site: _____)

What other VIZ properties have you purchased/own? _____

_____

How many anime and/or manga titles have you purchased in the last year? How many were VIZ titles: (please check one from each column)

ANIME
- [ ] None
- [ ] 1-4
- [ ] 5-10
- [ ] 11+

MANGA
- [ ] None
- [ ] 1-4
- [ ] 5-10
- [ ] 11+

VIZ
- [ ] None
- [ ] 1-4
- [ ] 5-10
- [ ] 11+

I find the pricing of VIZ products to be: (please check one)
- [ ] Cheap
- [ ] Reasonable
- [ ] Expensive

What genre of manga and anime would you like to see from VIZ? (please check two)
- [ ] Adventure
- [ ] Comic Strip
- [ ] Science Fiction
- [ ] Fighting
- [ ] Horror
- [ ] Romance
- [ ] Fantasy
- [ ] Sports

What do you think of VIZ's new look?
- [ ] Love It
- [ ] It's OK
- [ ] Hate It
- [ ] Didn't Notice
- [ ] No Opinion

Which do you prefer? (please check one)
- [ ] Reading right-to-left
- [ ] Reading left-to-right

Which do you prefer? (please check one)
- [ ] Sound effects in English
- [ ] Sound effects in Japanese with English captions
- [ ] Sound effects in Japanese only with a glossary at the back

THANK YOU! Please send the completed form to:

NJW Research
42 Catharine St.
Poughkeepsie, NY 12601

All information provided will be used for internal purposes only. We promise not to sell or otherwise divulge your information.